KING

OF CAPITAL

KING
OF CAPITAL

**THE REMARKABLE RISE, FALL, AND
RISE AGAIN OF STEVE SCHWARZMAN
AND BLACKSTONE**

DAVID CAREY AND **JOHN E. MORRIS**

CROWN
BUSINESS
NEW YORK

Library of Congress Cataloging-in-Publication Data

Carey, David (David Leonard), 1952–

King of capital / David Carey and John E. Morris. — 1st ed.

p.   cm.

Includes bibliographical references and index.

1. Blackstone Group.   2. Private equity.   3. Consolidation and merger of
corporations.   4. Leveraged buyouts.   5. Financial services industry—United States.
6. Investment advisors—United States.   I. Morris, John E., 1957–   II. Title.

HG4571.C37 2010

338.8'3–dc22

2010018286

ISBN 978-0-307-45299-3

Printed in the United States of America

Design by Leonard W. Henderson

1 3 5 7 9 10 8 6 4 2

First Edition

Dedicated to our parents, Robert B. and Elizabeth S. Morris and Miriam Carey Berry, and to the memory of Leonard A. Carey

CONTENTS

viii   Contents

CHAPTER 1

The Debutants

M ore Rumors About His Party Than About His Deals," blared the front-page headline in the *New York Times* in late January 2007. It was a curtain-raiser for what was shaping up to be the social event of the season, if not the era. By then, the buzz had been building for weeks.

Stephen Schwarzman, cofounder of the Blackstone Group, the world's largest private equity firm, was about to turn sixty and was planning a fête. The financier's lavish holiday parties were already well known in Manhattan's moneyed circles. One year Schwarzman and his wife decorated their twenty-four-room, two-floor spread in Park Avenue's toniest apartment building to resemble Schwarzman's favorite spot in St. Tropez, near their summer home on the French Riviera. For his birthday, he decided to top that, taking over the Park Avenue Armory, a fortified brick edifice that occupies a full square block amid the metropolis's most expensive addresses.

On the night of February 13 limousines queued up and the boldface names in tuxedos and evening dresses poured out and filed past an encampment of reporters into the hangarlike armory. TV perennial Barbara Walters was there, Donald and Melania Trump, media diva Tina Brown, Cardinal Egan of the Archdiocese of New York, Sir Howard Stringer, the head of Sony, and a few hundred other luminaries, including the chief executives of some of the nation's biggest banks: Jamie Dimon of JPMorgan

Chase, Stanley O'Neal of Merrill Lynch, Lloyd Blankfein of Goldman Sachs, and Jimmy Cayne of Bear Stearns.

Inside the cavernous armory hung "a huge indoor canopy . . . with a darkened sky of sparkling stars suspended above a grand chandelier," mimicking the living room in Schwarzman's $30 million apartment nearby, the *New York Post* reported the next day. The decor was copied, the paper observed, "even down to a grandfather clock and Old Masters paintings on the wall."

R&B star Patti LaBelle was on hand to sing "Happy Birthday." Beneath an immense portrait of the financier—also a replica of one hanging in his apartment—the headliners, singer Rod Stewart and comic Martin Short, strutted and joked into the late hours. Schwarzman had chosen the armory, Short quipped, because it was more intimate than his apartment. Stewart alone was known to charge $1 million for such appearances.

The $3 million gala was a self-coronation for the brash new king of a new Gilded Age, an era when markets were flush and crazy wealth saturated Wall Street and especially the private equity realm, where Schwarzman held sway as the CEO of Blackstone Group.

As soon became clear, the birthday affair was merely a warm-up for a more extravagant coming-out bash: Blackstone's initial public offering. By design or by luck, the splash of Schwarzman's party magnified the awe and intrigue when Blackstone revealed its plan to go public five weeks later, on March 22. No other private equity firm of Blackstone's size or stature had attempted such a feat, and Blackstone's move made official what was already plain to the financial world: Private equity— the business of buying companies with an eye to selling them a few years later at a profit—had moved from the outskirts of the economy to its very center. Blackstone's clout was so great and its prospects so promising that the Chinese government soon came knocking, asking to buy 10 percent of the company.

When Blackstone's shares began trading on June 22 they soared from $31 to $38, as investors clamored to own a piece of the business. At the closing price, the company was worth a stunning $38 billion—one-third

JPMorgan Chase soon shed the private equity subsidiary that had bid on the drug company and Credit Suisse barred its private equity group from competing for large companies of the sort that Blackstone, TPG, and Kohlberg Kravis target.

To some of Blackstone's rivals, the public attention was nothing new. Kohlberg Kravis, known as KKR, had been in the public eye ever since the mid-1980s, when it bought familiar companies like the Safeway supermarket chain and Beatrice Companies, which made Tropicana juices and Sara Lee cakes. KKR came to epitomize that earlier era of frenzied takeovers with its audacious $31.3 billion buyout in 1988 of RJR Nabisco, the tobacco and food giant, after a heated bidding contest. That corporate mud wrestle was immortalized in the best-selling book *Barbarians at the Gate* and made Henry Kravis, KKR's cofounder, a household name. Carlyle Group, another giant private equity firm, meanwhile, had made waves by hiring former president George H. W. Bush and former British prime minister John Major to help it bring in investors. Until Schwarzman's party and Blackstone's IPO shone a light on Blackstone, Schwarzman's firm had been the quiet behemoth of the industry, and perhaps the greatest untold success story of Wall Street.

Schwarzman and Blackstone's cofounder, Peterson, had arrived late to the game, in 1985, more than a decade after KKR and others had honed the art of the leveraged buyout: borrowing money to buy a company with only the company itself as collateral. By 2007 Schwarzman's firm—and it had truly been his firm virtually from the start—had eclipsed its top competitors on every front. It was bigger than KKR and Carlyle, managing $88 billion of investors' money, and had racked up higher returns on its buyout funds than most others. In addition to its mammoth portfolio of corporations, it controlled $100 billion worth of real estate and oversaw $50 billion invested in other firms' hedge funds—investment categories in which its competitors merely dabbled. Alone among top buyout players, Blackstone also had elite teams of bankers who advised other companies on mergers and bankruptcies. Over twenty-two years, Schwarzman and Peterson had invented a fabulously profitable new form of Wall Street powerhouse whose array of investment and advisory services and financial standing rivaled those of the biggest investment banks.

Along the way, Blackstone had also been the launching pad for other luminaries of the corporate and financial worlds, including Henry Silverman, who as CEO of Cendant Corporation became one of corporate America's most acquisitive empire builders, and Laurence Fink, the founder of BlackRock, Inc., a $3.2 trillion debt-investment colossus that originally was part of Blackstone before Fink and Schwarzman had a falling-out over money.

For all the power and wealth private equity firms had amassed, leveraged buyouts (LBOs or buyouts for short) had always been controversial, a lightning rod for anger over the effects of capitalism. As Blackstone and its peers gobbled up ever-bigger companies in 2006 and 2007, all the fears and criticisms that had dogged the buyout business since the 1980s resurfaced.

In part it was guilt by association. The industry had come of age in the heyday of corporate raiders, saber-rattling financiers who launched hostile takeover bids and worked to overthrow managements. Buyout firms rarely made hostile bids, preferring to strike deals with management before buying a company. But in many cases they swooped in to buy companies that were under siege and, once in control, they often laid off workers and broke companies into pieces just like the raiders. Thus they, too, came to be seen as "asset strippers" who attacked companies and feasted on their carcasses, selling off good assets for a quick profit, and leaving just the bones weighed down by piles of debt.

The backlash against the buyout boom of the 2000s began in Europe, where a German cabinet member publicly branded private equity and hedge funds "locusts" and British unions lobbied to rein in these takeovers. By the time the starry canopy was being strung in the Park Avenue Armory for Schwarzman's birthday party, the blowback had come Stateside. American unions feared the new wave of LBOs would lead to job losses, and the enormous profits being generated by private equity and hedge funds had caught the eye of Congress.

"I told him that I thought his party was a very bad idea before he had his party," says Henry Silverman, the former Blackstone partner who went on to head Cendant. Proposals were already circulating to jack up taxes on investment fund managers, Silverman knew, and the party could only fan the political flames.

Even the conservative *Wall Street Journal* fretted about the implications of the extravaganza, saying, "Mr. Schwarzman's birthday party, and the swelling private equity fortunes it symbolizes, are manifestations of . . . rising inequality. . . . Financiers who celebrate fast fortunes made while workers face stagnant pay and declining job security risk becoming targets for a growing dissent." When, on the eve of Blackstone's IPO four months after the party, new tax proposals were announced, they were immediately dubbed the Blackstone Tax and the *Journal* blamed Schwarzman, saying his "garish 60th birthday party this year played into the hands of populists looking for a real-life Gordon Gekko to skewer." Schwarzman's exuberance had put the industry, and himself, on trial.

It was easy to see the sources of the fears. Private equity embodies the capitalist ethos in its purest form, obsessed with making companies more valuable, whether that means growing, shrinking, folding one business and launching another, merging, or moving. It is clearheaded, unsentimental ownership with a vengeance, and a deadline.

In fact, the acts for which private equity firms are usually indicted—laying off workers, selling assets, and generally shaking up the status quo—are the stock in trade of most corporations today. More workers are likely to lose their jobs in a merger of competitors than they are in an LBO. But because a buyout represents a different form of ownership and the company is virtually assured of changing hands again in a few years, the process naturally stirs anxieties.

The claim that private equity systematically damages companies is just wrong. The buyout business never would have survived if that were true. Few executives would stay on—as they typically do—if they thought the business was marked for demolition. Most important, private equity firms wouldn't be able to sell their companies if they made a habit of gutting them. The public pension funds that are the biggest investors in buyout funds would stop writing checks if they thought private equity was all about job destruction.

A growing body of academic research has debunked the strip-and-flip caricature. It turns out, for instance, that the stocks of private equity–owned companies that go public perform better than shares of newly public companies on average, belying the notion that buyouts leave companies hobbled. As for jobs, private equity–owned companies turn out to be about on par with other businesses, cutting fractionally more jobs in the early years after a buyout on average but adding more jobs than the average company over the longer haul. In theory, the debt they pile on the companies they buy should make them more vulnerable, but the failure rate for companies that have undergone LBOs hasn't differed much from that of similar private and public companies over several decades, and by some measures it is actually lower.

Though the strip-and-flip image persists, the biggest private equity profits typically derive from buying out-of-favor or troubled companies and reviving them, or from expanding businesses. Many of Blackstone's most successful investments have been growth plays. It built a small British amusements operator, Merlin Entertainments, into a major international player, for example, with Legoland toy parks and Madame Tussauds wax museums across two continents. Likewise it transformed a humdrum German bottle maker, Gerresheimer AG, into a much more profitable manufacturer of sophisticated pharmaceutical packaging. It has also staked start-ups, including an oil exploration company that found a major new oil field off the coast of West Africa. None of these fit the cliché of the strip-and-flip.

Contrary to the allegation that buyout firms are just out for a quick buck, CEOs of companies like Merlin and Gerresheimer say they were free to take a longer-term approach under private equity owners than they had been able to do when their businesses were owned by public companies that were obsessed with producing steady short-term profits.

Notwithstanding the controversy over the new wave of buyouts and the brouhaha over Schwarzman's birthday party, Blackstone succeeded in going public. By then, however, Schwarzman and others at Blackstone were nervous that the markets were heading for a fall. The very day Blackstone's stock started trading, June 22, 2007, there was an ominous sign of what was to come. Bear Stearns, a scrappy investment bank long admired for its trading prowess, announced that it would bail out a hedge fund it managed that had suffered catastrophic losses on mortgage securities. In the months that followed, that debacle reverberated through the financial system. By the autumn, the lending machine that had fueled the private equity boom with hundreds of billions of dollars of cheap debt had seized up.

Like shopaholics who hit their credit card limits, private equity firms found their credit refused. Blackstone, which had bought the nation's biggest owner of office towers, Equity Office Properties Trust, that February for a record $39 billion and signed a $26 billion takeover agreement for the Hilton Hotels chain in July 2007, would not pull off a deal over $4 billion for the next two and a half years. Its profits sank so deeply in 2008 that it couldn't pay a dividend at the end of the year. That meant that Schwarzman received no investment profits that year and had to content himself with just his base pay of $350,000, less than a thousandth of what he had taken home two years earlier. Blackstone's shares, which had sold for $31 in the IPO, slumped to $3.55 in early 2009, a barometer for the buyout business as a whole.

LBOs were not the root cause of the financial crisis, but private equity was caught in the riptide when the markets retreated. Well-known companies that had been acquired at the peak of the market began to collapse under the weight of their new debt as the economy slowed and business dropped off: household retailer Linens 'n Things, the mattress maker Simmons, and Reader's Digest, among others. Many more private equity–owned companies that have survived for the moment still face a day of reckoning in 2013 or 2014 when the loans used to buy them come due. Like homeowners who overreached with the help of subprime mortgages and find their home values are underwater, private equity firms are saddled with companies that are worth less than what they owe. If they don't recover their value or renegotiate their loans, there won't be enough collateral to refinance their debt, and they may be sold at a loss or forfeited to their creditors.

In the wake of the financial crisis, many wrote off private equity. It has taken its hits and will likely take some more before the economy fully recovers. As in past downturns, there is bound to be a shake-out as investors flee firms that invested rashly at the top of the market. Compared with other parts of the financial system and the stock markets, however, private equity fared well. Indeed, the risks and the leverage of the buyout industry were modest relative to those borne by banks and mortgage companies. A small fraction of private equity–owned companies failed, but they didn't take down other institutions, they required no government bailouts, and their owners didn't melt down.

On the contrary, buyout firms were among the first to be called in when the financial system was crumbling. When the U.S. Treasury Department and the Federal Reserve Bank scrambled to cobble together bailouts of financial institutions such as Lehman Brothers, Merrill Lynch, and American International Group in the autumn of 2008, they dialed up Blackstone and others, seeking both money and ideas. Private equity firms were also at the table when the British treasury and the Bank of England tried to rescue Britain's giant, failing savings bank Northern Rock. (Ultimately the shortfalls at those institutions were too great for even the biggest private funds to remedy.) The U.S. government again turned to private equity in 2009 to help fix the American auto industry. As its "auto czar," the Obama administration picked Steven Rattner, the founder of the private equity firm Quadrangle Group, and to help oversee the turnaround of General Motors Corporation, it named David Bonderman, the founder of Texas Pacific Group, and Daniel Akerson, a top executive of Carlyle Group, to the carmaker's board of directors.

The crisis of 2007 to 2009 wasn't the first for private equity. The buyout industry suffered a near-death experience in a similar credit crunch at the end of the 1980s and was wounded again when the technology and telecommunications bubble burst in the early 2000s. Each time, however, it rebounded and the surviving firms emerged larger, taking in more money and targeting new kinds of investments.

Coming out of the 2008–9 crisis, the groundwork was in place for another revival. For starters, the industry was sitting on a half-trillion dollars of capital waiting to be invested—a sum not so far short of the $787 billion U.S. government stimulus package of 2009. Blackstone alone had $29 billion on hand to buy companies, real estate, and debt at the end of 2009 at a time when many sellers were still distressed, and that sum would be supplemented several times over with borrowed money. With such mounds of capital at a time when capital was in short supply, the potential to make profits was huge. Though new fund-raising slowed to a trickle in 2008 and 2009, it was poised to pick back up as three of the largest public pension funds in the United States said in late 2009 that they would put even more of their money into private equity funds in the future.

The story of Blackstone parallels that of private equity and its transformation from a niche game played by a handful of financial entrepreneurs and upstart firms into an established business of giant institutions backed by billions from public pension funds and other mainstays of the investment world. Since Blackstone's IPO in 2007, KKR has also gone public and Apollo Global Management, one of their top competitors, has taken steps to do the same, drawing back the veil that enshrouded private equity and cementing its position as a mainstream component of the financial system.

A history of Blackstone is also a chronicle of an entrepreneur whose savvy was obscured by the ostentation of his birthday party. From an inauspicious beginning, through fits and starts, some disastrous early investments, and chaotic years when talent came and went, Schwarzman built a major financial institution. In many ways, Blackstone's success reflected his personality, beginning with the presumptuous notion in 1985 that he and Peterson could raise a $1 billion LBO fund when neither had ever led a buyout. But it was more than moxie. For all the egotism on display at the party, Schwarzman from the beginning recruited partners with personalities at least as large as his own, and he was a listener who routinely solicited input from even the most junior employees. In 2002, when the firm was mature, he also recruited his heir in management and

handed over substantial power to him. Even his visceral loathing of losing money—to which current and former partners constantly attest—
shaped the firm's culture and may have helped it dodge the worst excesses
at the height of the buyout boom in 2006 and 2007.

Schwarzman and peers such as Henry Kravis represent a new breed
of capitalists, positioned between the great banks and the corporate conglomerates of an earlier age. Like banks, they inject capital, but unlike
banks, they take control of their companies. Like sprawling global corporations, their businesses are diverse and span the world. But in contrast to corporations, their portfolios of businesses change year to year
and each business is managed independently, standing or falling on its
own. The impact of these moguls and their firms far exceeds their size
precisely because they are constantly buying and selling—putting their
stamp on thousands of businesses while they own them and influencing
the public markets by what they buy and how they remake the companies they acquire.

CHAPTER 2

Houdaille Magic, Lehman Angst

To Wall Street, the deal was little short of revolutionary. In October 1978 a little-known investment firm, Kohlberg Kravis Roberts, struck an agreement to buy Houdaille Industries, an industrial pumps maker, in a $380 million leveraged buyout. Three hundred eighty million bucks! And a public company, no less! There had been small leveraged buyouts of privately held businesses for years, but no one had ever attempted anything that daring.

Steve Schwarzman, a thirty-one-year-old investment banker at Lehman Brothers Kuhn Loeb at the time, burned with curiosity to know how the deal worked. The buyers, he saw, were putting up little capital of their own and didn't have to pledge any of their own collateral. The only security for the loans came from the company itself. How could they do this? He had to get his hands on the bond prospectus, which would provide a detailed blueprint of the deal's mechanics. Schwarzman, a mergers and acquisitions specialist with a self-assured swagger and a gift for bringing in new deals, had been made a partner at Lehman Brothers that very month. He sensed that something new was afoot—a way to make fantastic profits and a new outlet for his talents, a new calling.

"I read that prospectus, looked at the capital structure, and realized the returns that could be achieved," he recalled years later. "I said to myself, 'This is a gold mine.' It was like a Rosetta stone for how to do leveraged buyouts."

Schwarzman wasn't alone in his epiphany. "When Houdaille came

along, it got everybody's attention," remembers Richard Beattie, a lawyer at Simpson Thacher & Bartlett who had represented KKR on many
of its early deals. "Up until that point, people walked around and said,
'What's an LBO?' All of a sudden this small outfit, three guys—Kohlberg
and Kravis and Roberts—is making an offer for a public company.
What's *that* all about?"

The financial techniques behind Houdaille, which also underlay the
private equity boom of the first decade of the twenty-first century, were
first hatched in the back rooms of Wall Street in the late 1950s and 1960s.
The concept of the leveraged buyout wasn't the product of highbrow financial science or hocus-pocus. Anyone who has bought and sold a home
with a mortgage can grasp the basic principle. Imagine you buy a house
for $100,000 in cash and later sell it for $120,000. You've made a 20
percent profit. But if instead you had made just a $20,000 down pay-
ment and taken out a mortgage to cover the rest, the $40,000 you walk
away with when you sell, after paying off the mortgage, would be twice
what you invested—a 100 percent profit, before your interest costs.

Leveraged buyouts work on the same principle. But while homeowners have to pay their mortgage out of their salaries or other income,
in an LBO the business pays for itself after the buyout firm puts down
the equity (the down payment). It is the company, not the buyout firm,
that borrows the money for a leveraged buyout, and hence buyout investors look for companies that produce enough cash to cover the interest
on the debt needed to buy them and which also are likely to increase in
value. To those outside Wall Street circles, the nearest analogy is an income property where the rent covers the mortgage, property taxes, and
upkeep.

What's more, companies that have gone through an LBO enjoy a
generous tax break. Like any business, they can deduct the interest on
their debt as a business expense. For most companies, interest deduc-
tions are a small percentage of earnings, but for a company that has
loaded up on debt, the deduction can match or exceed its income, so
that the company pays little or no corporate income tax. It amounts to a

huge subsidy from the taxpayer for a particular form of corporate finance.

By the time Jerome Kohlberg Jr. and his new firm bought Houdaille, there was already a handful of similar boutiques that had raised money from investors to pursue LBOs. The Houdaille buyout put the financial world on notice that LBO firms were setting their sights higher. The jaw-dropping payoff a few years later from another buyout advertised to a wider world just how lucrative a leveraged buyout could be.

Gibson Greeting Cards Inc., which published greeting cards and owned the rights to the Garfield the Cat cartoon character, was an unloved subsidiary of RCA Corporation, the parent of the NBC television network, when a buyout shop called Wesray bought it in January 1982. Wesray, which was cofounded by former Nixon and Ford treasury secretary William E. Simon, paid $80 million, but Wesray and the card company's management put up just $1 million of that and borrowed the rest. With so little equity, they didn't have much to lose if the company failed but stood to make many times their money if they sold out at a higher price.

Sixteen months later, after selling off Gibson Greeting's real estate, Wesray and the management took the company public in a stock offering that valued it at $290 million. Without leverage (another term for debt), they would have made roughly three and a half times their money. But with the extraordinary ratio of debt in the original deal, Simon and his Wesray partner Raymond Chambers each made more than $65 million on their respective $330,000 investments—a two-hundred-fold profit. Their phenomenal gain instantly became legend. Weeks after, *New York* magazine and the *New York Times* were still dissecting Wesray's coup.

Simon himself called his windfall a stroke of luck. Although Gibson Greeting's operating profits shot up 50 percent between the buyout and the stock offering, Wesray couldn't really claim credit. The improvement was just a function of timing. By early 1983 the economy was coming back after a long recession, giving the company a lift and pushing up the value of stocks. The payoff from Gibson was testament to the brute power of financial leverage to generate mind-boggling profits from small gains in value.

At Lehman, Steve Schwarzman looked on at the Gibson IPO in rapt amazement like everyone else. He couldn't help but pay attention, because he had been RCA's banker and adviser when it sold Gibson to Wesray in the first place and had told RCA the price was too cheap. The Houdaille and Gibson deals would mark the beginning of his lasting fascination with leveraged buyouts.

The Gibson deal also registered on the radar of Schwarzman's boss, Lehman chairman and chief executive Peter G. Peterson. Virtually from the day he'd joined Lehman as vice-chairman in 1973, Peterson had hoped to coax the firm back into the merchant banking business—the traditional term for a bank investing its own money in buying and building businesses. In decades past, Lehman had been a power in merchant banking, having bought Trans World Airlines in 1934 and having bank-rolled the start-ups of Great Western Financial, a California bank, Litton Industries, a technology and defense firm, and LIN Broadcasting, which owned a chain of TV stations, in the 1950s and 1960s. But by the time Peterson arrived, Lehman was in frail financial health and couldn't risk its own money buying stakes in companies.

Much of what investment banks do, despite the term, involves no investing and requires little capital. While commercial and consumer banks take deposits and make loans and mortgages, investment bankers mainly sell services for a fee. They provide financial advice on mergers and acquisitions, or M&A, and help corporations raise money by selling stocks and bonds. They must have some capital to do the latter, because there is some risk they won't be able to sell the securities they've contracted to buy from their clients, but the risk is usually small and for a short period, so they don't tie up capital for long. Of the core components of investment banking, only trading—buying and selling stocks and bonds—requires large amounts of capital. Investment banks trade stocks and bonds not only for their customers, but also for their own account, taking big risks in the process. Rivers of securities flow daily through the trading desks of Wall Street banks. Most of these stakes are liquid, meaning that they can be sold quickly and the cash recycled, but if the market drops and the bank can't sell its holdings quickly enough, it can book big losses. Hence banks need a cushion of capital to keep themselves solvent in down markets.

Merchant banking likewise is risky and requires large chunks of capital because the bank's investment is usually tied up for years. The rewards can be enormous, but a bank must have capital to spare. When Peterson joined in 1973, Lehman had the most anemic balance sheet of any major investment bank, with less than $20 million of equity.

By the 1980s, though, Lehman had regained financial strength and Peterson and Schwarzman began to press the rest of management to consider merchant banking again. They even went so far as to line up a target, Stewart-Warner Corporation, a publicly traded maker of speedometers based in Chicago. They proposed that Lehman lead a leveraged buyout of the company, but Lehman's executive committee, which Peterson chaired but didn't control, shot down the plan. Some members worried that clients might view Lehman as a competitor if it started buying companies.

"It was a fairly ludicrous argument," Peterson says.

"I couldn't believe they turned this down," says Schwarzman. "There was more money to be made in a deal like that than there was in a whole year of earnings for Lehman"—about $200 million at the time.

The two never gave up on the dream. Schwarzman would invite Dick Beattie, the lawyer for the Kohlberg Kravis buyout firm whose law firm was also Lehman's primary outside counsel, to speak to Lehman bankers about the mechanics of buyouts. "Lurking in the background was the question, 'Why can't Lehman get into this?'" Beattie recalls.

All around them, banks like Goldman Sachs and Merrill Lynch were launching their own merchant banking divisions. For the time being, however, Peterson and Schwarzman would watch from the sidelines as the LBO wave set off by Houdaille and Gibson Greeting gathered force. They would have to be content plying their trade as M&A bankers, advising companies rather than leading their own investments.

*   *   *

Peterson's path to Wall Street was unorthodox. He was no conventional banker. When he joined Lehman, he'd been a business leader and Nixon cabinet member who felt more at home debating economic policy, a consuming passion, than walking a trading floor. A consummate networker, Peterson had a clearly defined role when he came to the firm in 1973: to woo captains of industry as clients. The bank's partners thought his many contacts from years in management and Washington would be invaluable to Lehman.

His rise up the corporate ladder had been swift. The son of Greek immigrants who ran a twenty-four-hour coffee shop in the railroad town of Kearney, Nebraska, Peterson graduated summa cum laude from Northwestern University and earned an MBA at night from the University of Chicago. He excelled in the corporate world as a young man, first in marketing. By his midtwenties, on the strength of his market research work, he was put in charge of the Chicago office of the McCann-Erickson advertising agency. His first big break came when he was befriended by Charles Percy, a neighbor and tennis partner who ran Bell & Howell, a home movie equipment company in Chicago. At Percy's urging, Peterson joined Bell & Howell as its top marketing executive, and in 1961 at age thirty-four, he was elevated to president. In 1966, after Percy was elected to the U.S. Senate, Peterson took over as CEO.

Through an old Chicago contact, George Shultz (later treasury secretary and then secretary of state), Peterson landed a position in early 1971 as an adviser to President Richard Nixon on international economics. Though Peterson had allies in the White House, most notably Henry Kissinger, the powerful national security adviser and future secretary of state, he wasn't temperamentally or intellectually suited to the brutal intramural fighting and stifling partisan atmosphere of the Nixon White House. He lacked the brawler's gene. At one point Nixon's chief of staff, H. R. Haldeman, offered Peterson an office in the West Wing of the White House, nearer the president. But the move would have displaced another official, Donald Rumsfeld (later George W. Bush's defense secretary), who fought ferociously to preserve his favored spot. Peterson knew Rumsfeld from Chicago and didn't want to pick a fight or bruise his friend's ego, so he turned down Haldeman's offer. Kissinger later told Peterson that it was the worst mistake he made in Washington.

Peterson soon found himself in the crosshairs of another headstrong figure: treasury secretary John Connally, the silver-maned, charismatic former Texas Democratic governor who was riding with President Kennedy when Kennedy was assassinated and took a bullet himself. Connally felt that Peterson's role as an economics adviser intruded on Connally's turf and conspired to squelch his influence.

A year after joining the White House staff, Peterson was named commerce secretary, which removed him from Connally's bailiwick. In his new post, Peterson pulled off one splashy initiative, supervising talks that yielded a comprehensive trade pact with the Soviets. But he soon fell out of favor with Nixon and Haldeman, the president's steely-eyed, brush-cut enforcer, in part because he loved to hobnob and swap opinions with pillars of the liberal and media establishments such as *Washington Post* publisher Katharine Graham, *New York Times* columnist James Reston, and Robert Kennedy's widow, Ethel. The White House saw Peterson's socializing as fraternizing with the enemy.

Nixon dumped Peterson after the 1972 presidential race, less than a year after naming him to the cabinet. Before leaving town, Peterson delivered a memorable parting gibe at a dinner party, joking that Haldeman had called him in to take a loyalty test. He flunked, he said, because "my calves are so fat that I couldn't click my heels"—a tart quip that caused a stir after it turned up in the *Washington Post*.

Peterson soon moved to New York, seeking a more lucrative living. Wooed by several Wall Street banks, he settled on Lehman, drawn to its long history in merchant banking. But two months after being recruited as a rainmaker and vice chairman, his role abruptly altered when an internal audit led to the horrifying discovery that the firm's traders were sitting quietly on a multimillion-dollar unrealized loss. Securities on its books were now worth far less than Lehman had paid and Lehman was teetering on the edge of collapse. A shaken board fired Fred Ehrman,

Lehman's chairman, and turned to Peterson—the ex-CEO and cabinet member—to take charge, hoping he could lend his management know-how and his prestige to salvage the bank.

The man responsible for the trades that nearly sank the firm was its trading department chief, Lewis Glucksman, a portly bond trader known for his combustible temper, who walked the floor with shirt flaps flying, spewing cigar smoke. There were some, particularly on the banking side of the firm, who wanted Glucksman's head over the losses. But Warren Hellman, an investment banker who took over as Lehman's president shortly before Peterson was tapped as chairman and chief executive, thought Lehman needed Glucksman. The trader was the one who understood why Lehman had bought the securities and what went wrong. "I argued that the guy who created the mess in the first place was in the best position to fix it," Hellman says. Peterson concurred, believing, he says, that "everyone is entitled to one big mistake." Glucksman made good on his second chance and, under Peterson, Lehman rebounded. In 1975 *Business Week* put Peterson's granite-jawed visage on its cover and heralded his achievement with the headline "Back from the Brink Comes Lehman Bros."

Despite his role in righting the firm, Peterson never fit easily into Lehman's bare-knuckled culture, particularly not with its traders. His cluelessness about the jargon, if not the substance, of trading and finance amazed his new partners. "He kept calling basis points 'basing points,'" says a former high-ranking Lehman banker. (A basis point is Wall Street parlance for one one-hundredth of a percentage point, a fractional difference that can translate into big gains and losses on large trades or loans. Thus, 100 basis points equals 1 percent of interest).

Peterson was appealing in many ways. He was honest and principled, and he could be an engaging conversationalist with a dry, often mordant, wit. He wasn't obsessed with money, at least not by Wall Street's fanatical norm. But with colleagues he was often aloof, imperious, and even pompous. In the office, he'd expect secretaries, aides, and even fellow partners to pick up after him. Rushing to the elevator on his way to a meeting, he would scribble notes to himself on a pad and toss them over his shoulder, expecting others to stoop down and gather them up for his later perusal.

At times, he seemed to inhabit his own world. He would arrive at meetings with yellow Post-it notes adorning his suit jacket, placed there by his secretary to remind him to attend some charity ball or to call a CEO the next morning. The off-in-the clouds quality carried over into his years at Blackstone, too. Howard Lipson, a longtime Blackstone partner, remembers seeing Peterson one blustery night sporting a bulky winter hat. Affixed to its crown was a note: "Pete—don't forget your hat." Lipson recalls, too, the terror and helplessness Peterson would express when his secretary stepped away and he was faced with having to answer his own phone. "Patty! Patty!" he'd yowl.

Peterson enjoyed the attention and ribbing that his absentmindedness provoked from others. In his conference room, he would later showcase a plaque from the Council on Foreign Relations given out of appreciation for, among other things, "his unending search for his briefcase."

"This was endearing stuff," says Lipson. "Some people said he was losing it, but Pete wasn't that old. I think it was a sign he had many things going on in his mind." David Batten, a Blackstone partner in the early 1990s who admires Peterson, has the same take: "Pete was probably thinking great thoughts," he says, alluding to the fact that Peterson often was preoccupied with big-picture policy issues. During his Lehman years, he was a trustee of the Brookings Institution, a well-known think tank, and occasionally served on ad hoc government advisory committees. Later, at Blackstone, he authored several essays and books on U.S. fiscal policy.

If he sometimes seemed oblivious to underlings, he was assiduous in cultivating celebrities in the media, the arts, and government—Barbara Walters, David Rockefeller, Henry Kissinger, Mike Nichols, and Diane Sawyer, among others—and was relentless in his name-dropping.

Far outweighing his shortcomings was his feat of managing Lehman through a decade of prosperity. This was no small achievement at an institution racked by vicious rivalries. Since the death in 1969 of its longtime dominant leader, Bobbie Lehman, who'd kept a lid on internal clashes, Lehman had devolved into a snake pit. Partners plotted to one-up each other and to capture more bonus money. One Lehman partner was rumored to have coaxed another into selling him his stock in a mining company when the first partner knew, which the seller did not, that the company was about to strike a rich new lode. In a case of double-dealing that enraged Peterson when it came to light, a high-ranking partner, James Glanville, urged one of his clients to make a hostile bid for a company that other Lehman partners were advising on how to defend against hostile bids.

The warfare was over the top even by Wall Street's dog-eat-dog standards. Robert Rubin, a Goldman Sachs partner who went on to be treasury secretary in the Clinton administration, told Lehman president Hellman that their two firms had equally talented partners. The difference, Rubin said, was that the partners at Goldman understood that their real competition came from beyond the walls of the firm. Lehman's partners seemed to believe that their chief competition came from inside.

The Lehman infighting amazed outsiders. "I don't understand why all of you at Lehman Brothers hate each other," Bruce Wasserstein, one of the top investment bankers of the time, once said to Schwarzman and another Lehman partner. "I get along with both of you."

"If you were at Lehman Brothers, we'd hate you, too," Schwarzman replied.

The bitterest schism was between Glucksman's traders and the investment bankers. The traders viewed the bankers as pinstriped and manicured blue bloods; the bankers saw the traders as hard-edged and low bred. Peterson tried to bridge the divide. A key bone of contention was pay. Before Peterson arrived, employees were kept in the dark on how bonuses and promotions were decided. The partners at the top decreed who got what and awarded themselves the lion's share of the annual bonus pool regardless of their contributions. Peterson established a new compensation system, inspired in part by Bell & Howell's, that tied bonuses to performance. He limited his own bonuses and instituted peer reviews. Yet even this meritocratic approach failed to quell the storm of complaints over pay that invariably erupted every year at bonus season. Exacerbating matters was the fact that each of the trading and advisory businesses had its ups and downs, and whichever group was having the stronger year inevitably felt it deserved the greater share of Lehman's profits. The partners' brattishness and greed ate at Peterson, whose efforts to unify and tame Lehman flopped.

Peterson had allies within Lehman, mostly bankers, but few of the firm's three dozen partners were his steadfast friends. He was closest to Hellman and George Ball, a former undersecretary of state in the Kennedy and Johnson administrations. Of the younger partners, he took a liking to Roger Altman, a skilled "relationship" banker in Peterson's mold, whom Peterson named one of three coheads of investment banking at Lehman. Peterson was also drawn to Schwarzman, who in the early 1980s chaired Lehman's M&A committee within investment banking. Schwarzman wasn't the bank's only M&A luminary. In any given year, a half-dozen other Lehman bankers might generate more fees, but he mixed easily with CEOs, and his incisive instincts and his virtuosity as a deal maker set him apart.

Those qualities were prized by Peterson, and over the years, the two developed a kind of tag-team approach to courting clients. Peterson would angle for a chief executive's attention, then Schwarzman would reel him in with his tactical inventiveness and command of detail, figuring out how to sell stocks or bonds to finance an acquisition or identifying which companies might want to buy a subsidiary the CEO wanted to sell and how to sell it for the highest price.

"I guess I was thought of as a kind of wise man who would sit down with the CEO in a context of mutual respect," says Peterson. "I think most would agree that I produced a good deal of new advisory business. But it's one thing to produce it, and it's another to implement it, to carry most of the load. I experimented with various people in that role, and Steve was simply one of the very best. It was a very complementary and productive relationship."

Schwarzman was more than just a deal broker. In some cases, he was integrally involved in restructuring a business, as he was with International Harvester, a farm equipment and truck maker, in the 1970s. Harvester's CEO, Archie McArdle, originally phoned Peterson, with whom he had served on the board of General Foods, and told Peterson he wanted Lehman to replace Morgan Stanley as his company's investment bank. Harvester was at death's door at the time, bleeding cash and unable to borrow. Peterson dispatched Schwarzman to help McArdle perform triage and over the following months Schwarzman and a brigade of his colleagues strategized and found buyers for a passel of Harvester assets, raising the cash the company desperately needed.

Similarly, Peterson landed Bendix Corporation as a client shortly before a new CEO, William Agee, came on board there in 1976. Agee wanted to remake the diversified engineering and manufacturing company by buying high-growth, high-tech businesses and selling many slower-growing businesses. Peterson handed the assignment off to Schwarzman, who became Agee's trusted consigliere, advising him what to buy and to sell, and then executing the deals. "Bill was a prolific deal-oriented person. I would talk to him every day, including weekends," Schwarzman says.

Peterson and Schwarzman made an odd couple. Apart from the twenty-one-year gap in their ages, the six-foot Peterson towered over the five-foot-six Schwarzman, and Peterson's dark Mediterranean coloring contrasted with Schwarzman's fair complexion and baby blue eyes. While Peterson could be remote and preoccupied, Schwarzman was jaunty, down-to-earth, always engaged and taking the measure of those around him. Whereas Peterson instinctively shied away from confrontation, Schwarzman could get in people's faces when he needed to. Their lives had followed different paths, too, until they intersected at Lehman. Schwarzman's family had owned a large dry goods store in Philadelphia and he had grown up comfortably middle-class in the suburbs—"two cars and one house," as he puts it—whereas Peterson was the small-town boy of very modest means from the American heartland.

While Peterson adored the role of distinguished elder statesman,

Schwarzman had a brasher way and a flair for self-promotion. That shone through in a fawning profile in the *New York Times Magazine* in January 1980 shortly after Schwarzman had added several M&A feathers to his cap, advising RCA on its $1.4 billion acquisition of CIT Financial Corporation and Tropicana Products' $488 million sale to Beatrice Foods. The *Times* proclaimed him "probably" the hottest of a "new generation of younger investment bankers," extolling his aggressiveness, imaginativeness, thoroughness, and "infectious vitality that make other people like to work with him." Peterson and Martin Lipton, a powerful M&A lawyer, sang his praises.

"Normally chief executives are reticent working with someone that age, but he is being sought out by major clients," Peterson told the *Times*. Schwarzman, Lipton said, possessed a rare "instinct that puts him in the right place at the right time." (Schwarzman offered little insight into his own drive, other than saying, "I'm an implementer" and "I have a tremendous need to succeed.") At a company outing that spring, colleagues presented him a copy of the story set against a framed mirror—so he could see his own image reflected back when he gazed at it. Not everyone at the firm responded to Schwarzman's vanity with amusement, though. As one Lehman alumnus puts it, "He was appreciated by some, not loved by all."

The *Times* feature may have been hyperbolic, but it was on the mark about Schwarzman's abilities. "He had a pretty good ego, but Steve was inherently a great deal guy," says Hellman, Lehman's president in the mid-1970s. "Steve had a God-given ability to look at a transaction and make something out of it that others of us would miss," says Hellman, who is not close to Schwarzman. Hellman goes so far as to compare Schwarzman to Felix Rohatyn of Lazard Frères, the most accomplished merger banker of the 1960s and 1970s who gained wide praise, too, for orchestrating a restructuring of New York City's debt in 1975 that spared the city from bankruptcy.

Ralph Schlosstein, another Lehman banker from that era, recalls Schwarzman's bold and crafty approach when he advised the railroad CSX Corporation on the sale of two daily newspapers in Florida in November 1982. After initial bids came in, Morris Communications, a small Augusta, Georgia, media outfit, had blown away the other bidders with a $200 million offer versus $135 million from Cox Communications and $100 million from Gannett Company. Another banker might have given Cox and Gannett a shot at topping Morris, but with the disparity in the offers it was unlikely Morris would budge.

Not that CSX would have been displeased. The newspapers generated only about $6 million in operating income, so $200 million was an extraordinarily good price. "CSX was saying, 'Sign them up!' " says Schlosstein, who worked on the sale with Schwarzman. Schwarzman instead advised CSX to hold off. Zeroing in on the fact that Morris had a major bank backing its bid, he reckoned Morris could be induced to pay more. Rather than reveal the bids, he kept the amounts under wraps and proceeded to arrange a second round of sealed bids. He hoped to convince Morris that Cox and Gannett were hot on its heels. The stratagem worked, as Morris hiked its offer by $15 million.

"That was $15 million Steve got for CSX that nobody else, including CSX, had the guts to do," says Schlosstein. Today sealed-bid auctions for companies are the norm, but then they were exceedingly rare. "We made it up as we went along," says Schwarzman, who credits himself with pioneering the idea.

As the economy emerged from a grueling recession in the early 1980s, Lehman's banking business took off and its traders racked up bigger and bigger profits playing the markets. But instead of fostering peace at the firm, Lehman's prosperity brought the long-simmering friction between its bankers and traders to a boil as the traders felt they were short-changed by the bank's compensation system.

At first Peterson didn't recognize how deep the traders' indignation ran. He sensed that Glucksman, who had been elevated to president in 1981, was restless in that role and thought Glucksman deserved a promotion, and in May 1983 he anointed him co-CEO. But that didn't placate Glucksman, who had long resented operating in Peterson's shadow and wanted the title all to himself. Six weeks later Glucksman organized a putsch with the backing of key partners. "He had a corner on the trad-ing area" and his traders had earned a bundle the previous quarter, Pe-terson says. "I guess he felt it was the right time to strike." Figuring the internal warfare might ease if he stepped aside, Peterson acquiesced, agreeing to step down as co-CEO in October and to quit as chairman at the end of 1983.

It was a humiliating ending, but Peterson never was one to push back when shoved. Schwarzman and other Lehman partners told him that if it came to a vote of the partners, he would win. But Peterson thought he might save the bank from further strife by stepping aside. He felt "that such a victory would be both hollow and Pyrrhic," Peterson later wrote. "Lew would take some of his best traders, leaving the firm seriously damaged."

Some of Peterson's friends believe his cerebral flights and preoccupa-tions may have contributed to his downfall, by desensitizing him to the firm's Machiavellian internal politics. For whatever reasons, former col-leagues say he was largely oblivious to—and perhaps in denial about—the coup Glucksman was hatching against him until the moment the trader confronted him in July that year and insisted that Peterson bow out. Peterson owns up to being "naïve" and "too trusting."

That summer, after his ouster, Peterson withdrew for a time to his summer house in East Hampton, Long Island. Schwarzman and most of his fellow bankers labored on amid the rancor. But in the spring of 1984, Glucksman's traders suffered another enormous bout of losses and Lehman's partners found themselves on the verge of financial ruin, just as they had a decade earlier. Glucksman, though still CEO, lost his grip on power and the partners were bitterly divided over whether to sell the firm or tough it out. If they didn't sell, there was a very real risk the firm would fail and their stakes in the bank—then worth millions each—would be worthless.

It was Schwarzman who ultimately forced the hand of Lehman's board of directors. The board had been trying to keep the bank's prob-lems quiet so as not to panic customers and employees while it sounded

out potential buyers. In a remarkable piece of freelancing, Schwarzman—
who was not on the board and was not authorized to act for the board—
took matters into his own hands. On a Saturday morning in March 1984
in East Hampton, he showed up unannounced on the doorstep of his
friend and neighbor Peter A. Cohen, the CEO of Shearson, the big brokerage house then owned by American Express. "I want you to buy
Lehman Brothers," Schwarzman cheerily greeted Cohen. Within days,
Cohen formally approached Lehman, and on May 11, 1984, Lehman
agreed to be taken over for $360 million. The merger gave Shearson, a
retail brokerage with a meager investment banking business, a major
foothold in more lucrative, prestigious work, and it staved off financial
disaster for Lehman's partners. (Years later Lehman was spun off and
became an independent public company again.)

It meant salvation for the worried Lehman bankers and traders, but
the deal came with strings attached. Shearson insisted that most Lehman
partners sign noncompete agreements barring them from working for
other Wall Street firms for three years if they left. Handcuffs, in effect.
What Shearson was buying was Lehman's talent, after all, and if it didn't
lock in the partners, it could be left with a hollow shell.

Schwarzman had no interest in soldiering on at Shearson, however.
He yearned to join Peterson, who was laying plans to start an investment business with Eli Jacobs, a venture capitalist Peterson had recently
come to know, and they wanted Schwarzman to join them as the third
partner. As Schwarzman saw it, he'd plucked and dressed Lehman and
served it to Cohen on a platter, and he felt that Cohen owed him a favor.
Accordingly, he asked Cohen during the merger talks if he would exempt him from the noncompete requirement. Cohen agreed.

"The other [Lehman] partners were infuriated" when they got wind
of Schwarzman's demand, says a former top partner. "Why did Steve
Schwarzman deserve a special arrangement?" Facing a revolt that could
quash the merger, Cohen backpedaled and eventually prevailed upon
Schwarzman to sign the noncompete. (Asked why Schwarzman thought
Shearson would cut him a uniquely advantageous deal, one person who
knows him replies, "Because he's Steve?")

Schwarzman desperately resented Shearson's manacles and felt he'd been wronged. In the months after Shearson absorbed Lehman, he showed up at the office but groused endlessly and sulked, according to former colleagues. For his part, Peterson still wanted Schwarzman to join him, and by now he needed him even more because he and Jacobs had fallen out. Peterson now says Jacobs never was his first choice as a partner. "Steve and I were highly complementary," he says. "I'd wanted Steve all along, but I couldn't get him." Peterson had to get him sprung from Shearson.

Eventually, Peterson and his lawyer, Dick Beattie—the same lawyer who had represented Lehman and Kohlberg Kravis—met with Cohen's emissaries at the Links Club, a refuge of the city's power elite on Manhattan's Upper East Side, to try to spring their man. It was going to cost Schwarzman and Peterson dearly, because Cohen did not want to lose more Lehman bankers. "It was a brutal process," says Peterson. "They were afraid of setting a precedent."

Shearson had drawn up a long list of Lehman's corporate clients, including those Peterson and Schwarzman had advised and some they hadn't, and demanded that Schwarzman and Peterson agree to hand over half of any fees they earned from those clients at their new firm for the next three years. They could have their own firm, but they would start off indentured to Shearson. It was a painful and costly agreement, because M&A advisory fees would be the new firm's only source of revenue until it got its other businesses up and running. But Schwarzman didn't have any good legal argument against Shearson, so he and Peterson buckled to the demand.

In Schwarzman's mind, Cohen had betrayed him, and to this day, friends and associates say, he has borne a deep grudge toward Cohen, both for making him sign the noncompete in the beginning when Cohen had agreed to make an exception, and later for demanding such a steep price to let Schwarzman out. "Steve doesn't forget," says one longtime friend. "If he thinks he's been crossed unfairly, he'll look to get even."

Peterson isn't much more forgiving about the episode. "The idea of giving those characters half the fees when they broke their word seemed egregious. But we couldn't get Steve out on any other basis."

They had survived the debacle of Lehman and now would have to labor under Shearson's onerous conditions, but at last the two were free to set out on their own as M&A advisers and to pursue the mission they had to put on hold for so many years: doing LBOs.

CHAPTER 3

The Drexel Decade

By the time Peterson and Schwarzman extricated themselves from Lehman and Shearson in 1985, the buyout business was booming and the scale of both the buyout funds and the deals themselves were escalating geometrically. Kohlberg Kravis Roberts and a handful of rivals were moving up from bit parts on the corporate stage to leading roles.

Several confluent factors were fueling the rise in buyout activity. Corporate conglomerates, the publicly traded holding companies of the 1960s that assembled vast stables of unrelated businesses under a single parent, had fallen out of favor with investors and were selling off their pieces. At the same time, the notion of a "core business" had penetrated the corporate psyche, prompting boards of directors and CEOs to ask which parts of their businesses were essential and which were not. The latter were often sold off. Together these trends ensured a steady diet of acquisition targets for the buyout firms.

But it was the advent of a new kind of financing that would have the most profound effect on the buyout business. Junk bonds, and Drexel Burnham Lambert, the upstart investment bank that single-handedly invented them and then pitched them as a means to finance takeovers, would soon provide undreamed-of amounts of new debt for buyout firms. Drexel's ability to sell junk bonds also sustained the corporate raiders, a rowdy new cast of takeover artists whose bullying tactics shook loose subsidiaries and frequently drove whole companies into the arms of buyout firms. Over the course of five years, Drexel's innovations revolutionized the LBO business and reshaped the American corporate establishment.

A decade earlier buyouts had been a cottage industry with just a handful of new and more established LBO boutiques. They typically cobbled together a couple of small deals a year, maybe $30 million at the biggest. Gibbons, Green, van Amerongen; E. M. Warburg Pincus, which mostly invested in start-ups; AEA Investors; Thomas H. Lee Company, started by a First National Bank of Boston loan specialist; Carl Marks and Company; Dyson-Kissner-Moran—it was a short list. But the scent of profit always draws in new capital, and soon new operators were sprouting up.

KKR, which opened its doors in 1976, was the most prominent. KKR's doyen at the time was the sober-minded, bespectacled Jerry Kohlberg, who began dabbling in buyouts in 1964 as a sidelight to his main job as corporate finance director of Bear Stearns, a Wall Street firm better known for its stock and bond trading than for arranging corporate deals. In 1969 Kohlberg hired George Roberts, the son of a well-heeled Houston oilman, and later added a second young associate, Roberts's cousin and friend from Tulsa, Henry Kravis. Kravis, whose father was a prosperous petroleum engineer, was a resourceful up-and-comer, small of stature, with a low golf handicap and a rambunctious streak. On his thirtieth birthday he fired up a Honda motorcycle he'd gotten as a gift and rode it around his Park Avenue apartment. In 1976, Kohlberg, then fifty, and Kravis and Roberts, thirty-two and thirty-three, respectively, quit Bear Stearns after a stormy showdown with Bear's CEO, Salim "Cy" Lewis, a lifelong trader who considered buyouts an unrewarding diversion.

The trio's inaugural fund in 1976 was a mere $25 million, but they quickly demonstrated their investing prowess, parlaying that sum into a more than $500 million profit over time. That success made KKR a magnet for investors, who anted up $357 million when KKR hit the fund-raising trail for the second time in 1980. A decade after KKR was launched, it had raised five funds totaling more than $2.4 billion.

While Lehman's executive committee had balked at Peterson and

Schwarzman's suggestion that Lehman buy into companies, other banks had no qualms and by the early 1980s many were setting up their own in-house buyout operations. In 1980, two years after KKR's landmark Houdaille deal was announced, First Boston's LBO team topped that with a $445 million take-private of Congoleum, a vinyl-flooring producer. Soon Morgan Stanley, Salomon Brothers, and Merrill Lynch followed suit and were leading buyouts with their own capital. Goldman Sachs stuck its toe in the water as well. Goldman's partners agonized over their first deal, a pint-sized $12 million takeover of Trinity Bag and Paper in 1982. "Every senior guy at Goldman obsessed about this deal because the firm was going to risk $2 million of its own money," remembers Steven Klinsky, a Goldman banker at the time who now runs his own buyout shop. "They said, 'Oh, man! We've got to make sure we're right about this!'"

The clear number two to KKR was Forstmann Little and Company, founded in 1978. It was only half KKR's size, but the rivalry between the firms and their founders was fierce. Ted Forstmann was the Greenwich, Connecticut–reared grandson of a textile mogul who bounced around the middle strata of finance and the legal world until, with a friend's encouragement, he formed his firm at the age of thirty-nine. He swiftly proved himself a master of the LBO craft, racking up profits on early 1980s buyouts of soft-drink franchiser Dr Pepper and baseball card and gum marketer Topps. Though he had less money to play with, his returns outstripped even KKR's, and like Kravis he became an illustrious and rich prince of Wall Street whose every move drew intense press scrutiny.

KKR remained the undisputed leader, though. Houdaille came to be recognized as the industry's Big Bang—the deal that more than any other touched off the ensuing explosion of LBOs. Doggedly gathering new capital every two years or so and throttling up the scale of its deals, by the mid-1980s KKR dominated buyouts in the way that IBM lorded over the computer business in the 1960s and 1970s.

In the early days of the buyout, many of the target companies were family-owned businesses. Sometimes one generation, or a branch of a family, wanted to cash out. An LBO firm could buy control with the other family members, who remained as managers. But as the firms had greater and greater amounts of capital at their disposal, they increasingly took on bigger businesses, including public companies like Houdaille and sizable subsidiaries of conglomerates.

In their heyday in the 1960s, conglomerates had been the darlings of the stock market, assembling ever more sprawling, diversified portfolios of dissimilar businesses. They lived for growth and growth alone. One of the golden companies of the era, Ling-Temco-Vought, the brainchild of a Texas electrical contractor named Jimmy Ling, eventually amassed an empire that included the Jones & Laughlin steel mills, a fighter jet maker, Braniff International Airlines, and Wilson and Company, which made golf equipment. Ling's counterpart at ITT Corporation, Harold Geneen, made what had been the International Telephone & Telegraph Company into a vehicle for acquisitions, snatching up everything from the Sheraton hotel chain to the bakery that made Wonder Bread; the Hartford insurance companies; Avis Rent-a-Car; and sprinkler, cigar, and racetrack businesses. At RCA Corporation, once just a radio and TV maker and the owner of the NBC broadcasting networks, CEO Robert Sarnoff added the Hertz rental car system; Banquet frozen foods; and Random House, the book publisher. Each of the great conglomerates— Litton Industries, Textron, Teledyne, and Gulf and Western Industries— had its own eclectic mix, but the modus operandi was the same: Buy, buy, buy.

Size and diversity became grail-like goals. Unlike companies that grow big by acquiring competitors or suppliers to achieve economies of scale, the rationale for conglomerates was diversification. If one business had a bad year or was in a cyclical slump, others would compensate. At bottom, however, the conglomerate was a numbers game. In the 1960s, conglomerates' stocks sometimes traded at multiples of forty times earnings—far above the historical average for public companies. They used their overvalued stock and some merger arithmetic to inflate their earnings per share, which is a key measure for investors.

It worked like this: Suppose a conglomerate with $100 million of earnings per year traded at forty times earnings, so its outstanding stock was worth $4 billion. Smaller, less glamorous businesses usually traded at far lower multiples. The conglomerate could use its highly valued shares to buy a company with, say, $50 million of earnings that was valued at just twenty times earnings. The conglomerate would issue $1 billion of new stock ($50 million of earnings × 20) to pay the target's shareholders. That would lift earnings by 50 percent but enlarge the conglomerate's stock base by just 25 percent ($4 billion + $1 billion), so that its earnings per share increased by 20 percent. By contrast, if it had bought the target for forty times earnings, its own earnings per share wouldn't have gone up.

Because stock investors search out companies with rising earnings per share, the acquisition would tend to push up the buyer's stock. If the conglomerate maintained its forty-times-earnings multiple, it would be worth $6 billion, not $5 billion, after the merger ($150 million of earnings × 40). If the buyer borrowed part of the money to buy the target, as conglomerates typically did, it could issue less new stock and jack up earnings per share even higher.

This sleight of hand worked wonderfully in a rising market that sustained the lofty multiples. But reality caught up with the conglomerates at the end of the 1960s, when a bear market ravaged stocks, the numbers game fizzled out, and investors cooled to the conglomerate model. They came to see that the earnings of the whole were not growing any faster than the earnings of the parts, and that the surging earnings per share was ultimately an illusion. Moreover, managing such large portfolios of unrelated businesses tested even very able managers. Inevitably there were many neglected or poorly managed subsidiaries. Investors increasingly began to put more store in focus and efficiency. Under pressure, the discredited behemoths were dismantled in the 1970s and 1980s.

In many cases, buyout shops picked up the cast-off pieces. A banner year for such deals was 1981, when interest rates spiked, the economy hit the wall, and stock prices fell, putting many businesses under stress. KKR bought Lily-Tulip, a cup company, from the packaging giant Owens-Illinois and also PT Components, a power transmission components maker, from Rockwell International, which by then made everything from aircraft to TVs and printing presses. Near the end of that year Forstmann Little struck a deal to buy Beatrice Foods' soft-drink bottling operations, and Wesray negotiated its deal to buy Gibson Greeting from RCA.

As the decade wore on and their bankrolls swelled, bigger LBO shops took aim at whole conglomerates with an eye to splitting them up, as KKR would do with Beatrice Foods in 1986. By then Beatrice had branched out from its roots as a dairy and packaged-food company to include Playtex bras and the Avis car rental chain once owned by ITT.

What turbocharged the buyout boom was a colossal surge in the amount of capital flowing into buyouts—both equity and debt.

As KKR, Forstmann Little, and other buyout firms chalked up big profits on their investments of the late 1970s and early 1980s, insurance companies and other institutions began to divert a bit of the money they had invested in public stocks and bonds to the new LBO funds. By diversifying their mix of assets to include buyouts and real estate, these investors reduced risk and could boost their overall returns over time. The money they moved into the buyout funds was used to buy the stock, or equity, of companies.

Equity was the smallest slice of the leveraged-buyout financing pie—in that era usually just 5–15 percent of the total price. The rest was debt, typically a combination of bank loans and something called mezzanine debt. The bank debt was senior, which meant it was paid off first if the company got in trouble. Because the mezzanine loans were subordinate to the bank loans and would be paid off only if something was left after the banks' claims were satisfied, they were risky and carried very high interest rates. Until the mid-1980s, there were few lenders willing to provide junior debt to companies with high levels of debt like the typical LBO company. A handful of big insurance companies, including Prudential Insurance Company of America, Metropolitan Life Insurance Company, and Allstate Insurance Company, supplied most of the mezzanine debt, and it was far and away the hardest piece of the financing for buy-out firms to round up.

The insurers' terms were punishing. They not only exacted rates as high as 19 percent but typically demanded substantial equity stakes, as well, so they would share in the profits if the investment turned out well. When Henry Kravis demurred to Prudential's demands on two deals in 1981 where the insurer's terms seemed extortionate to him, a Prudential executive bluntly told him there was nowhere else for KKR to turn. At the time, he was right.

The financing landscape began to shift in 1982 and 1983 as the American economy recovered from the traumas of the previous decade—the 1973 oil embargo followed by a deep mid-decade recession, a stagnant stock market, and double-digit inflation. Inflation was finally choked off when the Federal Reserve Board ratcheted up short-term interest rates to nearly 20 percent, triggering a second recession at the beginning of the new decade. The harsh medicine worked and by late 1982 inflation had been tamed and interest rates headed down. That jump-started the economy, stoked corporate earnings, and set the stage for a potent bull market in stocks that lasted most of the 1980s. This combination of lower interest rates and rising corporate valuations put the wind at the backs of the buyout firms for much of the rest of the decade. "It was like falling off a log to make money back then," says Daniel O'Connell, a member of the First Boston buyout team.

On the debt side of the LBO equation, U.S. banks flush with petro-dollars from oil-rich clients in the Middle East and Japanese banks eager to grab a piece of the merger business in the States began building their presence and pumping huge sums into buyout loans. At the same time, a new form of financing emerged from the Beverly Hills branch of a second-tier investment bank. The brainchild of a young banker there named Michael Milken, the new financing was politely called high-yield debt but was universally known as the junk bond, or junk for short.

Until Milken, bonds were the preserve of solid companies—the sort of companies that investors could feel confident would pay off their obligations in installments steadily for ten or twenty or fifty years. Milken's insight was that there were lots of young or heavily indebted companies that needed to borrow but couldn't tap the mainstream bond markets and that there were investors ready to provide them financing if the interest rate was high enough to compensate for the added risk. Renowned for his work ethic, he put in sixteen-hour days starting at 4:30 A.M. California time, an hour and a half before the markets opened in New York.

Milken built Drexel's money machine in increments. In 1974 he assembled a small unit that traded existing bonds of so-called fallen angels, once profitable companies that had fallen on hard times. In 1977 his group began raising money for companies that finicky top-end investment banks wouldn't touch, helping them issue new bonds. In that role, Milken's team bankrolled many hard-charging, entrepreneurial businesses, including Ted Turner's broadcasting and cable empire (including, later, CNN) and the start-up long-distance phone company MCI Communications.

After a breakout year in 1983, when Drexel sold $4.7 billion of junk bonds for its corporate clients, the bank saw the chance to move into the more lucrative field of advising on and financing mergers and acquisitions. Drexel would no longer just finance expansion but now threw its weight behind LBOs and other corporate takeovers. By then the Drexel organization had become a master at selling its clients' bonds to investors, from insurance companies to savings and loans, tapping a broad and deep pool of capital, matching investors with an appetite for risk and high returns with risky companies that needed the money. Milken had such sway with Drexel's network of bond investors that he could muster huge sums and do it faster than the banks or Prudential ever could.

KKR was one of the first clients to test Drexel at this new game, accepting Milken's invitation to help finance a $330 million buyout of Cole National, an eyewear, toy, and giftware retailer, in 1984. Though Drexel's debt was expensive, the terms still beat those of Prudential, and KKR soon stopped tapping insurers altogether and drew exclusively on Drexel's seemingly bottomless well of junk capital. Kravis called Drexel's ability to drum up big dollars in a flash "the damnedest thing I'd ever seen." Before long, the insurance companies' mezzanine debt mostly disappeared from large deals, replaced by cheaper junk from Drexel.

At their peak in the mid-1980s, Milken and his group underwrote $20 billion or more of junk bonds annually and commanded 60 percent of the market. The financial firepower they brought to bear in LBOs and takeover contests redefined the M&A game completely.

At the same time, a robust economy and a steadily rising stock market were yielding a bonanza for buyout investors. Investors in KKR's first five funds saw annual returns of at least 25 percent from each and nearly 40 percent from one. They earned back six times their money on the firm's 1984 fund and a staggering thirteen times their investment on the 1986 fund over time, after KKR's fees and profit share. The buyout game became impossible for pension funds and other investors to resist, and when KKR passed around the hat again in 1987 it raised $6.1 billion, more than six times the size of its largest previous fund. The buying power of that capital would then be leveraged many times over with debt.

With Drexel's backing, KKR went on from Cole National to execute five buyouts in 1986 and 1987 that would still be large by today's standards, including Beatrice Foods ($8.7 billion), Safeway Stores ($4.8 billion), glass maker Owens-Illinois ($4.7 billion), and construction and mining company Jim Walter Corporation ($3.3 billion). The scale of the takeovers—made possible by Drexel and the mammoth new fund KKR raised in 1987—propelled the firm into the public light. With $8 or $10 of debt for every dollar of equity in its fund, KKR could now contemplate a portfolio of companies together worth $50 billion or $60 billion. The media took to calling Kravis "King" Henry, and he quickly came to personify the buyout business. (Kravis's press-shy cousin Roberts lived and worked in faraway Menlo Park, California, off the New York media and social radar. Jerry Kohlberg resigned from KKR in 1987, after clashing with his former protégés over strategy and lines of authority.)

When KKR chased by far the biggest buyout of all time, that of RJR Nabisco in 1988, that too was largely with Drexel money. At bottom, Kravis's power and celebrity, like the deals KKR did, were magnified by the billions put up by Drexel.

* * *

Buyout specialists weren't the only financial players benefiting from and dependent on Milken. At the same time that LBO firms were proliferating, Drexel was also staking a new, rude, and belligerent horde that emerged on the corporate scene. The corporate establishment and a skeptical press coined a string of equally unflattering names for the new intruders: corporate raiders, buccaneers, bust-up artists, and, most famously, barbarians.

Like wolves, the raiders stalked stumbling or poorly run public companies that had fallen behind the herd, and they bought them in LBOs. Like the buyout firms, the raiders were forever on the lookout for companies whose stocks traded for less than they thought the companies were worth—because they had valuable assets that weren't reflected in the stock price or because the companies were inefficiently managed. Both the raiders and the buyout firms sought hidden value that could be captured by splitting up companies to expose the latent value of their parts. But, despite their assertions to the contrary, the raiders generally had little interest in taking control of the firms they targeted, and—unlike buyout firms, which usually wooed the top executives of the companies they sought—the raiders dedicated themselves to taunting and eventually ousting management.

The hunted and the hunters each portrayed the other side in stark caricatures, and there was more than a grain of truth to what each side said. Many corporate bigwigs did in fact fit the raiders' stock image. The eighties were an era of the imperial CEO, who packed his board with cronies, kept a private jet (or two or three), and spent millions on celebrity sporting events and trips that added little to the bottom line. Doing right by shareholders wasn't high on every CEO's agenda, so it wasn't hard for the raiders to cast themselves as militant reformers intent on liberating businesses from the clutches of venal, high-living CEOs who cared more about their perks than about shareholders.

To the corporate world, the raiders were a ragtag band of greedy predators whose aim was to pillage companies and oust management for personal gain.

No one embodied the raider role better than Carl Icahn, a lanky, caustically witty New York speculator whose tactics were typical. After buying up shares, he would demand that the company take immediate steps to boost its share price and give him a seat on its board of directors. When his overture was rebuffed, he'd threaten a proxy fight or a takeover and rain invective on the management's motives and competence in acidly worded letters to the board that he made public. Often these moves would cause the stock to rise, as traders hoped that a bid would surface or that the company would act on its own to sell off assets and improve its performance. Sometimes his tactics did in fact spark other companies to bid for the company he had in his sights. But either way, Icahn could cash out at a profit without having to actually run the target. Other times, the company itself paid him a premium over the market price for his shares just to get him to go away—a controversial practice known as greenmail.

Icahn's peers were equally colorful: T. Boone Pickens, a flinty Texas oilman who launched raids on Gulf Oil, Phillips Petroleum, and Unocal; Nelson Peltz, a New York food merchant's son known for his takeovers of the vending-machine company Triangle Industries and National Can; James Goldsmith, an Anglo-French financier who went after companies on both sides of the Atlantic, including Goodyear Tire and Rubber Company and British-American Tobacco, and whose marriages and affairs filled the gossip pages; and Ronald Perelman, a Philadelphia-bred businessman who won a heated bidding fight for the cosmetics maker Revlon, Inc., in 1985.

Milken backed them all as they pursued LBOs of companies whose shares they thought were cheap. For all their talk of overhauling badly run companies, the raiders seldom demonstrated much aptitude for improving companies. Peltz ran National Can ably enough, but Icahn ran Trans World Airlines into the ground after gaining control of it in 1986. (Icahn and Peltz were still plying their trade into the second decade of the twenty-first century.)

While buyout firms typically enlisted management in their bids, the corporate raiders' instrument of choice was the uninvited, or hostile, tender offer, a takeover bid that went over the heads of management and appealed directly to shareholders. The device wasn't new. In the 1960s and 1970s, Jimmy Ling of the conglomerate LTV, United Technologies CEO Harry Gray, and other acquisitive industrialists had used it now and again to seize control of unwilling corporate targets. But the raiders were a different breed, bent on shaking up the status quo, not building industrial empires. The executives of the growing companies that Milken helped finance were fiercely loyal to the banker, but his ties to the raiders earned him the enmity of most corporate CEOs. A giant of the M&A bar, Martin Lipton, inveighed against the evils of "bust-up, junk-bond takeovers." And Lipton's law firm took the lead in contriving legal defenses—"shark repellants" and "poison pills"—to ward off Milken's marauders. Some banks such as First Boston attempted to straddle the fence, advising and financing corporations while also backing the raiders on particular deals, but as the raiders gained clout and cast their nets wider, Wall Street was forced to choose sides. Goldman Sachs assured its blue-chip corporate clients that it would never stoop to enabling a hostile takeover.

Even though the buyout firms used the same type of financing for their takeovers as the raiders, their aims and tactics were different. For starters, their intention was to gain control. Their investors put up money to buy companies, not to trade stocks. And unlike the raiders, buyout firms almost never pressed hostile bids against the wishes of management. In LBO circles, launching an all-out raid was all but taboo. KKR touted itself as sponsoring friendly collaborations with existing managers, which it dubbed "partnerships with management." More than once—most famously in the case of Safeway in 1986—KKR played the "white knight," joining forces with management in an LBO to repel a belligerent bidder. Indeed, the buyout firms were often kept in check by their own investors, for many public and corporate pension plans insisted that the firms they invested with do only friendly deals. But such opportunism hardly helped their image. They were seen as just one wing of the same disruptive, rapacious army making war on the corporate status quo. "We came into a contested situation, so we looked like a raider," says KKR's longtime lawyer Dick Beattie.

In some cases, in fact, they did the nearest thing to a hostile takeover, by publicly announcing unsolicited offers for companies. Even if they didn't bypass the board, the move usually put the target in play and put intense pressure on the company to do something to boost the share price. KKR used this tactic, known on Wall Street as a bear hug, a number of times, including with the Kroger Company, Beatrice Foods, and Owens-Illinois and eventually struck deals to buy the last two. To the lay observer, and the CEOs and directors who had to respond, the distinction between that and a genuine hostile bid made straight to shareholders was largely academic.

Moreover, the buyout firms, like an Icahn or a Perelman, did not shy from whacking excess costs at the companies they'd taken over. Both shared a view that corporate America was riddled with inefficiencies. ("We don't have assistants to assistants anymore," the chairman of Owens-Illinois told *Fortune* magazine in 1988, the year after KKR bought the glass and packaging company. "In fact, we don't have assistants.") The fact that both groups had developed symbiotic relationships with Michael Milken ensured that they would be lumped together in the public's consciousness. True or not, the image of LBO artists as a pernicious force on the corporate landscape was being permanently etched.

Egged on by the corporate establishment and labor unions, Congress explored ways to combat hostile takeovers and junk bonds. In a series of hearings from 1987 to 1989, buyout industry executives, corporate moguls, and others trooped to Capitol Hill to defend or deride the takeover wave. There was serious talk of abolishing the tax deductibility of the interest costs on junk bonds in order to kill off the alleged menace. At a meeting with Kravis and Roberts in 1988, Senator Lloyd Bentsen, who later that year ran unsuccessfully as the Democratic nominee for vice president, was said to have tossed a study prepared by KKR about the impact of LBOs in the trash. Congress in the end took no action to rein in takeovers, but some states did.

Apart from the tactics and the pursuit of companies that didn't want to be bought, junk bonds stirred controversy for another reason: Many feared that Drexel and the LBO firms were piling too much debt on too many companies, putting them at risk in an economic downturn. Though he had made his name and fortune in LBOs, Ted Forstmann became a vocal critic of junk financing. The fiery-tempered Forstmann's dislike of Kravis by the late 1980s had ripened into a deep-seated loathing. In op-ed pieces and in interviews, Forstmann fulminated about a culture of unbridled excess and a mounting dependency on junk bonds, arguing that it was ruining the LBO business and threatened to destabilize the broader economy. To his way of thinking, an honorable industry grounded in financial fundamentals and discipline had devolved into a quick-buck racket fueled by what he called "funny money" and "wampum." Forstmann believed that the easy credit provided by the junk-bond market had pushed deal prices to loony levels and that target companies ended up laden with debt they couldn't afford. Though he didn't finger Kravis and Drexel publicly, the targets of his wrath were clear.

It was easy to see why Forstmann was upset by Drexel, because Forstmann Little didn't rely on the junk market. Forstmann raised his own debt funds in tandem with his equity funds, in effect lending money from one hand to the other. That gave Forstmann Little great flexibility in formulating bids, but the firm couldn't begin to marshal the masses of debt that the Drexel junk machine was feeding to its competitors. Forstmann's firm was simply eclipsed by the scale of the Drexel operation. The competition between it and KKR had now transcended the win–loss column. Forstmann would privately rant that Kravis ("that little fart") was leading the buyout business's race to perdition. Kravis, for his part, was quoted snarkily telling associates that Forstmann suffered from an "an Avis complex."

CHAPTER 4

Who Are You Guys?

On October 1, 1985, weeks after the Links Club accord that sprung Schwarzman from Shearson, Peterson and Schwarzman formally launched the Blackstone Group, with Peterson as chairman and Schwarzman as CEO. The name, Schwarzman's invention, reflected their ethnic roots, combining the English equivalents of *schwarz*, German and Yiddish for black, and *peter*, Greek for stone. They opened an office on the thirty-fourth floor of the Seagram Building, the elegant Mies van der Rohe– and Philip Johnson–designed skyscraper on Park Avenue just north of Grand Central Station. Their quarters were conspicuously austere: just 3,067 square feet, which they outfitted with two desks and a used conference table. There was one other employee, Peterson's secretary.

The funding was similarly frugal: $400,000, half from each partner, to pay Blackstone's bills until cash started coming in. That was nothing to Peterson, who had pocketed more than $13 million in severance pay and from his cut of the money from Lehman's sale to Shearson. Schwarzman, too, had made a bundle, $6.5 million, from the sale of his Lehman shares. But though the amount they staked to Blackstone was comparatively small, they were determined not to risk any more. They worried that if they ran through the money before Blackstone started to pay for itself, it would bode ill for their venture.

It was the same cautious approach to risking money that would become a hallmark of Blackstone's investing style—and helps explain why

Blackstone avoided the kind of brazen, outsized gambles that caused some high-flying rivals to run aground.

Schwarzman and Peterson had a breakfast ritual, convening at eight thirty nearly every morning in the cafeteria of the former Mayfair Hotel, on Sixty-fifth Street and Park Avenue, now the site of the celebrated restaurant Daniel. There they mapped out their plans for a hybrid business—part M&A boutique, part buyout shop.

They had no wish to emulate investment banks or brokerage firms, which need sturdy capital foundations to back the commitments they make to their clients and to tide them through when they lose money in the markets. "We didn't want to have a lot of capital tied up in low-margin businesses," Schwarzman says. "We wanted to be in businesses where we could either drive very high assets per employee or operate with very high margins." Giving M&A advice was the ultimate high-margin work—enormous fees with very little overhead. Managing a buyout fund was appealing because a relatively small team could oversee a large amount of money and collect a commensurately large management fee along with a share of the profits on the investments.

They also hoped to tack on related businesses that made their money from fees. They weren't sure yet what those would be, but they thought they could attract like-minded entrepreneurial types from other niches of the financial world who could benefit from a collaboration. They lacked the dollars to hire top talent, however, or to stake another business. Nor did they want to share the ownership of Blackstone. The memory of the feuding at Lehman was still all too fresh, and they wanted absolute control of their business.

The solution they ultimately hit on was to set up new business lines as joint ventures—"affiliates," they called them—that would operate under Blackstone's roof. To lure the right people, they would award generous stakes in the ventures. In time, that arrangement was the foundation for two of Blackstone's most successful affiliated businesses, its real estate investment unit, built by John Schreiber, and the bond investment business that was later spun off as BlackRock, Inc., now one of the preeminent publicly traded investment managers in the world, which Laurence Fink, who started it, still leads.

Such was their long-term vision. But the first task was to land some M&A work to pay the rent. It would take time to raise a fund to invest in buyouts and years more before the new firm would garner any profits from its investments. In the meantime, Peterson and Schwarzman needed a source of near-term revenue.

Their M.O. on the M&A front was the same one they had employed at Lehman. The fifty-nine-year-old Peterson, with his entrée to executive suites around the country, would get Blackstone in the door and Schwarzman, then thirty-eight, would make the deals happen. Peterson and Schwarzman would cozy up to management to get "deal flow."

With the financial world polarized by the wave of hostile takeover bids, Peterson and Schwarzman knew that they would have to choose sides. In 1985 the backlash against the raiders and Drexel had not reached its peak, but it was clear to them how they would ally themselves in the battles over corporate control. From day one, Blackstone pledged its loyalty to management. "Drexel was viewed by many in both the business and the financial establishment in a very unfavorable way, because they were like uninvited guests at many parties and they insisted on staying," Schwarzman says. "We wanted to be consistent with what we were doing at Lehman, and we didn't see how we could be counseling corporations one day and then turning around and attacking them the next. We wanted the corporate establishment to trust us."

They soon discovered that it was one thing to pitch clients with the prestige of Lehman behind them. It was quite another to win business for a new firm no one had heard of.

For several months, they couldn't scare up a single advisory assignment. By the time they landed their first, a project for Squibb Beech-Nut Corporation in early 1986, the $400,000 they'd started out with had dwindled to $213,000. The Squibb Beech-Nut job paid them $50,000. A pittance compared with the fees they'd commanded at Lehman, it was manna for the starving. Soon after that, Blackstone won two other assignments that paid modestly more, from Backer & Spielvogel, an advertising agency, and Armco Steel Corporation. "We were starting to earn back what we'd been losing," says Schwarzman. "Those were the streams of revenue between us and oblivion."

Starting in April 1986, Blackstone's M&A work picked up markedly. Yet even as its income rose, the firm continued to bump up against a prejudice in the corporate world against independent M&A boutiques. Not even CSX, which had collected an extra $15 million for its newspaper subsidiary thanks to Schwarzman's cunning years earlier, was entirely comfortable using Blackstone. CSX supplied Blackstone its first major M&A assignment, hiring it to help craft a takeover offer for Sea-Land Corporation, a shipping company that was seeking a friendly buyer after receiving a hostile bid from a corporate raider. However, when it came time to order a fairness opinion—a paid, written declaration that a deal is fair that carries great weight with investors—CSX's chairman Hayes Watkins sought out a brand-name investment bank, Salomon Brothers, instead.

Disheartened that his client had looked elsewhere, Schwarzman asked Watkins why he wouldn't accept Blackstone's opinion when Schwarzman's opinions had always sufficed when they were issued on Lehman's letterhead. "I hadn't thought of that," Schwarzman remembers Watkins responding. Schwarzman then prevailed upon Watkins to commission fairness letters from both firms. Though Blackstone hadn't managed to handle the deal solo, at least it won equal billing with the much more established Salomon.

At the same time as the two men were selling their services as M&A sages, they were also pounding the pavement, trying to drum up money for a buyout fund. By now the LBO business was no longer a backwater industry, and many others, including their former Lehman colleague Warren Hellman, were flocking to this hot corner of the investment world. The lure was easy to understand. KKR, the buyout front-runner, had just collected $235 million—four times what it had invested—selling Golden West, a Los Angeles TV broadcaster. Not long after, KKR pulled off its twenty-seventh buyout, capturing a much larger broadcaster, Storer Communications of Miami, for $2.4 billion, setting a new record.

But if winning M&A work had been harder than Peterson and Schwarzman had imagined, the fund-raising was downright demoralizing. The magic of their collaboration at Lehman, their accomplishments and renown as bankers, meant little now.

They'd set a most ambitious target for themselves: a $1 billion fund. KKR, the biggest operator at the time, was managing just under $2 billion. If Blackstone reached its goal, it would smash the record for a first-time fund and rank third, behind only KKR and Forstmann Little, in the amount of capital it had to invest. Schwarzman admits that the advertised figure was partly bravado, but it served a tactical purpose. Many potential investors had caps that barred them from providing more than, say, 10 percent of any one fund's capital. By setting a lofty total figure, Schwarzman figured, investors might be persuaded to make larger pledges.

Moreover, a large fund would throw off a fortune in fees to Blackstone as its general partner. For investing the money it rounded up from insurance companies, pension funds, and other financial institutions and overseeing the investments, Blackstone would rake in management fees of 1.5 percent of the fund's capital, or $15 million a year if the fund reached $1 billion. (The investors, who become limited partners in a partnership, don't write a check for their full commitment at the outset; they merely promise to deliver their money whenever the general partner issues a demand, known as a capital call, when it needs money for a new investment. Even so, the general partner collects the full 1.5 percent from the limited partners every year no matter how much of the money has been put to work. When the funds themselves begin to wind down after five or six years, the management fee is substantially reduced.)

Richer yet was the potential bonanza Blackstone stood to make in "carried interest." By the conventions of the business, private equity firms take 20 percent of any gains on the investments when they are sold. If Blackstone raised the hoped-for $1 billion and the fund averaged $250 million in profits a year (a 25 percent return) for five years running—a not impossible mark—Blackstone would be entitled to $50 million a year, or $250 million over five years.

On top of that, the companies Blackstone bought would reimburse Blackstone for the costs it ran up analyzing them before it invested and for its banking and legal fees. Its companies would also pay advisory fees to Blackstone for the privilege of being owned by it.

A more lucrative compensation scheme was hard to imagine. The fee structure ensured that if the fund was big enough, the financiers would become millionaires even if they never made a dime for their investors. The management fees alone guaranteed that with a large fund. If they made good investments and collected their 20 percent carried interest, they stood to make a lot more. While the individual partners at a successful midsized firm such as Gibbons, Green, or van Amerongen might earn $2 million in a good year, the industry's kingpins, Henry Kravis and George Roberts, overseeing multibillion-dollar funds, each took home upward of $25 million in 1985. This was several times more than what the CEOs of Wall Street's most prestigious investment banks made at the time, and it dwarfed what Peterson had earned as CEO of Lehman.

Getting their hands on the money in the first place, though, proved to be a struggle for Peterson and Schwarzman. Though LBOs were generating a great deal of talk and curiosity, most pension managers viewed them as too risky. The few investors who had the stomach for LBO funds preferred to place money only with tried-and-true firms such as KKR, Forstmann Little, and Clayton Dubilier & Rice. Not even a Wall Street grandee like Pete Peterson could overcome that bias.

"The problem was that a lot of pension fund managers had financial advisers, and the first question they asked us was, 'What is you track record?'" Peterson says. "Well, we didn't have one. They had to accept us on faith, nothing more. It was one of the toughest things I've ever been involved in."

Shortly after they opened shop, they drew up a two-page promotional letter describing their business plan, which they mailed to hundreds of corporate executives and old Lehman clients. They then waited. And waited. And waited. "Pete and I expected business to come flooding in.

Of course, it didn't," Schwarzman says. "We got a few 'Congratulations, nice letter' responses. That was it."

The pair's fund-raising trips were often fruitless. They were treated cavalierly, sometimes boorishly. Schwarzman, who arranged the trips, dragged Peterson with him to pitch the Delta Airlines pension plan in Atlanta one brutally hot day. Their taxi driver got lost and left them to walk the last half mile to the office. Peterson, weighed down with a suitcase, a bulky briefcase, and a suit bag, was drenched in sweat when they arrived. They were greeted by two pension officials, who escorted them to a room in the basement of the building and offered to get them coffee—and then asked them to chip into the coffee fund. At the end of their long presentation, Peterson and Schwarzman asked for the managers' reaction, only to learn Delta's fund didn't invest in LBO funds. "They said they had just wanted to meet us because we were well known," Schwarzman says. "The walk back was even hotter than the walk there. I thought Pete was going to kill me."

An excursion to Boston was equally galling. They flew there one Friday for a 4:00 P.M. meeting Schwarzman had lined up with officials at the Massachusetts Institute of Technology's endowment. When they arrived at MIT, the receptionist informed them she had no record of the appointment, and there was no one remaining in the office on the eve of the weekend. The two partners left, muttering imprecations under their breath. Adding insult to injury, they emerged from the building to find themselves in a torrential downpour with no umbrellas. They retraced their steps in order to call a cab from the endowment office, but it was locked. They took up positions on opposite street corners, hoping to hail a taxi in the driving rain, but to no avail. Finally, Schwarzman, ever the bargainer, rapped on the window of a cab stopped at a red light and offered the passenger a deal: $20 to have the driver take him and Peterson to the airport. It was the only pitch they made that day that succeeded.

After months crisscrossing the country, their quest had yielded only a single, $25 million pledge from New York Life Insurance Company. Eighteen institutions they'd considered strong candidates to invest with

Blackstone had rebuffed them. By the winter of 1986, a year into the fund-raising, they were "about out of tricks," says Schwarzman.

There were few targets left, so they decided to take a long shot and approached Prudential Insurance. The Pru had close ties to KKR, so they weren't optimistic. "It didn't seem the highest probability they'd want to invest with a start-up," Schwarzman says. But Peterson had done business with Prudential's chief investment officer, Garnett Keith, and was a close friend of Keith's old boss and mentor, Raymond Charles. He arranged a lunch at Prudential's headquarters in Newark, New Jersey.

Keith knew his way around leveraged buyouts at least as well as Peterson and Schwarzman, having financed twenty-five to thirty of them by that point. Under Charles in the 1960s and 1970s, the insurer had became the biggest lender for "bootstrap" acquisitions of small, family-owned businesses in which the buyer borrowed most of the purchase price—the forerunners of buyouts. Keith himself had helped fund a number of KKR's early deals, including the landmark Houdaille LBO, for which Prudential furnished nearly a third of the total capital.

Over lunch, Keith proved to be receptive. Between bites of a tuna sandwich, he trained his eyes on Peterson and said, "I've thought about this, Pete. We've worked together. I'm going to put $100 million in your fund, and we would like to be the lead investor." Keith, it turned out, had come to believe that the Pru was too closely identified with KKR and was in fact eager to forge new relationships. Furthermore, Ray Charles "had a lot of respect for Pete, and that rubbed off on me," Keith recounts.

At last, after more than a year of brush-offs, humiliations, and gnawing doubts about whether Blackstone would make it, Peterson and Schwarzman's luck had turned for the better. They were stunned. "That luncheon was the biggest day of our Blackstone lives," says Peterson.

As an anchor investor, Prudential drove a hard bargain, though. Back then, buyout shops laid claim to 20 percent of the investment profits from each individual company their fund bought. But that meant that if one very large investment in a fund was written off—say, an investment that consumed a third of the fund's capital—investors might lose money even though other investments worked out. The manager, though, would still collect profits on the good investments. It was a kind of heads-I-win, tails-you-lose clause.

Prudential insisted that Blackstone not collect a dime of the profits until Prudential and other investors had earned a 9 percent compounded annual return on every dollar they'd pledged to the fund. This concept of a "hurdle rate"—a threshold profit that had to be achieved before the fund manager earns any profits—would eventually become a standard term in buyout partnership agreements. Prudential also insisted that Blackstone pay investors in the fund 25 percent of the net revenue Blackstone made from its M&A advisory work, even on deals not connected to the fund. At the time, Blackstone still was forking out much of that revenue to Shearson under Schwarzman's severance agreement, which would end the following year.

In the end, these were small prices to pay for the credibility the Pru's backing would give Blackstone. The Prudential name could open doors at top financial institutions in the United States and abroad, and Peterson and Schwarzman quickly parlayed Keith's endorsement into further investments. It paid off particularly in Japan, where Prudential was a major player and where Peterson's status as a former cabinet member carried weight. Peterson was scheduled to give a speech in April 1987 at a gathering of top American and Japanese politicians and business leaders in Tokyo, and he and Schwarzman took advantage of the trip to trawl for money.

There, with the help of First Boston and Bankers Trust, top U.S. banks with a presence in Tokyo that Blackstone had hired to help on the fund-raising, they lined up meetings with Japanese brokerage houses. Schwarzman knew that brokers like Nomura, Daiwa, and Nikko were hankering to do business on Wall Street, and he hoped Blackstone could leverage its Wall Street lineage into a capital commitment.

Schwarzman's hunch turned out to be right. In Tokyo, an exploratory meeting with Yasuo Kanzaki, executive vice president of Nikko Securities, Japan's third-largest broker, went well. Kanzaki signaled that Nikko was willing to discuss an investment and asked the two not to talk to any other Japanese brokers. Unbeknownst to Peterson and Schwarzman, First

Boston had scheduled a meeting the next morning with one of Nikko's big competitors, Nomura. The two Americans weren't sure what to do. They feared insulting Nomura by canceling on short notice but didn't want to renege on their word to Nikko.

Schwarzman and Peterson called Kanzaki from their car phone outside Nomura's headquarters before the meeting and asked him how to resolve the awkward situation. Kanzaki responded by asking them how much money they wanted. Peterson cupped his hand over the phone while he and Schwarzman discussed how much to ask for. Finally they settled on $100 million. "No problem," Kanzaki declared. "Done deal!" He then suggested they keep their appointment with Nomura so as not to breach Japanese business protocol.

Nikko got what it desired from Blackstone, a collaboration to help its tiny band of New York bankers get up to speed on Wall Street. For Blackstone the surprise investment was even more valuable than it first seemed, for Nikko was part of the Mitsubishi industrial group, one of four enormous Japanese business combines that are linked by cross-ownership, commercial synergies, and a shared mind-set. As Schwarzman and Peterson trooped to meetings with other parts of the Mitsubishi network, they were greeted warmly. Mitsubishi Trust, Tokio Marine & Fire, and other group firms ponied up for the new fund.

Peterson and Schwarzman hadn't recognized how intimately linked the institutions were when they headed into these meetings. "We'd congratulate ourselves on being such great presenters," Schwarzman says. "I came to realize later we could have sent monkeys in to make those presentations. The fact was, they tended to trust the lead investor, Nikko." Even a member of a rival industrial group, Mitsui Trust, pledged $25 million. He and Peterson headed home with an additional $175 million in hand.

Their hot streak continued upon their return. In June, Peterson bumped into an old friend, General Electric chairman and chief executive Jack Welch, at a birthday party for *Washington Post* publisher Katharine Graham. "Where the hell have you been?" Welch inquired. "I know you and Steve have started this business, and I haven't heard from you."

Peterson answered, "Dear God, Jack, we've called and called on GE, and they said you're not interested." Said Welch, "You should have called me directly." Peterson did so the next morning, picking up $35 million.

Even more momentous was the $100 million General Motors' pension fund put up. GM, like GE, had brushed off Blackstone several times, but a First Boston banker tapped a church connection to get Blackstone access to GM, and the firm soon captured another $100 million pledge. The GM imprimatur brought Blackstone a raft of smaller commitments—$10 million to $25 million—from other pension funds.

Blackstone had now won anchor investments from three of the most important sources of investment capital at the time: the insurance industry, pension funds, and Japanese financial firms.

By early autumn 1987, the Blackstone buyout fund had reeled in a total of more than $600 million. That was well short of their $1 billion target, but Peterson and Schwarzman began to think they should lock that up while they could. It was a perilous time, though it was not yet clear just how perilous. By the second week of October, the stock markets were jittery. Inflation was headed up, fanning talk of an interest rate hike, which would slow the economy and put a damper on a business such as a buyout firm that relied on borrowed money.

"I was exceptionally nervous and putting pressure on everyone to close," Schwarzman says. He worked the phones, and on Thursday, October 15, 1987, Blackstone wrapped up the fund at around $635 million, with some mop-up legal work on Friday.

The following Monday the U.S. stock markets nose-dived 23 percent. Black Monday, as it became known, was the biggest one-day drop since 1914, outstripping even the 1929 sell-off that ushered in the Great Depression. If Blackstone hadn't tied up contractual loose ends before the crash, undoubtedly many investors would have backed out. Instead, Blackstone could boast of raising the largest first-time leveraged buyout fund up to that time.

No longer would Peterson and Schwarzman live off the unpredictable bounty of M&A fees. Blackstone now would collect 1.5 percent of the fund's capital every year as a management fee for at least six years.

This not only ensured Blackstone's near-term survival, but it also meant that Blackstone, finally, could staff up and take on the trappings of a bona fide business.

After an exhausting, two-year struggle, Blackstone had arrived.

"We got in just under the wire," Schwarzman says. "It was probably the luckiest moment" in Blackstone's history.

CHAPTER 5

Right on Track

Peterson and Schwarzman's new firm had sailed through the 1987 crash in good shape and they were free of nagging financial worries after raising their fund. But the stretch ahead would be rocky not just for Blackstone but for the buyout business as a whole. A treacherous turn in the capital markets and misfires on the deal front would doom some of Blackstone's fellow start-ups and imperil even some seasoned buyout firms. Through it all, Blackstone would struggle to establish footing. It didn't help that turnover at Blackstone was notoriously high in the early years, owing partly to Schwarzman's mercurial and demanding personality. The young firm, too, would make some bum bets on companies and people. But it would do more right than wrong.

With its $635 million safely in the bag, Blackstone immediately ramped up its operations. Soon it spilled over with fresh hires and filing cabinets. In the autumn of 1988, the firm moved to 345 Park Avenue, a bland, hulking, cream-colored skyscraper right across Fifty-second Street from its former offices in the Seagram Building. It took a ten-year lease on sixty-four thousand square feet, twenty times the size of its original quarters. Surveying the cavernous new expanse, Schwarzman wondered if he'd been batty to sign a lease for so much more space than the firm needed at the moment.

In rapid succession, Schwarzman and Peterson recruited three high-ranking partners with imposing pedigrees. The first, Roger Altman, forty-two, the Lehman banker, joined as vice-chairman. Peterson and

Schwarzman had tried hard to lure him in 1986 and 1987, but their old colleague held off until Blackstone at last raised its fund and was financially stable. Altman's coyness irked them, but they knew the well-connected banker would be a magnet for M&A fees. Lean, with a shaggy mane and suave manner, Altman was as adept as any Wall Street banker at winning over big-ticket corporate clients. His fascination with public policy clicked with Peterson, even though Altman was a staunch Democrat who had worked on Robert F. Kennedy's 1968 presidential campaign and had put his Lehman career on hold from 1977 to 1981 to work in Jimmy Carter's Treasury Department.

In February 1988, Blackstone corralled Laurence Fink, thirty-five, who had helped create mortgage-backed securities—bonds backed by packages of home mortgages—and built First Boston's successful mortgage securities unit. Securitization, as the process of making bonds out of mortgages was called, transformed the home lending business and created a huge new addendum to the debt markets. The next month, David Stockman, forty-one, a former Reagan administration budget czar, arrived.

As Reagan's first budget director, Stockman, a former two-term congressman from Michigan, was the point man for the supply-side economics the new administration was pushing—the theory that taxes should be lowered to stimulate economic activity, which would in turn produce more tax revenue to compensate for the lower rates. With his wonky whiz-kid persona, computer-like mental powers, and combative style, he browbeat Democratic congressmen and senators who challenged his views. But he soon incurred the wrath of political conservatives when he confessed to *Atlantic* reporter William Greider that supply-side economics was really window dressing for reducing the rates on high incomes. Among other acts of apostasy, he called doctrinaire supply-siders "naive." The 1981 article created a sensation and prompted Reagan to ask him over lunch, "You have hurt me. Why?" Stockman famously described the meeting as a "trip to the woodshed."

Though the president himself forgave him, Stockman's loose lips undercut his power at the White House, and in 1985 he left government to

become an investment banker at Salomon Brothers. He was recruited to
Blackstone initially by Peterson, who had known Stockman from Washington circles and, like Stockman, was deeply concerned about the federal deficit. Peterson and Schwarzman hoped to put Stockman to work
with corporate clients on big-picture strategic, economic, and trade issues, but ultimately he evolved into one of Blackstone's main LBO deal
makers.

Fink, tall and engaging, with a shrinking periphery of hair and old-
fashioned rimless spectacles, was a well-regarded Wall Streeter whose
star had fallen. A pioneering financier and salesman, he was considered
the second leading figure, after Salomon Brothers' Lewis Ranieri, in the
development of the mortgage-backed bond market. At the time, Fink
was about to lose his job at First Boston after his unit racked up $100
million in losses in early 1988. But Schwarzman and Peterson had from
the start hoped to launch affiliated investment businesses and thought
Fink was the ideal choice to head a new group focused on fixed-income
investments—the Wall Street term for bonds and other interest-paying
securities. They accepted Fink's explanation that flawed computer software and bad data inputs had triggered the stunning trading losses, and
they were further reassured by a conversation Schwarzman had with
Bruce Wasserstein, First Boston's cohead of M&A, who had become a
friend and frequent tennis partner of Schwarzman's. "Bruce told me that
Larry was by far the most gifted person at First Boston," Schwarzman
says. Peterson and Schwarzman offered Fink a $5 million credit line to
start a joint venture called Blackstone Financial Management, or BFM,
which would trade in mortgage and other fixed-income securities. In exchange for the seed money, Blackstone's partners got a 50 percent stake
in the new business while Fink and his team, which included Ralph
Schlosstein, a former Lehman partner and a good friend of Roger Altman's,
owned the other 50 percent. Eventually, the Blackstone partners' stake
would fall to around 40 percent as the BFM staff grew and employees
were given shares in the business. Fink also got 2.5 percent interest in
the parent, Blackstone.

The arrangement with Fink reflected the Peterson and Schwarzman approach to building up Blackstone. They wanted to recruit top talent, but they were not about to surrender any significant part of Blackstone's ownership. The implosion at Lehman had convinced them that they should keep tight control of the overall business. This was going to be their show. Altman, who might have gotten a bigger stake if he had joined his friends sooner, received a comparatively meager ownership interest of around 4 percent. Stockman's piece was even smaller.

By the spring of 1988, Blackstone had larded its buyout fund with an extra $200 million from investors who signed up after the original closing, pushing the fund's total capital to about $850 million, and it was now scouring the country for investments. It was a heady time for the LBO business, stoked by Drexel's junk-bond factory, and the larger corporate world was undergoing one of its periodic paroxysms of mergers and consolidation. There were more than sixteen hundred mergers in the United States worth nearly $90 billion in the first half of 1988, more than triple the dollar volume five years earlier and on a par with the frenzied level in early 1987. The slump in M&A following the October 1987 stock market crash was swiftly fading from memory.

Blackstone was as yet only a midsized player in a field that had become more crowded since its launch. A Wall Street bank, Morgan Stanley, had raised $1.1 billion, while Merrill Lynch would close a $1.5 billion fund later that year, and two new Blackstone-style, M&A-cum-buyout boutiques had burst onto the scene with far more hoopla than Blackstone had aroused.

The first was formed by First Boston mergers superstars Bruce Wasserstein and Joseph Perella, who jolted Wall Street when they left First Boston in February 1988 to form Wasserstein Perella and Company. They talked the cream of First Boston's M&A bankers into joining them, and their names carried enough cachet that they quickly lined up $500 million toward a $1 billion buyout fund.

More than anyone else, Wasserstein, forty, a rumpled, paunchy figure with a chess genius's command of tactics, had restyled the genteel M&A business into a sophisticated, high-stakes sport of aggression. He first gained wide attention in 1981 in the $9 billion takeover battle for the oil company Conoco, Inc., in which he outflanked Mobil Oil Corporation and the liquor giant Seagram Company Ltd. to win the target for E. I. du Pont de Nemours and Company, his client, despite a lower bid. (The intricate tactic he hatched to capture Conoco, called a front-end-loaded, two-tier tender offer, was later banned by the U.S. Securities and Exchange Commission.) After Conoco, Wasserstein had a hand in some of the biggest takeovers of the mid-1980s, including Texaco's hotly contested $10.8 billion purchase of Getty Oil Company in 1984 and Capital Cities Communications' $3.5 billion acquisition of the ABC television network in 1985. He was known for exhorting gun-shy clients to pull the trigger on topping bids, which earned him a nickname he hated, "Bid 'Em Up Bruce." Perella, forty-seven, the diametric opposite of his partner in height, girth, and sartorial savoir faire, was more of a traditional relationship banker in the mold of Peterson and Altman.

Wasserstein Perella soon won the backing of Japan's largest stock brokerage, Nomura Securities Company, which that July put up $100 million for a 20 percent stake in the firm. Most or all of that money ended up being funneled into Wasserstein Perella's buyout fund. Nomura issued a press release expressing its delight at the chance to be an early investor in a firm so obviously "destined to be an international M&A powerhouse." Wasserstein Perella looked to be halfway there already, raking in $30 million of M&A fees in its first four months. With those fees and the $100 million from Nomura, Wasserstein and Perella were spared the hand-to-mouth existence Peterson and Schwarzman endured for their first two years.

The other headline-grabbing new firm was Lodestar Group, formed the same month as Wasserstein Perella by Ken Miller, Merrill Lynch's M&A chief and vice-chairman and its highest-paid banker. Miller was not as lionized as Wasserstein and Perella, but he had secured his reputation by making Merrill a first-tier power in M&A and shepherding several high-profile LBOs that Merrill had led, including those of truck trailer maker Fruehauf Corporation and drugstore operator Jack Eckerd Corporation. In July, a day after Nomura announced its investment in Wasserstein Perella, Lodestar unveiled a comparable deal: Yamaichi

Securities Company, Japan's fourth-largest brokerage, would put up $100 million of the $500 million LBO fund Miller was raising and separately inject an undisclosed sum in Lodestar itself for one-quarter of the firm.

Blackstone would have to vie for investors, talent, and deals with these flashier upstarts. None of the new players held a candle to KKR, though. It had recently amassed a $6.1 billion war chest—far and away the biggest buyout fund ever—and controlled about a third of the $15 billion to $20 billion of equity the buyout industry had stockpiled to date. It was no easy task to compete, for KKR was raking in profits on a scale its founders couldn't have imagined a decade earlier. In May 1988, Henry Kravis and the other KKR partners personally pocketed $130 million in profits on just one investment: Storer Communications, a broadcaster they had bought just three years earlier, which they sold for more than $3 billion. KKR had pulled off gargantuan buyouts of name-brand companies—a $4.8 billion deal for the supermarket chain Safeway in 1986 and the $8.7 billion buyout of Beatrice Foods the same year. Late in 1988 KKR would reassert its dominance when it cinched by far the largest buyout ever, the $31.3 billion take-private of the tobacco and food giant RJR Nabisco—a bid that would define the era, crystallize the public image of private equity investors as buccaneers, and set a record that would not be matched for eighteen years.

Unlike KKR, though, Blackstone had its M&A business, which by 1988 was capturing its share of plum M&A assignments. Early that year Blackstone took in more than $15 million from two jobs alone: handling negotiations for Sony Corporation's $2 billion purchase of CBS Records, an assignment Blackstone picked up from Sony founder Akio Morito, an old friend of Peterson's, and from Sony's top U.S. executive, whom Schwarzman knew; and advising Firestone Tire & Rubber when it sold out to Japan's Bridgestone, Inc., for $2.6 billion, a deal Schwarzman guided. As Peterson and Schwarzman hoped, the M&A business gave the firm access to executives that eventually turned up LBO opportunities.

Blackstone's first buyout developed that way. It was puny compared with KKR's big deals—a mere $640 million—but it would have an immense impact on the young firm's image and fortunes.

It began when Altman telephoned Donald Hoffman, a top official at USX Corporation, the parent of U.S. Steel. USX was battling for its corporate life with Carl Icahn, the much feared corporate raider. In 1986 Icahn had amassed a nearly 10 percent stake in USX and launched an $8 billion hostile takeover bid. U.S. Steel was three months into a strike that was crippling steel production and had pummeled the stock. Over the next year, Icahn hectored USX to off-load assets and take other steps to boost its share price. To back itself out of a corner and persuade Icahn to go away, USX eventually announced that it would sell more than $1.5 billion in assets and use the money to buy back some of its shares. (Companies often buy in shares to boost their share price because that increases the earnings attributable to each individual share.) Among the assets USX tabbed for full or partial sale were its rail and barge operations. The plan assuaged Icahn.

Altman, Peterson, and Schwarzman flew to Pittsburgh to meet with USX's top brass to see if they could strike a deal for the transport business, which Hoffman headed. In addition to Hoffman, USX chairman and chief executive David Roderick and Charles Corry, the steelmaker's president, were at the meeting. USX hoped to raise $500 million from the sale, but two conflicting goals made it tricky to structure a deal. USX wanted to sell more than 50 percent of the transport business to an outside party so that under accounting rules it could take the unit's debt off its books. However, it didn't want to give up too much control. More than half the railway's business came from other shippers, but U.S. Steel was almost wholly reliant on its subsidiary's train and barges. The system hauled all the raw materials to U.S. Steel's Midwest plants and 90 percent of the company's finished products passed over its lines on the way to customers. Roderick couldn't agree to a sale if the businesses would end up in unfriendly hands.

"They told us, 'This is our lifeline. If anything goes wrong with this, if we sold it to a buyout firm unwilling to invest enough capital or that held us up for higher transport rates, it could bankrupt us,'" Schwarzman recalls. Rather than focus on price at the outset, the three Blackstone partners zoomed in on USX's anxieties and how to allay them. "The first meeting was not about price," Peterson says. "It was about governance. We went over some major operating decisions we'd face—spending levels to maintain the equipment, how we'd set rates, a determination of what to do if either of us wanted to sell our interests and various other issues."

That approach alone wouldn't have won Blackstone the deal, Roderick says: "Governance was extremely important to us, but so was price." But the attentiveness Altman, Peterson, and Schwarzman showed to USX's concerns gave the company comfort. The trio convinced Hoffman "that they understood our problem very well," he says. "They were head and shoulders above any other investment group that I saw. We saw probably five or six."

Not everyone at Blackstone was keen on the deal. Back in New York, David Stockman was dead set against it. The partners agonized over doing it. The big concern was how the business would perform if there were a severe slump in the steel market—a common event in that highly cyclical industry that could ravage revenues and profits of the transport unit. It fell to James Mossman, a brilliant, twenty-nine-year-old banker Altman had lured from Shearson, to digest the patchy data Blackstone had been given. After crunching the numbers, he was enthusiastic about the deal and made his case at a staff meeting.

"James raised his hand and said, 'We need to do this deal. We're going to make a lot of money!'" says Howard Lipson, a young staffer at the time who helped Mossman draft the financial model. Mossman explained that even though steelmaking is notorious for its ups and downs, the business of shipping steel was much steadier. "We showed that most of the wild cyclicality in steel companies' profits was due to what happened to pricing as volume rose or fell," says Lipson. "Despite that, the railroads are affected only by steel volume, not prices, and volume is not nearly as volatile as prices."

Mossman sketched an imaginary worst case. He assumed that steel volume tumbled to its lowest point in twenty years and stayed there for two years. He showed that, even then, the railroad and barge unit would be able to meet its costs and turn a profit. "James did a perfect analysis," says Schwarzman.

Convincing the Blackstone partners was one thing. Persuading banks to finance the deal was another matter. Blackstone needed $500 million of loans or bonds for the spinoff, but it had no track record in buyouts, and bankers were unnerved at the prospect of lending to a highly leveraged business that was dependent on the boom-and-bust cycles in steel. They weren't moved by Mossman's analysis. "Their mind-set was they didn't want to go anywhere near a cyclical business," Lipson says.

Schwarzman put out calls to all the big New York banks that financed buyouts: Manufacturers Hanover, Citibank, Bankers Trust, Chase Manhattan, and J.P. Morgan. All but J.P. Morgan turned him down flat. The House of Morgan, whose name radiated prestige, had been U.S. Steel's banker since the turn of the century, when J. Pierpont Morgan bought the steelmaker's predecessor from the industrialist Andrew Carnegie. It offered to finance the deal with USX, but it declined to give a firm commitment to come up with the money, and its proposal was loaded with conditions. "We loved the J.P. Morgan name," Schwarzman says, but reputation alone wouldn't get the deal done.

A sixth bank offered much better terms, however. Chemical Bank, like Blackstone's founders, had aspired for years to break into the LBO business, but it had been a distant also-ran in the world of high finance. Mocked for its dismal lending record, Chemical deserved its popular sobriquet, "Comical Bank." It would shed that reputation only in the late 1980s under the leadership of Walter Shipley and his successor as CEO, Bill Harrison. The two gave Chemical's new commercial lending chief, James Lee, a thirty-something banker, free rein to invigorate Chemical's loan operation and lead the charge into LBOs.

Chemical simply wasn't big enough to finance large buyouts alone, but Lee got around that limitation by mustering a network of banks that would back the deals he signed up. Canvassing loan officers he'd befriended in Australia, Japan, and Canada, he assembled a corps of banks that trusted Chemical and could be counted on to ante up quickly when new lending opportunities came along. By 1984 Lee's syndication apparatus was in place, and he conducted trial runs on a handful of high-rated, low-risk corporate loan packages before he ventured into the dicier realm of buyouts. By the time of the USX rail and barge deal, Lee had notched a handful of small loan syndications for LBOs.

To steal a march on other banks, Lee loaded Chemical's $515 million debt package for Blackstone with seductive features. Most important, he gave Blackstone an iron-clad promise to provide all the debt, and to do so at a lower interest rate than Morgan. By contrast, Morgan had offered only to make its "best efforts" to round up the requisite funds, not a binding commitment. To sweeten Chemical's proposal, Lee agreed to drop the interest rate by half a percentage point if the company's profits sprang back to prestrike levels. To tide the business over if it ran into trouble, Lee further offered $25 million of backup capital in the form of a revolving credit facility—a now-conventional part of LBO financing that Lee helped popularize. This was credit the company could draw on if needed and pay back as it could, unlike the regular loans, whose amounts and due dates were fixed.

"When I walked into Blackstone's offices, I knew I could give them what they wanted," says Lee. "I had a firm grip on how much money" Chemical could pledge to any deal.

Schwarzman, still angling to obtain the imprimatur of the more august J.P. Morgan, went back and asked Morgan to match Chemical's terms. To no avail.

"Steve let us know he thought J.P. Morgan was classy, and we were not," says Lee. "But he said our offer was vastly more clever and creative," and Chemical won the day.

First announced on June 21, 1989, the deal closed in December. That month, Blackstone and USX formed a new holding company, Transtar Holding LP, to house the rail and barge operations. As with the famous leveraged buyout of Gibson Greeting in 1982, equity was just a tiny sliver of the total financing package for Transtar. Blackstone shelled out just $13.4 million, 2 percent of the buyout price, for a 51 percent ownership stake. The new debt Chemical provided replaced much of the railroad's equity, so USX was able to take out more than $500 million in cash. (USX also lent Transtar $125 million in the form of bonds—a kind of IOU known in the trade as seller paper because it amounted to a loan by USX to help Blackstone finance the purchase.) Roderick and USX got what they asked for: Despite holding just 49 percent, USX shared decision-making power over budgeting, financing, and strategy on equal terms with Blackstone.

The transaction was not a classic LBO at all. Strictly speaking, it was a leveraged recapitalization—a restructuring where debt is added and the ownership is shuffled. But whatever the label, it helped advertise the company-friendly approach that Peterson and Schwarzman had been touting for three years now. "We really wanted to put meat on our corporate partnership idea, and we hoped this deal did that," Peterson says. "It sent a signal that we were good guys who did thoughtful, friendly deals as a real partner."

Blackstone got everything it bargained for: a sturdy business on the rebound, which it had snared for an extraordinarily low price of four times cash flow. That was one-third to one-half below the stock market valuations of most railroads.

For a buyout investor, cash flow is the axis around which every deal turns. It determines how much debt a company can afford to take on and thus what a buyer can afford to pay. Net earnings, the bottom-line measure mandated by accounting rules for corporate financial statements, factors in interest costs, taxes, and noncash accounting charges such as the depreciation of assets. Cash flow is the deal maker's raw "show me the money" measure—the amount that remains after operating expenses are paid. The financial structure of an LBO is built upon it.

One way that buyout firms make profits is to use the cash flow to pay down the buyout debt. In the industry's early days, deals were formulated with the aim of retiring every dollar of debt within five to seven years. That way, when the business was finally sold, the buyout firm reaped all the proceeds because there was no debt to pay off. A second way to generate a gain is to boost cash flow itself, through revenue increases, cost cuts, or a combination, in order to increase the company's value when it is sold. Using cash flows, there is also a third way to book a gain, without an outright sale. If a company has paid down its debt substantially, it can turn around and reborrow against its cash flow in order to pay its owners a dividend. That is known as a dividend recapitalization.

In Transtar's case, Blackstone used all three means to manufacture a stupendous profit. In 1989, in line with Mossman's expectations, Transtar's cash flow reached nearly $160 million, enabling it to repay $80 million of debt by year's end. By March 1991 Transtar had pared $200 million of its original buyout debt. With substantially less debt than it had when the business was spun off and with Transtar's cash intake growing, the company was able to borrow again to cover a $125 million dividend to Blackstone and USX. A little more than two years after the deal closed, Blackstone had made back nearly four times the $13.4 million it had invested. By 2003, when Blackstone sold the last of its stake in a successor to Transtar to Canadian National Railroad, the firm and its investors had made twenty-five times their money and earned a superlative 130 percent average annual return over fifteen years.

If this seems a bit like conjuring profits from nothing, that's largely what happened. Transtar, like Gibson Greeting, was a prime example of buying at the right time, leveraging to the hilt, and milking every drop of cash flow for profit. Soon enough, rising prices and a floundering economy would change the rules of the game, forcing buyout firms to focus more intently on improving fundamental corporate performance to generate profits and less on financial sleights-of-hand.

That's not to say the Transtar buyout served no purpose. It delivered a hefty profit to the pension funds and other institutions that put their money with Blackstone. The deal also assisted USX, allowing it to keep control of Transtar even as it restructured itself and sold off the subsidiary and other operations to increase the value of its stock. As to Transtar itself, the buyout didn't particularly strengthen the company, but it certainly didn't weaken it.

*   *   *

Transtar's success showed the rest of Wall Street that Peterson and Schwarzman could excel at the buyout game. The deal also was a landmark for a second reason. It forged an abiding tie between Blackstone and Chemical Bank's Jimmy Lee that would be of enormous consequence to both. A gregarious spark plug of a man who resembled a back-gelled Martin Sheen and was known for his spiffy silver-dollar suspenders, Lee soon emerged as a kingpin of leveraged finance, a banker's banker to other LBO luminaries such as Henry Kravis and Ted Forstmann. Just as Drexel Burnham's Michael Milken had created the junk-bond market, tapping the public capital markets to finance the corporate raiders and buyout shops of the 1980s, Lee reinvented the bank lending market with his syndicates, which allowed risk to be shared and thereby allowed much larger loan packages to be assembled. At Chemical and its later incarnations (Chase Manhattan Bank, the name Chemical adopted in 1996 after buying Chase, and later JPMorgan Chase, after Chase bought J.P. Morgan in 2000), Lee would go on to play as critical a role in the stupendous growth of LBO activity in the 1990s and 2000s as Milken had with junk bonds in the 1980s.

Even though Lee would do brisk business with all the major LBO shops, he would work most closely with Blackstone. Beginning with Transtar and for the next fifteen years, Lee functioned as a kind of house banker to Blackstone, financing a great many of its deals and never siding with a competing LBO firm in a deal on which Blackstone was bidding. Theirs was a truly synergetic relationship, which helped propel both Chemical/JPMorgan Chase and Blackstone to the top in their fields.

"You could argue that Blackstone made JPMorgan Chase as much as JPMorgan Chase made Blackstone," says one of Lee's counterparts at another bank. "Neither would be where they are today without the other."

Transtar also advertised Blackstone's readiness to ally itself with corporate chieftains in the war against raiders, and just how far it would bend to accommodate corporate America's financial and strategic imperatives. It helped establish Blackstone's reputation as "an operating problem solver," in Peterson's words.

"In every way, it was a perfect first deal for us," says Lipson. "It was

highly successful quickly, and it showed we weren't looking to antago-
nize corporations but to be friends. Corporate partnerships became our
calling card." Whereas competing buyout shops typically exercised dic-
tatorial control over their acquisitions, Blackstone was adaptable. Its
openness to splitting power or even taking a back seat to a corporate
collaborator bolstered its deal flow, as Schwarzman and Peterson had
hoped: Of the dozen investments that Blackstone went on to make with
its 1987 buyout fund, seven would be partnerships akin to Transtar.

In addition to differentiating Blackstone from the competition, Schwarzman also believed the partnerships heightened Blackstone's odds of success. Having a co-owner intimately familiar with the business—typically
one that was a major customer or supplier and therefore had an interest
in its thriving—would give Blackstone an advantage over competing
buyout firms, staffed as they were with financial whizzes who had never
run a business or met a payroll. With the prices for whole businesses escalating in step with the stock market in the late 1980s, Schwarzman felt
Blackstone "needed an edge to safely do deals in a higher-priced environment."

"That's really why we came up with the corporate partnership strategy. I just couldn't figure out how to make money buying companies
unless we brought unusual efficiencies to a company by way of cost improvements or revenue synergies."

The partnership approach also fit with Schwarzman's innate cautious-
ness. In some partnerships, Schwarzman went so far as to barter away
some of Blackstone's potential upside for downside insurance, in the form
of a right to sell out to its partner several years later at a preset price or
valuation. Some of the firm's rivals viewed such trade-offs with bemuse-
ment. To their way of thinking, ceding power and profit to hedge the
downside was downright lily-livered. "We always thought Blackstone's
corporate model was bullshit," sniffs one. "It was like they couldn't stand
on their own; they needed help and made a lot of concessions to get it."

Schwarzman's preoccupation with the possible downside was more
than a reasoned response to the market dynamics of the day. It was a gut-
level reflex, a kind of bête noire or obsession, former colleagues say. The

rudimentary rule of investing, that one must risk money to make money, "is something Steve always had a hard time coping with," says one former partner. For a world-class investor, "his risk-aversion was really extra-ordinary."

Schwarzman acknowledges as much. "We are more risk-averse than other private equity firms, and part of it is visceral. I don't like failure, and losing money is failing. It's a personal thing that has turned into a strategy here."

Over the next two decades, the corporate partnership deals had a mixed record. But the strategy was pivotal to Blackstone's success early on, producing most of its early home runs, including investments in the Six Flags amusement parks and a second railroad, the Chicago and North-western Railroad.

Schwarzman's caution sometimes worked against Blackstone by de-nying it promising deals. But it also spared it from perpetrating some of the colossal blunders that in the 1990s would damage and doom a few bullish (or bull-headed) rivals. Call it what you will, knee-jerk trepida-tion or prudence, Schwarzman's instincts would be central to Blackstone's success.

CHAPTER 6

Running Off the Rails

The Transtar triumph produced a warm afterglow. But it didn't last long. Two misguided investments quickly ran off the tracks in 1989 and forced the young firm to rethink the way it vetted its investment options. The failures also established a harsh new unwritten rule: Slip up badly enough, just once, and you're out. Everyone was on notice. Not even partners were exempt.

The first misfire was Wickes Companies, an unwieldy amalgam of three dozen disparate businesses that Blackstone took private for $2.6 billion in December 1988 in partnership with Wasserstein Perella, Blackstone's rival as an M&A boutique and buyout shop. Conglomerates like Wickes, once stock market darlings, had fallen out of favor and were being ripped apart. David Stockman, Blackstone's point man and strategist on Wickes, thought that Wickes would be worth more dismembered than intact.

Stockman was a relentless advocate for his own deals, bombarding his colleagues with minutiae—the actuarial details of pension plans, consumer vehicle preferences, or whatever other imaginative product of his research would be the key to making an investment successful. He became legendary inside and outside the firm for calculating and writing out voluminous spreadsheets by hand, often faxing the sheets of numbers to underlings at Blackstone who would type them into computer spreadsheets, as most other deal makers did from the outset. A banker who worked on one of Stockman's deals remembers being dumbfounded as page after endless page of figures spat out of the fax machine during negotiations.

Stockman had cracked the Wickes nut, or so he thought. He plotted to break up the company, whittling it down to a single business: Collins & Aikman, a maker of textiles, carpeting, and wallpaper. Blackstone and Wasserstein Perella each sank $122 million into the buyout, which closed the same month as Transtar—the largest investment by Blackstone for the next seven years.

Things went awry almost from the start, in early 1989, when the U.S. economy started to soften. An early sign of trouble came that spring, when Wickes put Builders Emporium, then the largest home-improvement retail chain in California, up for sale. Blackstone expected it to fetch as much as $250 million, one former employee says. "But we ended up having to sell it over time for like $50 million." Slowing auto sales also dug into the auto fabrics side of the business.

The buyers also soon discovered that Wickes's former CEO Sandy Sigoloff—a corporate turnaround artist and notorious cost slasher nicknamed Ming the Merciless—had hacked away rather too exuberantly at Wickes's managerial ranks. "What we found was that Sigoloff was used to getting rid of whole layers of management for companies that were in trouble. But this company wasn't in trouble," says Schwarzman. "He fired a lot of people anyhow, so there was nobody around to do the work." Nearly from the start, then, the company was a problem.

Far uglier and more damaging than Collins & Aikman, though, was Blackstone's third investment, an ill-conceived $330 million LBO of Edgcomb Metals Company, a Tulsa steel distributor. In the space of just a few months, Edgcomb threatened to demolish Blackstone's investors' faith in the firm.

The Edgcomb acquisition was the brainchild of Steven Winograd, a thirty-one-year-old M&A prodigy Blackstone lured away from Drexel. At Drexel, Winograd had played a role in a $150 million, management-led LBO of Edgcomb in 1986 and later that year helped take the steel fabricator public, making a rich man of Edgcomb's CEO, Michael Scharf, and huge profits for Texas's Bass family and other backers of the buyout.

From the moment Winograd settled in at 345 Park Avenue, he pressed the idea of a second buyout of Edgcomb, whose stock had languished after it went public. Schwarzman quickly said yes. In May Blackstone negotiated a $330 million deal to take Edgcomb private for $8 a share, $2 above the IPO price of 1986. Like Transtar, the Edgcomb buyout was leveraged to the rafters, with Blackstone contributing just $23 million for a 65 percent equity stake. The buyout closed in June.

David Stockman opposed the deal. Since his arrival at Blackstone a year earlier, Stockman had carved out a role for himself as a devil's advocate and doomsayer, and he argued fervently against the Edgcomb buyout. Stockman's input didn't win him many fans at headquarters. "He had a habit of criticizing other people's deals, particularly in the early years," says one former Blackstone partner. "Right or wrong, David was never in doubt," says David Batten, another ex-partner. Stockman's Cassandra act soon wore thin not only because it put him at loggerheads with his partners, but because he often was just wrong.

But not this time. Edgcomb made its money buying raw steel, milling and shaping it, and selling it at a markup to auto factories, aircraft makers, and other users. Its profit margins, Stockman pointed out, were directly linked to steel prices, and if business turned down sharply, Edgcomb would find itself selling its steel inventory at a loss and its cash flow would vanish.

"I had them both in my office," Schwarzman says of Stockman and Winograd. "Winograd argued that the company's profits were of a repeat nature, and that it had very interesting expansion prospects. Stockman said it was a dangerous deal to do and it wasn't worth the price. I could see both sides, and I voted with Winograd. It turned out to be a catastrophically wrong decision."

Indeed, almost as soon as Blackstone completed the deal in June 1989, the same economic softening that had undermined the firm's breakup plans for Wickes doomed Edgcomb, just as Stockman had predicted. The company was saddled with inventory that was worth less than it paid. The business situation turned very bad so quickly that Edgcomb had trouble making its first interest payment that summer, a humiliating state of affairs for Blackstone. Right out of the gate, the buyout was racing toward insolvency.

Schwarzman soon threw his energies into trying to rescue the deal. He cajoled Blackstone's fund investors to stump up another $16 million of equity to try to keep the business afloat and worked tirelessly to ensure that the creditors didn't lose a dime. If Edgcomb defaulted on its debt, it might irreparably taint the new buyout firm's reputation in the credit markets. He was beside himself at that possibility and made his anxiety clear around the office.

In July 1990, Schwarzman arranged to sell the nearly bankrupt company to a subsidiary of France's Usinor Sacilor SA, then the world's largest steel company, at a steep discount to the original price. Edgcomb's senior lenders were repaid, but there wasn't enough money left to repay Blackstone. Its fund investors wound up losing $32.5 million of the $38.9 million they'd put into the deal.

That Schwarzman ultimately salvaged even one-sixth of the limited partners' money was little short of miraculous in the circumstances, an ex-partner recalls. "That's where I saw Steve's brilliance," this person says. "That's where I saw how good he was. He saw the problem and he worked doggedly to resuscitate the company."

Many Blackstone fund investors viewed the entire affair less charitably. In a phone conversation, Shirley Jordan, the chief investment officer of Presidential Life Insurance, called Schwarzman "a complete idiot" and fumed, "I never should have given you a dime!" Schwarzman says he responded, "I may not be a complete idiot, but I certainly was on this transaction." Other limited partners rendered similar judgments in less-barbed language.

Schwarzman may have taken responsibility in talking to outsiders, but internally he blamed Winograd and turned on him. He castigated him savagely for his deficient judgment and other supposed failings and fired him with a bazooka blast of invective. The brutal dismissal fueled anxiety among the rank and file and contributed to the firm's reputation for being a difficult and even volatile place to work. Anything from misspelling a word in a legal document or failing to rustle up enough business could evoke Schwarzman's ire. But Winograd's experience sent the chilling message that losing money could be a capital offense.

In the early years, "there was an atmosphere where every deal on the principal, or LBO, side was do-or-die," says former partner Howard Lipson, who logged eighteen years at Blackstone. "Like life or death."

At the same time Schwarzman was wrestling with problems at Collins & Aikman and at Edgcomb, the firm faced a third major setback in 1989: an ill-timed detour into stock trading that took a generous bite out of the partnership's own capital.

The new business was launched on a victorious note in December 1988, when Blackstone procured another $100 million from Nikko, the Japanese bank that had made a crucial early commitment to Blackstone's first fund. This time the money would go not to the buyout fund, but to Blackstone itself. As with Wasserstein Perella's headline-grabbing pact with Nomura six months earlier, Nikko was putting up $100 million for a 20 percent cut. But Schwarzman extracted sweeter terms from his Japanese backer than Bruce Wasserstein, his friendly rival and tennis partner, had.

"After Bruce did that deal," Schwarzman says, "I went back to Nikko and said I wanted another $100 million, like he got, but I wanted it in the form of a joint venture with our advisory business." He knew how avidly Nikko and other Japanese brokers wanted a piece of the M&A banking business, and he and Nikko both knew that allying with a well-connected American firm was the quickest way to obtain it. Nikko resisted at first but eventually acceded to his terms: Instead of taking a straight 20 percent ownership interest in the Blackstone partnership and all its operations, as Nomura had in Wasserstein Perella, the Japanese accepted a 20 percent share of the net earnings of Blackstone's M&A advisory business over the next seven years. In addition, Nikko would receive 20 percent of any returns Blackstone earned investing the $100 million. In 1995, if either party chose not to extend the investment, Blackstone would repay the $100 million along with any returns Nikko was still due.

For Nikko the deal had loads of promise. Mergers had rebounded smartly from the brief lull after the 1987 stock market fall, and in 1988

M&A was Blackstone's main fee engine, yielding close to $29 million in income. Japanese corporations and banks were snapping up American businesses and real estate, and through Peterson's ties to Japanese industrial titans, Blackstone snagged lucrative assignments, advising on two of the biggest such deals that year: Sony's purchase of CBS Records and Bridgestone Corporation's purchase of Firestone Tire and Rubber Company. Nikko had visions of trading on Peterson's ties to Japanese managers to capture a bigger share of the cross-border merger market.

Conceivably Blackstone could have used Nikko's money to fund expansion and hire top-tier talent, or tucked it away as a rainy-day reserve. But Schwarzman wasn't eager to embark on a hiring spree and was thinking more short term. Soon after Nikko wired Blackstone the money in early 1989, he hit on a moneymaking formula that would throw off hefty dividends to Blackstone and his partners as well as to Nikko. (By this time, the burdensome M&A fee-sharing arrangement with Shearson had expired and only Nikko and the buyout fund's investors shared in Blackstone's M&A fees. What's more, Nikko's cut was of M&A earnings after expenses, including the payments to fund investors.)

Schwarzman decided to sink half of Nikko's money into risk arbitrage, or trading in stocks of takeover targets. Arbitrageurs—arbs for short—bet on the likelihood and timing of takeovers and mergers that have been announced but not yet completed. Typically, a target's stock will sell for less than the offer price to reflect the risk that the deal may not go through and the fact that, even if the deal is completed, the shareholder can't collect until sometime in the future. If something goes wrong with a deal, the target's stock can plummet, but in spite of the risk, many big brokerages wagered tens of millions of dollars on takeover stocks and earned a pile of profits in the eighties with the explosion of takeover activity.

That March Schwarzman lured a seasoned arb, Brian McVeigh, along with his team from Drexel. McVeigh's résumé was blemished. Smith Barney and Harris Upham and Company had dumped him and his crew after they suffered massive losses in the October 1987 stock market crash. Overall, though, his record sparkled. From February 1983 to September 1987 at Smith Barney and then from May 1988 to March 1989 at Drexel, McVeigh's arbitrage funds had returned on average 39 percent a year. Blackstone formed a joint venture with McVeigh along the lines of the one it had formed with Larry Fink for the fixed-income investment affiliate. McVeigh and his group were allotted a 50 percent interest in Blackstone Capital Arbitrage and were handed custody of about $50 million of Nikko's money and were told to go at it.

Blackstone couldn't have picked a worse moment to ramp up in arbitrage. The economy was just beginning to slow, putting the brakes on takeovers, and by October 1989 LBOs and most takeover activity had screeched to a halt. The death knell for the M&A boom was the unexpected collapse of a $6.8 billion, employee-led buyout of UAL Inc., the parent of United Airlines, that October. McVeigh's group, which had amassed a large position in UAL's stock, lost a bundle when the airline's shares plunged from a high of $294 to less than $130. Many other of his holdings nose-dived, as well. The arb unit took an 8 percent loss.

Schwarzman's reaction was quick and severe. Ten months after McVeigh had arrived at Blackstone, he and his team were axed, Blackstone Capital Arbitrage was shuttered, and the $46 million that remained of the original $50 million was stowed away in the very safest kind of securities: certificates of deposit.

Blackstone wasn't the only firm with heavy arbitrage losses in October. Nor was it alone in firing traders or bolting the arbitrage business. Some of Wall Street's best-known arbs lost their jobs in the winter of 1989 when the takeover market evaporated. But it's safe to say that few received a tongue-lashing on their way out the door like the one Schwarzman gave McVeigh. As Schwarzman saw it, McVeigh, like Winograd, had made an avoidable blunder that cost the partnership dearly. Few sins were worse in Schwarzman's world.

Winograd and McVeigh were just the first of many partners and lesser employees hired and jettisoned from 1989 to 1991. Hotshot investment bankers the firm had lured away from First Boston, Shearson, and Morgan Stanley came and went in less than a year, let go for failing to rustle up deals and revenue in a down market. The best-known casu-

alty was Richard Ravitch, a business executive and public official renowned for revitalizing New York City's derelict subway system in the
mid-1980s, when he was chairman of New York's Metropolitan Transportation Authority. Like Felix Rohatyn, who had helped New York
City stave off bankruptcy in the 1970s, Ravitch was a local legend with
a dazzling résumé. (In 2009 he was named the state's lieutenant governor, one of the few nonpoliticians ever to be offered the post.)

But his talents didn't translate well to Blackstone's deal-driven,
pressure-cooker culture. "He was a terrific manager. He was not a great
deal guy," says a former Blackstone partner.

Not all who left were summarily executed. Some who fell from grace
were eased out quietly or quit. Others were exiled from the thirty-first
floor, where Schwarzman and Peterson held court, to humbler quarters
one floor below before getting the ax. The move to the thirtieth floor was
brutally symbolic. Ringed by partners' offices, the upper floor was the
seat of activity and power, whereas the sparsely populated lower floor
was home to accounting and payroll and a place to warehouse documents. After a few had been kicked downstairs, the thirtieth floor came
to be seen as a departure lounge for those about to be sent packing, a
death row for the condemned. Junior staff members jokingly dubbed the
space the Aloha Suite.

"Steve was a very tough boss," says Henry Silverman, the former
CEO of the travel and real estate conglomerate Cendant Corporation
and a billionaire financier, who was a Blackstone partner from early
1990 to late 1991. "At one point I was in my office, working on a deal
with the team, and Steve walked in and shook his finger at us and said,
'Remember, I don't like to lose money!' I heard that many times from
him over the years. He needed to remind us that he wasn't among the
minority who likes to lose money."

Beyond the message Winograd's summary termination sent to others
at the firm, Edgcomb had another lasting and more beneficial repercus-
sion. Realizing that a second costly stumble could do lasting harm to
Blackstone, or perhaps even consign it to an early grave, Schwarzman
decided that the firm's process for vetting investments needed to be

formalized. From then on, partners would have to submit a researched and tightly reasoned proposal that would be shared with all other partners. Schwarzman would remain the final arbiter, but henceforth there would be a full airing of every deal's possible pitfalls before he decided whether to go forward.

"I didn't want people lobbying me at my desk or whispering to me in a corridor. Every deal would get vetted in front of the entire partnership, and not just once," Schwarzman says. "It would be the job of the partners to poke holes and lay out the risks, without anyone getting huffy or defensive. It wasn't a personal attack. People had to realize it wasn't *their* deal being criticized; it was the *firm's* deal, and the process was to protect the firm. Had we not had Edgcomb, people might still be lining up at my door."

Though the new procedures didn't immunize Blackstone from making bad investments, Schwarzman is convinced they cut down their frequency. The more formalized review process also made the decision to invest a collective one. This insulated individual partners from blame— and from Schwarzman's wrath—if deals went sour.

CHAPTER 7

Presenting the Steve Schwarzman Show

B y 1989, less than four years after Blackstone's founding, Schwarzman was the firm's uncontested leader. Peterson, who'd arguably done more than his young partner to give life to Blackstone, continued to wine and dine clients and initiate deals. Indeed, some of Blackstone's most profitable LBOs in those early years stemmed from Peterson's network of corporate connections, and he still reeled in fat M&A paychecks. In 1989, a year when the new firm would be tested by bad investments and the downturn of the credit markets, Peterson once again drew on his friendship with Sony's Akio Morita to land a prime M&A assignment: advising Sony on its $5 billion purchase of Columbia Pictures Entertainment, Inc., for a $9.9 million fee. But it was Schwarzman who performed the majority of the grunt work at the firm: hiring, firing, executing the business plan the two had devised, deciding which LBOs to pursue and trying to pick up the pieces of Edgcomb.

By decade's end, Peterson had forged a parallel career as a big-picture thinker and author, a shift he says that he and Schwarzman anticipated. "I was extremely active in the building years, raising money and getting clients and attracting people. But Steve was the CEO and ran the business. I already had that CEO experience at Bell & Howell and Lehman, and I was very confident he could do the job. I had equal powers in major decisions, and if I learned something about the business that troubled me, I'd talk to him. I wasn't going to second-guess him."

Starting with essays he wrote for the *New York Times* and the *New*

York Review of Books, and an article in the October 1987 *Atlantic* that won a National Magazine Award, Peterson took to blasting away at Washington's spendthrift ways and its addiction to raising money by selling treasury bonds to foreigners. He extended his crusade to speeches and books. The thrust of his argument was that the ballooning federal debt inevitably would sap America's competitiveness in the world economy. The irony of Peterson's political passion was not lost on the press at the time. *Newsday* columnist Allan Sloan pointed up the disconnect between Peterson and Stockman's "inveigh[ing] against government deficits" and "corporate overborrowing" and the fact that a surfeit of debt had ruined Edgcomb. An article in *Barron's* dubbed Peterson a "Cadillac Cassandra" and remarked, "Like many a social scold before him, Peterson's admonitions do not always match his actions." (Peterson says government borrowing is different from LBO debt. The former, he says, is done off the books or through "fictitious trust funds," and the public that foots the bill has little understanding of its scope or consequences. By contrast, LBO borrowing is a controlled procedure carried out by "more or less sophisticated and knowledgeable" parties who are "far better able to assess the facts, the risks, and the rewards.")

Often it seemed like Peterson's mind drifted to those larger public issues. During investment committee and management committee meetings he would scrawl away furiously on yellow legal pads, preparing his next speech or book. But his brain could entertain more than one intricate line of thought at a time. Jonathan Colby, who worked at Blackstone from 1989 to 1996 before moving to another buyout firm, Carlyle Group, describes his first job interview with Peterson. It began in Peterson's office, then shifted to a limo that took Peterson to an event where he was to speak. Peterson drafted his speech in the car, "scribbling away on his legal pad the whole time," while Colby talked on, Colby says. Later that evening, Colby met with Schwarzman back at Blackstone's offices.

"Steve asked me how it went with Pete. I told him I don't think Pete had heard a word I said. So Steve called up Pete at home and asked him what I'd said. Pete was able to repeat all of it, virtually verbatim."

Peterson rarely deigned to shoot the breeze with junior or midlevel employees. One, who spoke with Schwarzman almost daily, says Peterson was remote, never once sitting down to talk. Many ex-staffers recall passing him on the way to the elevator accompanied by luminaries like Henry Kissinger, who sometimes stopped by for lunch. They remember the annual Blackstone Christmas bashes Peterson hosted where, decked out as Santa Claus, he would distribute Hermès ties to the men and scarves to the women.

For one party, Blackstone chartered a boat with a helipad to navigate the waters off Manhattan. Peterson was perceptibly uncomfortable mingling with anyone under the age of thirty, says a former associate, then in his twenties. "The joke was that Pete wanted a helipad so he could make a quick getaway and not have to spend time talking to younger people."

Nevertheless, Peterson continued to shape the firm by his tone, veterans say. "He was absolutely a presence, a day-to-day presence, really throughout the nineties" through his role on the investment and management committees, says partner Lawrence Guffey, who calls Peterson a "compass for the firm." It was Schwarzman, though, who set the agenda. And no one would ever accuse him of being aloof or detached. He was a ferociously engaged boss.

His ambition was manifest while he was growing up in Huntington Valley, Pennsylvania, a Philadelphia suburb. In a revealing anecdote in a 2008 magazine profile, Schwarzman recounted how as a teenager he had urged his father to develop the family store, which sold linens and housewares, into a chain. The elder Schwarzman retorted that the business was fine just as it was and he intended to keep it that way. Unsatisfied with that answer, young Steve kept hectoring his father.

"I saw the business as a model you could expand nationally. If you look at how Bed Bath & Beyond has done, that probably wasn't a terrible judgment," Schwarzman says. "My dad had no interest whatsoever in doing it. He was a very bright person, but he was not aggressive."

In school, Schwarzman's competitive drive was funneled into sports. "He could fly, man!" says Bobby Bryant, who ran track with Schwarzman at Huntington Junior High School and who remains a friend. "In junior high, he was only two-tenths of a second off the national junior-high record for the hundred-yard dash. He anchored our relay team. He was a short guy, but he could jump up and grab the basketball rim."

Schwarzman also excelled academically at Abington High School and won a spot at Yale in 1965, where he majored in social sciences. He was a solid A and B student, recalls Jeffrey Rosen, a Yale classmate and friend, who today is deputy chairman of Lazard, the investment bank. "Steve was an intense, competitive athlete," Rosen says, who loved to play touch football and soccer in the large, interior courtyard at Davenport College, where he resided.

He was also something of a ladies' man, which was no small achievement given that Yale was still an all-male school at the time. He struck up a friendship with Davenport's dean, Horace Taft, a prominent physicist, and his wife, Mary Jane, who loved the ballet. She kindled a fascination in Schwarzman for dance. In his junior year, Schwarzman started a club, the Davenport Ballet Society, and arranged for its members to see a dress rehearsal of the *Nutcracker Suite* by George Balanchine's New York City Ballet at Lincoln Center. Later that year, Schwarzman staged a dance festival at which students from nearby women's colleges performed. Rosen suspected Schwarzman started the club at least in part "as an excuse to meet girls," yet the event was a big hit. Schwarzman also won an invitation to join Skull and Bones, the secret and elite society of Yale seniors whose alumni include both Presidents Bush. (George W. Bush joined Skull and Bones in 1968, a year before Schwarzman, and the two knew each other but not well, Schwarzman says.)

Fresh out of Yale and off the family dole in June 1969, Schwarzman set off to try his luck on Wall Street. Through a contact in the Yale admissions office, he landed a position at Donaldson, Lufkin & Jenrette, an investment bank. There was little glamour or glitz to this young banker's life, though. As a penny-pinching plebian, he rented tiny flats by the month in gritty neighborhoods. His first was a fourth-floor walk-up on the Lower East Side, next to the precinct house where the opening sequence of the 1970s television series *Kojak* was shot.

Cockroaches skittered away when he arrived home and flipped on the lights. A subsequent rental, on Second Avenue and Forty-ninth Street, above the Midtown Shade Company, was one and a half rooms with no kitchen and a common bathroom down the hall.

The living conditions were a comedown from the ivied world of Yale, as was his stint at DLJ, where his energy and cleverness didn't make up for his cluelessness about finance. At Yale, he'd studied psychology, sociology, and anthropology; the business world was terra incognita. "They gave me an office and a secretary, but I was utterly unprepared for any commercial enterprise, let alone a fast-moving one like DLJ and the securities business. I had no knowledge of accounting. I didn't even know what a common stock was before I went there."

He calls his time at DLJ "a very searing experience." Even so, he says, he showed enough raw talent to earn a farewell lunch with DLJ senior partner Bill Donaldson. "I'm not sure I did anything to merit that lunch, other than the fact that Bill had hired me," Schwarzman says. "I asked him why he had hired me, because in my view, I had provided no value-added for his firm." Donaldson, Schwarzman says, answered: "I make bets on people on my own instincts, and my instinct is that someday you're going to be the president of DLJ." (Donaldson says he has no memory of the lunch or of making such a statement but says Schwarzman was a hardworking and promising young man.)

He was accepted to business school at Harvard and got his MBA in 1972. After graduating, he entertained offers from Lehman Brothers and Morgan Stanley. Back then Wall Street still was ethnically divided into the WASP firms of Morgan Stanley and First Boston; the mostly Catholic Merrill Lynch; and the elite Jewish houses of Lehman, Goldman, and Salomon Brothers. Those divisions would begin to break down later in the 1970s, but Schwarzman claims he was only the third Jew to receive a job offer from Morgan Stanley. When the bank's president, Robert H. B. "Bob" Baldwin, extended the offer, he qualified it, telling Schwarzman he would have to "change [his] personality to fit in." Schwarzman told him he wouldn't do that, and chose Lehman.

The Steve Schwarzman who became the driving force of Blackstone

reflected the verve and talent of that younger man. He also had para-
doxical qualities.

In Blackstone's early years he worked tirelessly, logging fourteen-
hour days, his mind constantly immersed in ways to strengthen the fledgling business. Associates and bankers fielded calls from him at all hours
to hash over ideas. "He would often call me on Saturday morning to ask
me what I thought of this or that, or I would call him," says Jimmy Lee,
the Chemical Bank lending chief. "He was building his firm, I was building mine, and we reinforced each other."

Former partner Bret Pearlman, who worked at the firm from 1989 to
2004, remembers as a young employee getting voice mails from Schwarzman left at 5:30 A.M. commenting on memos Pearlman had left him the
night before. The calls spoke volumes, both about Schwarzman's attentiveness and about the work ethic he demanded. "Steve never expected
more out of you than he expected out of himself," says Pearlman.

To many, the desire and drive were linked uncomfortably to a less
attractive quality. On Wall Street, where money is the yardstick of success, greed is as ubiquitous as exhaust fumes at Daytona. But even by the
standards of the Street many considered Schwarzman a money grubber.
"When I worked with Steve, he was aggressively greedy," says one former partner. "But he didn't try to hide it. He was always honest and
straight, and his word was his bond. A lot of people motivated by money
are elliptical and disingenuous. They will put their arm around you and
reach into your pocket. Whereas Steve would come up to you and say,
'I'm going to try and take your wallet.'" A banker recalls once asking a
Blackstone partner about Schwarzman's athletic prowess. "I asked him
if what I'd heard was true, that Steve was good at basketball and could
jump really high," the banker says. "He said, 'Yeah, if he's jumping for
a bag of money!'"

As he grew richer, the displays of his wealth became more conspicu-
ous, and irksome, even to other financial types. The head of another private equity firm recalls walking along a white-sand beach in St. Barts in
the Caribbean with his children in the 1990s when an enormous yacht
pulled into the harbor and weighed anchor. Two Jet Skis piloted by crew

members emerged from the boat and motored in with a cargo of a folding table and chairs, big umbrella, tableware, a wine bucket, and fancy
food. After laying the table, the two buzzed back to the yacht to retrieve
a tall and striking woman and a shorter man. Moving in to see who was
responsible for this strange scene, the witness recognized Schwarzman and
his wife. "Here I am schlepping my kids around, drenched in sweat, and
Schwarzman pulls up in a yacht to have lunch. To say it was ostentatious
is an understatement. I'm not pleading poverty here, but I really did feel
like there should be a revolution."

Schwarzman had a softer side. The same person who mercilessly
hounded Steven Winograd from Blackstone over the Edgcomb debacle
also cultivated warm relations with young recruits such as Howard Lipson, David Blitzer, and James Mossman, furthering their careers. He
took pains to remember subordinates' wedding anniversaries and birth-
days. "If you were going through something tough personally, Steve
made a point of calling. He was good about stuff like that," Lipson
says. He could be compassionate, too. When Steven Fenster, a friend
and former Lehman partner, came down with a fatal form of pancreatic
cancer, Schwarzman saw to his medical treatment. After Fenster died,
Schwarzman and Allan Kaplan, another Lehman alumnus, raised money
to endow a professorship in his name at Harvard Business School.

He was also free of airs. He enjoyed working directly with young analysts and associates, for instance, and often solicited their views directly.
On the eve of an investment committee meeting, former partner Bret
Pearlman says of his early years at the firm, Schwarzman would often call
to get Pearlman's views about a proposed deal. "He always did that with
the younger people," Pearlman says. "He knew he needed that other avenue of conversation."

Early on Schwarzman stood out in a field of aspiring buyout moguls,
says one investor who first met him in the early 1990s. "I just remember
thinking this guy is a friggin' dynamo. Holy moly! He was all energy, all
these different insights and thoughts," says Mario Giannini of Hamilton
Lane, which advises pension funds and other investors. "Who is this
guy? He has this sort of blend of self-confidence and self-deprecating

style that was interesting. At the time it was a very different style from a lot of his buyout peers. He can be so self-deprecating, and you don't normally hear that from people in the industry. It's disarming sometimes. And yet as you listen to him, he's just very smart."

Schwarzman had an "unfiltered" quality, as the head of another private equity firm puts it. He was enthusiastic and spontaneous and at times just plain brash and oddly insensitive. His manner could thus charm or irritate, accordingly. "There's something impishly, immaturely admirable about Steve," this person says. Even friends and partners who were fond of him found themselves rolling their eyes at the ill-considered thoughts that escaped his mouth on occasion.

Internally, there was no question that Schwarzman was the boss, but he didn't dictate decisions from the top. "Steve is not the sort to lay down the law and say, 'I think we should do this,'" says former partner Simon Lonergan. He didn't need to dominate the room; he preferred to hear views from around the table before making a decision.

Still, an arrogance could shine through at times. In 1990 he told a *Wall Street Journal* reporter that Blackstone's success derived from his ability to "explain financial stuff to morons," and he had a penchant for putting down competitors and others behind their backs. His seeming compulsion to brag—about being the first Jew admitted to Skull and Bones and the first banker in history to orchestrate a sealed-bid corporate auction—rubbed many the wrong way.

Despite his savvy as a banker and manager, even after years as a CEO he could be strangely tone-deaf and tactless at times. At Blackstone's annual meeting with its fund investors in Florida in the spring of 2008, he put his foot in his mouth while explaining why a buyout Blackstone had planned of a residential lender, PHH Mortgage, had collapsed that spring. "Trying to buy a mortgage bank in the midst of the subprime crisis was the equivalent of being a noodle salesman in Nagasaki when the atomic bomb went off," he said. "Not a lot of noodles left, or even a person, and that's what happened to us on this deal." The radioactive jest, which quickly leaked out to the press, could not have come at a worse time, as the firm was trying to catch up to competitors like Carlyle and Texas Pacific Group in Asia.

Schwarzman "always has a few off-the-cuff zingers that leave heads shaking," says a limited partner who was there.

As the firm grew larger and went public, that blindness to the way he was perceived became a serious liability.

CHAPTER 8

End of an Era, Beginning of an Image Problem

T he merger mania that had heated up in 1988 intensified in early 1989, fueling Blackstone's M&A unit, which advised on $8 billion of deals that year, taking in fees from clients such as Sony, PepsiCo, French computer maker Société des Machines Bull, and Varity Corp. The firm also lined up a buyer for the *National Enquirer,* the supermarket tabloid. Another fountain of fees was Larry Fink's bond-investment affiliate, Blackstone Financial Management, which turned profitable within months of its launch. Fink used just $150,000 of the $5 million credit line Blackstone had provided to start the joint venture, and he quickly repaid that. By the end of 1989 Fink was managing $2.7 billion of outside investors' money, more than four times the $585 million his group had raised a year and a half earlier. That year Fink's team pulled in $13.4 million in management fees, posting a $3.9 million net profit. Blackstone's partners had struck gold. They collectively owned 40 percent of a successful, fast-growing money manager, and it had cost them next to nothing.

But the waning months of the decade were marked by mounting anxiety over a faltering economy and what that would mean for leveraged buyouts. In the early fall of 1989, fears began to surface that a raft of recent LBOs would buckle under their onerous debt loads. As the year wore on, panicked lenders started to cut off financing for future LBOs altogether.

The brewing economic storm battered Blackstone early. It had aggravated the financial ills of Wickes, the textiles and home improvement conglomerate Blackstone had bought, and triggered the demise of both Edgcomb and Blackstone's risk-arbitrage operation. The turn of mood in the markets would clobber the firm a fourth time that year, nearly capsizing Blackstone's $1.6 billion buyout of Chicago and Northwestern, a regional railroad, and threatening the very existence of Donaldson, Lufkin & Jenrette, Schwarzman's first employer out of college and one of the main lenders for the purchase.

In the CNW deal, like Transtar, Blackstone stepped in as a white knight—an ally of management—for a company facing a hostile takeover bid. In April 1989, Japonica Partners, a Drexel-backed corporate raider, launched a hostile offer for CNW Corporation, the railroad's publicly traded parent, after buying up nearly 9 percent of CNW's shares in the open market. Immediately after catching wind of Japonica's move, CNW chief executive Robert Schmiege reached out to potential investors he thought would be friendly toward management to see if they'd be willing to trump Japonica's $44-a-share bid. Both Blackstone and DLJ expressed interest, and at Schmiege's suggestion they pooled forces and started crafting a joint offer.

Soon after, a third potential coinvestor surfaced: Union Pacific Railroad, the nation's third-largest railroad. UP, whose tracks from the West Coast ended at Omaha, had long coveted CNW, whose lines ran from there to Chicago, the nation's rail hub and the connection to eastern lines. UP's chairman, Drew Lewis, transportation secretary in the Reagan administration and an old friend of Peterson's, called Peterson and said UP wanted in.

UP was the obvious ultimate owner of CNW, but under federal rules it could not buy more than 25 percent without obtaining regulatory approval, a process that could stretch on for years. UP collaborated with CNW on shipments to and from the East, and Lewis was horrified at the thought of CNW's falling into Japonica's hands, fearing that the raider would slash upkeep and hurt service. The federal railroad merger rules prevented UP from topping Japonica's offer. Taking a stake in a Blackstone buyout of CNW would serve UP's purposes nicely.

"I asked Lewis, 'What would you do if you owned it?'" Peterson says. Lewis said that CNW's railbeds hadn't been upgraded and that UP wanted to be able run trains at up to fifty-five miles per hour. "So we said, why don't we make that railbed investment part of the deal?" Lewis also requested that CNW hand off to UP some of its highly lucrative business hauling low-sulfur coal from mines in Wyoming's Powder River basin. "We told him that if his prices were competitive, that would be fine with us," says Peterson.

Together Blackstone, DLJ, and UP put a $45.50-per-share offer on the table and on June 6, Japonica dropped out—collecting a nice profit as the shares rose during the bidding. (Illustrating again that in the corporate raider game you can win by losing.) Although the $1.6 billion price was rich—Blackstone was paying eight times cash flow, twice what it had paid for Transtar—it was risking comparatively little: Blackstone injected $75 million of equity for a 72 percent ownership stake, while DLJ's buyout arm put in $25 million for 24 percent. Union Pacific invested $100 million in preferred stock that paid a dividend. Though the preferred didn't have the potential to rise (or fall) in value like common stock, UP had an option to convert it after five years into common shares for 25 percent ownership. Lenders, led by Chemical Bank and DLJ's investment banking operation, furnished most of the remaining $1.4 billion.

On June 23, the buyout, Blackstone's fourth, was put to bed.

But not to rest. Three months later, a nightmare set in.

In the intervening months, lenders and bond investors became nervous that the market had overheated, and the trading prices of junk bonds tumbled as investors ran for the hills. As in the financial crisis two decades later, credit suddenly tightened. Leverage wasn't just out of fashion; it had become next to impossible to obtain. Indeed, the whole financing apparatus that had given rise to leveraged buyouts was sputtering, and the CNW deal looked like it might die along with it. The problem was a $475 million bridge loan DLJ had provided to finance the deal until CNW could arrange to float new bonds.

Bridge financing had been invented to compete with Drexel's junk bonds. The process of issuing bonds was cumbersome and could take months: Elaborate prospectuses had to be prepared and circulated and buyers had to be lined up. Drexel was so adept at hawking junk, however, that companies and other banks involved in a deal would go forward with a takeover based solely on Drexel's assurance that it was "highly confident" it could sell the necessary bonds. Other banks couldn't do that, so instead they offered short-term loans that allowed the buyer to close the deal immediately and issue bonds later to repay the bridge loans. By 1988, DLJ, Merrill Lynch, and First Boston had each nibbled away at Drexel's market share in leveraged takeovers this way.

But bridge lending was risky for the banks, because they could end up stuck with inventories of large and wobbly loans if the market changed direction or the company stumbled between the time the deal was signed up and the marketing of the bonds. The peril was magnified because bridge loans bore high, junk bond–like interest rates, which ratcheted up to punishing levels if borrowers failed to retire the loans on schedule. The ratchets were meant to prod bridge borrowers to refinance quickly with junk, and up until the fall of 1989, every bridge loan issued by a major investment bank had been repaid. But the ratchets began to work against the banks when the credit markets turned that fall. The rates shot so high that the borrowers couldn't afford them, and the banks found themselves stuck with loans that were headed toward default.

The perils of bridge lending hit home that September and October when Robert Campeau, a Canadian financier and real estate developer, struggled valiantly to refinance a $400 million bridge loan he had taken out the year before with First Boston and two other banks to buy Federated Department Stores, the parent of the Bloomingdale's, Abraham & Strauss, Filene's, and Lazarus stores. After the abrupt failure of the $6.8 billion United Airlines buyout on October 13, the leveraged finance business all but ceased, Campeau couldn't arrange borrowings to pay back the bridge, and Federated filed for bankruptcy. First Boston came close to toppling that year because of its loan to Campeau and two other bridge loans it made, for a takeover of the Long John Silver's restaurant chain and for a buyout of Ohio Mattress Company, the parent of Sealy.

The Ohio Mattress debacle was quickly dubbed "the burning bed" and remains, along with Campeau, a pivotal episode in takeover lore.

DLJ found itself in similarly precarious straits. It had planned to market CNW bonds to refinance the CNW bridge loan the third week of October 1989, but the United employee buyout cratered the week before and spooked the markets. DLJ now was saddled with two enormous bridge loans: the $475 million one for CNW and a $500 million loan to TW Services, owner of the Denny's restaurant chain. Some of the money had been furnished by other institutions, but the bulk had come from DLJ and its corporate parent, Equitable Life. DLJ's very survival now hinged on its bond desk's ability to peddle CNW and TW Services bonds at a time when investors were scared to bet on highly leveraged companies.

To no one's surprise, bond buyers demanded much higher interest rates than DLJ had bargained for—and much higher rates than CNW had expected to pay. So it was that one dark, blustery morning in mid-October, Schwarzman trekked downtown to DLJ's headquarters across from the World Trade Center to hash out the terms for the bonds.

The senior banker on DLJ's side of the table was Hamilton "Tony" James, who was the boss of both DLJ's buyout group and its junk-bond sales force. Thirty-eight years old, he was composed under fire and, many who have worked for him attest, ferociously intelligent. In addition to creating and running the bank's LBO and junk units, he led M&A and restructuring. Ostensibly the number-three executive, he was considered by many inside and outside the bank to be its de facto chief executive. Their tense face-off that morning was the first time that James, who years later would become Blackstone's president and chief operating officer, had met Schwarzman.

Failing to refinance the bridge would be calamitous for DLJ and Blackstone alike. It would leave DLJ holding a giant, risky debt that it never expected to keep, and it would slam CNW with escalating interest payments that could sink the company and obliterate Blackstone's equity. But James and Schwarzman had different ideas about how to solve the problem. DLJ was so desperate to get the bridge loan paid off that it was willing to offer bond buyers the moon. Blackstone, by contrast, was fixated on protecting its equity investment and didn't want to endanger CNW with sky-high rates.

"DLJ was scared silly; there was fear in the room," Schwarzman says. After some heated give-and-take, they reached a middle ground, with Blackstone agreeing to raise the rate on the junk bonds from 14.5 percent, already very high, to 14.75 percent and to award bond buyers a 10 percent equity share in CNW as well. But James and his team wanted yet another inducement for bond buyers: an offer to raise the interest rate on the bonds after a year if the bonds had declined in value. It was known as a reset clause, and as the junk-bond market turned increasingly jittery, investors had begun to insist on resets to limit their risk. DLJ demanded that one be added to the CNW package.

Reset notes were akin to adjustable-rate home mortgages, but instead of being tied to a broad index of borrowing costs, as adjustable mortgages typically are, the rates on reset notes are adjusted to reflect the going market value of the notes or bonds themselves. Suppose investors buy $1,000 bonds that pay $147.50, or 14.75 percent, annual interest, and the bonds' market value falls to $970 a year later because interest rates in general have risen, making the old 14.75 percent bonds less desirable, or because the particular company is in trouble. The fall in value means that for an investor who buys them at $970, the bonds effectively are paying 15.2 percent interest. The reset clause would restore the bonds to their face value. To make up for the drop in price, the company would be required to boost the interest 3 percent to $152 a year, returning the bonds' market value to $1,000, making the original bond buyers whole and happy.

As hard as DLJ pushed for a reset, Schwarzman pushed back just as hard. What if the bonds traded down to 90 cents on the dollar, triggering a rate hike to 16.4 percent? The market was capricious and Schwarzman was leery of open-ended risks: "I said, 'I'm not doing a reset. I have to know my cost of money. What if there's a bad economy? You could bankrupt the company!' This was terrible corporate finance. But DLJ said, 'We need a reset or we won't do the deal.'"

Eventually Schwarzman said he could agree to a reset provided that there was a 15.5 percent cap on the adjusted rate. After a back-and-forth, James agreed. The DLJ bankers insisted that the odds were strongly against the bonds' falling so much in value that CNW would have to pay 15.5 percent. Schwarzman worried, though, that someone would figure out how to depress the bond price temporarily near the reset date so the new rate would hit the cap. A trader buying the bond then at a discount could make a killing when the interest rate was reset.

"I said that, somehow, some trader will find a way to make sure the bonds reset at the top of the cap," Schwarzman recalls. "I said, 'I'll personally bet you $100,000 it will reset at the top.' There was stunned silence. 'Nobody is good for $100,000? What about $50,000?' Again, silence. 'How about $25,000?' Finally, Tony James bet $5,000."

James, too, recalls the exchange vividly. "We went back and forth a long time. This was the last issue we got hung up on. We couldn't get Steve off it. Eventually, I said, 'All right, Steve, I'll bet you $5,000 this gets reset below the cap.'" (Asked if the wager started at $100,000 and descended in increments, James responds, "I'm going with my version.")

The reset still wasn't enough to sell all the bonds, and DLJ was stuck holding a lot of them in its own account, as well as a big slug of TW Services bonds. With DLJ still struggling, many employees received unsold CNW and TW bonds in lieu of cash bonuses that year. But DLJ staved off bankruptcy.

As for the reset, Schwarzman's prediction was borne out. CNW's bonds fell sharply, sending the interest rate up to 15.5 percent.

"Steve won the money, because the market continued to deteriorate," says James. "He was gracious and had me give the money to charity."

The seize-up of the markets and the turmoil that followed the downfall of the Campeau-Federated and United Airlines deals foreshadowed the credit crisis the financial world experienced a generation later. Though the downturn that began in 2007 lasted longer and inflicted far wider damage than that of the early 1990s—no major commercial or investment banks foundered in the early nineties as Bear Stearns and Lehman

Brothers did in 2008—both shared a root cause: overexuberant borrowing. In both cases, scores of lending institutions went under and buyout firms strained to keep debt-laden holdings afloat. Then, as later, buyout players that had binged on leverage would have a nasty hangover.

Within months of the Federated and United problems, the biggest LBO ever—the deal that had come to symbolize the buyout business—was teetering on the verge of collapse.

KKR's buyout of RJR Nabisco, the tobacco and food giant that peddled Oreo cookies, Ritz crackers, and Winston and Salem cigarettes, embodied the raucous, rapacious ethos of the late 1980s. It had everything: an imperial CEO who maintained a fleet of ten corporate jets, doled out $1,500 Gucci watches to employees, and surrounded himself with celebrities at company-funded golf events; Wall Street sharks circling the prey; and a teeming supporting cast of bankers and lawyers craving a cut. It was a tale of greed, excess, and hubris, with no small measure of farce. In the words of M&A banker Bruce Wasserstein, it was "the Roller Derby of deals."

It began in October 1988 with the CEO, F. Ross Johnson, who was frustrated that RJR's stock wouldn't budge even though profits were up, lodging a bid. That month, with backing from Peter Cohen at Shearson Lehman Hutton, Johnson won his board's support for a $75-a-share management-led buyout. Management would put up equity and would borrow the balance. His bid, one-third higher than RJR's stock price, was far from stingy, but Johnson saw value in a company that could not win the stock market's love. He calculated that if they bought at the right price, he and his financial backers could all make a fortune selling pieces of the business, capturing the hidden value for themselves.

For Cohen, the deal was a chance to resuscitate the M&A franchise Shearson had acquired with Lehman. But Johnson and Cohen quickly lost control of the situation, and of Johnson's company. Henry Kravis and George Roberts thought Johnson had made a low-ball bid. Some outsiders figured that RJR could be worth as much as $100 a share if it were split up, and Kravis and Roberts calculated that they could top Johnson's offer and still make a bundle by shedding parts of RJR and slashing fat.

KKR decided to crash Johnson's party, bypassing him and RJR's board with a $90-per-share tender offer aimed directly at shareholders.

The sidewalk fisticuffs soon became a full-blown rumble. Ted Forstmann allied himself with Johnson, offering to help save the company from the clutches of Kravis, Forstmann's nemesis. Most of Wall Street lined up on one side or the other with offers of financing. When it was all over, six weeks after it began, KKR had been forced to raise its offer to $109 per share, which the board accepted over a $112 bid from Johnson. Both bids offered shareholders a mix of cash and promissory notes—short-term bonds, in effect—but KKR's terms on its notes were more generous.

By then Johnson had been publicly pilloried both for the rich golden-parachute package he had negotiated so he would be paid millions if he were deposed after a takeover and for trying to buy his company from his own shareholders at an unfairly low price. In this winner-take-all game, Johnson found himself without a job, and Cohen, his dreams of ascendancy dashed, resigned as chairman of Shearson Lehman in January 1990.

The takeover was *the* defining moment for the buyout industry. From the opening skirmish, it was seen for what it was—a battle between corporate America and a new breed of Wall Street titan. "The firm's partners each take home in the neighborhood of $50 million a year, according to people close to the firm," the *New York Times* gushed when KKR made its opening bid, pointing out the $2 billion KKR had made breaking up Beatrice Foods over the preceding years.

More significant in the long term, KKR emerged from the RJR battle perceived as a raider. Technically, KKR's was not a hostile bid. In Wall Street parlance, a hostile bid is one made at a time when the company has not put itself up for sale, and KKR came in only after RJR's board had put the company in play by entertaining Johnson's offer. But that was a legalism. The fact was that KKR had bid against the management and won. It had snatched control away from the CEO and now promised to slash costs and carve up the company. To the man in the street, that was no different from what corporate raiders did.

At $31.3 billion, the RJR buyout smashed all records. It was more than three times the size of the next biggest, KKR's $8.7 billion LBO of Beatrice in 1986. But KKR ended up paying a dangerously high eleven times cash flow, and there was a time bomb buried in the complicated mix of debt behind the buyout: $6 billion of reset notes whose interest rates were up for adjustment in February 1991. Like the CNW reset notes that had alarmed Schwarzman when Blackstone was arranging debt for that deal in October 1989, the interest on the RJR notes had to be readjusted upward if the notes traded below their face value. But unlike the CNW notes, where Schwarzman had insisted there be a ceiling on the maximum interest rate, the RJR reset notes had no limit on rates: RJR would have to pay whatever rate it took to restore the bonds to their original value so bondholders wouldn't suffer a loss. With the investors fleeing risky securities, interest rates spiked and the notes were trading at such deeply depressed prices that RJR faced the prospect that the rate on the notes might jump from 13.71 percent to 25 percent. The hit would be lethal—adding more than $670 million in yearly interest costs that RJR could in no way afford.

By the spring of 1990, the situation was grave enough that Martin Lipton, a famed takeover attorney, warned Henry Kravis that Chapter 11 might be RJR's only option. "There's no way we'd do that," Kravis retorted. If the company defaulted, KKR stood to lose its entire $1.5 billion of equity. In July, KKR did the only thing it could do to stave off bankruptcy: It doubled down, investing another $1.7 billion of equity to bail out RJR as part of a debt refinancing.

RJR managed to fend off insolvency, but the investment came to be seen not as a triumph but as the all-time booby prize, Exhibit A in the case against the LBO. The rip-roaring bestseller *Barbarians at the Gate*, by *Wall Street Journal* reporters Bryan Burrough and John Helyar, released in 1990, cemented the deal's reputation as a monument to twisted thinking, greed, and megalomania. Years later, when KKR finally extricated itself from the last of its investment, it had lost more than $700 million. Investors in KKR's record $6.1 billion 1987 fund ended up with a mediocre 9 percent return after KKR collected its cut.

A devastating front-page story in the *Wall Street Journal* that year completed the picture of KKR and the buyout business from another angle. The lengthy piece about KKR's 1986 buyout of Safeway by Susan Faludi focused not on jousting executives and financiers but on the rank-and-file employees who lived through the buyout of the supermarket chain and the layoffs and divestitures that followed. The story was awarded a Pulitzer Prize the next year for "reveal[ing] the human costs of high finance."

It was an ugly picture the *Journal* painted. KKR and Safeway's management made four times their money when the chain went public again in 1990.

> Employees, on the other hand, have considerably less reason to celebrate. . . . 63,000 managers and workers were cut loose from Safeway, through store sales or layoffs. . . . A survey of former Safeway employees in Dallas found that nearly 60% still hadn't found full-time employment more than a year after the layoff.
>
> James White, a Safeway trucker for nearly 30 years in Dallas, was among the 60%. In 1988, he marked the one-year anniversary of his last shift at Safeway this way: First he told his wife he loved her, then he locked the bathroom door, loaded his .22-caliber hunting rifle and blew his brains out.

The new management philosophy was poetically summed up in the change in the company's motto, from "Safeway Offers Security" to "Targeted Returns on Current Investment."

Coming the same year as *Barbarians,* the story helped crystallize the reputation of buyout moguls as ruthless job cutters who looted companies of cash and assets for the sake of short-term profits.

It was not just the layoffs that made the Safeway buyout emblematic of the eighties. The Safeway saga had all the ingredients of a classic LBO of its era. The deal emerged after a father-and-son team of raiders began circling the chain, which they viewed as a lumbering business run by complacent managers who didn't appreciate the company's undervalued, underutilized assets. There was a bidding war and the company emerged with debt heaped upon it.

The true consequences of the Safeway buyout, however, were rather different from what the *Journal* portrayed. The first three years under KKR were indeed tumultuous, as Safeway shrank its business by 30 percent and sold 40 percent of its stores. Tens of thousands of employees did pay a steep price. But KKR reshaped a languishing company and positioned it to thrive in the next decade. In that way, it was a case study in the economic payoff from the upheaval and restructuring wrought by the raiders and buyout firms.

Safeway may have been a "a company legendary for job security," as the *Journal* said, but that was another way of saying that it had become bloated. Its labor costs had shot up and were a third higher than those of its competitors (most of which were also unionized) because Safeway had been preoccupied with expansion rather than profitability. Management had been virtually hereditary. Safeway's CEO at the time, Peter Magowan, had succeeded his father at age thirty-seven, and his grandfather, Charles Merrill, a founder of Merrill Lynch, had been instrumental in assembling the chain through mergers in the 1920s and '30s as an investor, a banker, and later as head of the company.

Safeway had a strong brand in its home market in northern California as well as the Pacific Northwest and Washington, D.C., but was competing ineffectively and losing money in many others. Moreover, it did not even have internal mechanisms to gauge the profitability of its divisions or its investments.

In 1986, Herbert and Robert Haft, two sometime corporate raiders whose family had owned the Dart Drug chain, thought they could do a better job running Safeway and began buying up the stock as a prelude to a hostile takeover bid. In July, after amassing a 6 percent stake, they went directly to shareholders with a $58-a-share bid, backed with a promise from Drexel to provide billions in financing.

KKR had already been eyeing Safeway, but Magowan had brushed off several feelers from the firm. Now, with his job threatened, he was receptive when KKR offered to be a white knight, allying with management to take the company private. Soon KKR and Magowan had formulated a $4.8 billion, $69-a-share offer, which Safeway's board recommended to shareholders when the Hafts refused to up their bid beyond $64. KKR would put up $132 million of equity for about a 90 percent ownership interest, with management taking a 10 percent stake. (Morgan Stanley and Bankers Trust backed KKR's bid since Drexel was spoken for.)

The Hafts were outbid but walked away with a $153 million profit—double the money they'd spent buying Safeway stock—including millions Safeway paid to settle a lawsuit over its defensive tactics during the battle. Other shareholders did well, too, for KKR's offer was 70 percent above the stock's price when the Hafts began buying up shares.

While KKR kept Magowan on as CEO, he would now be playing according to KKR's script as Kravis, Roberts, and their partners put Safeway through radical reconstructive surgery.

Lowering labor costs was only one piece of KKR's strategy. Equally important was getting out of markets where Safeway was an also-ran. Safeway quickly sold off its Los Angeles and San Diego stores, where it had small market shares, to stronger competitors. Soon its Salt Lake City, Arkansas, Oklahoma City, and Kansas City stores were off-loaded, also to other chains. Out went the profitable British subsidiary, sold to reduce debt. Meanwhile, a British wine retailer that wanted to branch into the United States bought Safeway's struggling Liquor Barn operation.

What made Safeway so ripe for an LBO was the fact that it had never scrutinized how it used its capital, whether its investments were paying off, or where it was making and losing money. KKR set to work at once analyzing Safeway's real estate to determine which properties were so marginal as grocery stores that the company was better off disposing of them. The test was not what the company had paid for properties years before, but what they were worth today. That was the real measure of the capital tied up in the property, and viewed that way, many of the stores didn't pass muster. Those were sold off.

Headquarters staff, meanwhile, was slashed 20 percent, and managers down through the ranks were given new financial incentives to increase profitability and returns on investment rather than just to increase sales, at whatever cost, as they had in the past.

At a time when no-frills warehouse stores were gaining big market shares with their low prices, Safeway's labor costs put it at a tremendous competitive disadvantage. Its rank-and-file workers thus inevitably bore the brunt of cost-cutting at the stores Safeway retained. The company succeeded in renegotiating terms with its unions in most regions, cutting wages for tens of thousands of employees. In the Dallas area, however, where Safeway's competitors were not unionized, Safeway's unions demanded that Safeway sell its stores to a unionized company and refused to grant concessions when their contracts expired. Without some break on labor costs, Safeway said it would not be able to find a buyer for the stores as a unit, and it opted to shut 131 stores and sold them piecemeal, mainly to smaller, nonunionized chains. Some 8,600 employees, mostly union members, were let go.

The slashing "cut plenty of muscle with the fat, both from [Safeway's] holdings and from its labor force, and deferred capital improvements in favor of the all-consuming debt," the *Journal* declared in its 1990 piece. But Safeway's growth in the nineties disproved that. When the restructuring was complete, Safeway had contracted from twenty-four hundred to fourteen hundred stores, and from $20 billion in sales to $14 billion—a shrinking act that would have been virtually unthinkable for a public company to attempt, because stockholders and investment analysts would never tolerate the risks. Yet, remarkably, cash flow rose 250 percent during the coming decade. Capital spending, which had been cut in half from 1987 to 1989 during the divestiture program, was restored in 1990 after Safeway's debt had been reduced and the company set out on a new expansion, this time targeting profitable markets.

The full history of the Safeway buyout actually debunks many of the clichés about LBOs. Yes, there were big job and pay reductions, but the company's workforce remained 90 percent unionized, and the asset sales, cuts, and new incentives had a dramatic impact on Safeway's profitability, which had lagged for years. By 1989, three years after the buyout, the chain's operating profit margin, which had been 2.2 percent in 1985, was up almost one half to 3.2 percent. Far from hamstringing the company, the brutal pruning of Safeway laid the foundation for an extraordinary run after the company went public in 1990. After a brief dip in the early nineties, Safeway's stock skyrocketed more than twenty times in value, going from $2.81 at its IPO in 1990, adjusted for stock splits, to $62 by 2000, the year KKR sold the last of its stake. The buyout had been leveraged in the extreme, with just 3 percent equity, so the payoff was huge: KKR made more than fifty times its money. The deal also flew in the face of the notion that buyout firms seek quick flips. Despite its big profit early on, KKR retained a stake in Safeway for nearly fourteen years.

The strategy behind KKR's restructuring of Safeway was not unique to buyout firms. Spurred by new business school teachings about measuring returns on capital, executives and boards of directors were increasingly reexamining their businesses. If we sold this factory, could we reinvest the money and make a higher return than we do now? Would we be better to focus on the fastest-growing and most profitable parts of our company? Could we raise money to invest in them by selling off other subsidiaries?

These were the same questions people like Kravis and Roberts had been asking as they sized up investments. The pressure exerted by the enormous debt loads on companies that had undergone LBOs accelerated the process greatly, but the same relentless, unsentimental reexamination of companies by their managers was becoming the norm throughout the American corporate world. Boards and CEOs knew full well that if they didn't perform the analyses and make the changes, someone else might take over their company, sack them, and do it themselves. A decade of looking over their shoulders at the raiders and the buyout firms enabled by Drexel's debt had brought that lesson home emphatically.

"These people were very influential," says Robert Bruner, the dean of the Darden School of Business at the University of Virginia. Not only did they help unlock resources and displace sleepy managements, he says, but "the buyout wave and the raiders really liberalized the way we look at the generation of value by companies and the delivery of that value."

It was the beginning of a new age in market capitalism, one with constant upheaval and less security for executives and workers alike. But it instilled a discipline and incited a new drive for efficiency with payoffs for the economy as a whole—so much so that it permanently reshaped the thinking of public company managers. No longer were the public stock markets populated with scores of companies worth less as a whole than the sum of their parts. As managers worked to eliminate that disparity, there were fewer and fewer easy pickings for the raiders and buyout firms.

Financing takeovers also grew harder. When the credit markets finally opened back up in the early nineties, lenders demanded that buyers front 20 or 30 percent or more of the entire price in equity, not 5 to 10 percent as in the 1980s. That sidelined many raiders, who had drawn sustenance from Drexel and typically did not have big pools of equity themselves. In the 1990s raiders largely ceased to be a force.

For buyout firms, the game had to change as well. No longer could they lean so heavily on the power of leverage to deliver gains or simply break apart what they'd bought. Now they would have to take companies more or less as they were and burrow deeper into the nitty-gritty of their operations to make them worth more. "Value creation" would be the new mantra.

CHAPTER 9

Fresh Faces

RJR Nabisco and other LBOs were not the only victims of the debt crisis that set in at the end of 1989. From KKR's Midtown Manhattan office to Drexel's posh Beverly Hills digs and small-town savings and loans across the Sun Belt, credit was suddenly in short supply. The Drexel junk-bond operation had been operating under a cloud since late 1986, when news surfaced that the Securites and Exchange Commission had begun an insider-trading investigation of Drexel and Michael Milken, who not only created the junk-bond market but had stabilized it through thick and thin. The bank pleaded guilty to criminal charges in December 1988 and agreed to pay a $650 million fine. Milken was indicted for his role in March 1989 and left Drexel. The impact was not immediate, but the elaborate set of relationships Milken had used to sustain the junk market, and to rescue his clients when they stumbled and were in danger of defaulting, was being undermined. No more could a troubled company have faith that Milken would refinance its debt to keep it going. No longer was he there to call in favors, tapping one client to buy another's bonds, as he often did.

The junk market had cooled in 1989, but that October it completely froze up. The precipitating event was the breakdown of the $6.8 billion employee-led buyout of United Airlines. When the senior lenders for that deal got cold feet, it spooked other banks, which, in turn, swore off LBOs. Across the board, investors began to take a new look at risks, and junk bonds were one of the riskiest forms of debt. It became nearly impossible to sell them.

The turn in the market sank Drexel. With losses piling up, the bank filed for bankruptcy in February 1990, putting a nail in the high-yield coffin and punctuating the end of the era. The junk-bond market, which had churned out $20 billion to $40 billion in new issues annually from 1986 to 1989, all but evaporated. In 1990, just $1.4 billion of new bonds were sold.

At the same time even larger problems were brewing far from the big-city banks. The savings and loan industry, which had been deregulated in the early eighties, was melting down. S&Ls had been instrumental in financing a decade-long real estate boom, and in a mix of incompetence, greed, and cronyism, they had used their deposits to make speculative loans. By the end of the decade, S&Ls were going bust in droves. Federal regulators seized 185 in 1988 and 327 in 1989. Real estate prices collapsed over wide swaths of the United States where the S&Ls had lent with abandon for new offices and subdevelopments. Many of the S&Ls had also fed at Drexel's trough, both issuing junk bonds and buying those of other Drexel clients. When they were taken over and their assets sold, there was that much less demand for the bonds.

The credit lockdown and the recession that followed in 1991 and 1992 put an end to the lavishly leveraged, big-ticket takeovers of the previous decade. Schwarzman embellishes only slightly when he likens DLJ's frenzied scramble to sell the CNW bonds in October 1989 to "catching the last helicopter out of Vietnam." Nearly three years would pass before there would be another sizable junk-bond-financed LBO, a $1.5 billion deal by KKR for the insurer American Re, and then KKR had to invest 20 percent of the price in equity—far more than it had been accustomed to stumping up.

Blackstone, too, had to lower its sights. While its first six deals had averaged $1.1 billion in size, the average from 1991 to 1995 fell to barely $300 million. Blackstone wouldn't attempt another deal on the scale of the $1.6 billion CNW deal until 1996.

The financial meltdown soon worked a Darwinian thinning of the ranks of LBO firms, crippling some, eviscerating others. The partners of Gibbons, Green, van Amerongen, a twenty-year-old pioneer of the LBO, split up in a bitter squabble over who was to blame for a string of wipe-outs. Adler & Shaykin, another established boutique, flamed out after most of its half-dozen investments bombed and its investors demanded to be released from their future funding commitments. Adler & Shaykin's second, $178 million fund also would be its last.

Ken Miller, the former Merrill Lynch M&A wunderkind who entered the buyout field in 1988 with his new Lodestar Group amid great fanfare, ended up funneling more than half his $300 million fund into one misguided investment, the 1989 purchase of Kinder-Care Learning Centers, a day-care-center operator. When Kinder-Care collapsed three years later, obliterating most of Lodestar's equity, Ken Miller's brief heyday as a buyout artist was over.

Wasserstein Perella, the other firm whose debut buyout fund in 1988 unleashed a blizzard of hype just as Blackstone's LBO business was getting under way, survived but was bloodied. Like Lodestar, it put too much of its money on one horse, risking—and ultimately losing—just over one-third of its $1.1 billion fund on a $3 billion buyout of England's Gateway supermarket chain in 1989. Though it wrung big profits from smaller bets on the cosmetics supplier Maybelline and Pneumo Abex, a landing-gear maker, Wasserstein Perella was indelibly tarnished by the Gateway debacle, and the firm, later renamed Wasserstein and Company, never raised a buyout fund as large as its first.

The savage shakeout forever altered the industry's power structure. Never again would KKR lord it over the business to the degree it had in the 1980s. Merely by surviving and safeguarding its investors' money as more ballyhooed firms bombed out, Blackstone was positioned to compete on a more equal footing in the years ahead.

The upheaval also set the stage for a new generation of players to come to the fore, some of whom had set up shop around the time Blackstone's buyout operation was launched. Four of the newcomers, along with KKR and Blackstone, became dominant players in the 1990s.

In Washington, D.C., in 1987, David Rubenstein, a brusque former lawyer and top Carter administration official, and William Conway, a former CFO of MCI Communications, formed the Carlyle Group, which carved out a unique niche through its knowledge of government's ins and outs. Carlyle notched its first big score in GDE Systems, a defense electronics business it bought in 1992 and sold in 1996 for eight times its money. Because it chalked up most of its other early successes in the defense and aerospace industries, it gained a reputation for Washington-centric deals even though it soon branched abroad and to other sectors.

In Texas, meanwhile, Tom Hicks, a charismatic deal maker who'd earned a fortune on LBOs of soft-drink makers Dr Pepper and Seven-Up, broke up with his longtime partner, Robert Haas, and raised a $250 million fund with a new partner, John Muse. In one of its early deals, Hicks, Muse and Company, the firm they formed in 1989, bought Morningstar, a perilously indebted Houston dairy. They injected $30 million of equity, shoring up its balance sheet, and took it public a little over a year later. From its quick flip, Hicks, Muse milked more than a fourfold gain.

Two of the biggest emerging stars, Leon Black and David Bonderman, stepped to the front of the pack a year or two later when the buyout business was shut down in the early nineties by demonstrating that they were shrewd opportunists who could seize on the crisis to buy up distressed businesses at fire-sale prices.

Black, a towering man with the intimidating bulk of a linebacker, had been one of Drexel's stars, rising by his midthirties to head Drexel's M&A bankers. Based in Drexel's New York office, he had instigated a host of takeover campaigns, which he passed off to Michael Milken in Beverly Hills for financing. Black emerged unscathed by Drexel's scandals and collapse and proved as adaptable as a chameleon. In 1991, with the economy at its worst and the junk-bond market at its nadir, state regulators in California seized Executive Life Insurance Company, a prime customer of Drexel's that had gone under as its bond holdings shriveled in value. When the state liquidated the company, Black, backed by money from a French bank, swooped in with a winning bid and snared the insurer's $8 billion junk-bond portfolio at less than 40 cents on the dollar. Black was perfectly situated to evaluate the bonds, for he had advised many of the companies behind them. When the economy revived, he unloaded the securities piece by piece for more than a $1 billion profit, winning him an enduring place in the top tier of vulture investors. Apollo Advisors, Black's new firm (later renamed Apollo Management and then Apollo Global Management), ultimately reaped more than $5.7 billion in gains on the $2.2 billion it raised from 1990 to 1992, from Executive Life and other distressed assets.

Bonderman was another child of the takeover boom who nimbly shifted course. A brainy ex-litigator known for his unorthodox sartorial getups—he often pairs plaid sports shirts with wildly clashing ties—Bonderman had executed a string of profitable takeovers as chief investment strategist to the Texas financier Robert M. Bass. But it was his pivotal role in Bass's 1988 purchase of the country's largest failed S&L, American Savings Bank, that brought him wide notice as a vulture investor of the first order. Bass invested $400 million, most of it borrowed, to buy American Savings. Less than a year later, with its bad debts handed over to the government, the thrift was solidly in the black. Bass would turn a fivefold gain on the investment.

Bonderman and another Bass alumnus, James Coulter, followed that in 1993 by buying Continental Airlines, Inc., out of bankruptcy with $400 million they'd rounded up from wealthy investors and institutions. Bonderman and Coulter ultimately came away with nine times their money on Continental. By then, they and a San Francisco business consultant, William Price, had launched their own buyout firm, Texas Pacific Group, based in Fort Worth and San Francisco, and raised a $720 million debut fund in 1994. They quickly became known as top-flight contrarians and turnaround artists who would take on financially or operationally hobbled companies most buyout firms wouldn't touch.

Bonderman did not conform to the Wall Street mold. Even as a lawyer, he had deviated from the conventional corporate career path, living in the Middle East, where he learned Arabic and studied Islamic law, and later doing a stint in the Civil Rights Division of the U.S. Department of Justice. Like Schwarzman, though, he had a flair for partying. Four years before the Schwarzman bash, Bonderman held his own even grander sixtieth birthday, flying scores of friends to Las Vegas, where they were entertained by the Rolling Stones, John Mellencamp, and Robin Williams at the Hard Rock Hotel. The event reportedly set back Bonderman by $7 million, but staged far from the press hordes in New York, it generated only a few scattered press reports.

With the LBO business on ice at the beginning of the new decade, Peterson and Schwarzman continued their quest to round out Blackstone's collection of businesses, bolstering the partner ranks with a string of high-profile hires. In addition to Henry Silverman on the buyout team, Schwarzman enticed David Batten, a seasoned capital markets executive, to join from First Boston in June 1990. The following year, Batten brought in Joseph E. Robert Jr., who had overseen the disposal of $2.3 billion worth of distressed real estate for the Resolution Trust Corporation, the federal agency changed with salvaging as much value as possible from the carcasses of failed S&Ls seized by the government. The inventory of troubled real estate, mortgage loans, and entire thrifts that the RTC was poised to auction off ran to tens of billions of dollars. Up and down Wall Street, people were salivating at the prospect of the RTC's liquidation sales, and Batten arranged to work with Robert on scooping up real estate at distressed prices. (Robert didn't join the Blackstone partnership, preferring to stay an independent contractor.)

A second new business emerged almost unintentionally, a by-product of the need to invest the $100 million Blackstone had received from Nikko. Blackstone's abortive risk-arbitrage fling in 1989 had eaten into the original hoard, but Schwarzman shuddered at the thought of putting the cash at risk in the turbulent markets. Still, the firm couldn't afford to leave the capital invested in low-paying certificates of deposit forever.

Batten, who had been charged with managing the money, hit on a solution. That summer he proposed that Blackstone divvy up the money and invest it with a half-dozen successful hedge funds, so named because they hedged their bets by deploying capital across an array of securities and currencies and could sell short when they thought the markets were headed down. The aim was to make money in down as well as up markets, and the best of the funds habitually had outstripped the stock market's performance. At the time, hedge funds were a small galaxy in the financial cosmos, but a handful of proven stars had emerged, including George Soros, Michael Steinhardt, Paul Tudor Jones II, and Julian Robertson.

Despite his initial reluctance, Schwarzman signed off on Batten's suggestion, and Batten proceeded to set up a fund-of-funds, taking stakes with six managers, the most illustrious being Robertson. But Schwarzman, who had never been a trader, was jittery as ever about losses and kept a sharp eye trained on the monthly results. "The first month the funds were up three percent and Steve was happy," recalls Batten. "The second month they were up four percent, and Steve was even happier." But around the fourth month Robertson posted a 4 percent loss and Schwarzman was beside himself.

"How could this happen?" he fumed to Batten. "Fire him! Fire Robertson!"

Batten answered by pointing out that Robertson was up substantially since Blackstone first placed money with him. Hedge funds' results, he explained, are inherently volatile, and one bad month does not necessarily a bad year make.

Robertson wasn't fired. Over the years, despite occasional setbacks, the fund-of-funds generated remarkably sturdy returns, and Blackstone later opened it up to outside investors, drawing in tens of billions of dollars, which created an important new source of fee income for the firm.

The buyout business remained the core, but it was still a source of headaches, notwithstanding the reforms Schwarzman had put in place in the wake of the Edgcomb fiasco. Blackstone's first major leveraged purchase of the 1990s, and its first foray into distressed investing, Hospitality Franchise Systems, very nearly self-destructed as quickly as Edgcomb had.

Henry Silverman, who steered the HFS deal for Blackstone, was versed in the hotel franchise business from his years working for the financier and corporate raider Saul Steinberg, for whom he had led a successful LBO of the Days Inn of America chain. Steinberg was one of the early raiders, having wrested control of Reliance Insurance Group via a hostile tender offer in 1968 when he was just twenty-nine, and following that the next year with an implausible and fruitless bid to buy Chemical Bank. In the eighties, Steinberg and Reliance became stalwarts in Drexel's troupe of marauders. For a six-year stretch in that period, Silverman led Steinberg's LBO fund, which did mostly friendly deals, including Days Inn. (Later Steinberg would be linked to Blackstone in another way: When his financial empire crumbled in 2000, he was forced to sell many personal possessions, including his sumptuous duplex apartment at 740 Park Avenue. The apartment's buyer, who paid a reported $30 million, was Steve Schwarzman.)

HFS was set up to take advantage of the financial ills of Prime Motor Inns, one of the world's largest operators and franchisers of midpriced hotels and motels. In 1990, Prime ran into trouble and needed to dump properties to pay down debt, and Silverman leaped at the chance to get control of Prime's two most prized possessions, the Howard Johnson franchise operation and an exclusive license to run the Ramada franchise. While the hotel business is cyclical, ebbing and spiking with the season and the economy, franchise fees are only partly tied to hotel earnings and are relatively steady, so it looked like a safe bet for an LBO. Moreover, Blackstone was buying in at a reasonable price: $195 million, or six times cash flow.

A month to the day after the buyout closed, however, on August 2, 1990, Iraq invaded Kuwait, an event that wasn't in any of Blackstone's investment scenarios. Almost immediately, as it became clear that the United States would lead a war to drive back Saddam Hussein's army, oil prices shot up and hotel bookings plummeted as people were daunted by the costs and risks of travel. "Our reservation volume fell off a cliff," Silverman says. "It was down 30 to 40 percent in one day."

This quickly threatened to sink the investment. The problem was that HFS didn't actually own the Ramada name; it simply licensed it from one of Hong Kong's biggest property conglomerates, New World Development, and New World, in turn, had the right to withdraw the license if HFS fell behind on its royalty payments—which HFS quickly did. Losing the right to the Ramada name would have rendered HFS largely worthless. At that stage in Blackstone's history, another failure could have threatened not just HFS but Blackstone itself. "Blackstone already had had issues with Wickes and Edgcomb when I got there," Silverman says. "The fund was too new for Blackstone's limited partners to start screaming, but they were very concerned. If this deal had blown up, it probably would have been the end of the fund, and maybe the end of Blackstone."

Silverman and Schwarzman tried to win some breathing room from New World. After an exchange of faxes with New World managing director Henry Cheng, whose father had founded the business, Schwarzman and Silverman flew to Hong Kong in September to see if a face-to-face meeting could prevent the situation from deteriorating.

Cheng started off by asking why he shouldn't rescind the license. Schwarzman countered by offering to give New World a higher percentage of HFS's income, a proposal he and Silverman already had made in a fax. "There must be some arrangement we can come to," Schwarzman said.

Dissatisfied with the offer, Cheng told them, "Okay, why don't you go and figure out whether there's anything that might be of interest to me." He then dispatched the two Americans to a nearby conference room, with a gargantuan tropical fish tank, to draft a proposal.

Schwarzman and Silverman pondered the fish and their predicament, eventually formulating what they thought might be a workable compromise. When they returned to Cheng's office, however, he dismissed it as unacceptable. "Try to come up with something better," he told them, and they returned to the conference room. Their second suggestion, offered a few minutes later, didn't win over Cheng either.

It was now a quarter to noon and Cheng told them he would be leaving soon. "I'm going to play golf at twelve. If we can't work out some arrangement by then, we're just going to take the company."

Back to the conference room they trudged. Schwarzman stared glumly at the brilliantly colored fish gliding through the water, thinking, "Here's my whole career about to disappear like those fish bubbles."

With only minutes to go, Schwarzman and Silverman returned and offered yet another revised proposal. This time Cheng swiftly endorsed it.

Before heading to the links, Cheng revealed that he'd been toying with them.

"You know, I never would have taken the company, because I had heard that Henry Silverman is a very good operator, and the U.S. is quite far away," Schwarzman recalls him saying. "I really was very pleased you bought this. Thank you for your proposal."

Schwarzman was so relieved, he didn't mind the ruse.

Though HFS was a problem, Blackstone's other early holdings—Collins & Aikman, CNW, Transtar, and a small investment in a chemical company—weathered the recession without crises. There was still no way to get financing for major new LBOs, but when the economy showed signs of improving in late 1992, the IPO market began to pick up and Blackstone had a chance to show just how well its investments were doing by taking some companies it owned public.

In an IPO, typically, big stockholders like Blackstone sell at most a small portion of their shares. The market often can't absorb all the stock of a company at one time, and investors will balk if they think existing investors want to cut and run. In many cases, the existing shareholders sell no shares, and the IPO consists solely of shares newly issued by the company equivalent to, say, a 15 or 20 or 25 percent stake. While the new stock waters down existing investors' stakes, the IPO raises new capital for the business and establishes a public-market value for the stock, opening an avenue for the company's backers to sell their shares and lock up profits later.

CNW was the first of Blackstone's companies to undergo an IPO. In

April 1992, the railroad sold a 22 percent stake to the public. The IPO price equated to 12.3 times CNW's cash flow, compared with the 7.2 times Blackstone had paid, and put CNW's overall worth at $3.2 billion, twice the LBO's original $1.6 billion price tag. The plum valuation partly reflected a 20 percent rise in CNW's cash flows, but more than anything it attested to the IPO market's ravenous appetite for new issues. "CNW didn't hit one of its [earnings targets]. Our operating projections were wrong. But our view of the overall value was right," says Howard Lipson. Blackstone, which sold the last of its CNW shares in August 1993, wound up with a profit of 217 percent on its original $75 million investment, and a gross annual return of 34.2 percent.

Amazingly, it was HFS that yielded the firm's second IPO bonanza. A year after Schwarzman and Silverman's gut-churning negotiation with Henry Cheng in Hong Kong, they had expanded HFS by buying another franchiser out of bankruptcy, Days Inn of America. Silverman's old boss Saul Steinberg had once owned Days Inn, and in 1989 Silverman had arranged the sale of the chain for $765 million to Tollman-Hundley Hotels, one of Days Inn's largest franchisees. The price was stratospheric: fourteen times Days Inn's cash flow. Silverman and Steinberg were happy to take the money, but Silverman thought the price was excessive and was convinced that Days Inn was bound to go bust.

"When Henry joined us, he told us one thing we'd probably be able to do is to buy Days Inn," Schwarzman says. "He said, 'I don't know why somebody paid fourteen times cash flow for it, but they'll never be able to meet their debt costs, because these businesses don't grow fast enough to outrun them.' "

As Silverman predicted, Days Inn filed for bankruptcy in September 1991, allowing Blackstone to grab it for $259 million—one-third the price Silverman had sold it for in 1989. Since HFS already had its franchising infrastructure set, there were huge cost savings to be gleaned from the merger. Most of the same staff that managed the Howard Johnson and Ramada franchises could readily handle Days Inn, too, and most of the Days Inn staff would be pink-slipped. A similar rationale would propel bank mergers later that decade—combine deposits and slash people—as well as thousands of corporate mergers driven by what CEOs euphemistically call "cost synergies." It was capitalism with a chilly heart. From a stockholder's standpoint, it also made HFS a far more valuable business with more staying power.

"Because of the people we already had in place, I thought we'd be adding $50 million of revenue at virtually no cost," Silverman says.

In December 1992, with the Persian Gulf War over and travel and hotel bookings back to prewar levels, HFS went public at $16 a share, 255 percent above Blackstone's investment cost of $4.50 a share. The shares jumped 17 percent the first day they traded and soared to $50 within a year. Blackstone exited HFS with a $362 million profit on its $121 million outlay, posting an annual gross return of 59.2 percent.

Almost battered into extinction in 1990, Blackstone had picked itself up off the canvas and was banging out gain after gain. In December 1993, on the strength of its performance in CNW and HFS, together with a smaller profit on a corporate partnership investment with Time Warner in Six Flags Theme Parks, Blackstone raised a new $1.3 billion buyout fund, nearly twice the amount it had raised in 1987. Rounding up pledges wasn't easy, though. By then Japan's markets and economy were stalling after a decade-long bubble in stock and real estate prices. The Japanese banks that had thrived in the boom years were now stuck with bad loans and assets that were shrinking in value, and they were retrenching on every front. Most every Japanese financial institution that had participated in Blackstone's first fund, with the exception of Nikko, took a pass on the second. But Blackstone filled the void, and then some, with money from new investors, including several state pension funds, which increasingly were adding buyout funds to their mix of investments.

The new fund propelled Blackstone past Clayton, Dubilier & Rice into the number-three slot among independent operators in the buyout game's capital hierarchy. Only the perennial kingpins, KKR and Forstmann Little, were larger.

CHAPTER 10

The Divorces and a Battle of the Minds

I f Peterson and Schwarzman at times seemed like polar opposites as personalities, they in fact shared a deep craving for public recognition. Schwarzman had something to prove, it was clear for all to see. Peterson's need to play the role of public-minded sage was more subtle but no less profound.

The personalities and ambitions of both, and the incongruity of their partnership, was never more apparent than in the Sunday *New York Times* on September 16, 1990. By a poetic coincidence of newspaper scheduling, both men occupied prominent spots in that issue. On the op-ed page, Peterson weighed in with an earnest, fourteen-hundred-word piece calling on Congress to enact a multiyear deficit-reduction program—the federal deficit having become an obsession with him. In a glossy "Men's Fashions of the Times" insert, meanwhile, Blackstone's CEO was on display in a three-quarter-page photo modeling a $1,300 Alan Flusser wool suit with matching silk Jacquard tie. To some people's eyes, Schwarzman's trousers, bunched at the shoes, accentuated his shortness. Peterson found Schwarzman's Manhattan-dandy act so achingly funny that the next day at 345 Park Avenue he pinned up Schwarzman's fashion shot in his office to draw laughs from those who dropped by. "Pete thought it was hilarious," says a former Blackstone partner. "Steve was really pissed off."

To those who knew Peterson, it was just another example of his irrepressible, impish reflex to tease those around him. He could be merciless, but for the frequently remote Peterson it was also a form of affection, a bonding ritual. Schwarzman, who could be thin-skinned, usually took Peterson's taunts in stride and gave as good as he got. In that era "Steve and Pete were very close," says Jonathan Colby, a partner at Carlyle who worked at Blackstone in the early 1990s. "Each knew what the other was thinking. It was like they communicated telepathically."

Over time, however, there were growing strains and their camaraderie faded. Pinpointing the source is hard, but some trace it to the time around 1992 when Peterson's slice of the profits was reduced. From the beginning, he and Schwarzman had had sole voting control over the buyout and M&A businesses and had an equal share in the profits, then about 30 percent each. As new partners arrived, they had each been given slices of what the firm made, which diluted Peterson's and Schwarzman's portions equally. That year the two founders agreed that, henceforth, as new partners joined, Peterson would cede more of his share to them. Thus, over time, his cut of the bottom line would steadily drop. By then, there was no dispute that Schwarzman was pulling more weight at the firm. Even so, the financial realignment marked the end of their equal partnership and an acknowledgment of Schwarzman's primacy at the enterprise they'd created and built together.

"I felt it was fair that our shares would be diluted as we added new partners, but my shares should be diluted somewhat more than his. That is what we did, and I fully agreed it was fair," Peterson says.

His career as a savant and writer was eating up much of his time, and he'd long ago ceded the top managerial role to his younger cofounder. What's more, his cut would remain substantial, within five points of Schwarzman's, and would remain well above any other partner's.

The profit split was not what pushed the men apart, says an investment banker who is a friend of Peterson's, but rather values and style. "With Pete, it wasn't the money. Money didn't matter to Pete the way it did to Steve," says the banker, who describes Peterson's material cravings as modest, certainly by Schwarzman's standards. "What eventually got to Pete was Steve's lifestyle, his flashing his wealth, his drawing attention to himself. That's not what Pete is about."

"Pete doesn't believe the point of making money is to let everyone know you made it," says a second person, who knows them both well. "Steve doesn't have a problem with that."

Though to this day both tout their relationship as "the longest-lasting partnership on Wall Street," by the 2000s their relations were frayed and they carped about each other to friends. Schwarzman would grumble about Peterson still collecting millions but contributing little, while Peterson would snipe about Schwarzman's crass displays of wealth.

There were other strains, too, at the top of an organization that shed partners faster than a dog sheds hair. In 1992, just two years after Schwarzman recruited him from First Boston for the buyout team, David Batten quit for a high-profile position at Lazard Frères, and Joe Robert, whom Batten had recruited in 1991 to buy distressed real estate in a joint venture with Blackstone, defected to Goldman Sachs. Yerger Johnstone, an M&A honcho hired from Morgan Stanley in 1991, lasted less than three years. Even by Wall Street's easy-go standards, the revolving door at Blackstone whirled fast.

Far more consequential than those losses were three others that gutted the leadership of Blackstone's core businesses: the departures of Henry Silverman, Roger Altman, and Larry Fink from 1991 to 1994.

Silverman was the first out, and not because he had blundered. On the contrary, Silverman oozed competence. Six years older than Schwarzman, he was shrewd, cool, and commanding, a master craftsman with an eagle eye for great deals. Schwarzman very much liked his style and to this day talks admiringly of the way Silverman foresaw when he joined Blackstone that the Days Inn hotel chain would get in trouble and that Blackstone would be able to buy it on the cheap.

There was no doubt about Silverman's contributions at Blackstone. But Prudential Insurance, the anchor investor for Blackstone's first fund, had it in for Silverman over a deal from his days at Reliance Capital, the investment arm of financier Saul Steinberg's Reliance Insurance. In 1987 Prudential bought John Blair Communications, a television ad business from Telemundo, which was owned by Reliance Capital. Prudential grossly overpaid and Blair began to founder not long after the purchase.

Prudential later sued Reliance and Telemundo, claiming they had misrepresented Blair's condition. The suit was still alive in 1991 when Prudential discovered that Silverman had resurfaced at Blackstone, and it urged Schwarzman and Peterson to boot him out.

"Pru felt it would be very difficult, as the lead investor in Blackstone, to be in litigation against one of the key managers of Blackstone's fund," says Gary Trabka, the Prudential executive who oversaw the insurer's investment in Blackstone's fund at the time.

Schwarzman looked into the matter and concluded that Silverman was likely blameless, but he and Peterson felt they had no choice but to accede to their investor. Silverman didn't have to go far to find a new job, however. He simply went to work full-time as chairman and CEO of Hospitality Franchising Systems, the hotel system he had helped Blackstone buy the year before. Blackstone gave him a chunk of HFS stock and free rein to run the business. As severance packages go, this one was a doozie, for HFS went public in 1992 and, over the next fifteen years, Silverman transformed it into Cendant Corporation, a franchising empire that controlled top brands such as the real estate brokerages Coldwell Banker and Century 21, Avis and Budget car rentals, Wyndham hotels, and the Travelport and Orbitz reservation systems. (Prudential's Blair Communications suit was ultimately settled for about $20 million, according to Silverman.)

Roger Altman's departure wasn't as cut-and-dried. With Altman, the primary bones of contention were loyalty and money. Schwarzman had always held something of a grudge against Altman for fending off his and Peterson's entreaties to join Blackstone until it had finished raising its first fund. Altman had paid dearly for his dillydallying, receiving only about a 4 percent stake in the firm. He had quickly become a powerful revenue magnet for Blackstone, generating a wealth of M&A fees and fathering two of its more successful early buyouts, Transtar and Six Flags, and resented his lowly stake.

"The genesis of the schism between Roger and Steve and Pete is that Roger was really unhappy about his equity," says a former Blackstone partner.

For years Altman agitated for a bigger piece of the pie, and in 1991 or early 1992 Schwarzman and Peterson relented, elevating Altman's share to around 7 percent.

The peace didn't last long. Altman, who had always been drawn to politics, had put his career at Lehman on hold to work for the Carter administration. Soon after his stake in Blackstone went up, he was working behind the scenes to help elect his friend and former Georgetown University classmate, Bill Clinton, president, which ate into the hours he gave Blackstone. Peterson, Altman's mentor at Lehman, was understanding about Altman's political involvements, remembers Austin Beutner, a former Blackstone partner and friend of Altman's. "When I left Blackstone to do my thing in government, Pete was one of the first to congratulate me on the opportunity," he says. "I'm sure he felt the same way for Roger."

Schwarzman was less forgiving. "Roger, right after the bump up in his equity, starts spending maybe one-third of his time on the campaign. Steve wasn't happy about it," one former partner says.

Events in Schwarzman's personal life fueled his sense of pique. In 1990, his wife, Ellen, filed for divorce and began angling for a hefty settlement. "This thing with Roger asking for more partnership points was going on while Steve thought he was losing half his net worth to Ellen," says a former Blackstone partner. Schwarzman would buttonhole partners and moan that Ellen wanted to dispossess him of "50 percent of his net worth," says another ex-colleague. "He complained a lot about that." (Because Schwarzman at the time was worth at least $100 million, Ellen Schwarzman presumably was asking for $50 million or more.)

The divorce steeled Schwarzman's resolve to safeguard his hard-earned fortune. He wasn't going to cede a fraction of his worth to a partner who then gave short shrift to Blackstone. "There is no one who ever got a scintilla of equity in Blackstone who didn't feel like it was pulling teeth from Steve. He's not one of these people who graciously hands out equity," the same former partner says.

In January 1993, when Altman took a job as deputy treasury secretary in the new Clinton administration, he locked horns again with Schwarzman and Peterson over money. The issue this time was Altman's potentially valuable 3 percent stake in Blackstone Financial Management, the fast-growing fixed-income venture that Larry Fink led. Altman fought tenaciously to hang on to his share of BFM, but Blackstone's founders said no because of the potential conflict of interest. For a high-level Treasury Department official to own a sizable piece of a firm that traded Treasury securities would flunk just about any smell test.

Altman's exit from Washington in 1994 was even bumpier. That August he resigned under pressure over his handling of congressional inquiries into Whitewater—a financial and political scandal that grew out of a dubious 1980s Arkansas land deal involving Bill and Hillary Clinton. Though the Clintons were never prosecuted for their roles in the affair, other Whitewater figures were convicted of fraud. When Altman returned to New York, says a friend, he fully expected Schwarzman and Peterson to cast aside bygones and ask him to rejoin the firm, but the invitation was never extended. Altman went on to start an M&A–private equity boutique of his own, Evercore Partners, which swiftly established itself as a top deal adviser.

"That he wasn't asked back had nothing to do with Whitewater," a former partner says. "It had everything to do with what had gone on before."

Altman's absence left a gaping hole in Blackstone's M&A operation, one that Peterson's diminishing involvement made wider. Other parts of the business grew by leaps and bounds after 1992, but the M&A group did not. Its inability to keep pace with the explosive growth in Bruce Wasserstein's M&A business exasperated Schwarzman, even though he had left Wasserstein behind in the dust in the leveraged buyout arena.

Significant as the loss of Altman was, the departure that hurt most on the bottom line was Larry Fink's. By early 1992, BFM's assets under management had rocketed to $8.1 billion and it was earning $13 million a year after taxes. It was doing so well that in mid-1992, Fink and Blackstone laid plans to raise outside capital through an IPO. At the time, Fink, Ralph Schlosstein, and other senior BFM managers jointly owned 45 percent of the business through a partnership while Blackstone Group and its partners owned another 35.3 percent. Fink and Schlosstein individually owned much of the rest.

But Fink and Schwarzman soon were at loggerheads over money. In order to corral top-notch talent, Fink insisted that he be able to award new hires a stake in BFM—the same lure Schwarzman had used to bring Fink under the Blackstone roof. Schwarzman and BFM's executives had been doing just that, steadily handing over part of their own stakes as the business added senior staff. But after Blackstone's stake slipped to around 35 percent, Schwarzman drew the line, telling Fink the parent company wouldn't drop its stake further.

Some trace Schwarzman's intransigence to his divorce battle. "He was obsessed about it," says one colleague from the time. "When money is as important to you as it is to Steve, and you think you're going to lose fifty percent of your savings, you become more difficult."

At an impasse, Schwarzman found himself negotiating a second divorce—between Blackstone and Fink's group. Convinced that Blackstone had become a drag on his grand designs, Fink shelved his plans for an IPO and demanded the outright sale of his unit. Schwarzman, despite his strong initial resistance, finally relented. In June 1994, the business, which in the interim had adopted the name BlackRock Financial Management and seen its assets climb to $23 billion, was sold to PNC Bank Corporation of Pittsburgh for $240 million. Blackstone's partners made out well, pocketing upward of $80 million in cash, in addition to about $30 million in dividends they'd collected from BFM over the previous six years. Schwarzman personally banked more than $25 million, enough to subsidize most if not all of his split from Ellen. (Though the size of the divorce settlement was never disclosed, *Business Week* put it above $20 million.)

BlackRock went on to surpass Fink's headiest dreams. Over the next dozen years it grew into an investment empire comprising $1.2 trillion of assets, mostly fixed-income and real estate securities, reshuffled its ownership, and went public in 2006. By 2010, BlackRock was the world's biggest publicly traded money manager, twice as big as its nearest rival, with $3.2 trillion in assets and 8,500 employees in 24 countries. Fink emerged as a Wall Street prince on a par with Schwarzman and became an adviser to the Obama administration on ways to resuscitate the U.S. economy.

Schwarzman would later freely admit he'd sold BlackRock too soon. Though he personally earned a tidy sum on the sale to PNC, if Schwarzman had held on to even 3 percent of BlackRock—less than a third of his ownership stake when BlackRock was sold to PNC—he'd have been about $1.3 billion richer by 2010.

After Henry Silverman's forced departure, Blackstone's complement of LBO specialists was skeletally thin. It now consisted of a cadre of bright, young strivers and a single middle-aged luminary, the brainy and difficult David Stockman.

A high-octane personality by nature, Stockman kept his mind in overdrive by consuming more caffeine and nicotine than a French existentialist. He was a two-fister, alternately guzzling coffee from a mug in one hand and taking deep drags from a cigarette in the other. He later quit smoking, but his caffeine habit remained. Blackstone partner Chinh Chu, then a junior staffer, recalls flying with Stockman to Kokomo, Indiana, fifty miles north of Indianapolis, to visit the headquarters of Haynes International, a machinery maker Blackstone owned. When they arrived and got in their rented car, Stockman started driving in the wrong direction. When Chu asked where they were going, Stockman replied, "There's not a Starbucks until Indianapolis." Two hours and a hundred-mile round-trip to the state capital later, they arrived at Haynes.

Stockman's febrile temperament alternately entertained and bemused his associates, who marveled at his mind's capacity to soak up oceans of data. Yet by the early 1990s, it was evident that the Reagan administration whiz kid was an unreliable judge of deals. Yes, he'd been dead right about Edgcomb, warning Schwarzman in advance of that buyout's perils. But he also had delivered similarly gloomy judgments on other Blackstone investments that later performed well, including Transtar, Days Inn, and Six Flags. Meanwhile, his Collins & Aikman (formerly Wickes) investment was struggling.

It wasn't just that he was sometimes wrong. His high-handed dismissals of his fellow partners' deals left him with few friends. At an investment committee meeting in 1991, Stockman arrived armed with two assistants, graphs, and spreadsheets, prepared to do battle over a proposed $81 million equity investment in Six Flags, an amusement park operator that had fallen on hard times under its previous owner, Wesray Capital. Blackstone and Time Warner, its corporate partner in the investment, had worked up a plan to boost TV advertising using Time Warner's popular *Looney Tunes* cartoon characters, which they believed would lure kids back to the parks and resuscitate the business. Everyone involved in the deal was convinced that Six Flags could be turned around: Time Warner; Roger Altman, who had spotted the opportunity and recruited Bob Pittman, a cofounder of MTV and a media marketing guru, to manage Six Flags; Henry Silverman, the deal's overseer; and Howard Lipson, who had helped Silverman vet the proposal. Stockman begged to differ.

"David came to the meeting with a fully baked counterargument" to the plan, a person at the meeting says. Stockman produced a graph showing that leisure spending by Americans had been rising as a percentage of economic activity and insisted that it inevitably would drop back to the historic norm. He also had an analysis of the cost of adding exciting new attractions—"the need to top yourself, the thrill factor—which he said was going up, so capital spending would be a problem," this person says.

"I think your attendance projections are too optimistic, and your capital spending assumptions are too light," Stockman asserted.

In fact, the transaction had been tailored to protect Blackstone in the event of just such problems. Blackstone had agreed that Time Warner would get a lopsided share of the profits if the company performed exceptionally well. In exchange Blackstone got what amounted to a guarantee that it would earn a minimum return of 25 percent so long as cash flows grew modestly. When Stockman was finished and it was Howard Lipson's turn to speak, he told Stockman, "You know, even if all your assumptions are right, and we plug your attendance and capital spending figures into our model, we still get a 25 percent return."

Flustered, Stockman stared at Lipson's spreadsheet and retorted, "Well, that's just because of the way you structured it."

"Exactly!" said Lipson.

Silverman, Altman, and Lipson won the argument, and in the coming months the investment played out exactly as they'd hoped. In December 1992, a year after the $760 million buyout, Time Warner exercised its option to buy out Blackstone's stake in the resurgent company for $104 million. Stockman's dyspeptic prophesy notwithstanding, Blackstone raked in a 27 percent return.

Because of his spotty record, Stockman never earned Schwarzman's unconditional trust. Nor did he ascend to the role of Schwarzman's chief deputy, which Silverman effectively had occupied until he left in 1991—a role to which Stockman's fame, experience, and age might otherwise have entitled him. Instead, that function gradually passed to a much younger man, who'd joined Blackstone from Shearson Lehman in 1987 as a lowly vice president.

James Mossman was twenty-nine years old in 1988, when he untangled the financial complexities of Transtar, USX's short-line railroad, and persuaded his superiors to make the investment that put Blackstone on the map. The next year, he solidified his status as a rising star with brilliant financial-modeling work and with his hard-bitten style while negotiating key elements of the CNW buyout. No one was more enamored of him than Schwarzman.

"James's IQ was off the charts," says Blackstone partner J. Tomilson Hill III, who joined Blackstone in 1993.

Away from the office, the University of Toronto graduate got his intellectual kicks dabbling in astrophysics and mathematical esoterica like string theory. A late 1987 photograph in a Blackstone newspaper ad shows a grinning Mossman in dark-framed glasses standing aside a group of colleagues, a ringer for Clark Kent minus the neck muscles. But unlike Superman's alter ego, Mossman was anything but fumbling and meek.

His primary social deficiency—some viewed it as a strength—was his unvarnished candor. If he thought an idea was flawed or dim-witted, he'd say so.

"James saw the world in black and white," says Kenneth Whitney, a longtime Blackstone partner. Mossman's personality was similarly split, Whitney says. "He had a great sense of humor, but as soon as he focused on something, he turned very serious. It was like Jeckyll and Hyde." He had an obsessive-compulsive side, sometimes going two or three days without sleep when immersed in a deal. Says Whitney: "He had the kind of personality that only had one speed, full speed ahead."

Inside 345 Park Avenue, verbal clashes between the equally headstrong Mossman and Stockman drew crowds. "People would show up at investment committee meetings to see David and James debate," says partner Chinh Chu. "It was intense." When Stockman was on the defensive, one could almost see steam blowing out of his ears. A leg bobbed rapidly up and down, his speech raced, his body trembled. Mossman kept his cool throughout, delivering logically elegant counterthrusts.

"James was professorial, but he could drive a point home," says Chu. "He could take a deck of analysis and zero in on the top three issues within minutes. That's an innate ability." By contrast, Stockman, the data-point and trend-line junkie, could spout decades of actuarial statistics for a pension plan or reams of figures on oil-refining capacity but often lost the forest for the trees, his former colleagues say.

Three years after his arrival, Mossman became a partner, and he evolved into the firm's de facto chief investment officer—the point man through whom all deals had to flow. In that role, he distanced himself entirely from the messy particulars and distractions of deal making. Aside from Transtar and CNW, he never involved himself in sourcing or spearheading buyouts. At most, he occasionally rigged up an ingenious asset-backed financing scheme or the like. He never met with the management of a prospective portfolio company, never spoke with limited partners. Instead, he holed up in his office, where he vetted his partners' investment proposals on paper.

It was a peculiar modus operandi for a chief investment officer, but it served a function in the organization, keeping Mossman at an emotional distance from the pitches he received and helping to keep the firm from succumbing to the momentum the investment process can take on when people have invested weeks or months probing a company. "He doesn't have deal fever," says Simon Lonergan, who worked at Blackstone from 1996 to 2004. "Doing nothing is as good as doing something in James's mind. He was an analytically rigorous guy—very disciplined."

Even though Schwarzman made the final call on investments, he seldom second-guessed his young adjutant. As a result, Mossman became the behind-the-scenes arbiter of which deals got done, and his cerebral approach had a quiet but profound impact on Blackstone's investment agenda over the rest of the nineties and into the next decade.

CHAPTER 11

Hanging Out New Shingles

While the buyout business was in suspended animation during the downturn of the early 1990s, Schwarzman set out to nurture new business lines more suited to a period of tumbling markets and a drought of leverage. In May 1991, he poached a six-member crew of debt-restructuring specialists from Chemical Bank led by Arthur Newman, an ace in the field. The move paid off quickly as assignments poured in from America West Airlines, R. H. Macy and Company, steelmaker LTV Corporation, and other bankrupt corporations needing advice on reorganizing their finances. In time Blackstone's restructuring advisory group would expand to forty-four professionals and would draw some of the most challenging restructurings in the early 2000s and again at the end of that decade.

Schwarzman had set out to establish a real estate investment arm, too, as the Resolution Trust Corporation—the federal agency charged with cleaning up the S&L mess—prepared to unload thousands of properties and distressed loans the government had taken over from failed savings and loans. The quick departure of Joe Robert in 1992 had set back that plan, but Schwarzman began looking for a replacement and soon found his way to John Schreiber, forty-six, who had retired from his job as head of acquisitions for JMB Realty Corporation, a Chicago-based real estate empire that specialized in syndicated real estate investments, a forerunner to today's multibillion-dollar real estate private equity industry. JMB had pioneered the kind of real estate private equity

Schwarzman had in mind, buying properties on the cheap or in need of upgrading, and selling them a few years later. Schwarzman first contacted Schreiber for advice on whom he might hire, but after talking with other property investors and bankers, he called Schreiber back in the summer of 1992 and tried to woo Schreiber for the position.

"I told him I had no interest," Schreiber says. Schreiber had promised his wife he wouldn't go back to work full-time, he was sick of managing, and there was no way he was moving to New York. But Schwarzman pressed him and pressed him. Finally, Schreiber's wife suggested that he make what seemed to both husband and wife to be ridiculous demands. He told Schwarzman he'd be willing to consult and help Schwarzman recruit a hands-on management team in exchange for an ownership stake, but he would work just forty days a year and from Chicago. To the Schreibers' amazement, Schwarzman agreed.

The business was structured along the lines of Blackstone Financial Management, Larry Fink's fixed-income operation. Blackstone owned 80 percent and Schreiber 20 percent, but Blackstone agreed to hand off part of its stake to managers as they were hired so that the business eventually would be owned fifty-fifty by its executives and Blackstone. Schreiber would remain, in his words, "third-base coach."

By late 1992, JMB Realty, which had once boasted $24 billion in assets, was in trouble as some of the highly leveraged deals it had engineered in the good times were unwinding, and many of its executives were looking for jobs. Schreiber targeted one of them, Barry Sternlicht, to head up the new business at Blackstone. "We had basically agreed on terms to bring Barry and his group," Schreiber says, "but at the last minute he changed his mind." Sternlicht went on to form Starwood Capital, his own property investment firm. In his place, Schreiber in 1993 recruited Thomas Saylak, who had worked at Trammell Crow Company, another big property firm, and a year later hired another JMB alumnus, John Kukral, to be his field commanders.

Schwarzman reckoned there was a windfall to be made in distressed real estate, as the property boom of the eighties came to a harsh end. Developers and lenders were struggling in the aftermath, and the government was shoveling billions of dollars of savings and loan property out the door to anyone who could make a solid bid. The problem was that Blackstone had scant capital to invest in such deals. The firm tried in 1991 to persuade the investors in Blackstone's first fund to plow up to $400 million—close to half the fund—into properties being auctioned by Resolution Trust. But because many of the limited partners were U.S. and Japanese institutions already freighted with troubled real estate, they nixed the idea. With a new team on board, Blackstone set out to raise hundreds of millions of dollars for a dedicated real estate fund.

In late 1993, Schreiber clinched his first trophy deal. Edward J. De-Bartolo Corporation, which owned stakes in fifty-seven regional malls, the Ralphs supermarket chain, and numerous parcels of land, had fallen on hard times, and DeBartolo's lenders were eager to rid their books of its debt. Through his long-standing ties to the First National Bank of Chicago, Schreiber arranged to buy $196 million of secured debt from the bank for 56 cents on the dollar. Because DeBartolo owned a mix of corporate assets and real estate, Blackstone could tap its LBO fund.

The deal turned into a winner. When a company defaults on its debt, creditors can often swap the debt they hold for equity when the company restructures. In April 1994, Blackstone did just that, and in 1996 it cashed out, more than doubling its $109 million investment.

Schreiber's next major deal involved a failed JMB Realty investment he knew all too well: Cadillac Fairview. The Canadian shopping mall owner had been JMB's crown jewel, owning Toronto's Eaton Centre and Toronto-Dominion Centre and the Pacific Centre in Vancouver. Schreiber had helped engineer JMB's $5.1 billion buyout of Cadillac Fairview, which was the largest real estate deal of the 1980s, but in 1991, with the economy in the dumps, the company was buckling under its debt. Cadillac Fairview's financial downfall, more than any other event, triggered JMB's demise. Now Schreiber would have a chance to try his hand at vulture investing. Just as Leon Black had established Apollo's reputation by picking up the broken remnants of deals he had fathered when he worked at Drexel, Schreiber would use his knowledge of Cadillac Fairview to make money from its restructuring.

With the confidence that comes from knowing the target, in February 1995 Blackstone's real estate team swooped down and bit off a $10 million morsel of Cadillac Fairview's bank debt. It ultimately was angling for equity in the restructured company. By this time, Schreiber's group was flush with money, having stockpiled $330 million in commitments in 1994 for the real estate investment fund, and later in 1995 it joined up with the giant Ontario Teachers' Pension Plan Board and pushed through a bailout plan for Cadillac Fairview that Schreiber had taken a hand in crafting. In exchange for injecting $200 million, the two acquired a combined 32 percent stake. Goldman Sachs, the largest creditor, swapped its bank loans for 22 percent. Two years later, Cadillac Fairview went public. The deleveraged company thrived, and when Blackstone later cashed out, it made a $73 million profit on its $65.5 million investment.

JMB had blazed the trail for real estate private equity long before Blackstone. But Blackstone was the first large corporate-LBO specialist in America to launch a real estate venture, and it was the only one that developed into a top-tier player. Apollo and the Carlyle Group launched their own units in 1993, but Apollo Real Estate Advisors eventually split from Leon Black and renamed itself, and Carlyle's property business remained relatively small.

The hiring of Schreiber, Saylak, and Kukral drew little attention at the time. Much more ballyhooed was the hiring of J. Tomilson "Tom" Hill III, an old friend and fellow partner of Peterson's and Schwarzman's at Lehman. Hill was a steely M&A gladiator who'd been in the thick of some of the most memorable hostile takeover battles of the 1980s, siding with Federated Department Stores in its defense against Robert Campeau and working with Ross Johnson, the CEO of RJR Nabisco, in the fight for control there. Hill had also been an architect of some of the most iconic friendly mergers of the age: Bendix Corp.'s $1.8 billion merger with Allied Corp. in 1983, American Stores' $2.5 billion takeover of Lucky Stores in 1988, and Time Incorporated's $14 billion merger with Warner Communications in 1989.

He dressed the part to perfection, from his back-combed coif to his impeccably tailored Paul Stuart suits and tasseled loafers. Rumor had it that Gordon Gekko in the movie *Wall Street* was styled after Tom Hill.

In 1993 Hill was ousted as Lehman's co-CEO, and Blackstone soon tapped him to cohead M&A and assume Roger Altman's mantle as a brand-name rainmaker. From the moment Altman left, Schwarzman and Peterson had searched doggedly for a worthy replacement, Schwarzman remarked when Blackstone hired Hill. "Tom fills that bill," he said.

The timing seemed propitious. Merger activity, which bottomed out in 1991 and 1992, was rebounding, nearly tripling from 1992 to 1995, and Hill spoke boldly of capitalizing on the upturn. Blackstone hoped it might even steal business from M&A powerhouses such as Goldman and Merrill Lynch. There was little doubt Hill would transform M&A into a stout fourth leg of Blackstone's business platform.

But it wasn't to be. Though a new merger wave was taking off, Hill and the group's other cohead, Michael Hoffman, never met Schwarzman's lofty expectations. Hill and Hoffman weren't wholly to blame. As the regulatory barriers between commercial banks and investment banks came down, investment banks became free to make commercial loans and commercial banks moved into the traditional preserve of the investment banks, advising on mergers and capital raising. Deregulation gave birth to so-called one-stop shopping, with one bank, or a small group, handling every financial element of a merger or acquisition, from strategizing and crafting it to the underwriting and marketing of both loans and bonds. LBO sponsors, in particular, were elated to be rid of the hassle of scraping together debt from multiple sources. But the new full-service banks siphoned off advisory work from boutique advisers such as Blackstone that didn't lend or underwrite.

A few long-established M&A boutiques such as Lazard Frères maintained strong franchises as pure advisers. Wasserstein Perella, an M&A-cum-private equity shop like Blackstone, also pulled in big fees.

But Blackstone's M&A group struggled, and it was a sore point with Schwarzman. Whenever a plum assignment fell through or anything bad happened, he would erupt. Schwarzman often would vent his fury at Hoffman, a former Smith Barney M&A executive who had been at Blackstone since 1989. "The animosity between Michael and Steve was unbelievable. You've got to give Michael credit. He endured it all. Every day, it seemed, he got dumped on," recalls one ex-partner.

What galled Schwarzman most, says Hoffman, was the fact that Bruce Wasserstein, his old rival, was eating Blackstone's lunch in M&A. "I thought we did well" considering the obstacles, Hoffman says. According to Hoffman, Blackstone's yearly M&A fees nearly tripled during the 1990s, rising from $25 million early in the decade to $70 million. Still, that was less than one-fifth the $400 million that Wasserstein Perella pulled in. Schwarzman "dumped on the fact that the M&A business was not as big as Wasserstein's," Hoffman says. Hoffman's unit turned a fair profit, but that fact didn't placate Schwarzman, he says. Hoffman left in 2001 to advise the State of California on a financial crisis and later moved to Riverstone Holdings, a private equity firm that specializes in energy investments.

Hill eventually would excel and leave a lasting mark at the firm, but not in M&A. By the mid-nineties, Blackstone's hedge fund-of-funds business, which David Batten had conceived in 1990 to invest the money Blackstone had received from Nikko, was managing money from outside investors, charging them a fee to screen hedge funds and spread their money across a variety funds, and had become a profit-making business in its own right. Called Blackstone Alternative Asset Management, BAAM for short, the unit would scuffle along under a series of overseers until the time Hill relinquished his M&A post and took charge of it in 2000. At BAAM, Hill would find his groove, and the business's assets under management would soar in size.

CHAPTER 12

Back in Business

The resuscitation of the buyout market was nothing like the violent crash that preceded it. There was no one deal that announced private equity was back in business. No clarion sounded. Instead, it was a gradual thaw.

The junk-bond market experienced a revival in 1992 and 1993, as Donaldson, Lufkin & Jenrette and other banks hired the best and the brightest out of Drexel Burnham after it went under in 1990 and put them to work. But little of the money raised via junk bonds was being used to finance new buyouts. LBO was still a dirty word. It was clear that the freehanded lending practices of the eighties were obsolete. Scarred by the failures of scores of businesses they'd helped lever to the hilt, the Wall Street banks wised up, imposing a stricter lending regimen. Unlike the old days, when buyout sponsors could get away with inserting a mere sliver of equity—10 percent or less of the purchase price—lenders now demanded that they have much more at risk. From 1993 through the early 2000s, lenders almost always demanded at least 20 percent and often 30 percent of the cost to be financed with equity.

That forced a new calculus on the LBO set. No longer could they take control of massive enterprises with a smidgen of their own money, as KKR had done with RJR and Beatrice. With less debt for the same quantum of equity, the average size of LBOs inevitably shrank. With less leverage, sponsors were also staring at lower returns, because minute gains in a company's value could no longer be multiplied ten or twenty times. The only good news was that the price tags for companies came down.

In the new environment, buyout firms were forced to reexamine how they went about making profits, and what the LBO game was all about. Slowly, they began to focus more on making operational improvements at their companies. Where they had once simply slashed costs and sold off assets whose value was masked inside a larger enterprise, they began focusing on the top line—revenue. They began asking how they might alter a company's mix of profits to emphasize higher-margin items, how they might expand its geographic reach or fill in gaps through acquisitions, or how they might improve relations with customers.

A few, like Clayton Dubilier & Rice, built up stables of executives they could parachute in to help reform the companies the firm bought. CD&R showcased its approach with an ambitious carve-out of IBM's office product lines in 1991. No office products division existed when IBM approached CD&R about taking on the assets. It was just a mishmash of slow-growth or dying products such as Selectric typewriters and dot matrix printers that IBM sought to sell. CD&R would have to create a company around them and then take on bigger, more nimble competitors such as Hewlett-Packard that dominated the inkjet printer business. It was a tall order—something other buyout firms would never attempt. But CD&R succeeded, building the IBM castoffs into a new company called Lexmark, accelerating product development and shaping it into a serious competitor in inkjet and laser printers before taking it public in 1995. (CD&R claims that when its partners first met with IBM chairman John Akers, he brandished a copy of *Barbarians at the Gate* and said, "The reason I am talking with you is because you are not mentioned in this book.") KKR had undertaken ambitious overhauls such as Safeway's, but few firms had experience with this sort of hands-on investing. It was an approach they would increasingly come to emulate—or at the least pay lip service to.

The new emphasis on value building was accompanied by a new terminology. "LBO" and "buyout" had become so tarnished that buyout firms started branding what they did as "private equity." British buyout firms, meanwhile, took to calling their deals "management buyouts" to highlight that the business would be run by familiar faces, though the managers seldom had a controlling stake.

"Private equity" had long been used for venture capital investments in start-ups and other young companies—an investment approach that was widely lauded as fueling innovation and growth. But now the phrase was appropriated for the more controversial process of buying companies with borrowed money. The new term took hold, but it did little to free the buyout business from the stigma of its signature deals in the eighties.

In its new incarnation—with less leverage, more equity, and more prudence—the buyout business began to emerge from hibernation in 1993 and 1994. The stock markets were still traveling sideways, but the economy was climbing out of the 1991–92 slump. It proved to be a fantastic time to invest.

In the four years after the CNW deal closed in late 1989, Blackstone had pulled off only three sizable buyouts: Hospitality Franchise Systems, Six Flags, and Great Lakes Dredge & Dock Company, a Chicago dredging contractor it bought for $177 million in October 1991. But in late 1994 it returned to the hunt and lined up two new investments, a tiny wager on a broadcaster, US Radio, and a big bet on steel. The latter, like Blackstone's maiden investment in iron ore and steel hauler Transtar, would yield a stratospheric return. Just as Blackstone had parlayed its success with Transtar into a bigger second fund, the $1.2 billion purchase of UCAR International, Inc., laid the groundwork for its third fund and Blackstone's ascendancy in the late nineties.

UCAR, a joint venture of Union Carbide and Japan's Mitsubishi Corporation, wasn't itself a steelmaker but was the world's largest maker of graphite electrodes used to produce steel: thick rods that, when heated to 5,000 degrees Fahrenheit and dipped into caldrons big enough to digest a house, could melt scrap metal into liquid steel. Because the rods had to be replaced often, UCAR was guaranteed a steady stream of orders so long as demand for steel held fast. But what particularly enthralled

Blackstone was the fact that UCAR and its main competitor, Germany's SGL Group, had slashed manufacturing capacity by about a third over the previous decade while aggressively boosting prices.

"David Stockman came up with an analysis showing that the price of electrodes was going up because there was no capacity left anywhere," says Howard Lipson. "He understood the business, had analyzed it in terms of the end markets and capacity. His analysis got us comfortable to do the deal."

By the time Blackstone set its sights on UCAR, its owners were just weeks away from taking the business public, and Blackstone had to race to preempt the IPO. Pete Peterson, who in 1991 had advised Union Carbide chief executive Bob Kennedy when it sold half of UCAR to Mitsubishi, reached out to his old friend about selling UCAR to Blackstone instead of taking it public. IPOs are inherently risky, because the offering price can change up to the last minute, and the seller can rarely sell more than a small minority of its shares at the outset. By contrast, a negotiated sale offers certainty and nets more cash for the seller because it can off-load as much of its holding as it wants.

Peterson suggested that United Carbide might want to retain a minority stake in case the company did well. "I told him it made sense to own some of it, because if we made a big profit on it, he'd wouldn't look dumb, the way RCA did after it sold Gibson Greeting to Wesray," he says.

Peterson sold Kennedy on the concept, but it was Chemical Bank's Jimmy Lee who made the deal fly. Working against the ticking IPO clock, Lee took a gamble no commercial bank had ever taken before, offering to arrange not only the loans for the buyout but also junk-bond financing. It was a first, and a sign of how the once-sharp line between the securities business of the investment banks and lending by the commercial banks was fading. Lee added another sweetener as well by putting Chemical's guarantee behind the entire $1.1 billion financing package.

"The only way we're going to talk Bob Kennedy out of taking it public is if we give them certainty of financing," Schwarzman told Lee. "You want to lead a big high-yield deal? Here is your chance."

Lee was petrified. If he couldn't syndicate the loans or sell the bonds and Chemical had to make good on the bridge financing, the bank would face far more exposure to a single company than it would ever ordinarily take. "We had never done a bridge of this size before, and I knew that if I took the bridge down and couldn't sell the bonds, I'd be gone. Vaporized. Jimmy Lee would be toast, and maybe Chemical, too."

Schwarzman eased Lee's fears by assuring him that if Chemical had to fund the bridge "we'd be in it together," Lee says. Though Schwarzman didn't spell out specifics, he seemed to imply that if the need arose, Blackstone might cough up more money to buy bonds or agree to concessions on the bridge loan. "Those were the magic words I needed to hear," says Lee. He was reassured, too, because he knew that Schwarzman had a vested interest in supporting Chemical. "He knew that if he could get me to be a major player in high-yield bonds, he would gain leverage" against other private equity firms. With Chemical in its corner, Blackstone would have an easier time trumping them in bidding contests.

The deal was signed in November 1994 and sealed two months later. Blackstone invested $187 million for 75 percent, taking half of Union Carbide's stake and all of Mitsubishi's.

UCAR proved to be a watershed for Wall Street. Lee's successful junk-bond offering for the buyout marked the birth of one-stop financing for large LBOs, a market that a small circle of banks, led by Chemical Bank and its successor, JPMorgan Chase, came to dominate. Lee had first concocted the debt-syndication model that transformed commercial banks from lenders into debt-distribution platforms, carving up loans and selling them to a multitude of investors, mutual funds, hedge funds, and the like. Now he had conjoined the lending and bond-issuing process under one roof.

Lee's debt-syndication machine would evolve into a font of profits for Chemical and other Wall Street banks. Now they could manage huge debt financings and rake off fees without packing their own books with risky loans. The market the banks built attracted a flood of capital from nontraditional lenders such as hedge funds, which triggered a surge in buyout activity and allowed larger and larger deals to be financed. By the late 1990s, loan syndications, including corporate loans not tied to buyouts, were a trillion-dollar-plus business, with Lee's group at Chase handling a third of that. In the 2000s, the one-stop financing and syndication model would funnel hundreds of billions of dollars into LBOs and set off a wave of record-shattering megadeals. As much as any single figure on Wall Street, Jimmy Lee set the stage for the great leveraged buyout extravaganza of 2005 to 2007.

UCAR was also a grand slam for Blackstone. The spring and summer after the investment was made, production cuts and price hikes drove up UCAR's earnings, and in August 1995 the owners moved to cash in by taking UCAR public. When Blackstone sold the last of its shares in April 1997 after a surge in the stock, it had bagged a walloping $675 million gain, 3.6 times its investment, and an average annual return of close to 200 percent. That day at 345 Park Avenue, spirits ran high.

But a cloud soon would be cast over the UCAR investment. On June 5, less than two months after Blackstone had cashed out, federal investigators subpoenaed UCAR as part of a price-fixing investigation. In March 1998 UCAR threw out its chairman and CEO, Robert Krass, and its COO, Robert Hart, and in April 1998 it pleaded guilty to antitrust violations and agreed to pay the U.S. government a $110 million fine. Krass and Hart were packed off to prison.

The production cuts and ensuing price hikes that had so captivated Stockman when he was first analyzing the company as a prospect, and which were the basis for much of UCAR's growth, turned out to have been the fruit of illegal collusion. Starting in 1992, before Blackstone acquired UCAR, the company and its chief rival, SGL, which together controlled two-thirds of the world market in graphite rods, had conspired to cut capacity in tandem. At least one Blackstone partner, Lipson, was questioned in the cases against Krass and Hart, but no one from Blackstone, Union Carbide, or Mitsubishi was ever charged. Says Lipson: "What we didn't know, and what you learn, is that many price-fixing schemes involve capacity-fixing schemes. It was a shock."

Fortunately, Blackstone had most of the commitments for its third buyout fund, Blackstone Capital Partners III, signed up by that summer, before the UCAR scandal fully unfolded. To investors, the stupendous profit on Blackstone's huge investment in UCAR was a mighty draw. Nearly all the 80 percent annualized return that Blackstone touted to investors was attributable to UCAR. It was a pattern that would recur with future funds: One or two great investments made at a trough in the business cycle could make a fund a huge success.

The $4 billion third buyout fund, which had its final closing in October 1997, elevated Blackstone to the number-two position in private equity. Only KKR, the industry's perennial kingpin, boasted a larger fund, a $5.7 billion vehicle raised in 1996. Forstmann Little, long KKR's leading competitor, had rounded up just $3.2 billion in 1997 for its latest fund. The other megafunds of the period were all a safe distance behind: a $3 billion pool at Donaldson Lufkin & Jenrette's private equity unit, Welsh Carson Anderson & Stowe's $3.2 billion, and Thomas H. Lee Company's $3.5 billion. Not until 1999, when Tom Hicks and John Muse's firm, which now was called Hicks Muse Tate & Furst, closed on $4.1 billion, did anyone edge ahead of Blackstone.

With the new fund, Blackstone was no longer an aspiring upstart. It now was a player, and Schwarzman wasn't shy about broadcasting the firm's success. In an April 1998 interview with *Business Week*, he drew the reporter's attention to Blackstone's complement of advisory, hedge fund, real estate, and buyout activities. By contrast, he said dismissively, KKR was a "one-trick pony." If there had been any doubt that Schwarzman was vying to steal Kravis's crown as the king of private equity, the put-down laid that to rest.

But the glow of triumph from UCAR and the new fund soon dissipated. Blackstone did make a handful of good investments in 1997 and 1998: Stockman's bet on transmission maker American Axle & Manufacturing along with three telecom investments led by the up-and-coming partner Mark Gallogly. But many of the deals it struck in those years turned into clunkers.

A funeral home and cemetery investment was a wipeout. Blackstone paid an inflated fourteen times cash flow for Prime Succession and Rose

Hills, which it bought in partnership with a funeral industry giant, Loewen Group, just as the funeral business was turning down. Blackstone had negotiated downside protection in the form of a put option that allowed it to sell its stake back to Loewen at a gain. But just when Prime Succession and Rose Hills were on the brink of insolvency, Loewen itself was teetering on the edge, succumbing to the industry's general malaise and a huge court judgment. Loewen filed for bankruptcy in 1999, rending the put option worthless. Blackstone walked away $58 million poorer. Adding insult to injury, as Loewen was failing, Blackstone was fined $2.8 million for not disclosing to antitrust regulators an internal document when it sought clearance to buy Prime Succession in 1996. The document highlighted that Loewen and Prime were competitors. Howard Lipson, who had certified to the government that Blackstone's application was complete, was personally fined $50,000.

Blackstone lavished a total of $441 million from its second and third funds on Allied Waste Industries, a trash hauler, landfill owner, and recycler in 1997 and 1990—up to then the most Blackstone had injected into one company. But the main premise of the investment proved to be flat wrong. Blackstone and Allied executives had predicted that a dwindling supply of unused landfill would jack up prices. Instead, a brutal price war erupted. More than ten years later, Blackstone was still sitting on its stake. "We preserved capital, but it was dead money," says Lipson, who led the deal.

Schwarzman can still painfully tick off the names of other late-nineties Blackstone duds: Haynes International, a producer of aerospace alloys; plastic-bottle maker Graham Packaging; and the ostentatiously named Imperial Home Decor, the world's biggest wallpaper maker. Haynes and Imperial—both Stockman deals—eventually went bankrupt, socking Blackstone with $127 million in losses.

Graham, another Lipson deal, survived but struggled. A strategic merger with another packaging company that Blackstone financed in the hopes of boosting Graham's market share utterly backfired. Some of Graham's main customers, food and beverage companies, were unnerved by the prospect of being too dependent on one company and took business elsewhere. Graham, like Allied Waste, would languish on Blackstone's list of holdings for more than a decade after the original investment—an eternity in the private equity business.

With hindsight, there was a pattern to the failures. All were highly cyclical companies whose fortunes seesawed with the economy. None were dominant, or even terribly competitive, in their fields. In some cases the opposite was true: The businesses had intractable problems that made it impossible for them to gain traction against bigger and stronger rivals. No one inside Blackstone really understood the businesses that well. On top of all that, Blackstone bought many of them at the wrong time in the economic cycle. It wound up overpaying and piling on too much debt. It had stacked the deck against itself.

"These were all medium-sized, cyclical businesses that we bought within two or three years of an economic top," says Schwarzman. "We paid too much for some of them. We had ambitious turnaround plans for them that turned out to be very difficult to execute." The losses taught the firm several lessons, he says. First, "don't pay too much when you're buying cyclicals," he says. Second, "don't have ambitious turnaround expectations for medium-sized companies. Don't expect to reinvent them." Third, if an investment calls for reengineering operations, "don't have it be a Blackstone-manufactured plan." Rather, develop a plan in consultation with seasoned executives and consultants knowledgeable enough to judge if the plan will fly.

Several of Blackstone's debacles had something else in common: They had been championed and overseen by David Stockman, whose midwestern roots had instilled in him a zeal for rejuvenating Rust Belt businesses.

His eleven-year career at the firm had been remarkably checkered. His conviction in 1997 that demand for sport utility vehicles would continue to soar led the firm in 1997 to buy American Axle, a spinoff of General Motors that specialized in drive trains for SUVs. When the company went public in January 1999, a little over a year after Blackstone bought it, the market valued American Axle at four times Blackstone's cost. But such hits were proving to be the exception, not the rule, and by the summer of 1999, Stockman's stock inside Blackstone had reached bottom.

The SUV thesis tied in with the premise of another 1997 investment, in Premcor USA, an oil refiner that was as problematic as American Axle was successful. When oil prices dropped in 1997 and 1998 because of oversupply, Premcor was stuck with old inventory it had bought at higher prices and its earnings turned negative. When oil prices rose again several years later, Stockman's belief that there would be a shortage of refining capacity was vindicated, but in 1999 it looked like another of his ornately argued investments had backfired.

At Haynes, which made alloy parts for planes and chemical refineries, his projections proved too rosy and by 1999 the company was headed toward bankruptcy. The story with Imperial Home Decor was equally disastrous but more comical. When Blackstone invested in 1998, Stockman projected big sales gains in post-Soviet Russia and Eastern Europe as incomes there rose. A young banker who worked on the original deal recalls Stockman explaining how people there would need wallpaper to cover up cracking plaster that was beyond painting. Not only did that seem far-fetched; to the twenty-something banker, just a year or two out of business school, wallpaper seemed passé. "I'm thinking, what do I know," he says, "but I don't know anyone who buys wallpaper." He was right. When Russia defaulted on its debt in 1998, the Eastern European economies sank and global wallpaper sales fell 10–15 percent. Sales in Western Europe and the United States remained anemic and the company resorted to bankruptcy in January 2000 to rid itself of its debt, taking $84.5 million of Blackstone's money with it.

Then there was Republic Technologies International, a much grander fiasco. Stockman had hatched a scheme to create a moneymaking specialty steel business out of unwanted subsidiaries of bigger steelmakers. He began his buying spree in April 1996 with a $30 million purchase of Bar Technologies, the former wire and rod division of Bethlehem Steel, and later annexed two much bigger businesses, Republic Engineering Steels and a steel-bar venture once owned by U.S. Steel and Japan's

Kobe Steel. When Bar Technologies merged with Republic in 1998, the businesses were in such rotten shape that one Wall Street wag likened the combination to "two garbage trucks in a collision."

Stockman's plan was to shutter plants and lay off thousands of workers, which he did. But the price of union cooperation was an agreement to pay $178 million into the union pension plan. When the drastic downsizing didn't produce the profits Stockman had forecast, the company found itself burdened with the pension liability and began to hemorrhage cash. "The pension payouts sucked it dry of liquidity," says a person who was involved in the deal. "The Kobe–U.S. Steel deal really killed the company. It was the bridge too far." In 1999, Republic was barely clinging to life, though it would be two more years before it declared bankruptcy.

Blackstone sank $190 million into Republic—the biggest investment in Blackstone's second buyout fund. The whole investment would go up in smoke.

In addition to the stream of worrying financial news from Stockman's portfolio, complaints about Stockman were filtering back to others at Blackstone from the managers of the companies, who were unhappy at his persistent meddling and niggling. Stockman questioned the judgment of executives who knew their businesses far better than he, and his suggestions sometimes seemed off-the-wall.

In August 1999, when Stockman was away on a two-week African vacation, Schwarzman decided to play detective. He personally hit the phones, calling executives at each of Stockman's companies to find out about their relations with Stockman. From those soundings, "Steve came to the realization that David was a little out of control," says a former associate. When Stockman returned, Schwarzman told him that he had in mind a new role for him, spotting trends and researching potential investments. His days overseeing companies, he was informed, were over.

Stockman was not booted out, but he could see that his role would be diminished. On September 16, 1999, he announced he was quitting Blackstone to form his own private equity firm, Heartland Industrial

Partners. In a press release, Schwarzman and Peterson extolled his fine work on American Axle. Blackstone invested some of its own capital in Heartland, and Peterson served on Heartland's board of advisers. The parting was smooth enough that even years later Stockman would still periodically drop by Blackstone's offices. But few, if any, of his Blackstone colleagues were sorry to see him go.

At Heartland, Stockman was free to pursue his convictions unchecked, and he poured his investors' money into midwestern manufacturers, many linked to the auto industry. Nearly all went bust. The most disastrous was an investment in the auto interiors and trims company that had launched his private equity career in 1988, Collins & Aikman (née Wickes), and that continued to hold an allure for him. Less than two years after he founded Heartland, he bought control of Collins & Aikman from Blackstone and Wasserstein and Company, which had taken the company public in 1994 but had never managed to cash out. After a dozen years, they were only too happy to get out even though they recouped less than half their original money.

Stockman appended other smaller parts makers to Collins & Aikman, but by 2003 it was being squeezed by rising raw-materials prices and falling profits at its customers, General Motors, Ford, and Chrysler. Stockman personally took the helm as CEO in 2003, but the company was taking on water and he could not keep it from sinking under the weight of the debt from its buyout and the acquisitions. In 2005 Collins & Aikman filed for bankruptcy, obliterating Heartland's $360 million investment. In 2007 Stockman was indicted on charges of hiding Collins & Aikman's true financial condition from investors while its situation turned dire. Two long years later, federal prosecutors dropped the charges, saying that "further prosecution of this case would not be in the interests of justice." But by then the onetime wunderkind's reputation as an astute wheeler and dealer in private equity lay in tatters.

CHAPTER 13

Tuning in Profits

So long as you didn't cast your gaze too far beyond the center of the financial universe in Manhattan, Blackstone seemed to be enjoying a golden era in the late nineties. On the back of the spectacular profits of its second fund from 1992, it raised a new $4 billion investment pool in 1998. The world's largest insurance company, American International Group, took a 7 percent stake in the firm, valuing Blackstone at $2.1 billion, and AIG promised to ante up $1.2 billion for Blackstone's investment funds. *Forbes* and *BusinessWeek* each ran cover stories proclaiming the resurgence of leveraged buyouts.

But the truth was, by then Blackstone and private equity were a sideshow. The prosaic, cash-generating businesses that traditionally had been the bread and butter of the private equity business—short-line railroads like Transtar, graphite makers like UCAR, and auto-parts makers like Collins & Aikman and American Axle—had fallen out of fashion. The "old economy" of boring, profitable, but slow-and-steady companies was being eclipsed by the high-tech "new economy."

The IPO of Netscape Communications in April 1995 is usually pegged as the turning point. At the time the Internet was still in its infancy. For most people, it meant e-mail and perhaps some America Online chat rooms. Netscape's browser, which the company gave away free, enabled a new generation of websites loaded with photos and snappy typefaces and introduced a generation to what many still called by its formal name, the World Wide Web. For Netscape's founders, the company was more than just a software business. They were on a mission to "democratize information" via the Internet, and they sold the public on the proposition—literally. The company went public at $28 per share, valuing the start-up at $1.1 billion. Investors who hadn't been able to buy shares in the IPO itself were so desperate to get a piece of the action that they drove the stock up to $75 on its first day of trading.

To the cash-flow-obsessed private equity mind—and, frankly, under any conventional form of economic analysis—the price was absurd. Netscape had taken in just $16.6 million in revenue in the previous six months and lost $4.3 million in the process. The IPO demonstrated just how hungry investors were for start-ups that promised to remake the world with their technology and prepared the way for a new era of investing. The next year Yahoo!, the web portal and search engine, followed in Netscape's footsteps, going public at a similar valuation despite revenues of just $1.4 million and a loss of nearly half that.

Make money? That was so *old economy.* There was no need to do that now. The mere *prospect* of huge profits down the road was enough to lure the public. Instead of profits, the financial metric became "burn rate"—how much of its backers' cash a company chewed through every month or year.

However fantastical the stock prices were, a profound technological revolution was in fact under way. Advances in personal computers and access to online information made workers more productive and created new pastimes. That, in turn, drove demand for more telecommunications services, which created a demand for new phone switching equipment and the software to go with it, which allowed more and more information and graphics to be moved across the Internet, in turn spawning the birth of new Internet businesses. Completing the virtuous circle, this led people to want more powerful computers and even faster connections to the Internet.

Private equity firms like Blackstone found themselves looking on from the sidelines of the revolution. The stratospheric profits from the IPOs of companies like Netscape, Yahoo!, Amazon.com, and eBay were flowing into the pockets of entrepreneurs and the venture capitalists who backed them. Those windfalls inevitably had a profound impact on buy-out firms—profound and disastrous in some cases.

Venture capital funds share the same legal structures as buyout funds. They are limited partnerships and their sponsors typically collect 1.5 or 2 percent a year as a management fee and 20 percent of invest-ment profits. They tap the same pension funds, endowments, and other institutions for money. But there the similarities end. The programmers, chip makers, biotech researchers, Internet merchants, and the venture capitalists, or VCs, who financed them operated in their own universe, on another coast, playing by their own set of rules.

The epicenter of the U.S. buyout industry is Midtown Manhattan, where Blackstone, KKR, Apollo, Warburg Pincus, and dozens of other firms are headquartered within a few blocks of one another in a world of starched shirts and Hermès ties, chauffeured Mercedes, and office tow-ers. Ground zero of the venture world is Sand Hill Road, a landscaped boulevard rising into the gentle, suburban hills behind Palo Alto, Cali-fornia. There capital flows in a dress-down world of khakis and golf shirts, low-rise office compounds surrounded by groves of live oaks and towering eucalyptuses. Venture capitalists drive themselves to work in Ferraris and Porsches.

The investment styles were as different as the dress codes. Venture investing involves an entirely different type of risk. VCs seed scores of small companies that often have little or no revenue, and many of those that do take in revenue are nonetheless losing money. No bank would lend to these businesses, but they need equity capital for research and to build out their businesses. The VCs know that many of their companies will fizzle but hope that a few will be spectacularly successful. It is a scat-tershot approach, like tossing apple seeds and hoping a healthy tree or two will spring up. VCs make bets on which entrepreneur will achieve a technological breakthrough first, who can get to market fastest, and whose product will dominate its market—events whose likelihood defies precise projections.

That is a world away from buyouts. If venture investing is a game of long, daring passes, many incomplete, the LBO game is fought a yard at a time on the ground. To be a private equity investor, you need to be a kind of control freak—someone who can patiently map out all the scenarios, good and bad, first to make sure your company won't go bust and, second, to see how it can be improved incrementally to lift its value. Buyout investing focuses on cash flow because banks won't lend money, and bond buyers won't buy bonds, unless they are confident a company will be able to pay its creditors through thick and thin. Private equity investing means burrowing into businesses and performing minutely tuned analyses. Could revenue be boosted a point or two? How much would pass through to the bottom line? What costs could be taken out to notch up the profit margin a fraction? Could we shave a quarter of a point off the interest rate on the debt? If the company has problems, how much of a cushion is there before it defaults? If private equity investors do their job right, things more often than not will play out more or less in line with their projections.

Because venture investments are so much more unpredictable, venture investing requires a degree of passion—a belief in the product and its potential and, very often, in its value to society. Venture capitalists talk of nurturing "disruptive technologies" that will upend existing industries and lay the groundwork for new ones, in the way that diesel locomotives displaced steam engines, personal computers and laser and inkjet printers rendered the typewriter obsolete, and digital photography supplanted film. No amount of number crunching can predict if a new website will capture the public's imagination or whether a biotech start-up's research will succeed in developing a drug to treat cancer. The pay-off comes from seeding dozens of long shots. To sustain the process, the VCs and the entrepreneurs they back have to *believe,* and during the boom of the 1990s they had that faith in spades. The buyout types, with their dense spreadsheets and elaborately engineered debt structures, never promised to transform the world. They had no religion to offer the investing masses.

The passion for the new technology became contagious in the second half of the 1990s and began to alter the calculus for buyout firms far removed from Silicon Valley, as capital that might have gone to LBO funds began flowing into venture funds. Executives and business school graduates, too, were gravitating to tech companies, hoping to be paid in stock so they could make a fortune when the companies went public.

Blackstone wasn't equipped to compete on the VCs' home turf in pure technology plays. But Mark Gallogly, the youngest deal-making partner in the buyout group, succeeded, partly by accident, in riding the Internet wave.

Gallogly was the odd one out among the larger-than-life personalities and egos there. He generated none of the electricity that the brilliant and overbearing David Stockman did. He had a penchant for analysis, but he was not an eccentric mad-scientist number-grinder like James Mossman. Nor could he compete for laughs with the outgoing, wise-cracking Howie Lipson. Gallogly, who began his career on the lending side at Manufacturers Hanover bank, was intense, reserved, and soft-spoken. Innately cautious, he retained a loan officer's fear of risk, measuring his words and agonizing over investments.

Inside the firm, he was seen as a good investor, collegial, and uncommonly concerned about morale. In a firm that was notoriously hard on junior employees, it was Gallogly who hosted summer parties at his house in Rhode Island and organized the annual firm ski outing. He even lobbied once to install a plaque in the lobby inscribed with the name of every young analyst who had ever warmed a cubicle seat at Blackstone. (The proposal went nowhere.)

Gallogly became intrigued by the cable TV industry in the mid-1990s and had his underlings running numbers. At the time, the business was beaten down. Customers were up in arms about rising rates, which politicians and regulators were threatening to rein in, and cable operators, which had long enjoyed monopolies in their territories, suddenly faced a new threat from satellite TV. "They were calling it the death star. Satellite was going to kill cable," says Blackstone partner Lawrence Guffey, who worked as an associate for Gallogly at the time. Gallogly thought the market had overreacted. Rural cable systems, in particular, looked like prime LBO material, with solid cash flows and very little threat of competition.

The first deal that came to fruition was a classic Blackstone corporate partnership. The cable subsidiary of Time Warner, the media conglomerate, was planning to merge some of its marginal rural cable systems with others run by Bob Fanch, a veteran cable executive whom Gallogly's team had cultivated. Blackstone already had ties to Time Warner through the Six Flags theme parks investment in 1991 and offered to come to its aid again with the cable subsidiary. Blackstone invested $50 million for a one-half interest in the merged Time Warner–Fanch system, which covered parts of Pennsylvania, West Virginia, Texas, Ohio, and North Carolina. The business then borrowed so that debt could replace some of Time Warner's equity, allowing Time Warner to take out cash. As a bonus, because it no longer held a controlling stake, Time Warner no longer had to report the system's debt on its own balance sheet, which was massively leveraged at the time.

Much of the combined network, which was dubbed TW Fanch-One, was antiquated, transmitting as few as thirty channels. The plan was to update it to offer more programming, much of it to be provided by Time Warner at advantageous rates, and convince customers to pay up for more channels.

"In some cases, the systems were quite primitive," says Gallogly. "We believed the business had real growth potential, both through price and through improved technology. Even if satellite TV took a greater share than we were expecting, the cable business was generating a lot of cash flow and we thought we could do well despite that."

What happened next was not in the business plan, but it was extraordinarily fortunate.

When the Fanch deal closed in 1996, most people who used the Internet dialed in on their regular phone lines to America Online, CompuServe, or another Internet provider. But as websites developed richer and richer content and it became possible to move images and other large files over the Internet, conventional phone connections were painfully slow and computer users demanded high-speed data hookups. Cable companies, whose video transmission networks already had enormous bandwidth (the capacity to send heavy streams of electronic signals), found they

could easily adapt their systems to carry phone calls and Internet traf-
fic. In fact, they could modify their systems to offer high-speed Internet
access more easily than traditional phone companies could.

"We didn't know in 1996 that the Internet was going to be a boom,
but we knew that we would be able to benefit from the fact that we'd be
one of only two direct lines into the home," Gallogly says. Offering Internet and phone service was icing on the cake.

Gallogly soon engineered a second deal combining other Time Warner
and Fanch systems and invested in two unrelated companies, InterMedia
Partners VI and Bresnan Communications, Inc., that were buying stakes
in rural cable systems owned by TeleCommunications, Inc., one of Time
Warner's big national cable rivals.

By that point, the cable industry, which had been all but written off
only a few years earlier, had become a crucial link in the Internet, and
"triple play"—phone, Internet, and cable over the same connection—
was the buzz in the telecom industry. The industry had also acquired its
own high priest of triple play, Paul Allen, the cofounder of Microsoft
Corporation. The billionaire combined the faith of a tech maven with
a personal fortune of some $20 billion to back his dream of becoming a
cable mogul of the first order. Beginning in 1998, with the purchase of a
small cable business, Charter Communications, Allen went on a three-
year shopping spree, leveraging Charter to the hilt and shelling out $24.6
billion to buy twenty cable systems. Soon he came knocking on Blackstone's door.

Blackstone and Time Warner had assumed that Time Warner would
one day buy back control of their systems, but in late 1999 Charter
dropped a $2.4 billion offer on them for the two TW Fanch operations—
an offer the two simply couldn't refuse. Charter soon bought Blackstone's InterMedia systems as well, and in February 2000, just a year
after Blackstone had invested in Bresnan, Charter snatched that up, too,
for $3.1 billion. Convinced that new technology would drive demand
for his cutting-edge networks, Allen paid an eye-popping $4,500 per
customer for the TW Fanch networks and $4,400 for InterMedia, about
twice the price Blackstone had paid just a couple of years earlier.

"Paul Allen seemed to believe at the time that there was a cure for cancer coming down the cable pipeline," says Simon Lonergan, then an associate who worked with Gallogly on the investments. "We couldn't believe the prices he was paying for those assets. It was hard to have a rational view that justified paying that amount of money for infrastructure."

"We used to get up every morning and thank Paul Allen," says Bret Pearlman, who worked on the InterMedia deal and became a partner in 2000, as Charter was forking over billions to Blackstone. "Hallelujah!"

In fact, the prices did *not* make a lot of sense: Two years later Charter was near bankruptcy. (It finally succumbed in the next recession, in 2009.) But Allen's folly was Blackstone's gain in 2000 and it walked away with $400 million—eight times its original investment—on TW Fanch-One, a bigger multiple of its investment than even UCAR had earned. It hauled in 5.5 times its money, or $747 million, on Bresnan.

On top of the cable deals, Gallogly logged another huge gain on a cell phone operator in Montana, Wyoming, the Dakotas, and Colorado. Like the cable systems, Blackstone was able to pick up CommNet Cellular cheaply in 1998 because its stock price was depressed owing to fears that new competitors would enter its markets. Gallogly was skeptical, calculating that it would not be economical to build new cell networks in CommNet's sparsely populated territories. In 1999, less than a year and a half after Blackstone completed the purchase, Vodafone AirTouch, an emerging national firm that had bought a cell operator in the Denver area several years earlier, agreed to buy CommNet for $1.4 billion. Blackstone collected a $463 million profit, or 3.6 times its money.

By mid-2000, Blackstone had cashed out of almost all its telecom investments. In the process, Gallogly had brought home $1.5 billion in profit on five deals, making him the firm's newest star. The successes were sorely needed, too, because the exits came just as the dud deals led by Stockman and Lipson in 1997 and 1998 had begun to founder: The funeral chain Prime Succession/Rose Hills, the wallpaper maker Imperial Home Decor, Premcor, the oil refiner, and steel-rod maker Republic Technologies were all in deep trouble.

Gallogly's very success created a problem, however. With investors clamoring for ways to invest in communications companies, Gallogly saw a chance to hang out his own shingle, and he told Schwarzman in 1999 that he planned to leave. It was the last thing Schwarzman wanted to hear at the time, for the firm could ill afford the loss of another senior deal maker. Glenn Hutchins, who had been brought in as a partner in 1994, left to form a new firm, Silver Lake Partners, at the end of 1998. Stockman and Anthony Grillo, a partner who had moved over to buyouts from the restructuring team, departed in 1999. Without Gallogly, the buyout group would be down to just two full-time partners, Lipson and Mossman, and Mossman never left his office!

"There was a growing concern over our reputation as a place with a lot of turnover," Peterson says.

"We hit a fork in the road," says Schwarzman.

Schwarzman worked on Gallogly first, persuading him to stay by offering to raise a new, specialized fund that would invest only in telecom and media companies and putting Gallogly in charge of it. Gallogly would get pretty much what he wanted but under Blackstone's banner. For Schwarzman, it kept Gallogly in the fold and allowed the firm to tap into the communications mania without having Blackstone's main fund put too much money at risk in one sector. The fund-raising, which kicked off in early 2000, went quickly, and Blackstone Communications Partners, known as BCOM, hit its $2 billion target by June of that year.

That still left the buyout ranks worryingly thin, however. Through the fall of 1999, the management committee and the private equity partners debated whether to hire from the outside and which associates to elevate. Ultimately, they decided to gamble on the home-grown talent and promote a big new class of partners.

"There was more risk bringing people in from the outside, where you don't know exactly how they'll fit culturally," Schwarzman says. In January 2000, the firm, which had only twelve partners at the time, expanded those ranks by five: David Blitzer, thirty, Chinh Chu, thirty-three, Larry Guffey, thirty-one, Bret Pearlman, thirty-three, and Neil Simpkins, thirty-three.

There were risks giving more responsibility to such a young crew. "It would require more supervision," Schwarzman says. "We'd have to work with them more." To keep an eye on them, Schwarzman recruited Robert Friedman, Blackstone's lead outside lawyer at Simpson Thacher & Barlett, to join the buyout team to make sure "nothing dropped through the cracks."

It also wasn't clear how good the new partners would be at generating business. "The whole corporate partnership model was [to] go out and call on and sit down with a CEO or a board as an equal," says Simon Lonergan, who was made partner in 2001. That had worked when it was Peterson, Schwarzman, and Stockman who were making the calls. "How do you do that when you're in your early thirties?"

It was a risk, but Schwarzman and the other partners felt they had no choice.

CHAPTER 14

An Expensive Trip to Germany

In the beginning it had looked like a West Coast fad, the technology boom that shifted into high gear when Netscape, Yahoo!, and the first generation of big Internet companies went public. By the end of the nineties, though, the technology industries, the venture capitalists that supported them, and the religion for which they proselytized had become as disruptive to finance as their new inventions had been to established companies. Microsoft had displaced General Electric as the world's most valuable company and seven of the top ten were in the computer or telecom industries. Coca-Cola, Toyota, and the oil and pharmaceutical companies—the old economy giants that had dominated the list for years—had been bumped off.

With some venture funds chalking up returns of 100, 200, and even 300 percent a year, the lure of venture investing proved irresistible, and pension funds and endowments began redirecting more money to investment funds that specialized in start-ups and other technology companies. To these investors, venture capital, private equity, and real estate were all in the category of "alternative assets"—alternatives that offered higher returns than their mainstay investments in stocks and bonds.

Venture firms, which had attracted a mere $10 billion in 1995, hauled in more than $59 billion in 1999, nearly the sum for buyout funds that year. More venture capital was raised in 1998 and 1999 than in the entire history of the industry through 1997, and in 2000 venture firms raked in $105 billion, for the first time surpassing buyout funds, which drew only $82 billion. Like a pile of poker chips pushed across the table from loser to winner, mounds of capital were being transferred away from traditional industries and investment firms to the technology and venture mavens—from New York to California.

This rearranged the map of wealth. Nearly one-quarter of the richest Americans were Californians, *Forbes* reported in 1998. The next year, John Doerr and Vinod Khosla of Kleiner Perkins Caufield & Byers, perhaps the best-known venture firm, were worth $1 billion each—as much as Henry Kravis and George Roberts, and considerably more than other buyout stars such as Teddy Forstman, Tom Lee, and Tom Hicks. Pete Peterson and Steve Schwarzman didn't even make the *Forbes* list.

Blackstone couldn't help but feel the pressure to jump on the bandwagon. Bret Pearlman, who became a partner in 2000, and other younger deal makers were lobbying to invest more in the tech sphere, and junior employees were clamoring to be paid partly in Internet company stocks, the preferred currency of New Economy workers.

The firm was hearing it from some investors, too. When Schwarzman hit the road in 1999 to raise money for Blackstone's new mezzanine debt fund, which would lend money to midsized businesses, one potential investor who preferred venture funds just scoffed. "I make more money in a month than you make in a year in your mezz fund if things go well," he told Schwarzman.

"We had enormous pressure here to be doing those deals," Schwarzman says. "We were viewed as not being modern."

It was all irksome to Schwarzman, who thought the prices being paid for Internet companies were ridiculous. But with firms like Doerr and Khosla's reaping stupendous returns selling their tech start-ups in IPOs, it was hard not to be tugged in that direction. "As you got to the 1999 period and into 2000, the amount of money people were making so quickly by putting capital in venture-type deals and flipping them in IPOs put enormous pressure on the buyout firms to participate in some level in that," says Schwarzman. "Or else you could lose your people or lose your competitive returns."

Competing with the VCs wasn't really an option, though. That took in-depth knowledge of tech industries ranging from semiconductors and software to websites and biotechs—sectors where private equity firms had little if any expertise and few contacts. Moreover, entrepreneurs flocked to the venture firms that had backed the most successful investments. Why would they come to Blackstone, which had no track record and was on the wrong coast? Buyout firms that tried to intrude on the Californian finance turf were likely to get only companies that had been rejected by the top VCs. KKR formed a joint venture with the venture firm Accel, and Carlyle launched venture funds, but they never left a big mark.

Schwarzman threw a bone to the troops by authorizing $7 million of the firm's own capital to be allocated for technology investments. The investment committee also gave the green light to a string of tech deals by the main buyout fund. Most were ultimately complete write-offs. Fortunately, they were all small. "To Steve's credit, no matter how many times people said we're sort of missing the boat here on the Internet, Steve insisted over and over, 'This is not what we do well,'" says Pearlman.

Telecommunications was a different matter, however. Many conventional phone companies and wireless and cable operators made money but needed additional capital. Many were large enough that private equity firms could put hundreds of millions of dollars to work at one company, which was nearly impossible with start-ups. So no sooner had Blackstone cashed out of the cable and cell companies it had bought in 1996 to 1998 than it waded back in, drawing on both its main 1998 fund and the new $2 billion media and telecoms fund that Mark Gallogly oversaw.

This time, though, many of the investments were a far cry from the stable, rural cable and cell systems of the nineties. Some of the new round of deals looked more like speculative venture plays on a grand scale—big bets on start-up businesses where Blackstone took only a minority stake and thus didn't control the business. And unlike a run-of-the-mill VC deal, these investments tended to be heavily leveraged.

It plowed $227 million into Sirius Satellite Radio, a start-up that was building a satellite broadcasting network, taking just a 9 percent stake. Another $176 million went into three "overbuilder" cable networks that hoped to compete with existing cable operators—ambitious and dicey deals premised on projections that the upstarts could steal away enough customers to pay for the huge build-out costs. "It was definitely a dare-to-be-great sector," Pearlman allows.

Another $187 million went for a small stake in an Argentine cellphone operator, and Blackstone wrote a $23 million check to a Brazilian online service.

The grandest plan of all the second round of telecom deals, and the first major investment for Gallogly's new fund, was in Germany. Richard Callahan, a cable executive from Denver whom Gallogly knew, had set up a private equity firm and invested in cable companies in France, Belgium, and Spain. In 1999, he approached Gallogly about backing his firm in a bid to take over two regional cable systems being sold by Germany's state-owned phone company, Deutsche Telekom. Regulators mandated the divestitures so that new owners could offer phone and Internet service over the cable lines, creating competition for Deutsche Telekom, which had long held a monopoly.

Blackstone had been investing heavily in European real estate for several years, but it did not yet have an office in Europe and was far behind Carlyle, KKR, TPG, and other American private equity firms in penetrating the buyout market there. The Callahan deals, which together were worth $5.2 billion, would be the largest private equity investments to date in Europe and a dramatic debut for Blackstone.

Blackstone and Quebec's public pension fund, Caisse de Dépôt et Placement du Québec, were the lead investors, with the private equity arm of Bank of America and the Bass family of Texas also writing checks. It was an unusual deal for Blackstone, because it would own just a 14 percent position amid a large consortium of investors, and Callahan's people would be taking the lead in managing the project. But Caisse de Dépôt and BofA had backed Callahan when he built a cable system from scratch in Spain and they thought highly of David Colley, the British executive who had spearheaded that project and was slated to head up the German business. The physical networks and the customer base were already in place, so it looked like a simpler undertaking than the one in Spain.

"We looked at this and said, 'Geez. It's a massive market, there's only one guy, Deutsche Telekom, offering local telephony. If we upgrade the infrastructure and get a small piece of the phone market,'" the pay-off could be huge, says Simon Lonergan, the associate who relocated to his native Britain in 2000 and was Blackstone's liaison to Callahan's managers.

The two networks, one in North Rhine Westphalia along the central Rhine and the other in Baden-Württemberg, stretching east from the southern Rhine to Stuttgart, covered some of Germany's densest and most prosperous urban areas. The twin deals were signed in early 2000 and Callahan closed the purchase of the North Rhine network in July 2000, and that of the Baden-Württemberg system the following year. Together, the third buyout fund and the communications fund shelled out $320 million, the second-largest sum Blackstone had ever invested.

Deutsche Telekom's phone rates were so high that the investors figured they could easily skim off some of its customers. "The basic economics were incredibly attractive," Lonergan says. "The basic thesis made a lot of sense. The problem was the execution."

Callahan and Colley planned $1 billion of capital spending the first year, in a race to get the new equipment in place. But the management team that had performed so ably in Spain struggled in Germany. Colley and other senior staff didn't speak German and commuted from Britain and Spain, arriving Mondays and leaving Fridays. Soon, everything that could go wrong did. There were delays getting the equipment and software running, so the revenue from new services that was supposed to help cover the ongoing upgrade costs didn't materialize as planned. They also found they were hostage to Deutsche Telekom, which owned the conduits through which the cable wires ran. Callahan's engineers had problems getting access, and they discovered the hard way that the phone company's maps of cable paths didn't always correspond to reality. When they installed their new equipment, they sometimes unwittingly blacked out whole neighborhoods. Once, much of Cologne lost its cable signal during a key soccer match and the company found itself pilloried on the front pages of the local papers.

Nor had Callahan's people factored in the housing cooperatives that own many big German apartment complexes and control the last leg of the network into tens of thousands of homes. Deutsche Telekom and Callahan relied on the co-ops to collect the phone and cable bills from their tenants, but the co-ops proved lackadaisical about dunning tenants who were in arrears, so revenues fell even further behind budget.

Through late 2001 Colley's team reported to Blackstone and the other investors that everything was more or less on track, when, in fact, the North Rhine Westphalia system was burning through money at an alarming rate and wasn't completing enough of the upgrade or selling enough new services to keep pace. Worse still, management didn't have proper accounting systems in place to monitor how much cash it had.

In early 2002, when the investors began pressing Colley and his people about the cash-flow situation, they couldn't get an answer. "It was only by going to some of the regular meetings with them and digging into the numbers with them, all of a sudden there was this aha moment—something's not right here," says William Obenshain, who oversaw the investment for Bank of America. "Either we were being misled or the management just didn't have a grip on it. . . . These [meetings] were very unpleasant."

When Callahan's crew finally did succeed in calculating its cash position, the company turned out to have more than a hundred million euros less than it should have had and was in imminent danger of violating the terms of its loans, which required it to have minimum cash flows and cash levels. Seemingly overnight, a massive investment had veered from on course to crisis. Two years earlier, at the height of the telecom boom, the company probably could have borrowed more money or refinanced its debt so it could complete the upgrade. But in 2002, that was impossible.

Gallogly, Lonergan, Obenshain, and the other investors scrambled to get things under control. Spending was reined in at the Baden-Württemberg company, where the upgrade had only just begun to get under way. But it was too late. Short on cash, the Callahan entities breached the terms of their loans. It was clear the equity was going to be erased, and Blackstone was forced to write off its entire investment at the end of 2002.

When Callahan arrived at Schwarzman's office to discuss what had happened, he got an earful from Schwarzman. "Where's my fucking money, you dumb shit?" were the first words out of Schwarzman's mouth, according to a person with ties to Callahan.

"I was really furious because he was personally working on a lot of other transactions rather than keeping his focus on this particular transaction," says Schwarzman, who calls it a "chilly meeting." "I told him I believed he had failed."

The loss was most devastating for the new media and telecom fund, because the $159 million it had contributed from its kitty represented more than 70 percent of its invested capital to that point. Two years after it was raised, the fund was in a deep hole and, with the entire telecom industry in a severe slump by 2003, it wasn't clear how it could dig its way out through new investments.

Callahan was only the biggest failure. Two-thirds of the investments Blackstone made in 2000, at the height of the market, were wipeouts. The write-offs were an object lesson in the dangers of wagering on companies in a frothy market—a lesson that would echo again when the credit markets crashed in 2007 and the economy began spiraling downward.

Most of the other mistakes were small, but not all. In addition to the Callahan setbacks, the Argentine cell operator CTI Holdings cost Blackstone $185 million and two companies that aimed to build new cable systems from scratch, Utilicom Networks and Knology, were complete losses. So was the investment in Sirius, the satellite radio company.

"The pain we took [on the investments of 2000] was a real turning point," says David Blitzer, who had joined Blackstone out of college not long after the disastrous collapse of the Edgcomb investment and become a partner in 2000, just as the firm again was about to stumble badly. "Losing money again was really a jolt to the system. How could we let this happen? What did we do wrong?" It was a time of "real soul-searching," he says.

Blackstone was hardly alone. The losses it suffered in 2001 and 2002 came as the technology and telecom bubbles were pricked, and air hissed out of the entire stock market. European stocks topped out in the winter of 1999 and 2000. In the United States, the IPO market cooled off in early 2000. The technology-heavy Nasdaq stock index crested in April 2000, at five times its 1995 level. The broader S&P 500 index, which had tripled in five years, inched up until that August. From there it was all downhill.

The skepticism that had poured cold water on the IPO market that spring spread to junk bonds. New issues were down by three-quarters in the spring of 2000 from their peak two years earlier. Across all the capital markets, worries grew that the economy might slow and that the miracle markets of the past five years might be coming to an end, just as they had at the end of the 1980s after a long run-up. Investors no longer wanted to roll the dice on profitless start-ups, and they didn't want to lend to highly leveraged companies whose cash flows might evaporate if the economy slowed.

The downturn was most catastrophic for tech companies and their investors, but buyout firms—particularly those that had forged deeply into telecoms—soon began to take their lumps. The dare-to-be-great telecom build-outs that Blackstone and others had funded began to totter and collapse, victims of both the buyout firms' overoptimistic projections and the slumping stock and debt markets, which made it impossible to raise new money if the projects hit a snag.

As stinging as Blackstone's losses were, they paled by comparison to the debacles of some competitors. At Hicks Muse Tate & Furst, the Texas firm that grew to be a major player in the later years of the nineties, well over $2 billion of its investors' money was incinerated in eleven disastrous deals over three years, mostly in telecoms.

Ted Forstmann, who had railed publicly against the risks KKR and others were taking with leverage in the 1980s, proved to be one of the most reckless gamblers of the nineties, plunking $2.5 billion—much of his funding—into just two companies, XO Communications and Mc-LeodUSA, which were building phone, cable, and Internet networks to compete with the Bell phone companies. Forstmann Little lost it all when both had to be restructured in 2002.

Welsh Carson, J.P. Morgan Partners, DLJ Merchant Banking, Madison Dearborn—some of the best names in the business—watched as one telecom investment of theirs after another cratered. Many found it harder to raise their next funds and were knocked down a peg or two in the pecking order. Forstmann's and Hicks's losses put their firms near death's door. Forstmann Little made only two significant investments after 2000 and slowly sold off old holdings. Exacerbating its woes, the state of Connecticut, which had invested in Forstmann's fund, sued in February 2002, claiming the firm had breached its agreements with investors by putting so much of its capital into just two risky investments. Ted Forstmann found himself on the witness stand in 2004, where he was grilled publicly about the calamitous decisions. (In a quirky outcome, the jury found that the firm had violated its investment contract but awarded no damages.)

When Tom Hicks tried to raise a new fund in 2000 to match his $4.1 billion pool of 1998, his investors balked. Most weren't convinced the firm deserved a second chance, and in 2002 it had to settle for $1.6 billion. In 2004, Tom Hicks announced that he plans to retire. The firm's London team, which had a good track record, split off in 2005. The remaining U.S. organization renamed itself HM Capital Partners and regrouped, focusing on smaller deals.

The carnage extended far beyond telecoms. In one of the biggest crack-ups, the $1.4 billion buyout in 1996 of the bowling equipment and bowling lane operator AMF Bowling Worldwide proved to be a $560 million gutter ball for Goldman Sach's private equity group, which had led the deal. Blackstone, which tagged along for the ride with a minority investment, lost $73.5 million of its money. Meanwhile, KKR, Hicks

Muse Tate & Furst, and DLJ kissed good-bye to more than $1 billion in the Regal Cinemas chain.

Sixty-two major private equity–backed companies went bust in 2001, vaporizing $12 billion of equity by one tally. Another forty-six failed in the first half of 2002, wiping out a further $7.6 billion, and there were many more, smaller deals that never came onto the public radar.

By the end of 2000, virtually no LBOs were being done in the United States. Then came the terrorist attacks of September 11, 2001, and the stock and debt markets, which had been sputtering for a year, had the final wind knocked out of them. With the public afraid to fly, airlines and the rest of the travel industry saw business dry up, setting off a domino-like line of bankruptcies, from the airlines themselves to Samsonite, the luggage maker, which was part owned by Apollo. Blackstone narrowly escaped losing one of its real estate jewels, the Savoy Group, which owned four of the poshest hotels in London. One day, no guests checked into Claridge's, perhaps the most exclusive hostelry in the city.

The mood was grim. With the World Trade Center ruins smoldering for five months after the attacks, people wondered out loud if New York would survive as a world financial center. As time went by, the slowdown took a growing toll on leveraged companies. By 2002, the default rate on junk bonds had shot to 13 percent. By September 2002 the broad S&P 500 index of U.S. stocks had fallen by almost half from its peak two years earlier, and the Nasdaq was 75 percent off its high.

Confidence was further sapped by corporate scandals. In December 2001 Enron Corporation, a pipeline operator and energy trading firm that had been a darling of Wall Street, imploded after it was revealed that the company had concealed billions of dollars of liabilities. WorldCom, a giant telecom that had grown through acquisitions to become AT&T's chief competitor in long-distance phone service, filed for bankruptcy in July 2002 after its books, too, turned out to be cooked. Adelphi Communications, a big cable operator, also went bust after disclosing that it had kept secret several billion dollars of loan guarantees to its controlling shareholders, the Riga family. When the U.S. government indicted the global accounting firm Arthur Andersen, which had audited both Enron and WorldCom, for destroying Enron documents, that only reinforced the growing suspicion that corporate financial statements meant nothing.

The downturn was a boon to Blackstone's restructuring and M&A groups, which won key roles in Enron's bankruptcy—one of the largest and most complex reorganizations ever. Arthur Newman's team was also tapped by Delta Airlines, whose bankruptcy was complicated by contentious labor relations, and by Global Crossing, one of the highest-flying international telecoms of the 1990s. But for the second time in a decade, Blackstone's LBO business was cast into limbo. It was virtually impossible to obtain financing and sellers couldn't accept that values had fallen. Big buyouts continued to be done in Europe, where the credit markets were healthier, and LBO activity there surpassed that of the United States from 2001 to 2003, but because Blackstone had been slow to focus on Europe, the opportunities went to its American competitors and big British buyout firms such as Apax Partners, BC Partners, CVC Capital Partners, Cinven, and Permira, which had the networks of connections and strong records there.

From the summer of 2000, Blackstone went nearly two years without closing a conventional buyout. After the Callahan projects in Germany in 2000, it was four years before Blackstone's communications fund invested in the equity of another company.

CHAPTER 15

Ahead of the Curve

While the stock and debt markets were still sliding in late 2001 and 2002, it was nearly impossible to pull off a buyout. Companies were still struggling and cash flows were tanking, so financing one was an ordeal. But Blackstone was sitting on billions it had raised in better times. Going into 2001, it still had more than $1 billion left from its $4 billion 1997 fund, as well as nearly all of the communication fund's $2 billion, and it was gearing up to raise a fourth generalist fund. Sooner or later it would have to deploy this money. It could wait until the credit markets recovered, or it could find alternatives to the classic leveraged buyout. The strategy that unfolded revealed a truth about private equity that is seldom observed by those outside the financial world: It is defined more by opportunism than by the conventional LBO. Other things being equal, buyouts are the norm. But things were anything but equal in 2001 and 2002.

In a rising market, leveraging equity with debt produces supercharged returns by amplifying any gain in the value of the equity. In troubled times, however, it can pay to invest instead at other levels of a corporation's capital structure, or to make unleveraged equity investments. Relatively low-risk senior debt of a company may pay as much as 15 percent—not too far short of the 20-percent-plus returns buyout firms typically aim for. Riskier, more junior debt may pay even more and may be swapped for equity down the road. When stock and bond markets fall, that's another way of saying that the price of capital has risen: Investors demand higher returns because they perceive more risk, and companies have to offer more stock to raise the same amount of new equity capital and must pay higher interest rates to borrow. When the world at large is preoccupied with what can go wrong and afraid to stake money, those brave enough to invest can exact a very high price. Blackstone's deal making in 2001 and 2002 reflected that fact of economic life.

The events of September 11, 2001, provided a case in point. One of the collateral casualties of the terrorist attacks was the insurance industry, which found itself staring at billions of dollars of unexpected claims not only from those hurt directly at the World Trade Center, but also from business interruption and other commercial policies covering companies far removed from New York and Washington. Overnight, capital reserves that had been built up over years as a cushion against losses were exhausted. Reinsurance companies, which protect other insurers against freak and catastrophic claims, were hit particularly hard because the attacks were so far outside any actuarial predictions, and the damage penetrated beyond the original insurers' coverage up into the reinsurers'. Because insurance companies are required by law to maintain reserves to back the policies they write, the losses forced many insurers to curtail business, writing fewer new policies. That sent premiums skyward.

Private equity firms pounced on the opportunity, pouring money into the sector—KKR, Hellman & Friedman, TPG, and Warburg Pincus, to name just a few. Rather than invest in existing companies that still had big claims to work off, however, they set up new reinsurers with clean balance sheets that now would face little competition from existing, wounded companies.

Two months after the terrorist attacks, Blackstone plowed $201 million into Axis Capital, a new reinsurer it formed with four other private equity firms. The next June it invested $268 million alongside the London buyout firm Candover Investments and others to form another new reinsurer, Aspen Insurance, around assets that a troubled London reinsurer, Wellington Re, was forced to sell. These were 100 percent equity investments in start-ups without leverage. In a crippled industry, they had the potential to match the returns Blackstone expected on LBOs in good times because the new players would be abnormally profitable.

At the time, it looked like "probably a three-year opportunity," says Schwarzman. After that, more capital would flow into the industry, boosting competition, driving down premiums, and causing returns to fall back to historical levels. "We would not make an amazing return, by the nature of the industry, but you could make twenty-one or twenty-two or twenty-three percent a year for a few years." Ultimately, Blackstone made a 30.2 percent annual return on Axis. Aspen might have matched that but it suffered big losses from Hurricane Katrina in 2005, so Blackstone ultimately earned only a 15 percent return.

In mid-2002, with the stock markets still falling, Blackstone veered even further from its customary investment formulae, detouring into vulture debt investing, a treacherous new territory where it had ventured only a few times before, such as when it bought debt of the shopping mall owner DeBartolo in 1993 and Cadillac Fairview, the Canadian property developer, in 1995.

Vultures, in financial jargon, are investors who scavenge bankrupt or distressed companies, buying up their loans or bonds. Investing in distressed debt entails many of the same analyses as an LBO—figuring out the value of a company's assets and whether it generates enough cash to cover its debt. But when a company is going down the drain, it's much trickier to estimate how much value will be salvaged and how much value creditors will come away with.

Under corporate law, creditors are ranked in a hierarchy that determines who gets what if the company becomes insolvent. At the top are banks, whose so-called senior loans are secured by the company's assets. They are followed by bondholders, suppliers, and employees. Shareholders stand at the back of the line, getting nothing unless the creditors are all paid off. When the company's assets are tallied up or sold off, creditors at the top of the ladder may be paid in full while those at the bottom may get little or nothing. In between, some creditors may be only partly paid off. Those groups often get to swap their debt for an ownership stake when the business is restructured, which gives them a chance to recoup their losses.

There are several ways to make money as a vulture, all risky. Some play the distress discount. For example, if a bond pays 10 percent interest on its face value and it's selling for 67 cents on the dollar because it might go into default, the buyer earns a 15 percent return on its investment; the effective interest rate is 50 percent higher than the nominal rate because of the discounted price. That alone might attract some investors. If the bond doesn't default and pays off in full at maturity, they also stand to collect the full $1 in principal and score a 50 percent gain on their 67-cent investment. The investor may not have to wait until maturity to cash in if the company's fortunes improve, because the bond's market price will rise and the investor can sell out at a gain.

Alternatively, you can gamble on layers of the company's debt that may not be paid off in full but which are likely to be exchanged for equity when the business is restructured. This, however, is a game only for the bold, because the payoff hinges not only on the legal position of the debt, but on the performance of a troubled business and the volatile market for distressed debt. Restructurings and Chapter 11 reorganizations often spawn bitter disputes among creditors about who will be paid how much and who will get what when the company emerges from bankruptcy—battles that can drag out the rehabilitation of the company. No matter how many numbers you crunch through a spreadsheet, the payoff for any individual class of debt is hard to predict.

"When you look at distressed deals, you have to think very differently," says Blackstone partner Chinh Chu. "The negotiations are much more complicated because you're playing three-dimensional chess with the creditors, the equity holders—many tranches of creditors."

With few LBO options on the horizon, though, Blackstone was ready to gamble. "We're value investors and we're pretty agnostic as to where we appear in the capital structure," Schwarzman says. "In 2002 it became pretty clear that subordinated debt in a whole variety of companies was a terrific place to be." In other words, buying distressed bonds on the cheap was as good as buying equity if you could turn a profit that way.

Blackstone tested its new strategy first on Adelphia Communications, the cable company that filed for bankruptcy in 2002 after admitting that it had fudged its books to conceal liabilities. Mark Gallogly, whose team had been steeped in the cable industry since the mid-1990s, understood the business and was comfortable betting on Adelphia's debt. Art Newman, the head of Blackstone's restructuring advisers, was called in to help strategize. "These guys knew the assets very well, and I understood the bankruptcy process," says Newman.

In the secondary market, Blackstone bought up a sizable portion of Adelphia's debt and won a seat on the creditors committee in the bankruptcy, where the firm pressed for a sale of the company.

A few months later, in September 2002, Blackstone began buying up debt of Charter Communications, Microsoft cofounder Paul Allen's cable giant, which had mortgaged itself to the hilt to buy cable systems at outlandish prices, including Blackstone's TW Fanch, Bresnan, and InterMedia holdings. In both cases, the underlying businesses were fundamentally sound. They simply carried too much debt, and that would be reduced in a restructuring.

"At that point, cable looked relatively well protected," says Schwarzman. "Its systems were built out. Its systems were difficult to replicate. Customers liked watching television, and many of the new entrants that had tried to challenge cable had gone bankrupt."

Blackstone splashed out a hefty $516 million from both the 1997 and communications funds for Adelphia and Charter debt. It was a massive bet, and for a while it looked like the investment had been badly mistimed. As Schwarzman looked on, the trading prices of the debt fell, recalls Larry Guffey, a young partner at the time who worked on the trades. "We were underwater. Painfully—particularly when Steve's calling you and asking you why it's underwater, which I remember very well."

It still wasn't clear if the Adelphia and Charter wagers would pay off in mid-2003 when Blackstone began weighing a third big investment in distressed cable debt. This one would be equally risky but also held the

promise of redemption, for the companies in question were the two Callahan systems in Germany that Blackstone had written off just months
earlier.

Like Adelphia and Charter, the North Rhine Westphalia and Baden-
Württemberg cable businesses were basically healthy. They had simply
run out of cash because they had spent too much too quickly to upgrade
their networks and hadn't signed up enough new customers to keep
pace. With new management and the costs under control, Blackstone
saw a chance to atone for the earlier loss.

Guffey, who had relocated to London in 2002, took over from Mark
Gallogly and Simon Lonergan, who had overseen the original German
cable investments. The banks hadn't formally foreclosed, but the businesses were in such grim straits that for all practical purposes they be-
longed to the banks. Together with its coinvestors from 2000, Quebec's
Caisse de Dépôt and Bank of America, Blackstone approached one of
the Baden-Württemberg system's banks and arranged to buy a big slice
of the company's loans at a meager 19 euro cents on the euro and then
bought more in the open market at deep discounts. The investor trio
also bought $20 million of debt of the sister company in North Rhine
Westphalia in the open market.

The timing was as perfect as it had been disastrous in 2000 and 2001.
The private equity firms swapped their debt in the Baden-Württemberg
company for equity when the company was restructured, and Blackstone then bought out Caisse de Dépôt and Bank of America's stakes,
giving it a controlling position. Working with a new CEO who had been
brought in at the tail end of Callahan's involvement, they kept new capital spending in sync with revenues. "We slowed it down until the revenue caught up," Guffey says.

The restructuring cut the company's debt to manageable levels and
the business was soon back on its feet. By 2005 profits were rising and
the company was able to borrow money to refinance its debt and pay a
huge dividend to Blackstone and other shareholders. By the time Blackstone cashed out its last piece of the two companies in 2006, it had
booked a profit of $381 million—three times what it had invested in the

second round. That more than made up for the $264 million loss on the original investment. On top of that, the communications fund raked in a $312 million profit on the debt of another troubled German cable firm, Primacom, in which Blackstone had not previously invested. Blackstone also made back some of what it had lost earlier on Sirius, the satellite radio company, by buying its debt on the cheap. The communications fund raised in 2000, whose situation had looked so dire in 2002, had been patched up and was now posting profits.

"We had just raised this $2 billion fund" when the original Callahan deal foundered, Guffey says. "This was 15 percent of the fund and it looked like it would be zero. We were down eight to one in the seventh inning and we turned the game around."

Adelphia and Charter yielded big windfalls as well. Altogether, Blackstone more than doubled the roughly $800 million it gambled on the distressed debt strategy.

The communication fund for years was the least profitable of all of Blackstone's funds, with an annual rate of return in the single digits. But thanks to the vulture plays and some later investments, by 2007 it had produced a respectable if not spectacular 17 percent annual return— better than Blackstone's 1997 fund.

Slowly it became possible, too, to make equity investments again, in many cases as a by-product of the economic strains of the retrenchment.

Across America and Europe corporations had binged on acquisitions in the late nineties, and they were still gripped by indigestion. Many mergers had not panned out, and even those that had worked operationally had often left the buyers overindebted. Many companies needed to sell assets to pay down debt and shore up their balance sheets, but there were few buyers. The markets had no appetite for IPOs, so they couldn't sell their subsidiaries that way. And the corporate world was generally reluctant to expand through acquisitions after the buying frenzy of the late 1990s. Flush with capital, Blackstone and other private equity firms were among the few buyers, and they began to fill the void.

It took some ingenuity to find deals that could get off the ground, and the first round of new equity investments Blackstone made deviated from the standard LBO model in one way or another.

When Blackstone took a minority stake in Nycomed, a Danish pharmaceutical company, as part of a consortium in October 2002, the buyers put up nearly 40 percent of the price in equity—far higher than the more typical 25 percent or 30 percent. They saw it as a growth play and calculated that the business would expand quickly enough that they could make LBO-level profits even without steep leverage.

Likewise, the financing for the $4.6 billion buyout of TRW Automotive, a parts maker, that autumn was unorthodox. Northrop Grumman, a defense contractor, was acquiring TRW's parent company, another defense supplier, and needed to off-load the auto subsidiary as quickly as it could to pay down the loans for the main takeover. Blackstone was unwilling to invest more than $500 million of its own, so Neil Simpkins, a young partner who was leading the deal, persuaded Northrop to keep a 45 percent stake while Blackstone tried to recruit other investors after the deal closed. In effect, the seller was offering installment financing for its own asset. Northrop even loaned Blackstone some of the money to buy its 55 percent stake. Still, it was hard to line up the debt needed to cover the balance. (Ultimately other investors joined Blackstone, allowing Northrop to sell down its stake to the 19 percent it wanted to retain.)

In another instance, Blackstone effectively provided financing for a public company to make an acquisition. There PMI Group, a bond insurer, wanted to buy Financial Guaranty Insurance Company, a municipal bond insurer, from General Electric, but PMI's bond ratings were lower than FGIC's and an outright purchase would have jeopardized FGIC's ratings. To insulate FGIC's credit rating from its new parent's, Blackstone and Cypress Group, another private equity firm, stepped in and agreed to take 23 percent stakes each so that FGIC was not deemed to be a subsidiary of PMI. The expectation was that PMI would one day be in a position to buy all of FGIC.

Blackstone also made two bets on energy prices. In 2004 it took a flier on a start-up oil and gas exploration company, Kosmos Energy, that planned to drill for oil off the west coast of Africa, and it bought Foundation Coal, the U.S. subsidiary of RAW, a German company that was shedding assets.

In late 2001 and 2002, when the markets were still staggering from the shock of the terrorist attacks, Blackstone managed to put out more than $1 billion of equity from its buyout funds, and put a further $1.5 billion to work in 2003.

Apart from the profits the investments earned Blackstone and its investors, those deals and others by private equity firms during that period injected much-needed capital into companies at a time when the capital markets were shut down. It was Blackstone's money, for example, that enabled Northrop and PMI to make key acquisitions. The firm helped fund the two start-up insurance companies as well as Kosmos Energy, another new company. In other cases, it bought assets that troubled companies badly needed to unload at a time when there were few other buyers. Its $1.7 billion deal with Bain Capital and Thomas H. Lee Partners to purchase the textbook publisher Houghton Mifflin in 2002, for instance, provided cash to the company's parent, the French media giant Vivendi, which was near collapse after an ill-considered campaign of takeovers. Another deal, for Ondeo Nalco SA, which made water-treatment products, grew out of a restructuring of its French parent, the utility Suez SA.

It wasn't just Blackstone that was stepping up when buyers were scarce. Across Europe, the United States, and Canada, private equity firms paid considerable sums for the phone book subsidiaries of big telecoms that had to pare their debt in those years. In Germany, KKR scooped up a grab bag of industrial businesses—a plastic extruding equipment company, a crane maker, and others—that the huge German conglomerate Siemens had acquired just a few years earlier.

The buyers were consummate opportunists, taking advantage of the disarray in the markets and the economic problems of the corporate world for their own and their investors' benefit. But the billions they invested at the bottom of the market supplied sellers with capital they needed to make it through the recession and helped set a floor under corporate valuations that had nose-dived. With a wealth of capital at their disposal, private equity firms performed a role the mainstream capital markets had relinquished at the time.

CHAPTER 16

Help Wanted

The upheaval in the markets wasn't the only challenge facing Schwarzman in the first years of the new millennium. He was also wrestling with a business that had long outgrown its management. No longer was Blackstone the small shop he and Peterson had managed on the fly for the first decade. Between 1996 and 2000 it had doubled to 350 people. In addition to its giant buyout fund, it now had one of the largest real estate investment operations on Wall Street, and it had just raised a new mezzanine fund, which would make loans to midsized businesses. The real estate group was running swanky hotels in London and buying up office towers and warehouses in France and properties in Germany. The firm had finally opened a London office and now hoped to push into private equity across Europe, an expansion that would raise a host of new business, cultural, and legal issues.

Back at home, meanwhile, there were problems. The M&A group had been languishing for years, and the buyout group was down to only two seasoned deal makers, Mark Gallogly, the communications specialist, and Howard Lipson, the veteran generalist, with the eccentric, office-bound James Mossman coordinating deals and rendering judgments.

For all intents and purposes, Schwarzman was senior management, and he was simply spread too thin. "I was working fourteen-hour days and much of Saturdays and Sundays. Ultimately, I would be a bottleneck to the growth of the firm. It became clear to me that I needed some help, and it was clear there was no internal person that was right for that. We talked about that among the partners. It wasn't a secret," he says.

Indeed, he was blunt about it with Mossman, Gallogly, and Lipson. "The truth is that none of the three of us were managers by nature," admits Lipson. "Steve said, 'Somebody has got to run this thing and I don't think it's going to be any of the three of you.'"

Resigned to looking outside, in 2000 Schwarzman thought he found the answer in the person of Jimmy Lee, the banker who had financed so many of Blackstone's deals. Lee was at the very top of his game. After building Chase Manhattan into a top player in M&A finance, he had been named head of investment banking at Chase, and that spring *Forbes* magazine put him on its cover with the headline "Meet the New Michael Milken."

Yet within weeks of Lee's anointment by the magazine, he was pushed aside when Chase absorbed the M&A boutique Beacon Group to fortify its investment banking business. Chase chairman Bill Harrison, Lee's mentor, put Beacon head Geoffrey Boisi, a onetime Goldman M&A hotshot, in charge of Chase's investment bank. Harrison asked Lee to stay on as business generator in chief, but the management responsibilities— and the title—were now Boisi's. Lee's status, like that of all Chase's investment bankers, was further clouded when Chase agreed to take over J.P. Morgan that fall. Chase coveted J.P. Morgan's top-flight M&A and securities business, which would complement Chase's own strength in lending, and it was anybody's guess how the inevitable power struggles would play out when the two institutions combined.

Lee's mastery of the leveraged loan and junk-bond markets, on which Blackstone's buyout and real estate businesses relied, was unparalleled, and he had an intimate knowledge of Blackstone's investments. Along the way, he had formed tight relations with its partners. "At the defining moments in Blackstone's history, it always felt like Jimmy was there with you," says former Blackstone partner Bret Pearlman, who worked at the firm from 1989 to 2004.

Lee, who had spent his career in far larger, more mature institutions, felt he could contribute immediately. "Most private equity firms had grown up like little, boutiquey law firms," Lee says. "The partners sat around and said, 'Let's do that deal, let's do this deal.' There was no structure, no infrastructure, no HR, no risk management. But by the year 2000 they'd been at it for fifteen years and they knew they were ratcheting up their activity level. They were going global. A lot was going on."

Peterson and Schwarzman offered to give him a substantial stake in Blackstone and to make him vice chairman and the hands-on day-to-day manager of the firm. By November they had hammered out a lengthy agreement, a press release had been drafted, and Lee was ready to make the move. Lee had informed Harrison that he was talking to Blackstone, but Lee told Schwarzman that he wanted to tell Harrison face-to-face that he was taking the Blackstone job before he signed on the dotted line. One day that month, Lee sent word to Harrison that the two of them needed to speak. Harrison broke out of a meeting with the bank's board of foreign advisers to hear what he had to say.

"I said, 'Hey, it's been a great run. I loved it. This is my favorite place in the whole wide world. But this is something I want to do and I'm going to say yes to it,'" Lee recounts. "He said, 'Would you please wait a day and let us circle the wagons and try to talk you out of it?'"

Harrison had shunted Lee out of administration, but he wasn't about to lose one of the keys to Chase's success if he could help it. Harrison pulled out all the stops, yanking on all the emotional cords. "They gathered together directors and other senior people," Lee says. "They put me in what I like to call the rubber room, where you take the employee who is about to go away and bombard him with, 'Oh! I remember you when you were just a kid.' The old guys play on your loyalty. 'This is your life, Jimmy Lee.'"

It worked. In the end, Lee couldn't bring himself to jump the Chase ship. That night Lee reached Schwarzman at the Ritz Carlton Hotel in Naples, Florida. Schwarzman took the call on the veranda. "Jimmy said, 'I just can't do it. Bill's asked me to stay. I've worked with Bill my whole adult career,'" Schwarzman says.

Schwarzman couldn't believe it. "He was like, 'Hey! What's going on? I thought you were going to resign and come back and sign,'" Lee recalls. "He said, 'Is it money? Do you need more money?'" Lee told him it wasn't about money.

"Jimmy's an exceptionally loyal person," Schwarzman says now, "both to people and to institutions." But Schwarzman was acutely disappointed, and he had no other candidates and so, for the time being, he abandoned the hunt for a number two.

The gap at Blackstone remained, however. The demands on Schwarzman only intensified when the firm went back on the fund-raising trail in 2001 and 2002 to sign up investors for its next fund, the $6 billion Blackstone Capital Partners IV. And so in mid-2002, two years after the go-around with Lee, Schwarzman set out again to see if he could find the right person. An executive recruiter, Tom Neff, suggested he meet Tony James, who had headed Credit Suisse First Boston's investment bank and alternative assets groups. Schwarzman and James had faced off over the CNW buyout back in 1989, when Donaldson, Lufkin & Jenrette, where James worked at the time, and Blackstone clashed over the bond financing, but their paths had not crossed since.

On paper, James had all the right qualifications. He had been a superstar at DLJ. Just seven years out of business school, in 1982, he was made head of the bank's M&A group—the same position Schwarzman attained at Lehman Brothers around the same time. Three years after that, James founded DLJ Merchant Banking, which mobilized DLJ's investment bankers to spot companies in which the bank could invest its own money. In the nineties, DLJ Merchant Banking raised money from outside investors for a succession of funds that were only slightly smaller than Blackstone's own. Along the way, James, who oversaw the investments closely until the late 1990s, put up some of the best numbers in the business. When Schwarzman reached out to him in 2002, investors in DLJ's $1 billion 1992 fund had earned an average annual return after DLJ's fees of more than 70 percent—an astronomical rate of return to sustain over such a long period. That was roughly twice the very respectable 34 percent Blackstone's 1993 fund had posted over the same span.

As a manager, too, James had excelled, rising to head all of DLJ's investment banking operations in 1995. Though there were a couple of

tiers of management above him, he was seen by many inside and outside the firm as DLJ's de facto head and the driving force behind the
bank's transformation from a scrappy research boutique into a major
player on Wall Street. "He wasn't running the firm," but he was "probably the most important person . . . to get the business from here to
there," says Sabin Streeter, a former DLJ banker who is godfather to one
of James's children. "Tony was the most valuable person who ever put
on his suit at DLJ."

"He was brilliant at DLJ," says another banker who worked there
in the 1990s. "He ran the investment committee, and DLJ [Merchant
Banking] was dominated by him in those periods when he ran it." James
was always seen as "the smartest guy in the room," this person says.

When Drexel Burnham Lambert imploded in 1990, James had
swooped in to snare many of its top bankers, including Ken Moelis, an
M&A star, and Bennett Goodman, a trader who helped DLJ build a
high-yield debt group. Under James, DLJ added a restructuring advisory
unit, a mezzanine lending arm, a fund-of-funds group, and even a modest real estate investment·unit—a stable of businesses very similar to the
one Schwarzman and Peterson had assembled.

In his pièce de résistance, James helped engineer the merger of DLJ
into Credit Suisse First Boston in 2000. CSFB's Swiss parent, Credit
Suisse, paid $11.5 billion, hoping to catapult its second-tier U.S. invest-
ment bank into the top ranks by capturing DLJ's bankers and clients.
James was made cohead of CSFB's investment bank and its alternative
assets business. By 2002, however, things had turned sour at CSFB. The
entire investment banking world, which had fed on the M&A and IPO
boom of the late 1990s, was in retreat. Banks were losing money hand
over fist and were laying off thousands of bankers. CSFB had greatly
overpaid for DLJ at the top of the market, and many of DLJ's biggest
rainmakers, who had pocketed millions from the sale of their DLJ shares,
had left soon after the merger. Some at CSFB blamed James for inducing
CSFB to pay so much and then letting the talent slip away. When a
new CEO, John Mack, was brought in after CSFB had a series of run-ins
with regulators, he bumped James upstairs to a newly created position

of chairman of global investment banking, where no one reported to him, and installed a new investment banking chief. James hadn't actually been sacked, as so many bankers were in that period. It was, in the words of a DLJ colleague, "death with dignity."

Owning 1.1 million DLJ shares from the merger that wouldn't vest until the summer of 2002, James had to sit tight until then, but it clearly was time for a new job.

To Schwarzman, James possessed the ideal background and skills: "Tony was, in effect, a natural entrepreneur. And he was also for many years at DLJ what they call a trigger puller—their master investor, who would do the go–no go decisions." The parallels in the businesses DLJ and Blackstone had built were striking, too. "In effect, his career was a carbon copy of mine. This was a very curious coincidence."

They had a preliminary discussion at Blackstone's offices. Both were a bit surprised but thought the relationship had promise. "We each walked out of that first meeting and said, 'Hmm. I didn't realize how good this fit was,'" James says.

Schwarzman wanted to probe deeper, and for that he wanted a more relaxed and discreet setting, so he invited James to dinner at his apartment at 740 Park Avenue. "I didn't want to meet him in a work setting. I wanted to really learn how his mind worked," Schwarzman explains.

Over a long meal they traded experiences and their takes on the world. "I really had a great time because we could speak shorthand about just about anything in the financial world," says Schwarzman. "Here's a situation. How did you think that worked out? What do you think went wrong? What would you have done there? I think we both found out there was an enormous convergence of investment style and outcome, and conservatism."

The conversation continued over several more dinners at Schwarzman's apartment as each man sized up the other. "There was a lot of talk with each other, without talking about the job so much," James says. "Just talking about the world, comparing notes, just getting on the same page, without really a sense of where it would go."

The rapport was there, but in many ways they made an unlikely pair.

The tall, lanky James—formally Hamilton E. James—was a prep-school New Englander from the suburban professional classes. His father had headed the management consulting practice at the elite consulting firm Arthur D. Little, Inc., and the younger James, who attended Choate prep school before collecting his bachelor's and MBA from Harvard, had a patrician patina that Schwarzman lacked. In the words of a woman who has worked with him, he is one of those rare men who can get away with wearing a seersucker suit to the office.

James had a more cerebral style than Schwarzman. While Schwarzman could devour the numbers his underlings generated and interrogate them about their analyses, at the end of the day he made decisions by instinct. James relished the analysis itself.

While Schwarzman found it hard to pretend he was interested in or cared about people when he didn't, James seemed to take an interest in everyone from the mailroom staff on up. He enjoyed playing teacher and mentor and happily performed scut work on a deal in a crunch—an attitude that was repaid with fierce loyalty from those under him. When engaged by work, his intensity and mental powers were downright intimidating. But he also liked to party and was equally at home with a beer in hand entertaining employees at his Connecticut home or raising eyebrows with his wild dancing at DLJ parties.

James had his own sizable ego—some people in other firms found him arrogant—but it expressed itself very differently than Schwarzman's. At DLJ, James had been happy to run the bank while more senior executives took the spotlight. He had no need to see his name in the paper and, indeed, it rarely appeared in print. Instead, he drew his satisfaction from keeping his subordinates perpetually in awe of his imposing intellect, his stamina, and his charm.

In a quiet way, too, he chafed at the conventions by which über-bankers were expected to abide. He rode the subway, and as a longtime director of Costco, the discount retailer, he often wore Costco dress shirts to the office. While Schwarzman vacationed at his homes in the traditional playgrounds of the super rich—the Hamptons on Long Island, Palm Beach in Florida, and St. Tropez in France, or on his yacht in the Caribbean—James was a die-hard fly fisherman who tied his own flies and ventured up the Amazon and to Mongolia on fishing trips with his friend David Bonderman, the iconoclastic founder of TPG.

In other ways, though, the men were much alike. Like Schwarzman, James had been a competitive athlete, playing varsity soccer at Harvard. Into his fifties, he would play on the weekends. He was every bit as competitive and ambitious as Schwarzman, and every inch as much an entrepreneur.

Because Schwarzman had begun his own financial career at DLJ after college, he knew many of the senior executives who were later James's bosses. After his initial dinner conversations with James, he decided to do a background check by calling up five of them, including DLJ founders Bill Donaldson and Dick Jenrette, to get their views on James.

"They all said exactly the same thing. They said that Tony was brilliant, he was a workaholic, that he was a great investor, he was a natural leader, that the people who worked for him were incredibly loyal. He was a brilliant manager and that he had tremendous loyalty to the institution. And, at a personal level, he would never betray you—meaning me. 'You two are a perfect fit.'" The fact that five people who had known both Schwarzman and James for decades thought the match would work was persuasive.

It was an enormous gamble for both men. Schwarzman had never been afraid to bring in big personalities with their own ambitions and agendas. He had wooed Roger Altman, David Stockman, Larry Fink, and Tom Hill to Blackstone in the early years. But this was different. This time he was not looking for a single rainmaker or someone to launch a new business line. This hire would have a much more profound impact across Blackstone. Blackstone had been the Steve Schwarzman show for a decade and now he would be sharing the role. It was more like finding a spouse than a deputy. None of his counterparts at other buyout firms had ever attempted to bring in someone at this level from the outside, and few had clear succession plans, so in every way it would be a first.

James understood what it represented. "It's a very intense firm with a very intense leader and intense people. If he meant what he said about turning over the core businesses to me, and helping him run the firm, it was a huge leap of faith for him—to [trust] any outsider that he didn't really know that well."

Blackstone wasn't James's only option. He had discussed forming a new firm with Garrett Moran and Bennett Goodman, two senior DLJ bankers. He also talked with TPG's founders, Bonderman and Jim Coulter, about joining their firm. He could see the Blackstone job carried special risks. Entrepreneurs and founders like Schwarzman often find it difficult to cede control and make a hash of things when they try to bring in deputies and designated heirs. The rising stars they hire often end up bloodied, dumped in the ditch at the side of the corporate road a year or two later. For James, who had enjoyed enormous autonomy at DLJ, this was a crucial issue.

"Does he really mean it? Is he going to give me the scope to do my thing? It was like I hadn't had a boss in twelve years. I'd been a very independent manager, running my businesses the way I thought. That's important to me. I'm not very respectful of hierarchy or authority. I like to make my decisions. I like to run a business my way and be held accountable for the result. I want to be able to make the decisions and refashion things my way."

Friends say that James had his doubts. Schwarzman's split over money with Larry Fink and Ralph Schlosstein, the BlackRock heads, was well known on Wall Street, as was the fact that there was no love lost between Schwarzman and Altman. The growing rift between Schwarzman and Peterson was known to many in the financial world, too. Certainly no one had ever called Schwarzman the dream boss. Was he capable of giving James real latitude to run the firm day to day? It was a theme that threaded through their dinner conversations.

"There's no epiphany or one thing he can say," says James. "When you're looking at a CEO and entrepreneur, you've got to take the measure of his intent and his ability to follow through emotionally and personally." Ultimately, James came to believe it could work. "I made the bet that he meant it and that he could, and he did."

By the last of their dinners, Schwarzman, too, was convinced. "At the end, I said, 'Really, this should be an absolutely perfect partnership.' I said, 'You and I are only going to have one type of disagreement working together. You're going to be interested in starting a lot of new businesses, some of which may not really be big enough to really affect us. That's because you're a better manager than I am. I prefer starting fewer things but having them be huge. But that's a matter of taste. That will be a difference in the way we approach things. We'll never disagree about deals or investments.' "

By the end of that summer, James agreed to join, lured in part by a major stake in the firm. (By the time of the IPO in 2007, he would hold 6.2 percent, slightly more than Peterson.) He agreed to finish the year at CSFB, but soon Schwarzman was pestering him for advice and help. "As soon as I accepted the job, Steve started calling, saying, 'We've got this crisis. Can you come up and think about this?' Or 'We're about to make this big investment' or 'We've got to pay people. You really should be a part of that process,' and so on." James simply couldn't juggle the two sets of responsibilities and moved to Blackstone ahead of schedule in early November.

James wasted no time putting his mark on the organization. "He arrived and you knew he was there," says former Blackstone partner Bret Pearlman. "He didn't spend six months behind closed doors" developing ideas of what he wanted to do.

His mandate from Schwarzman was to manage the entire firm, but Schwarzman wanted him to focus initially on reinvigorating the M&A business and whipping the private equity group into shape.

One of James's first moves was to impose more discipline on the investment process. He instituted a screening regimen so that partners, who had been free to pursue investment possibilities for weeks or even months without supervision, were required to submit an outline at the outset so management could decide if an opportunity was promising enough to warrant the partner's time.

He also pressed partners to analyze the risks of deals more rigorously. Like their counterparts at other firms, Blackstone's partners were accustomed to producing voluminous projections, often a hundred to one hundred and fifty pages, forecasting "every item of every division, down to how many Coca-Colas they're buying in their conference rooms and the price of Coke," as James puts it, to come up with the base case—the minimum projected financial performance. But he insisted that they take the analysis a step farther, factoring in more carefully the possibility of fluke events that could sink a company or turn the investment into a success—what economists dub optionality.

He cites a hypothetical investment in an airline: "You say there's a chance there's a major terrorism event blowing up an airline, but that happens once in twenty years, so that doesn't affect the base case because it's one in twenty. Then there's a chance that oil goes from $30 to a $140 a barrel in a year. It's never happened before—the most oil has ever gone up is twenty bucks in a year. How could it go up a hundred? But there's a probability to that." There is a risk of labor problems, "but, geez, we've got good relations with the unions and we've got three years before [the contract is up].

"All these unlikely things are one in ten, one in twenty, one in fifty, whatever they are, so you don't put them in your base case because they're very unlikely." But they are hazards nonetheless. "The chance of any one of them happening is tiny, but the chance that none of them will happen is also tiny. You multiply it out and you find that there's [say] a 55 percent chance that one of them will happen, and it kills you."

The same analysis worked on the upside. Some investments were like call options on a stock, which give you the right to buy shares at a fixed price at some point in the future. If Blackstone could leverage a deal enough that it had little money at risk and the freak possibilities on the downside were few and the payoff from an unlikely event on the positive side of the ledger was huge—such as Paul Allen's grabbing up Blackstone's U.S. cable holdings in 1999 and 2000 at inflated prices—it was like a cheap call option. James hammered home the point that "there was enormous option value for us in getting lucky," says Larry Guffey, the partner who led the distressed round of investing in the German cable companies.

The concept wasn't new, but the rigor and consistency with which the analysis was performed, on both the upside and the downside, was. (Schwarzman had his own, more colloquial way of framing the same issue. "What's the tooth fairy scenario?" he liked to ask partners about the investments they were pitching.)

At the same time, James started a series of internal workshops and strategic reviews. Despite the new procedures, he also sped up decision making, which had been as sluggish as molasses in the past. Before he instituted the screening process, Mossman was the gatekeeper through which everything passed. "Eight train tracks ran to one station," in the words of partner Chinh Chu, with every proposed investment passing Mossman's desk over and over before the investment committee signed off. James was just better at making decisions and moving on than the Blackstone veterans.

James also set out to improve the personal dynamics in a culture he saw as "edgy." He put his weight behind "360 reviews" in which part-ners were reviewed by peers and those under them as well as senior management. He "wanted to judge people not just on their talent but on how you trained people, et cetera," says Guffey.

He commissioned an exhaustive study of the firm's past investments to find out exactly where and how the firm had made its money—and how it had lost it. The report contained some provocative conclusions.

It came as no surprise that the firm had profited mightily by timing the markets shrewdly—buying during troughs and selling at the peaks. But there were some surprising patterns over the years. It turned out, for instance, that partners had a tendency to overestimate the abilities of those managing the companies Blackstone bought. In deals where the partners in charge had rated management highly at the outset, returns tended to be disappointing. "Management acumen drives ability to meet the plan," the headline in the summary read. "Unfortunately, we don't seem to be able to accurately determine this and calibrate the operating projections up front," the subhead wryly noted. The results led the firm to turn to outside consultants and psychologists to evaluate executives at potential portfolio companies. The study also made clear that Blackstone was lagging behind competitors at improving operations at its companies—a discovery that led to the expansion of its in-house consulting and management support group.

James also reexamined Blackstone's relations with its bankers. He began tracking how much Blackstone paid to individual investment banks so it could see which bankers were bringing it deals, and which weren't. At the same time, he made overtures to the banks, hoping to counter the reputation the firm had gained for being a hard-nosed and difficult customer.

"Tony said, 'We're not in this for the last basis point' "—haggling over fractional differences in interest rates—remarks one banker. "You know Steve—that's not really his speech."

Across the board, there was more structure. Before James arrived, "we were run like a small company that had gotten big—like five boutiques," says real estate partner Chad Pike. "We had no standard operating procedures." Now, Pike says, "the back of the house is kind of catching up to the front of the house."

Everyone could recognize the improvement, not least Schwarzman. He occasionally would bite his tongue when he disagreed with something James said, but he quickly came to see that James was indispensable. For his part, James never questioned that Schwarzman was the ultimate boss, and he respected Schwarzman's prerogatives. Over time the two developed a bond, talking or leaving long voice mails for each other ten or twelve times on a typical day. Schwarzman could often be seen slouched comfortably in a chair in front of James's desk.

Schwarzman understood that it would be a delicate matter to insert James at the top of the organization between Schwarzman and the partners, and it would have to be handled carefully.

"This was not Tony [coming] in as president with everyone reporting to him, like a corporate appointment," Schwarzman says. "That is not how this worked." It had been Schwarzman's decision to hire James, but he had discussed the hire with other partners so they wouldn't feel it was imposed on them. He understood, too, that it would shake up the existing relationships within the ranks. It would require "my strategizing how that would work in terms of his relationship with each important person at the firm," Schwarzman says.

Some partners were anxious as they tried to decipher what James's arrival would mean for them. Mossman was the person most directly affected. He had always taken a narrow view of his job as chief investment officer, which frustrated Schwarzman. Not only did Mossman not deal with outsiders, but he also had no interest in supervising people internally, and he wanted to work one day a week from home. Beyond his personal quirks, his very role—the funnel through which all investment proposals had to pass—was becoming impractical as the firm expanded and became more global. Now James had arrived, effectively running private equity. Mossman stayed on for a while but in 2003 he left, retiring to Connecticut to pursue his studies in the sciences.

There was no bloodletting, no corporate-style purges. But the truth was that while Schwarzman was still the top boss, everyone *did* now report to James. On the few occasions when people tried to go over him to Schwarzman, Schwarzman backed James. For many of the veterans, things just felt different.

"Before, everyone had their own relationship with Steve—their own understanding of how they fit in the organization," says ex-partner Howard Lipson. "For the senior guys to be in what looked much more like a hierarchy" was a shock.

One by one, they began to filter out. The motives and feelings were complex. It ran from " 'I don't know if I want to work at all,' like James [Mossman], to 'I need to be my own boss and I want to run my own show,' like Mark [Gallogly], to somewhere in between in that spectrum," says Lipson.

They recognized that Blackstone needed to grow up and that James was taking the firm "to the next level"—the business cliché they nearly all invoke for the transition. But they were no longer sure they wanted to go along for the ride. "People had made their money and they had families and weren't kids anymore," says Lipson. "So they said, 'If I'm going to do something different, now is the time.'"

The fact that they had become fabulously wealthy helped, as did the fact that Blackstone's partners did not forfeit their share of the firm's profits on past investments, as partners at many other buyout firms do once they depart. They could start new careers and continue to collect checks from Blackstone for years to come as investments from their time there were sold off.

For Bret Pearlman and Mark Gallogly, the boom in private equity in the years that followed James's arrival enabled them to raise their own funds, as investors deluged the private equity world with new capital. Pension funds and other institutions that a few years earlier would not have considered handing over money to a firm with no past record were suddenly open to doing so. In 2004, Pearlman, who had pressed Schwarzman to wade deeper into the technology and media sectors in the late 1990s, teamed up with a group of Silicon Valley executives and investors and Bono, the lead singer of the rock group U2, to form Elevation Partners to invest in media, entertainment, and consumer companies. The next year Elevation raised $1.9 billion. In October 2005, Gallogly, who had mulled going out on his own in 1999, finally took the plunge, forming Centerbridge Partners with a veteran vulture investor. By the next year they had a $3.2 billion fund at their disposal—half again as big as the 2000 Blackstone communications fund Gallogly had headed.

Lipson left that year, too, to join Bob Pittman, an ex–Time Warner executive Lipson had known from the Six Flags theme park deal, at Pilot Group, a private equity firm specializing in media deals. John Kukral, who had returned from London when his cohead of the real estate group, Thomas Saylak, left in 2002, served notice the same month as Gallogly. Other than Peterson and Schwarzman, by the end of 2005 there was just one partner who had joined the firm before 1990: Kenneth Whitney, who oversaw relations with Blackstone's investors.

Soon there were some fresh faces in the senior ranks, too. In 2003, Prakash Melwani, a highly regarded investor who had cofounded Vestar Capital Partners, was recruited to the buyout team. Paul "Chip" Schorr IV, who had led technology investments at Citigroup's private equity unit, joined in 2005. The same year James hired Garrett Moran, one of his key lieutenants at DLJ, to be chief operating officer of the buyout group, putting James's stamp even more firmly on the unit. James Quella, a seasoned management consultant who had advised DLJ Merchant Banking on its investments, was also hired that year to build an in-house team of corporate managers to work with the buyout operation.

Three years after James arrived, Blackstone was a very different place—more disciplined, more collegial, and a little less colorful. In private equity, the partner class of 2000—the thirty-somethings on whom the firm had gambled in a clutch situation—had firmly assumed the mantle. As junior partners, their worlds were altered less by James's assumption of the reins, and the departures of Mossman, Lipson, and Gallogly cleared the way for their ascension. Even before Gallogly and Lipson left, the new partners were taking the lead on many of Blackstone's biggest investments in 2003 and 2004—deals that would establish new records for profits and set the stage for Blackstone's own ascendancy later in the decade. It was the final step in a transition away from the freewheeling, personality-driven culture of the firm's first early years.

Meanwhile, Kukral's departure made room for Jonathan Gray and Chad Pike, the next generation in real estate, to take over as joint heads of that unit. They, too, were soon steering their group in new directions, buying whole real estate companies rather than individual buildings.

The successful integration of James into the firm was plainly due in part to his talents. But the process revealed even more about Schwarzman's evolution over the years. Schwarzman had pulled off a feat that none of his peers—and few other entrepreneurs—had managed: bringing in a successor from the outside and sharing real power with him.

Moreover, he engineered the transition without the turmoil, bitterness, and recriminations of the firm's first decade. The raw, and raw-edged, ambition he had shown in driving Blackstone to the top of the private equity heap with time had tempered.

"He's pretty self-aware," one banker says of Schwarzman's decision to bring in James. "He hides it well."

CHAPTER 17

Good Chemistry, Perfect Timing

As they sized up each other over their dinners at Schwarzman's apartment in 2002, one of the issues on which Schwarzman and James saw eye to eye was the state of the market. They shared a conviction that they were looking at the opportunity of a decade to buy assets cheaply. James had cemented his reputation as a private equity investor with DLJ's spectacularly profitable 1992 fund, raised when the economy was still in recession. Likewise, Blackstone's 1993 fund, much of it invested early in the 1990s upturn, was the firm's most successful to date. Blackstone was putting the finishing touches on a fresh $6.9 billion fund the summer they began talking. When the debt markets would allow it, both men wanted to dive back into the old-fashioned LBO business. What attracted them most was cyclical businesses—companies whose fortunes ebb and flow sharply with the economic tides.

Theirs was a contrarian view at the time, when most buyout firms were still nursing wounds from their mistakes of the late nineties, but Schwarzman's conviction was visceral. "I recall Steve very early in that particular cycle [saying], 'Look what's going on! You've got to be buying,'" says Mario Giannini of Hamilton Lane, a firm that advises pension funds and others on private equity investments.

It would be risky. Timing is everything when you are borrowing to buy a cyclical company. Like cliff diving in Acapulco, plunging in too soon or too late can be disastrous, which is why many private equity firms steer clear of cyclical businesses. Nimbly timed, however, a leveraged investment at the bottom of the cycle can magnify any earnings gains. In addition, valuation multiples for cyclical companies tend to rise at the same time that profits do because buyers will pay a higher multiple of cash flow or earnings when those are on the upswing. Harness both the earnings growth and the increase in valuations, and returns can shoot off the charts. The exit must be timed as deftly as the entry, however, because in a declining economy multiples can recede at the same time earnings are falling. A company that sold for seven times earnings in good times could easily trade for just six times in a down market. If earnings drop at the same time, the two factors together could slice the value by a third, leaving the company worth less than its debt and wiping out the value of the equity, at least on paper. That is the inherent risk of leverage.

Despite the perils, instinctively Schwarzman and James wanted to pounce. "We got very active, very aggressive, and went out and bought big, chunky, industrial assets," says James. In 2003, the year the economy turned the corner and began expanding again, Blackstone far outpaced its rivals, signing up $16.5 billion worth of deals. Goldman Sach's private equity unit was the only other buyout investor that came close. The totals for TPG and Apollo, Blackstone's next closest competitors, were only half Blackstone's.

The first big cyclical play was the TRW Automotive deal. Neil Simpkins, one of the five new partners promoted in 2000, was already talking to the company's parent, the defense contractor TRW Inc., about buying the parts business in 2002 when Northrop Grumman, another defense firm, made a hostile bid to take over TRW Inc. The latter eventually relented and agreed to be absorbed into Northrop, but Northrop had no interest in the parts business and moved to sell it even before it had completed the TRW acquisition. Since Simpkins knew the business, he was able to cut a quick $4.6 billion deal with Northrop.

At the same time, Chinh Chu, another member of the new crop of partners from 2000, was chasing two other companies in the chemicals industry, which was at least as cyclical as the car business.

Chu had followed an unusual route to Blackstone. While most of his peers were the products of affluent families and Ivy League schools, Chu's family had fled Vietnam when the United States pulled out, and he had earned his bachelor's degree from the University of Buffalo. After a short stint as a banker, he joined Blackstone in 1990 and soon was apprenticed to the mercurial David Stockman. Chu didn't shy from questioning his superior's views and earned a place in Blackstone lore for an incident in 1996 when he was working with Stockman on a proposed investment in an aerospace components maker, Haynes International. When Stockman made his pitch to the investment committee, Schwarzman asked Chu what he thought about Haynes. Chu replied frankly that he didn't think it would be a good investment. Stockman was so incensed that his underling would undercut his position that he refused to talk to Chu for weeks. Finally Schwarzman had to take Stockman aside, pointing out that it would be nearly impossible to close the deal if he wasn't communicating with the associate who had worked on the project from the beginning.

Chu turned out to be right about Haynes: Blackstone lost $43 million of the $54 million it invested. With Stockman's departure, Chu and the rest of the class of new partners from 2000 and 2001 would be put to the test as they led their first deals.

The first buyout Chu signed up, in September 2003, was Ondeo Nalco, known as Nalco, an Illinois-based maker of water-treatment chemicals and equipment owned by Suez SA, a French water, electricity, and gas utility that was selling off peripheral businesses.

Long before he began pursuing Nalco, though, another company had caught Chu's eye: Celanese AG, a publicly traded, Frankfurt-based chemical company. It would take two years to get it to agree to a buyout and another two years to complete the last step of the transaction, but when it was all over Celanese would generate by far the biggest profit Blackstone had ever seen. It would prove to be a showcase for the art of private equity, a brilliant mix of financial wizardry with a hefty dose of nitty-gritty operational improvements. Together with Nalco, which also repaid

Blackstone's money many times over, Celanese secured Chu's position as the fastest-rising star of the buyout group.

When Chu first began running the numbers on Celanese in 2001, the company was in a slump. With the economy ailing, demand was down for its key products: acetyl derivatives used in paints, drugs, and textiles; acetates for cigarette filters and apparel; plastics used in automobiles; farming chemicals and detergents; and food and beverage additives.

Celanese was also something of an orphan. Originally an American company, it had been acquired by the German chemical and drug maker Hoechst AG in 1987. When Hoechst agreed to merge with a French pharmaceutical company in 1999, it sold off Celanese via an IPO on the Frankfurt stock exchange. More than half Celanese's operations and revenue were in the United States, however, and only 20 percent or so in Europe, so it was a German company in name only and never found much favor on the German market. Moreover, German stock valuations tended to be lower than those in the United States. The logical thing, it seemed, would be to shift Celanese's main stock listing to New York. Chu figured that Celanese would trade for one multiple more there: five times cash flow, for example, if it traded for four times in Germany.

Beyond that, Celanese looked ripe for cost cutting. "We believed there were significant costs that could be taken off Celanese because Celanese was the [product] of a number of acquisitions and mergers," Chu says.

Identifying the target was one thing; buying a public company in Germany was another. Private equity had received a frosty reception in Germany, where managements were reluctant to sell out to investors who would unload their companies again in a few years. It was a cultural matter, in part. German firms tend to be paternalistic, guarding their workforces and preserving corporate traditions. In addition, large German companies are required by law to give nearly half the seats on the boards to employee representatives, who uniformly regard private equity firms with suspicion. As a result, private equity firms had made many more investments in Britain and France, even though their economies were much smaller.

Twice Chu approached Celanese and twice he was rebuffed, first in 2001 and again in 2002. In May 2003 he came back a third time, this time allied with General Electric, the American industrial and financial conglomerate. They proposed to merge Celanese's plastics businesses—about a quarter of the total business—into GE's global plastics division, leaving the rest of Celanese for Blackstone. Celanese's stock was trading for around four times its cash flow at the time, a bargain price for a company whose profits were sure to soar if the economy picked up speed.

With GE at Blackstone's side this time, Celanese's board was finally willing to grant Blackstone a hearing, and Celanese soon allowed Blackstone and GE to begin the process of due diligence, talking to managers and combing through internal records to understand the business and unearth any problems.

But no sooner was that under way than GE's management did an about-face and decided it did not want to invest more in the plastics industry. (Four years later GE sold its plastics business.) The talks continued with Blackstone, but Celanese seemed to be dragging its heals and Chu began to worry that he was going to find himself rejected again and back at square one. To keep up the momentum, he did an end run around management, appealing to Celanese's biggest shareholder, the Kuwait Petroleum Corporation, which owned 29 percent. The Kuwaitis signaled to management that they supported a buyout, and the process got back on track.

Celanese's executives were deeply divided over the idea of selling the company and working for American financiers. "It did take some time to become comfortable with how such a deal would be structured, managed, and create value for shareholders," says David Weidman, then Celanese's chief operating officer.

Winning over the company was only the first challenge. Nothing about Celanese would be simple.

The financing and the mechanics of the takeover were complicated by Germany's takeover laws. Like most LBOs, Blackstone's purchase would take place via a new holding company, which would borrow money to buy the operating business and use profits from that to cover the cost of the debt. But German law bars a buyer from taking cash out of a company until any remaining public shareholders have approved the move—a vote that could take a year or more to arrange. Blackstone therefore had to inject extra cash into the business at the outset so there would be money to pay the interest on the buyout debt in the interim.

Scaring up the equity also proved to be a problem. Blackstone needed about $850 million of cash to close the deal, but that would amount to 13 percent of Blackstone's new fund—far more than it was willing to risk on any single investment. Chu had assumed he would be able to bring in other buyout firms to take smaller stakes but soon found that he was alone in his conviction that the chemicals market was turning up. All six of the competitors he approached turned him down. "A lot of them thought the cycle would get worse before it got better and told us, 'You guys overpaid,'" Chu recounts. Ultimately he lined up $206 million from Blackstone investors, which invested directly in Celanese in addition to their investments through Blackstone's fund. Bank of America, Deutsche Bank, and Morgan Stanley, the lenders for the buyout, agreed to buy $200 million of preferred shares—a cross between equity and debt—to fill the remaining hole.

In December 2003 the pieces finally came together and Celanese's board agreed to sell the company to Blackstone for 32.50 per share, for a total of 2.8 billion ($3.4 billion). It was by far the biggest public company in Germany ever to go private. The 32.50 was 13 percent above the average price of the stock in the prior three months, but it still looked good to Chu, for that was just five times cash flow.

There was still one more hurdle: getting the shareholders to agree. The Kuwaitis had committed to sell their 29 percent, but other shareholders were free to refuse the 32.50 offer, and German takeover rules gave them a perverse incentive to do so.

In the United States and many other European countries, once a buyer gets 90–95 percent of the shares of a company, it can force the remaining shareholders to sell out at the price the other shareholders accepted. In Germany, by contrast, shareholders can hold out and insist on an appraisal, and the arcane formulas mandated for the appraisals almost always yield a far higher price—sometimes well above the stock's highest price ever. Until the appraisal process was complete, Blackstone therefore wouldn't know exactly what it would cost to buy Celanese.

Because of the holdout right, Chu found himself playing a multibillion-euro game of chicken with the hedge funds and mutual funds that owned most of Celanese's stock.

Blackstone had conditioned its offer on winning at least 75 percent of the shares at 32.50. Any less than that and the whole deal was off. The hedge funds and mutual funds didn't want that to happen, because Blackstone was paying a premium, and the stock would likely fall back well below 32.50 if the deal was scotched. However, it was in each investor's interest to demand an appraisal so long as most of the other shareholders opted for the 32.50.

"I remember sitting in my office negotiating with every hedge fund who had a stake and all the mutual funds," says Chu. "They all wanted the deal to go through, but they did not want to be part of the 75 percent."

On March 29, 2004, the day the offer expired, the outcome still wasn't clear, and Schwarzman was on pins and needles. "[Steve] walked into my office around three thirty and just sat there, because he was obviously concerned about the deal," says Chu. "We had run up something like $25 million in expenses, which was no small matter. Steve said, 'Chinh, how is it going?' I'd say, 'Steve, I'm on the phone negotiating with everybody. I don't know how it's going!'"

Schwarzman returned again with only minutes to spare till the 6:00 P.M. deadline. "We were 15 percent short. At six o'clock, Steve asked me, 'What is the official tally?' At that point, we were 1.5 percent short, but I told Steve, 'I think we're going to be fine when you wake up in the morning because a lot of guys came in at the last minute, and there is still stuff stuck in the computer system.'"

The next morning Blackstone learned it had garnered at least 80 percent of the shares, and the final tally the following day was 83.6 percent. Blackstone controlled Celanese. It would take another four months before a shareholder vote could be held, however, two additional months before Celanese's cash flow could be tapped to service the buyout debt, and more than a year and a half to buy up the rest of the German shares. In the fall of 2004 Blackstone offered 41.92 a share to the shareholders who had refused to sell out, but there were no takers. Two American hedge funds that owned almost 12 percent, Paulson and Company and Arnhold and S. Bleichroeder Advisers, held out for more. Finally, in August 2005, they both agreed to sell at 51 a share. A few stragglers stuck it out and ultimately got 67 per share. Paulson and Company would later gain fame for making billions in 2007 betting that the mortgage market would crash.

Blackstone didn't wait for the last of the holdouts before setting about to reshape the company. That began as soon as it won control in April 2004.

The first step was to, in effect, de-Germanize the company, both to invigorate the management culture and to make the company more appealing to American investors for an eventual IPO. Celanese's CEO, a thirty-eight-year veteran of Celanese and Hoechst, was slated to retire, and Blackstone wanted to install a brisk American-style leader. It settled on David Weidman, the company's chief operating officer, an American who'd joined just four years earlier from Honeywell/AlliedSignal and thus represented fresh blood.

German companies have a reputation for being plodding and bureaucratic. The problem was exacerbated at Celanese by the fact that the company had three power centers: the head office in Frankfurt and large satellite offices in Somerset, New Jersey, and Dallas that it had inherited over the years and never bothered to consolidate. Some key executives were based in the U.S. offices, and the three duchies often bickered and tripped over one another. One of the first moves under Blackstone was to centralize power in Dallas, an action it hoped would reduce the organization's inertia and reduce overhead.

The move to Dallas saved $42 million a year. Retooling at the North American plants sped up production and allowed more jobs cuts, saving another $81 million annually. Celanese also off-loaded a money-losing business that made glasslike plastics and sold its stake in an unprofitable fuel-cell venture, two drains on profits. It saved another $27 million annually by shifting most of its production of acetate fibers used in cigarette filters to China, where cigarette sales were rising and labor is cheaper.

To augment its business, meanwhile, in October 2004 Celanese struck a deal to buy Acetex Corporation, a Canadian company, for $490 million and the next month agreed to buy Vinamul Polymers for $208 million. Acetex brought new facilities in France, Spain, and the Middle East and made Celanese the number-one producer of acetyl products, with a 28 percent market share worldwide. That pushed cash flow up by another $60 million. Blackstone also endorsed Weidman's plans to increase the capacity of several plants Celanese already was building in Asia.

The rapid-fire asset sales and acquisitions, the operational changes, and the switch of headquarters "would have been extremely difficult to carry out as a German public company," says Weidman, because the costs—including payments to laid-off workers and investments in new plants—would have cut deeply into Celanese's earnings in the short term. Celanese's bureaucracy at the time also would have thwarted the changes, adds Weidman, who remained on as CEO long after Blackstone exited Celanese.

As the company was trimming fat and expanding through acquisitions, business was taking off as the global economy improved. Even before the deal closed in April 2004, demand had picked up enough that Celanese had begun raising prices. Over the course of that year it publicly announced thirty price increases, which helped lift its top line to $4.9 billion from $4.6 billion the year before and pushed cash flow up 42 percent. On the strength of that, Celanese was able to borrow more money in September 2004 to pay out a dividend. With that, Blackstone recouped three-quarters of the equity it had invested in April. Thereafter, most of what it would collect would be pure profit.

Two months after the dividend, in November, Celanese filed papers for an IPO to go public and in January 2005, only eight and a half months after Blackstone won control of the company, Celanese went public again on the New York Stock Exchange. As Chu had predicted, American investors valued the company more highly: at 6.4 times cash flow, or 1.4 "turns" more than Blackstone had paid. Celanese raised close to $1 billion in common and preferred stock, $803 million of which went to Blackstone and its coinvestors, on top of the dividend they received earlier. Blackstone and the coinvestors had now collected $700 million in profit on their $612 million investment, and they still owned most of Celanese. By the time they sold the last of their Celanese shares in May 2007, Blackstone and the coinvestors raked in a $2.9 billion profit on Celanese—almost five times their money and by far the biggest single gain Blackstone has ever booked.

Celanese was a tour de force of financial engineering. By Chu's reckoning, the cyclical upswing of the industry and the higher multiple the stock commanded in the United States accounted for roughly two-thirds of the Celanese profit. The remaining third traced to the operational changes, such as pruning costs, selling the money-losing operations, and adding Acetex and Vinamul. Much of that was accomplished in the eight and a half months between the takeover and the IPO.

Those enhancements rather than the economy were responsible for roughly half the increase in the company's cash flow from 2003 to 2006, Chu contends, and that appears to be corroborated by a comparison with other chemical companies. Celanese's cash flow rose 80 percent in that period while none of its chief competitors—BASF, Dow Chemical, and Eastman Chemical—managed a gain of more than 50 percent.

More than eleven hundred jobs were cut along the way, but Celanese also created new jobs at the same time, so the net loss was four hundred jobs, or about 4 percent, while Blackstone was in control. Meanwhile, the productivity of Celanese's workforce shot up by more than 50 percent, from $495,000 in revenue per employee in 2003 to $750,000 in 2006. Perhaps half of that resulted from the run-up in the chemical cycle, but much was due to the operational improvements and strategic changes on Blackstone's watch.

Celanese sustained its performance for years after it went public. Its shares more than tripled over the next three years, from $16 in the IPO to a peak of almost $50 in mid-2008, outperforming its competitors substantially. The economic slowdown took a toll on the company in 2008 and 2009, but Celanese entered the downturn "a fundamentally stronger company," its CEO, Weidman, says. As evidence he cites its cash flow, which never dipped below $800 million in 2008–2009, double its level in the 2001–2002 recession.

Even relisting in the United States—the ploy that at first glance looks like a financial sleight of hand—benefited the company. By shifting to the U.S. market, where its shares were more highly valued, Celanese gained access to cheaper capital, a crucial advantage if it wanted to expand or acquire other companies. To raise a given amount of money, it now has to sell fewer new shares than it would if it still traded in Germany.

The Nalco investment played out along similar lines. The company rode the rebound in the chemical markets, borrowed to pay a dividend to Blackstone, Apollo, and Goldman Sachs Capital Partners, and then went public in November 2004, two months before Celanese. At the IPO price, Blackstone's investment was worth three times what it paid a year earlier. By the time Blackstone sold the last of its shares in Nalco in 2007, its profit was 1.7 times its investment in Nalco.

"You've got to have a lot of respect for the cycles," Chu says, looking back. "No matter how smart an investor you are and no matter how great the company and its management team are, if you invested in U.S. or European chemicals in 2007 and exited in 2010, you'd take a loss."

It was a lesson Blackstone failed to heed with TRW Automotive. Auto sales bottomed out in 2003, right after Blackstone bought the company, and began trending upward. When the company went public in February 2004, a year after Blackstone bought it, Blackstone recouped much of its investment and showed a huge paper gain on its remaining shares. For several years after that, the company grew rapidly, even though car sales were flat in both the United States and Europe after 2005. The stock never progressed too far from its $28 IPO price, though, as Blackstone held on to a 45 percent stake. At the stock's peak of around $40 per share in 2007, Blackstone's stake was worth $1.9 billion and the investment still looked like a success. But it had held on too long. Car sales plummeted in 2008 and 2009, dragging TRW's sales down by a quarter. In the spring of 2009, when TRW shares troughed out at $1.52, Blackstone's remaining stake was worth just $70 million. The stock rose back above $30 in 2010. Blackstone seized the opportunity and sold $264 million in shares. Its remaining stake rebounded in value to $1.2 billion, restoring much of its gain on paper. But it would now take much longer to exit TRW, and because Blackstone has had its capital tied up for so long, the absolute gain will equate to only a modest annual rate of return. Timing really is everything.

CHAPTER 18

Cash Out, Ante Up Again

To understand the explosion of buyouts in 2006 and 2007 and the unprecedented quantity of capital and power amassed by big private equity firms in that era, one must understand what happened several years earlier.

The year 2003 proved to be an economic inflection point, and Celanese, Nalco, and TRW were harbingers of a gush of profits to come. Other private equity firms, too, were able to cash out of investments as the economy and markets turned up, and the gains they showered on their investors in 2004 and 2005 ensured that the next round of buyout funds would attract far larger sums than the last. Together with the availability of credit on an unparalleled scale, the stage was set for a wave of LBOs that would mesmerize the business world across the United States and Europe.

The mood shift was abrupt. Between March 2003, when Blackstone kicked off its new $6.9 billion fund by investing in TRW Automotive, and the end of that year, American stocks rose nearly 40 percent, and investors became hungry again for IPOs. But their tastes had changed since the tech bubble ended in 2000. This time investors wanted no part of visionary dotcoms with no revenues or profits. They were perfectly content, thank you, to invest in mundane businesses provided that they produced steady income—precisely the kind of companies buyout firms tended to buy.

Blackstone raced to take advantage of the situation. In May 2002, when the IPO market first opened briefly, it pulled off an IPO of Prem-cor, the oil refiner David Stockman had bought in 1997. A couple of years earlier Premcor had looked like it would be a money loser for Blackstone. After a supply glut drove down oil prices in 1997 and 1998, the company began leaking cash. Then, in 2000, it was indicted for en-vironmental violations. But by 2002 oil prices were up, the company was on the mend, and Stockman's original premise for the investment—that Premcor would benefit from a chronic shortage of refining capacity in the United States—had been borne out. Premcor went public at a price two and a half times what Blackstone had paid, and the firm made six times its money selling down its stake as the stock rose in the follow-ing years.

After demand for IPOs became more sustained in late 2003, Black-stone prepped six more of its companies to go public. Centennial Com-munications, a Caribbean cell phone operator it backed in 1999, held its IPO in November 2003. Then Centerplate, Inc., a catering company Blackstone had bought from KKR eight years earlier, followed by Aspen Insurance, the reinsurer Blackstone had helped set up after 9/11. That December, Foundation Coal went public, just five months after Black-stone had bought the American mining company from a German utility. Nalco and Celanese rounded out the IPO list. In none of these cases did Blackstone cash out even half of its holding, but the IPOs began the pro-cess of locking in profits and set the stage for it to take its gains over time by selling shares.

Taking companies public wasn't the only way to cash in on the mar-ket turnabout. There was also the dividend recapitalization—leveraging up the company more to pay a dividend. Together, the surging economy and the resuscitated credit markets made those the profit-taking meth-ods of choice in many cases. Suppose a company had been acquired for $1 billion with relatively little leverage in 2002, when credit markets were tight, and it had debt of just $500 million. If the improving econ-omy had pushed cash flows up 20 percent, the company could now bor-row an additional $100 million (20 percent of $500 million) assuming its bankers applied the same debt–to–cash flow figure they had when they financed the deal originally. That money could then be paid out to the company's owners.

But the takings were even larger than that because bankers had grown more generous as the debt markets improved. With a given annual cash flow, you could now borrow much more than you could in 2002. The high-yield bond market reopened in 2003 and 2004 and quickly matched its peaks in 1997 and 1998, sending interest rates tumbling as money cascaded in. A company issuing junk bonds at the beginning of 2003 had to offer an interest rate 8 percentage points over the rate on U.S. treasury bills. By December 2003 that spread had narrowed to just 4 percentage points. With their interest costs falling, companies could shoulder more debt and replace their old debt with new, cheaper loans and bonds. Thus the hypothetical company above might well be able to take on, say, $200 million of additional debt, paying back its owners 40 percent of the $500 million they originally had invested. Presto! An instant return. And the recapitalization might not even increase the company's interest costs.

That's what happened with Nalco. The buyout was quite highly leveraged from the start, with debt at six times Nalco's cash flow going in, but within a week of the deal's closing in November 2003, Blackstone and its coinvestors, Apollo and Goldman Sachs Capital Partners, were peppered with calls from bankers offering to lend Nalco even more money. "This was a wake-up call, evidence to me that something new was unfolding," says one investor in the deal. "Between the time that we signed the Nalco deal in the summer and the time it closed in November, the availability, pricing, and structure of this kind of credit had undergone a big change for the positive in the market."

The recaps were an irresistible move for buyout firms, because they allowed them to earn back part of their investment quickly, without the drawn-out process of an auction or an IPO, and the faster they returned money to their investors, the higher their annual rates of return.

To the uninitiated, the recaps could look like financial gymnastics. In fact, they were a tried-and-true move in the private equity playbook, and if the new debt simply reflected a healthier business with better prospects, or lower interest rates, there was nothing nefarious about the practice. It was no different from owning an apartment building where rents and the property's value had risen sharply. There would be nothing irresponsible about refinancing the building to take out equity if the increases looked permanent or mortgage rates had fallen.

Still, there had never before been a spate of recaps like this. Buyout firms big and small sucked $86 billion of cash out of their companies this way between 2004 and 2007—money that largely flowed straight back to their limited partners.

The recaps were in part a necessity at first, because it was still hard for private equity firms to find buyers for their holdings. Corporations had pursued so many misguided acquisitions in the late nineties that they were slow to resume buying once the recession ended. Merger activity didn't match its 1999 and 2000 heights again until 2007.

To compensate for the lack of corporate buyers, private equity firms also created their own M&A market, buying companies from one another in what are known as secondary buyouts.

The secondary buyouts of the mattress makers Simmons Company and Sealy Corporation within months of each other in the winter of 2003 to 2004 advertised the strange tendency of some companies to be handed off repeatedly from one private equity firm to another. When Thomas H. Lee Partners bought Simmons from Fenway Partners for $1.1 billion, it was Simmons's fifth consecutive buyout over seventeen years. A few months later KKR bought Sealy from Bain Capital and Charlesbank Capital Partners for $1.5 billion and became Sealy's fourth private equity owner in fifteen years.

Again, it looked peculiar to outsiders. It called to mind Milo Minderbinder, the wheeling-and-dealing mess officer in *Catch-22* who made a profit buying eggs from himself at 7 cents apiece and selling them for 5 cents. Were they just playing a financial shell game among themselves?

Secondary buyouts were usually not too baffling if you delved into the financials of the companies. Both mattress makers had steadily improved and expanded their businesses over the years under their successive private equity owners. They had consolidated smaller companies and launched new products, their businesses got a lift from a slow but steady increase in the number of bedrooms in the average American home, and they had expanded overseas. Their cash flows were predictable enough that they could be highly leveraged, generating gains for their owners from even relatively small improvements.

But the mattress company flips illustrated the risks of overleveraging companies. Two of the previous seven buyouts of the companies had ended badly: Simmons and Sealy had each defaulted once when their owners overpaid and loaded the companies up with too much debt. (Simmons would go bankrupt in 2009 for the same reason, and Sealy would later need a huge shot of additional equity from KKR to stay alive.)

Nevertheless, Simmons's three other prior buyouts had been very profitable, largely because of its superlative financial performance: From 1991, when Merrill Lynch bought Simmons, to 2007 its annual cash flow rocketed more than sixfold, from $24 million to $158 million. Even though Sealy's growth wasn't as steady, its cash flow tripled over the same stretch, and the cumulative increase in both companies' value over nearly two decades was remarkable. Given the expansion of the mattress businesses and the aggregate profits made by private equity firms from them over time, it wasn't surprising that when the companies were put up for sale, the buyers turned out to be other private equity firms.

With all the IPOs, recaps, and secondary buyouts, private equity firms and their investors were awash in incoming cash that they funneled right back into new investments. In 2001, the nadir of the market cycle, Blackstone's buyout funds managed to pay out just $146 million to its limited partners. In 2004, it returned $2.7 billion, then $4.2 billion in 2005, and another $4.7 billion in 2006—testimony to the heady combination of a rising market and leverage. Competitors were cutting even larger checks. Carlyle touted in a press release that it had paid out $5.3 billion in 2004 and KKR returned $7 billion that year. Carlyle paid out another $7 billion in 2005. For four or five years private equity became self-sustaining, as investors recycled the distributions immediately back into new buyout funds. The sums matched up almost perfectly.

It wasn't just the raw totals that were astonishing. The rates of return on buyout funds shot to the sky because firms were able to earn back their investments and begin taking profits so quickly. If you double your money in five years, your uncompounded annual rate of return is 20 percent, but if you double it in two years, it jumps to 50 percent. The economic turnaround was a godsend for everyone in the business, but Blackstone outpaced its big rivals. By the end of 2005 the firm's fourth fund, which it began investing in early 2003, had earned an annual return of more than 70 percent after Blackstone's share of the profits was taken out, about two and a half times the 20 percent annual rise in the stock market over that period. Funds raised by rivals such as Apollo, KKR, and TPG around the same time as Blackstone's also outperformed the stock market, but not by nearly as much. Their returns were about 40 percent, and returns on most other buyout funds of the early decade were below that, so Blackstone stood out in the crowd.

Blackstone's 2002 fund sustained its lead among the biggest buyout funds, generating roughly a 40 percent annual return through the end of 2008, or two or three times the returns on competitors' funds raised at the bottom of the business cycle in 2001 to 2003. That performance was the payoff from Schwarzman's and James's gut feeling in 2002 that things were bottoming out then and from Chinh Chu's two knockout deals: Celanese and Nalco. As Blackstone geared up to raise its next fund, its returns gave it a competitive edge.

It's a law of finance and human nature that investment managers who make money for their clients attract more capital over time. With bucket loads of profits coming in and extraordinary rates of return, Blackstone and other private equity firms with good records were assured of raising gargantuan investment pools the next time they hit the fund-raising trail. Another factor magnified the effect: the quotas big pension funds and other investors set for private equity.

The mix of institutions investing in buyout funds looked very different in the 2000s from what it had when Peterson and Schwarzman first went rapping on doors in 1986 and 1987. Back then they called first on insurance companies and Japanese banks and brokerage houses. Only at the end did they raise money from two corporate pension funds, General Motors' and General Electric's. By the late 1990s, banks and insurers together were providing only 15 percent or so of the money in buyout and venture funds, and state and local government pension funds had emerged as the leading backers of buyouts, furnishing roughly half the investment capital. The typical pension fund still kept half or more of its money in ordinary stocks, and a large slice in bonds, but pension managers increasingly were adhering to an economic model known as modern portfolio theory. This taught that overall returns could be maximized by layering in small amounts of nontraditional, high-returning assets such as buyout, venture, and hedge funds and real estate. Although they were riskier and illiquid (the investor's money was tied up longer), adding these so-called alternative assets diversified a pension portfolio so that the overall risks were no greater, the theory held.

Giant pensions such as California's state employee and teachers funds, CalPERS and CalSTRS, led the way, sprinkling billions of their beneficiaries' money across alternative assets in the 1990s, setting percentage targets for each subclass of assets. By the beginning of the new century, CalSTRS and CalPERS were allocating 5 percent and 6 percent, respectively, to the category that included buyout and venture funds—$13.6 billion between them—and they bumped the amounts up every few years. In 2003 the targets were lifted to 7 percent and 8 percent, shifting an extra $4.6 billion from other types of investments. Both California plans were major Blackstone investors, and they set a precedent with their large allocations that others copied. Between 2003 and 2008, state pension funds overall raised their private equity allocations by a third, from 4.2 percent to 5.6 percent. After the tech bubble burst in 2000, the great bulk of the money earmarked for alternatives went to LBO funds rather than venture capital.

Along with the rising quotas, the total assets of the pension funds were swelling as the population aged and the stock market roared back, so that year by year a given quota, whether 5 percent or 8 percent, equated to an ever-larger absolute amount. The formulas mandated that the pension managers pump billions and billions more into the next generation of buyout funds.

The stepped-up quotas made it possible for Blackstone partners such as Bret Pearlman and Mark Gallogly to strike out on their own and quickly raise multibillion-dollar funds, even though they had no independent investment record. In the main, though, the money flowed disproportionately to a handful of elite firms like Blackstone that had long outshone the stock market and their competitors. Contrary to the common admonition, in the case of private equity, past investment performance is a good predictor of future performance. There was a welter of mediocre private equity firms that didn't outrun the public stock market by a sufficient margin to justify the risk or the illiquidity of investing in their funds, and some even fell short of public stocks' returns. But those whose profits landed them in the top quarter of the rankings tended to stay there year in, year out, and investors clamored to gain entry to their funds. As a consequence, the top ten firms controlled 30 percent of the industry's capital in 1998 and held that position for the next decade.

The planets were all aligned in private equity's favor, and the forces converged to produce a fund-raising frenzy in 2005 and 2006. From the low ebb in 2002, fund-raising quadrupled by 2005. Blackstone's record $6.9 billion fund was soon eclipsed when Carlyle closed a pair of new funds in March 2005 totaling $10 billion. The next month Goldman Sachs Capital Partners, an arm of the investment bank that raises money from outside investors as well as from the bank itself, rounded up $8.5 billion. That August, Warburg Pincus raised $8 billion, and Apollo was closing in on $10 billion. Across the Atlantic, Permira and Apax Partners, two British buyout firms with strong records, raised funds of more than $14 billion apiece. Soon KKR, TPG, and Blackstone vied to top those, laying plans to raise funds surpassing $15 billion. (Blackstone eventually would close on a record $21.7 billion in 2007.) The industry wasn't as concentrated as it had been in the eighties, when KKR single-handedly dominated the field and was behind most of the largest deals of the decade, but the dozen-odd firms that were able to raise megafunds enjoyed a hegemony, because they controlled so much buyout capital and they alone could compete for the new megadeals.

The breathtaking sums pouring in changed the business in several ways. With such large war chests, the top buyout firms would not be content to buy a $500 million company here and a $1 billion company there. It would simply take too long and involve too much work to invest their money at that rate. They would have to find bigger targets, and now the debt markets allowed them to finance deals on a much grander scale.

Private equity had enjoyed a revival in the late 1990s, but it was nothing like this. In the previous decade, merger activity was dominated by huge corporate takeovers, with buyouts accounting for merely 3 percent to 4 percent of all mergers most years, measured by total dollar value. That figure, though, began to tick upward in the 2000s. Even with financing hard to come by, private equity led 10 percent of all takeovers worldwide in 2002, a level achieved only once before, in 1988, when the buyout numbers were skewed by the mammoth RJR Nabisco deal.

Private equity's share kept ascending even after corporations began pursuing mergers again. By 2004 it hit 13 percent in the United States and 16 percent in Europe, and it would rise past 20 percent before the cycle was over. With plenty of cheap debt at its disposal, private equity became a potent force in the markets and the economy. The mere prospect of becoming a buyout target could lift the price of a stock that was otherwise languishing, and corporations began to rethink their own capital structures. If a buyout firm could put more debt on the company so that any gain in the company's value was magnified in the value of its stock, companies began to ask themselves, why couldn't we do the same to give our public shareholders a higher return on their shares? In some cases, hedge funds and other activist investors urged companies to perform their own dividend recaps, borrowing more money to pay a dividend or to buy in some of their shares.

The sheer magnitude of the funds and the deals had another side effect on the business, one that troubled some investors. The fixed 1.5

percent to 2 percent management fees the firms charged their investors, and the transaction fees they tacked on when they bought or sold a company, had grown so large in absolute dollar terms that they had become a wellhead of income at large private equity houses, rather than just a way of ensuring that some money was coming in the door in tough times. By mid-decade, firms like Blackstone and KKR were deriving roughly a third of their revenue from the fixed fees rather than from investment profits, enough to make the firms' partners exceedingly rich regardless of the fate of their investments. Cynics began to wonder if the partners' cushy income was undercutting their motivation to make money for their investors. The driving force of the business, they feared, had become asset accumulation for its own sake, not investing for profit.

CHAPTER 19

Wanted: Public Investors

From its earliest days, the buyout investing game had been the private reserve of institutions and the super rich. There was no way for the American public or even mutual funds to get a piece of the action. Pension plans could invest, yet the man in the street could not add private equity to his own retirement savings account. There was a small number of publicly traded companies in Britain and Canada that invested in buyouts, but American securities law had made it effectively impossible to raise money to invest in LBOs by selling stock to the public, and the foreign investment funds were barred from selling their shares to Americans.

With the business commanding headlines every week, and word spreading of the enormous profits being churned out by buyout funds, the broader investing world wanted in, and it is an immutable law that when Wall Street senses an appetite for "product," it will find a way to fulfill that desire.

The product in this case would take the form of the business development corporation, or BDC. The BDC was a creature of the U.S. tax code, which gives tax breaks to certain kinds of investment funds that lend to midsized businesses. As long as a BDC pays out almost all of its income each year to shareholders, it is exempt from most corporate taxes. BDCs already existed, but in 2004, egged on by the investment bankers who would collect fees for selling shares to the public, major private equity firms started to perceive the BDC as a way of roping in more capital.

Leon Black's Apollo Management moved first, filing papers in February 2004 to raise $575 million for a new entity, Apollo Investment Corporation. Apollo Investment would not buy control of companies the way that a conventional buyout fund would. Instead, it would be a mezzanine lender, making loans to small and midsized companies. Mezzanine debt—the type of debt that insurance companies provided for LBOs in the early days of the business—is subordinated to senior debt such as bank loans, so the interest rates are higher, and mezzanine lenders usually demand a slice of equity in their customers as well, so they can share in the profits if the customers' stocks take off.

The BDC was a classic case of brand extension. Just as Procter & Gamble dreams up new soaps and toothpastes and sells them under established brands like Ivory, Tide, and Crest, Apollo was transferring the know-how and cachet of its buyout operations to a business that could sell shares to the public. Apollo, like other buyout firms, already had legions of analysts studying industries and potential target companies, and its knowledge of the debt markets was deep. Here was a way to capitalize on that expertise and collect management fees and profits on ever larger amounts of capital. The parent Apollo's cut was similar to an LBO fund's, a 2 percent management fee based on the total assets and up to 20 percent of the profits after investors had received a certain minimum.

The appeal of the BDCs to their sponsors was not just new capital to manage but permanent capital. The private equity business had long ago progressed from raising money deal by deal to amassing funds that could invest over many years. But sponsors still had to go on the road every few years, hat in hand, visiting limited partners to convince them to re-up in a new fund. The process consumed an enormous amount of time—time that the Leon Blacks and Steve Schwarzmans would rather have spent doing deals and raking in profits than justifying themselves. BDCs had to pay out most of their profits each year, but they retained their original capital in perpetuity and could raise new capital at any time by selling additional shares to the public, a process that could be handled by bankers and lawyers without senior management having to press the flesh.

The BDC was the closest thing to a publicly traded buyout fund anyone had formulated that was legal in the United States. (A company that buys companies but doesn't plan to keep them indefinitely falls under the Investment Company Act of 1940, which governs mutual funds and other passive asset managers. That law limits the amount of debt an investment fund can use and restricts the fees it can pay to its management firm, constraints that are deal breakers for a normal private equity firm.) The BDC wasn't a perfect substitute, but the prospect of permanent capital raised on the public markets was irresistible.

Apollo was the first out of the gate, and the usual suspects were close on its heels. When Apollo said in early April that it would boost the target size of its BDC to $930 million—a sign that there was market appetite—competitors rushed to launch their own BDCs. KKR filed for one on April 12, Blackstone on April 14. Within a month, more than a dozen were in the works from private equity firms like Thomas H. Lee Partners and Ares Capital Management and banks. It was "the pack moving and Wall Street was pushing, and there was no downside," says one adviser involved in several of the offerings.

As things played out, though, Apollo Investment Corporation was the undoing of the BDC. The banks that underwrote the IPO shaved 6.25 percent off the top in fees and commissions, so that there was barely $14 left to invest for every share the public had bought at $15. Had investors been optimistic enough about the prospects for profits, the stock price might have held at the IPO price, but they began to have doubts, and by May, Apollo Investment's shares fell below $13, dampening interest in the other BDCs in the pipeline. Why would anyone want to buy into an IPO if the shares were destined to fall? Some big investors began to grumble, too, about the fees that Apollo and the others would charge, though the charges weren't any higher than those for buyout funds.

The market had proved fickle, and it soon became clear that the other offerings would meet a hostile reception. One by one, the other BDC deals were withdrawn or recast. Blackstone called off its plans on July 21. Ultimately, Apollo Investment paid dividends and by early 2005 its shares rose past $17, but it was too late to salvage most of the others. The BDC would not be private equity's means to mine the public markets. Only a few smaller BDCs made it to market after Apollo.

"The golden goose only laid one big egg and left foie gras all over the place," one banker said when the BDC rush had faded in late 2004.

Apollo had won round one in the quest to tap the public markets, garnering nearly $1 billion of new capital. For the rest, the BDC turned out to be a dead end.

It was a painful lesson in how quickly the markets could turn, but the broader investment world's thirst for private equity, and the industry's desire to slake that thirst, didn't go away. American buyout firms would soon look for another means, in Europe, to corral public investors' money.

In March 2005, Ripplewood Holdings, an American private equity firm that had invested extensively in Japan, made the next move, transferring seven of its investments to a new holding company, which then sold $1.85 billion of shares to the public on the Belgian stock exchange. The new entity, RHJ International, would manage and then sell off its holdings over time and reinvest the proceeds. In effect, it was a buyout fund with perpetual capital. Although quirks in Belgian law deterred others from following in Ripplewood's footsteps, the seed was sown. In early 2006, Goldman Sachs, which had engineered the Ripplewood deal along with Morgan Stanley, hatched a plan for KKR to raise a $1.5 billion fund on the Amsterdam stock market that would invest directly in companies alongside KKR and also would invest indirectly as a limited partner in KKR's buyout funds.

This was the private equity manager's dream, the Holy Grail—true permanent capital raised in the public markets, obviating the need for laborious fund-raising campaigns and broadening the class of investors sponsors could tap.

Just as they had scrambled to catch up with Apollo to market BDCs, KKR's rivals were close on its heels, mobilizing their own teams of bankers and lawyers to float their own Amsterdam funds. "There were twenty other Amsterdam deals ready to go thereafter," says Michael Klein, a senior banker at Citibank, who worked on the KKR deal. Blackstone was secretly readying its own plans for a publicly traded fund in Amsterdam, a project code-named Project Panther. While KKR was raising a fund to supply equity for its funds and its buyouts, Blackstone's would be a mezzanine debt fund, offering loans.

KKR had a head start on the others, and it pressed its advantage to the fullest, stepping up the size of its offering week by week as its bankers lined up more and more investors for the offering. When KKR Private Equity Investors went public on May 3, 2006, it raised a whopping $5 billion.

At the original $1.5 billion target, the KKR fund "would not have been enough to have a huge impact on the [private equity] industry," Schwarzman says. At $5 billion, "it was a potential game changer." This was a bona fide public buyout fund, and on a scale approaching the biggest traditional LBO partnerships. The BDC had been just a poor cousin.

KKR had pulled off a double coup. Not only had it secured a huge new pool of money to manage, but in the process it had foreclosed that option for its big rivals. Henry Kravis had crossed the public bridge first and raised the bridge behind him.

Competitors soon found that KKR had soaked up all the demand in the market for this kind of stock and surrendered the field to KKR. The subsequent anemic performance of the KKR fund's stock also quashed demand for competitors' products. KKR Private Equity Investors suffered from the same problem Apollo's BDC did: The underwriters took their fees and commissions off the top, and investors came to understand that the fund might not earn cash profits for years. The shares, sold at $25 in the IPO, quickly slumped to the low $20s and never traded over the offering price. The IPO had sated the world's appetite for a private equity stock, but it had also left a sour taste in investors' mouths. Blackstone gave up on its plans for a public mezzanine fund.

There were mixed emotions at Blackstone. "Steve from the early days didn't like the [public investment fund] idea," says Edward Pick, a senior banker at Morgan Stanley who was advising Blackstone about public market options at the time. Blackstone had good relations with the investors in its funds, Pick says, and Schwarzman didn't see the need to turn to the public markets to raise investment capital.

Still, KKR had raised $5 billion of permanent capital on which it would collect fees and carried interest. Round two in the race to the public markets had gone to KKR. The lesson Schwarzman drew: "Being the prime mover is critical."

CHAPTER 20

Too Good to Be True

For Chinh Chu, the first sign that something was askew came in 2005 when Blackstone was weighing a bid for Tronox, which made titanium dioxide pigments used in paints. Like most chemical companies, Tronox's cash flow had soared as the economy picked up speed. Lehman Brothers, the bank handling the sale for Tronox's parent, Kerr-McGee, was offering buyers a generous package of guaranteed financing they could take advantage of if they wished.

With the Celanese and Nalco deals, Chu had earned a reputation as perhaps Blackstone's most astute buyout investor. The $2.6 billion in gains on those deals accounted for more than a third of the profits that Blackstone's 2002 fund realized through the end of 2008. Having snagged Celanese and Nalco at the bottom of the market, Chu understood well the swings of the chemicals industry. He was dumbfounded to learn that Lehman was offering debt of up to seven times Tronox's current cash flow. He figured the chemical industry was near a crest and that if business slacked off, the company wouldn't be able to handle such a huge debt load. If earnings fell back to what one might expect at the midpoint in the business cycle instead of the peak, he reckoned, Tronox's debt could suddenly equate to fourteen times cash flow—a perilous level.

"The debt [offered] on that deal was twice what I thought the company was worth," Chu says.

With Lehman's backing, Blackstone could have paid what Chu considered an absurd price, but Blackstone walked away. No other bidders took Lehman's bait either, and Kerr-McGee ultimately took Tronox public that November. After peaking that year, Tronox's cash flow nose-dived 40 percent, back to 2002 recession levels, sending it into bankruptcy in 2009. By then, Lehman itself was out of business.

Tronox was not an isolated case. Lehman's wildly optimistic package was symptomatic of the forces that were igniting a new buyout blitz that would eclipse that in the 1980s. The $10 billion and $15 billion LBO funds raised in 2005 and 2006 may have turned the ignition key, but it was the banks and the credit markets that shifted the buyout business into overdrive and jammed the pedal to the floor.

The first sign of the escalation to come was a buyout engineered by Glenn Hutchins, the Blackstone partner who left in 1998 to cofound Silver Lake Partners. In the spring of 2005, Silver Lake made headlines by leading a buyout of publicly traded SunGard Data Systems, which provides computer services to financial institutions and universities. At $11.3 billion, it was the second-largest LBO ever, upstaging the old number two, KKR's $8.7 billion buyout of Beatrice Foods in 1986. Only the RJR Nabisco buyout in 1988 was bigger.

The SunGard deal was notable not only for its size but for the unusual and potentially unwieldy, seven-firm coalition that Silver Lake corralled in order to come up with the $3.5 billion of equity needed. It was a who's who of the buyout world: Bain Capital, Blackstone, KKR, TPG, Goldman Sachs, and Providence Equity Partners. Private equity firms had occasionally teamed up in twos or threes in the past, but one firm usually had a larger stake and took a lead role. SunGard set a new precedent by including so many marquee names with roughly equal shares. No other consortium ever quite matched SunGard's, but increasingly firms that competed on one deal allied on the next in order to come up with the requisite capital.

SunGard also signaled that the banks would fund deals on a scale far beyond anything in the preceding fifteen years. It was their debt packages that were pushing the envelope on deal sizes, and even the biggest private equity firms sometimes had to scramble to round up the equity.

SunGard was a turning point, but it wouldn't hold its place in the record books for long. Soon Clayton Dubilier, Carlyle, and Merrill Lynch topped that with a $14.4 billion deal to buy Hertz Corporation, the rental car company, from Ford Motor Company. It seemed every time one blinked in 2005, another household name was being snapped up in a buyout: the retailer Toys "R" Us ($7 billion: Bain Capital, KKR, and Vornado Realty Trust), Neiman Marcus, Inc., the tony department store chain ($5.1 billion: TPG and Warburg Pincus), and the doughnut and ice-cream chains Dunkin' Donuts and Baskin-Robbins ($2.4 billion: Bain, Carlyle, and Thomas H. Lee).

Apart from the size, the other striking thing about the rash of mega-deals in 2005 was that, except for Hertz and Dunkin' Donuts, the companies were all publicly traded. The sheer scale of the new LBO funds all but dictated that their sponsors go after public companies, because there simply weren't enough big subsidiaries and private companies for sale to soak up the billions that the firms had to deploy. That meant the focus would shift heavily back from Europe to the United States, where big targets were more plentiful and there were fewer legal impediments to taking public companies private.

The take-privates, as they were known, also reflected a new social acceptance of private equity. CEOs who had once looked askance at buyout artists were now only too happy to offer up their companies. The Sarbanes-Oxley law enacted after the Enron and other corporate scandals early in the decade had imposed new disclosure obligations and new liabilities on companies and their managers, which executives groused were a distraction and a drain on their time. Offered the chance to answer only to private equity executives, and not to stock analysts and hedge funds that always seemed to think they knew better than management what to do, many CEOs found the going-private option tempting. At least as important, the private equity firms offered executives equity stakes that potentially could make them much richer than they could ever hope to become collecting stock options in a public company. "Sign me up!" CEOs said.

As the pace of deal making picked up in 2005, the buyout wave became an epic land grab by the private equity shops. What set it off, in addition to their piles of equity capital, were innovations in the debt markets that were at least as profound as those wrought by Michael Milken in the eighties.

Milken's achievement had been to tap the bond markets to fund takeovers. Until Drexel created the junk-bond market, buyers had to scrounge up credit from individual commercial banks and, for unsecured junior debt, insurers. Drexel displaced the insurers by acting as a conduit, funneling money from the bond market to growing companies, corporate raiders, and buyout firms. Even before Drexel's collapse, Jimmy Lee at Chemical had begun to assemble networks of banks to buy parcels of bank loans, channeling capital from banks around the world to M&A financing and distributing the risks.

By the 2000s, lending syndicates and bond financing were merging through a process known as securitization. Banks still made loans up front, but rather than divvying them up with other banks, they bundled them with scores of loans to other companies and sold slices of those bundles to investors. The process was known as securitization because it repackaged loans as widely sold securities similar to bonds or stocks.

Securitization had been a staple of the financial system since the 1980s, when it was first used for residential mortgages, auto loans, and, later, credit card receivables. Lenders would pool thousands of loans and sell them to newly created entities that would then issue debt securities, using the principal and interest on the underlying mortgages to pay interest to the investors. The process allowed banks to sell the loans they had made, raising cash they could then loan out again. On the buyer's side, investors who wanted to own assets such as mortgages and credit card loans could buy them in a form that was freely tradable and relatively safe because the securities were backed by thousands of mortgages or credit card debts that collectively were supposed to pay more than enough to cover the principal and interest payments.

In the 1990s and 2000s, a similar process was later applied to corporate loans and bonds. Those bundles, dubbed collateralized loan obligations, or CLOs, functioned like bank loan syndication had in the past, distributing slices of bank loans, thereby drawing on a wider pool of capital sources and spreading the risks of the loans. Soon corporate bonds as well as loans were being bundled into new instruments.

CLOs quickly came to drive the lending process, absorbing an estimated 60–70 percent of all big corporate loans between 2004 and 2007, including the riskier leveraged loans backing LBOs. Hedge funds and banks across the globe poured money into CLOs and their mortgage counterparts, collateralized debt obligations, or CDOs, because their leveraged structures allowed them to pay higher rates of return than the investors could earn buying straight loans and bonds, and the diversified pools of debt backing the securities provided a hedge against defaults. Demand for CLOs and CDOs was so strong, and the fees for creating them so great, that the banks couldn't raise the money and lend it fast enough. Banks were making loans just so they could satisfy the CLO and CDO appetite. This flooded the economy with credit and drove down interest rates. In early 2005, rates on high-yield debt were just 3 percent above those on U.S. treasury bonds, implying that they carried little risk. That spread was near its all-time low of 1987, and it stayed near there for the next two years.

The surplus of money had another effect. In their rush to make loans, the banks put few conditions on them. Historically, loans had come with covenants—clauses that allowed the lender to exert more control or even take over a borrower if it got in trouble and was merely in danger of defaulting. If a borrower's cash flow fell below, say, 150 percent of its interest costs, the banks might be able to move in. No more. A new era of "covenant lite" loans had dawned, and the investors who bought the securities backed by the covenant-free loans didn't seem to care.

There were several unintended, and ultimately ruinous, consequences of the explosion of securitized debt, sometimes called structured finance. One was that banks ceased seeing themselves as creditors and became mere middlemen between the market and borrowers, risking little of their own money. They therefore had less incentive to worry about defaults. (In fact, they had not escaped the risks because they also invested in CLOs and CDOs themselves and took them as collateral for some loans.)

The other side effect of the new financing machinery was to push up the prices of companies. Just as homeowners and speculators were bidding up house prices with the help of subprime and no-strings mortgages that were bundled up and sold into the bond markets, buyout firms were driving values higher because the banks were throwing so much debt at them that it didn't cost the buyers anything to offer more.

The run-up in prices was startling. In 2004 the average large company that went through a buyout was priced at 7.4 times its cash flow. By 2007, the average had shot up to 9.8 times. But it wasn't that buyout firms were cutting larger equity checks. Most of that rise in multiples consisted of debt, as banks promised bigger loans and larger bond packages for a given sum of cash flow. With the same amount of equity, a buyout firm could afford to buy a much more expensive company in 2007 than in 2004.

To private equity firms it was like having a credit card without a limit, and they went on a shopping spree, setting their sights higher and higher. Hertz was followed by a $15.7 billion take-private of Denmark's main phone company by a consortium including Blackstone. Then Carlyle and Goldman Sachs offered more than $20 billion for Kinder Morgan, Inc., a publicly traded pipeline operator, to become the new second-biggest buyout ever, in May 2006. Two months later the all-time record set by RJR Nabisco in 1988 finally fell, narrowly edged out of first place by a $33 billion buyout of HCA Corporation, a hospital chain. Fittingly, KKR led the HCA deal.

Public companies were stampeding into the arms of buyout firms, lured by all-cash buyout offers well above their current stock prices. In a two-day span the week before Christmas 2006, no fewer than four public American companies agreed to go private: building supplies company Elk Corporation (Carlyle for $1 billion), orthopedic device maker Biomet, Inc. (Blackstone, Goldman Sachs, KKR, and TPG for $10.9 billion), real estate brokerage franchisor Realogy (Apollo for $9 billion), and Harrah's Entertainment, a casino operator (Apollo and TPG for $27.8 billion). There had been competing bids for Elk and Biomet from corporations, but the corporations simply couldn't match the prices or couldn't afford to pay entirely in cash, as the private equity firms did.

In economic terms, debt had become overwhelmingly the cheapest source of capital. Investors always expect higher returns for investing in stocks—from dividends and the expected rise in the share price—because stocks are riskier than bonds or loans. But debt had become so inexpensive, and the terms so lax, that private equity firms could borrow money to buy a company's stock from its shareholders and offer them substantially more than the company was worth on the stock market. At bottom, the LBO frenzy was a colossal substitution of debt for equity.

"Inevitably when people look back at this period, they will say this is the golden age for private equity because money is being made very readily," Carlyle's cofounder David Rubenstein told an audience at the beginning of 2006.

It was indeed private equity's moment. That year private equity firms initiated one of every five mergers globally and even more, 29 percent, in the United States. Blackstone's partners, though, had decidedly mixed feelings about the bonanza. They began to worry that the market was overheating.

"It's not that you see problems coming. You never see problems coming at that point, or no one would be giving you ten times leverage," James says with hindsight. "There are no clouds on the horizon. What you see is too much exuberance, too much confidence, people taking risks that in the last 145 years wouldn't have made sense. What you say is, this feels like a bubble."

The firm conducted no grand study of the economy. It was a consensus that emerged gradually from the partners' scrutinizing many potential investments and asking over and over, "Where is this industry in its cycle? How would this company fare in a downturn?" The outcome was a decision to avoid heavily cyclical companies.

By early 2007, "we told our [investors] that, notwithstanding the fact that everyone else thinks it's a fantastic time, the economy is rocking, there are no problems, we're pulling back," says James. "We're not going to be investing, we're going to be lowering the prices, we're going to be changing the kinds of companies that we're going to buy, because when everything feels good and you can't see any problems, historically you've been near a peak."

By then Chinh Chu, the firm's chemicals industry guru, had shifted his focus to pharmaceuticals and medical devices, where demand tends to be more steady across the business cycle. For the same reason, Neil Simpkins, who specialized in industrial companies like the auto-parts maker TRW, was spending his time scoping out health services businesses, which had the same characteristics. Food looked like a safe bet, too. Prakash Melwani, who had worked on three highly cyclical energy investments in 2004, oversaw the purchase of Pinnacle Foods, the parent of Duncan Hines cake mixes and Mrs. Butterworth's syrup, and in London, David Blitzer led buyouts of the British cookie maker United Biscuits and the soft-drink bottler Orangina.

But the temptation for Blackstone to grab what it could while the money was flowing so freely was hard to resist, and Blackstone continued to take part in fiercely contested auctions where prices ran up. The buyout group's biggest deal in 2006, negotiated in a torrent of bids and counterbids for two companies, was one that would have been unthinkable in a tighter credit market. It would later be seen as a case of reaching too far.

It began in May 2006 when Paul "Chip" Schorr IV approached Freescale Semiconductor, Inc., about going private. Schorr had joined Blackstone as a partner the year before from the private equity arm of Citigroup, where he led technology buyouts. For several years at Citi, he had cultivated the management of Freescale and its former parent, Motorola Corporation. Schorr had offered to invest in Freescale before Motorola spun it off as an independent company in 2004, and in late 2005, shortly after moving to Blackstone, he had discussed the possibility of investing in Freescale to help finance an acquisition. In May 2006, with the capital of Blackstone behind him, Schorr was prepared to buy the company outright and he approached Freescale's chairman and CEO, Michel Mayer, about doing so.

Freescale agreed to let Schorr's team look at confidential business information to size up the company. No sooner had they begun to burrow into the business, however, than the Dutch company Philips Electronics announced that it planned to sell its semiconductor business, known as NXP, complicating the choices for Schorr. The two companies were similar. Like Freescale, NXP made a range of chips used in everything from cars to cell phones, and NXP and Freescale executives had even explored a merger. Schorr let the Philips bankers know that Blackstone was interested in NXP, and the firm teamed up with TPG and London's Permira for a bid. It could buy one or the other or, conceivably, both.

Like many subsidiaries of big European companies, NXP seemed ripe for restructuring, and other buyout firms, too, soon flocked to Philips's headquarters in Eindhoven in the Netherlands to scope out the operation. Many of the bidders had been allies in the SunGard buyout earlier that year but were now competitors in the NXP auction. The Blackstone group found itself pitted against two other consortiums, one made up of KKR and Silver Lake (both in SunGard) and the Dutch buyout firm AlpInvest, and a second consisting of Bain Capital (also in SunGard), London's Apax Partners, and Francisco Partners.

No one else—not even Blackstone's bidding partners in NXP, TPG and Permira—knew that Blackstone was wooing Freescale at the same time as NXP. "We were working Freescale alone and we were not allowed to tell anyone we were doing it," Schorr recounts. "We'd be in Eindhoven looking at NXP and then we'd have to fly down to Austin for Freescale meetings, but we couldn't tell our partners." Not only was Schorr evaluating each company on its own, but also what synergies there might be if they merged.

It would have been a stretch to buy both, though, and in the summer, when it appeared that the Blackstone group was in the lead to win NXP, Blackstone slowed down work on Freescale. "We went a little cold on Freescale in July," says Schorr. "We had kind of a three-week walk in the woods." When KKR and Silver Lake ultimately prevailed in the NXP auction with a $10.6 billion bid on August 3, Schorr threw himself back into Freescale again.

Blackstone told Freescale initially that it expected to offer $35.50 to $37 a share, but Freescale held out for more, and over the course of August Blackstone inched up its offer until the two sides agreed on $38. Blackstone would need more than $7 billion of equity to pull off the buyout—more than one firm could afford to risk on a single deal—so on August 31, Freescale gave Blackstone permission to reach out to TPG and Permira, its partners in the NXP bid. It also approached Carlyle, another SunGard backer, which quickly signed up as well.

Blackstone's and Freescale's bankers and lawyers were hammering out the final details when they were blindsided. Out of the blue, KKR wrote Freescale on September 7 to say it had gotten wind of the Blackstone talks and wanted to make its own bid. Three days later it told Freescale's board it expected to make an offer with Silver Lake of $40 to $42 a share, well above Blackstone's offer, which hadn't yet been revealed publicly.

"It was a completely proprietary deal until the eleventh hour, fifty-ninth minute, fifty-ninth-and-a-half second, when they threw in this letter over the transom on the evening we were supposed to sign the contract," Schorr says. "It was pretty audacious because they were in the middle of buying NXP. The combined equity [for] the deals was $12 billion."

Schorr and his team knew that many duplicate costs could be squeezed out if NXP and Freescale merged. They had run those calculations a few months earlier. In theory, then, KKR could afford to pay more for Freescale than Blackstone could because KKR could capture those savings if it owned both companies. But Blackstone had a four-month head start understanding Freescale's business, an advantage it would have to preserve if it hoped to prevail.

"We were prepared to sign a contract. They were not," says Schwarzman. "If we gave them sufficient time, they'd see the same kind of synergies that we thought existed because we had almost bought NXP."

Blackstone needed to preempt a bidding war. To do that, it huddled with Carlyle, Permira, and TPG and quickly countered with a $40 per share offer on September 14. It was less than the upper range of KKR's bid, but it was a firm offer.

Blackstone also played hardball. It vowed to walk away if Freescale didn't respond by the following night. It further put the screws to Freescale with what amounted to a threat. By now there had been leaks in the press and Freescale had been forced to confirm that it was in talks. Blackstone told Freescale that if it bowed out and Freescale didn't disclose publicly that it had, Blackstone might do so itself. In other words: Take our deal or you'll be left with a nonbinding offer from KKR, and we'll let KKR know that we're not in the running anymore.

The tactics worked. On September 15, Freescale's board opted for the bird in hand, accepting the $18.8 billion offer from Blackstone, Carlyle, Permira, and TPG rather than gamble that KKR and Silver Lake would eventually make a better offer. The next day KKR said it was no longer interested, and no one else emerged to trump Blackstone's offer.

Schorr had captured the company he had been pursuing for four months, but KKR's last-minute spoiler bid had cost the Blackstone consortium an extra $800 million. It was a steep price to pay for a semiconductor business that was notorious for its ups and downs, and Freescale had some worrisome problems. Cell phone chips sales for Motorola accounted for 20 percent of its revenue, but sales of Motorola's wildly popular Razr model were cresting as competitors began to steal market share with snazzier models, and Motorola didn't have any big product innovations in the pipeline. Freescale was also exposed to the vicissitudes of the auto industry, which provided another 30 percent of its sales.

In ordinary times, those vulnerabilities would have made Freescale an unlikely LBO candidate. But the Blackstone consortium put an unusually large amount of equity into the buyout, $7.1 billion, or 38 percent of the price, so that Freescale would have a large cash reserve as a cushion. Blackstone's lenders, Credit Suisse and Citigroup, took care of the rest with extraordinarily liberal financing terms. Virtually none of Freescale's debt was due until six years out, and much of it didn't mature until even later. Moreover, the debt had no covenants to speak of. Even if Freescale's business deteriorated badly, the lenders had few rights unless Freescale actually stopped making debt payments.

To give the company yet more breathing room, the banks also recycled a trick from the 1980s and included payment-in-kind notes, or PIKs. A popular type of bond in the Drexel era, they paid interest not with cash but with more bonds. In other words, the company could take on more debt instead of paying cash to its creditors. In an added, company-friendly feature, these notes had a "toggle": Freescale could pay in cash or with more notes as it wished. If sales plunged, Freescale could exercise the PIK option to conserve cash.

For Blackstone, the fine print of the financing made the investment a safe bet.

"Semiconductors, you knew, was cyclical—incredibly cyclical," says James. "We knew we were buying nearer the peak than the trough, so we built a capital structure with no covenants, long maturities, tons of liquidity. We said, it's going to be a wild ride, but the long-term trends for the industry were positive as electronics permeate everything. You're going to have your down cycles, but you'll have some great up cycles, too, so build yourself a bulletproof capital structure so you can ride through any down cycle and then harvest in the up cycle."

Even with the hefty equity investment, Freescale's balance sheet was torn up and rewritten, its debt load ballooning from $832 million before the buyout to $9.4 billion. It would now pay close to $800 million a year in interest, about ten times more than it had before.

Blackstone stretched and won Freescale, but in the ensuing months it just couldn't stretch far enough to win other bidding contests. In virtually every major auction over the next year, it was trounced, often by a wide margin. "It was frustrating sometimes," says Chinh Chu, "looking in the mirror with a little self-doubt when we didn't have resolve."

One of the most frustrating cases was Clear Channel Communications, a deal that became a poster child for the excesses of the decade. Blackstone lost the deal despite having nearly a two-month jump on the competition.

In late August, as Schorr was still haggling with Freescale over price, Blackstone partner David Tolley began talking to Clear Channel, one of the nation's largest radio chains and a major billboard owner. Tolley and

Blackstone's partner on the bid, Providence Equity Partners, which invests primarily in media and communications companies, managed to keep those talks a secret until October, when Thomas H. Lee Partners crashed the party, approaching the company. Soon, Clear Channel's bankers began conducting a full-fledged auction.

The situation quickly escalated into the buyout equivalent of a swingers party, with two of Blackstone's coinvestors from Freescale and SunGard—TPG and Carlyle—switching partners to compete against Blackstone while the ink was barely dry on the Freescale agreement. First, TPG paired up with Thomas H. Lee Partners and Bain Capital. Then Carlyle partnered with Apollo on a third bid. If that weren't promiscuous enough, KKR, which beat out Blackstone for NXP and tried to grab Freescale, was an on-again, off-again ally this time, twice joining and then pulling out of the Blackstone–Providence consortium. Cerberus Capital Management and Oak Hill Partners, which had no part in Freescale or SunGard, also joined the fray.

When the final round of bidding came in November, Blackstone's $36.85-per-share offer fell short of Bain and Thomas H. Lee's $37.60. (TPG dropped out along the way.) "The banks were offering us ten times debt to cash flow," says James. "No company can support that kind of debt. We wouldn't take all the leverage because it didn't make economic sense and, as a result, didn't get to the price the board wanted."

In its scale and its reed-thin equity base, Clear Channel was a high watermark, testimony to the extraordinary lengths to which lenders were willing to go. Bain and Lee's agreement called for them to put up just $4 billion of equity while a sprawling syndicate of banks—Citigroup, Deutsche Bank, Morgan Stanley, Credit Suisse, Royal Bank of Scotland, and Wachovia Corporation—agreed to supply $21.5 billion of debt. The buyers would put up a mere 16 percent of the price in equity.

After a group of hedge funds and mutual funds that owned Clear Channel shares complained that $37.60 a share was too little and threatened to vote down the offer, Bain and Thomas H. Lee upped their offer to $39 a share in April 2007 and then, when that still looked like it might not be enough, to $39.20 the next month. When the details of the financing for the revised offer were revealed, it turned out that the buyers had actually reduced their equity investment from $4 billion to $3.4 billion and the banks had offered an extra $1 billion in debt to make up the difference and top up the offer. Clear Channel's long-term debt would go from $5.2 billion to $18.9 billion after the closing, and it would spend $900 million annually on interest payments.

Similar scenarios played out time and time again that fall and into 2007, with Blackstone's bids falling short of rivals'. It lost the electronic transaction processor First Data Corporation to KKR, which offered $34 a share, or $29 billion, versus Blackstone's $30 a share. The cell phone carrier Alltel went to TPG and Goldman Sachs for $71.50 per share, or $27.5 billion. Blackstone had proposed $67 to $70 a share.

Bain and Clayton Dubilier won Home Depot Supply, the wholesale arm of the building supplies giant, with a $10.3 billion bid, roughly a billion more than Blackstone had offered. Textbook publisher Thompson Learning. Commercial caterer U.S. Foodservice. British food distributor Brake Brothers. Blackstone was outbid on them all.

"We lost seven out of eight in a row in early 2007," remembers Prakash Melwani, who sits on Blackstone's investment committee. "We kept losing by miles. It was very depressing."

Blackstone outspent rivals like KKR and Apollo in 2006, writing equity checks totaling more than $7.5 billion for Freescale and other big buyouts that closed earlier in the year, such as VNU NV (later known as Nielsen Company), Biomet, and Michaels Stores, and it plunked down nearly as much in 2007, $6.3 billion. Equity Office Properties and Hilton and other deals soaked up another $8.2 billion from the firm's real estate funds that year.

For all the calculations and worries about the markets heading out of control, there was an irreducible human factor at work—the ambition and competitive drive of Blackstone's partners.

"It's very hard when everyone around you is bidding on things and buying a lot of things to stick to your guns and say, 'No, no, I think it's overpaying,'" says James. "Your people start pushing back. They're deal people; they want to do deals. We allowed ourselves—the pull pressures from our own people and the push pressures from the market—to be dragged along. We had the brakes on but the car was still being pushed."

The brakes took hold firmly in the buyout group only in late 2006. After playing lead roles in four of the twenty-five largest buyouts that year, Blackstone's buyout team had a hand in just one of the top twenty-five in 2007, Hilton Hotel Corporation, and that deal was spearheaded by Jonathan Gray and the real estate operation. As the market was hitting its highs, it was Gray's group that would lead the two biggest buyouts Blackstone ever attempted.

CHAPTER 21

Office Party

Y ou should buy EOP," Jordan Kaplan casually told Jonathan
Gray, the young cohead of Blackstone's real estate operations. If
Blackstone acquired Equity Office Properties Trust, the nation's
biggest office property company, Kaplan went on, his company would
be happy to buy EOP's West Los Angeles buildings from Blackstone.

It was an offhand remark but a tantalizing thought for Gray. It was
October 23, 2006, and Kaplan, the CEO of Douglas Emmett, Inc., a Los
Angeles–based real estate investment trust, had stopped by Blackstone's
offices with Roy March, a top commercial real estate banker. Unbeknownst to Kaplan and March, Gray had been mulling a bid for EOP
for more than a year.

Gray deflected Kaplan's suggestion, but it intrigued him. Kaplan said
he would pay top dollar for the L.A. buildings. He said he would buy
them at a rich capitalization rate of 4—real estate terminology for a
price at which the buildings would generate a 4 percent cash return.
A cap rate is the inverse of a cash-flow multiple, so a lower rate means a
higher valuation. A cap rate of 4 was equivalent to twenty-five times
cash flow—two or three times the going rate for companies and enough
to set Gray's imagination to work.

As Gray walked with March and Kaplan toward the elevator, he
tapped March on the shoulder and asked him to stay behind. Back in his
office, an excited Gray peppered March with questions about how much
the other parts of EOP might fetch if they were sold off on their own.

Equity Office Properties was the creation of Sam Zell, one of the most colorful investors on the American landscape. He'd made his mark originally in the 1970s, scooping up real estate on the eve of foreclosure. In all, he bought some $3 billion in assets that no one else wanted, putting up fractional down payments and waiting for the market to revive. He emerged with a fortune, and a reputation as perhaps the bravest and most astute property investor of the era. Zell's personality had also ensured his prominence. In an industry of larger-than-life personalities, Zell stood out, shunning ties and suits, taking long motorcycle trips to strange corners of the world, and reliably shocking employees and audiences with off-color remarks.

EOP had been Zell's bid to move up-market. Over two decades, from its base in Chicago, EOP collected 622 prime buildings in seventeen cities. Trophy holdings included the Chicago Mercantile Exchange headquarters, New York's Verizon building overlooking Bryant Park, and the One Market Plaza complex across from San Francisco's Ferry Building. But EOP's stock had been a laggard, even as property values took off in the mid-2000s. The company owned too much in less-than-prime areas, and an ill-timed $7.2 billion investment in Silicon Valley property had dented EOP's reputation. Real estate stocks were on the rise in 2006, but EOP hadn't made up much of its lost ground.

Twice before Gray had tried to line up backers for a bid for EOP. First he had approached CalPERS, the California state pension plan, and later Mort Zuckerman, the head of Boston Properties, Inc., and the publisher of *U.S. News & World Report* and the *New York Daily News*. More recently, just six weeks before Kaplan and March showed up at Gray's door, Gray had lunched with EOP's chief executive, Richard Kincaid, and its chief operating officer, Jeffrey Johnson, and asked them point-blank what it would take to get them to sell the company. When they told him only a "godfather offer"—an offer EOP couldn't refuse—Gray figured they weren't interested in selling. He dropped the idea to focus on a bid for Hilton Hotels Corporation instead.

By the time Jordan Kaplan mooted the idea of Blackstone buying

EOP, the Hilton plans had fizzled out and Gray had time to think about taking another run at EOP. A beguiling proposition began to take shape in his head. If people like Kaplan would now buy buildings at a cap rate of 4, Gray could afford to pay a godfatherly price for EOP and sell off a third or so of its assets, leaving Blackstone owning the balance for a song. In effect, Blackstone would buy wholesale and sell retail. His team had recently done just that with two other publicly traded office property companies, CarrAmerica Realty and Trizec Properties, Inc., where the whole had proved to be worth less than the sum of the parts. If Blackstone bought EOP, Gray would want to unload many of its buildings anyway because he coveted only its properties in four key markets—New York, Boston, West Los Angeles, and the San Francisco Bay Area—where geography and zoning restrictions prevented the kind of overbuilding that periodically plagues many other cities.

Though Kaplan couldn't know it at the time, his impromptu remark would launch the biggest, most daring, and most complicated deal Blackstone had ever attempted—a gutsy bet that would pit the mild-mannered, thirty-six-year-old Gray and his thirty-something partners against two of the wiliest veterans of the real estate business, and would draw Blackstone into a public bidding war for the first time ever. Like Freescale and Clear Channel, the final price was far higher than the winning bidder expected at the outset. Unlike those investments, however, Blackstone in EOP would use the overinflated valuations to its advantage, selling most of the company so it could snare a small portion of EOP's assets for a bargain-basement price.

Blackstone was a pioneer in a type of investing that became known as real estate private equity: raising funds to buy properties and improve them or ride the market cycle up, and selling them a few years later. In the recession and savings-and-loan crisis of the early nineties, when Schwarzman recruited John Schreiber to set up the business, the firm had bought distressed properties. But over time it had adopted an approach more like the buyout group's. In 1998, for instance, the real estate funds bought Britain's Savoy Group hotel chain, which included the namesake

hotel plus three of London's other most swanky inns, Berkeley's, Claridge's, and the Connaught. Together they accounted for about half the
ultraluxury class rooms in London, but the family-run company hadn't
maximized their potential. Blackstone took office's, closets, and other
space that didn't make money and created two hundred new rooms at the
four buildings, upgraded the decor, and hired new chefs to create a buzz
around the establishments before selling the company in 2003.

The private equity approach to real estate had produced an average
return of 36 percent across Blackstone's various real estate funds by 2006,
on a par with the buyout funds, but the real estate group's record had
been more consistent. Only a dozen or so of its two hundred–odd deals
had ever lost money, and those had been relatively small.

The buy-and-sell strategy contrasted with the approach of most traditional property firms, which hold buildings for the long term and
manage them to maximize income rather than sell them at a profit.
Goldman Sachs, Lehman Brothers, and Merrill Lynch had funds with
strategies similar to Blackstone's, but real estate private equity was still
a small niche in the investment world, and Blackstone seldom faced the
intense bidding wars there that it did when buying other businesses.

Gray, a lean six feet, with boyish features and cropped black hair,
looked and acted more like an Eagle Scout than a Master of the Universe. He walked to work from his apartment twenty blocks straight up
Park Avenue from Blackstone's headquarters. His attire—a cheap digital
watch from Wal-Mart, sedate ties and suits, sturdy wingtips—completed
the quotidian effect. He joined Blackstone in 1992 as a research analyst
straight from college at the University of Pennsylvania. He and his
London-based counterpart, Chad Pike, who took over as coheads of real
estate in 2005, had both been tutored by Schreiber from their early days
at the firm. Within Blackstone, the group saw itself as having a distinct
culture, based on geographic roots. Gray, a Chicagoan, and Pike, a native of Toledo, never missed a chance to point out that their team was
dominated by midwesterners, beginning with Schreiber, its éminence grise,
who had remained in his home Chicago all along.

In the three years after Gray and Pike were put in charge of the group, they led it down a new path. Drawing on the firm's buyout know-how, they had shifted from buying individual buildings to acquiring whole real estate companies. In two years starting in March 2004, Blackstone bought eleven public real estate investment trusts, or REITs, in the United States. (REITs have tax advantages, so many businesses that have substantial property assets, as well as firms that invest solely in properties, structure themselves as REITs.) Those included a string of hotel chains: Extended Stay America, Prime Hospitality, Wyndham International, La Quinta, and MeriStar. In the United Kingdom, the real estate and buyout groups teamed up to invest in three businesses that were rich with real estate that in one way or another had not been fully exploited or was inefficiently financed: Spirit Group, a pub chain with scores of underutilized buildings in prime urban locations; Center Parcs, a chain of upscale weekend holiday camps; and NHP and Southern Cross, two nursing home chains that Blackstone merged.

Buying entire public companies not only allowed Blackstone to mine treasures buried inside them; it allowed the firm to invest larger wads of capital in one fell swoop. "That's when our business took a step forward," Gray explains. "It's like when you're turning a lock and all the tumblers all fall into place. We went from buying individual buildings to a business that was much more scalable."

In 2006, the U.S. team began to train its sights on office buildings, inking a deal to take CarrAmerica private for $5.6 billion and a $1.8 billion deal for much of Trizec. Those deals convinced Gray and the two other partners who worked on them, Frank Cohen and Kenneth Caplan, then thirty-two and thirty-three, respectively, that most publicly owned office companies managed their buildings to keep them full so they could maintain steady dividends and didn't hold out for the highest possible rents, which might create temporary vacancies. They had also learned from Carr and Trizec that many publicly traded property companies were valued by the market at less than the sum of their parts. Before it acquired Trizec in October 2006, Blackstone had lined up buyers for thirteen of Trizec's buildings, which it sold for $2.1 billion, earning an instant $300 million gain over its purchase price for the whole company.

Perhaps, Gray thought, Blackstone could now work the same magic on a grander scale with EOP, a company six or seven times the size of Carr. A few days after Kaplan and March had visited Gray, he called back EOP's banker, Douglas Sesler at Merrill Lynch. "What exactly would qualify as a godfather offer?" he asked.

Though EOP's CEO, Richard Kincaid, had been coy when Gray sounded him out about a buyout over lunch in September, Kincaid and Zell in fact felt that the office market was overheating and had begun to think that, if they were going to sell the company, now was the time they could fetch the best price for shareholders.

After consulting with Zell and Kincaid, Sesler got back to Gray. EOP wasn't going to name a price to Gray. "Sam's a trader," Sesler explains. "He's never going to give you his exact number." Instead, Sesler told Gray that any bid would have to be at least $45 a share to get the EOP board's attention.

Blackstone now had a target to shoot for, and Gray, Caplan, and Cohen set to work poring over the detailed tables of properties in EOP's public filings, comparing the data there with information they had gleaned from owning CarrAmerica and Trizec to see if they could justify a price over $45.

Gray was jittery about the bid. Not only would it be by far the biggest he had executed; it would be the largest LBO ever, and he was looking at writing a check for $3.5 billion or more, the most Blackstone had ever risked in a single deal. The firm's buyout group was already nervous that prices for corporations were getting out of hand and had begun to pull back, and Gray had the same concerns about real estate. If this was going to work, everything—the bid itself, the choreography of the asset sales, and the swift reduction of EOP's debt after the buyout—had to be executed perfectly. It would be disastrous if Blackstone paid top dollar and then found itself stuck with overpriced assets it couldn't unload.

For reassurance, Gray put in a call to Alan Leventhal, the head of the real estate investment firm Beacon Capital Partners, who had been a mentor and sounding board over the years. Leventhal had a pet theory that he had expounded to Gray in the past, and Gray wanted to hear it again. Leventhal's view was that, in the best markets, where it was hard to build new offices, you would make money over the long run if you bought buildings below their replacement cost, because prices had a natural tendency to rise where the supply couldn't expand much. Gray didn't tell Leventhal what he had in mind. He simply asked Leventhal to walk him through the theory again. Leventhal happily launched into a speech about how an explosive rise in construction costs on the coasts made it a good time to invest, even though building prices had been shooting up.

"He gave me a pep talk. It was like a revival meeting," Gray says. "In life, sometimes you need a little confidence booster when you're thinking about risking your entire career."

By November 2, Gray's team was ready to make a preliminary bid. Gray called Sesler, EOP's banker, to say that Blackstone was prepared to offer $47.50 a share, or about $35.6 billion, including the value of EOP's debt. Five days later, Blackstone signed a confidentiality agreement with EOP allowing it access to EOP's internal books, which revealed rents, when leases expired, who the tenants were, and other information that wasn't public. With that information, Gray could project how much additional income might be squeezed out of the buildings as space came off lease and was relet at higher prices.

The Blackstone team mobilized dozens of in-house analysts and outside lawyers to comb the data in a blitz, which confirmed the surmises that Cohen and Caplan had made from EOP's public reports to shareholders. The deal was viable. Six days later, on November 13, Blackstone put a formal $47.50 proposal on the table. EOP held out for an extra dollar, which would raise the total value to $36 billion. Blackstone soon agreed.

Zell drove a hard bargain on a technical issue, too: the breakup fee that EOP would have to pay Blackstone if it opted to accept a higher bid. Zell was adamant that the deal have a low breakup fee so that other bidders would not be deterred from making offers. (A company that trumps the original deal with a higher offer effectively must absorb the breakup fee, because the target's value is reduced by the amount of the fee it pays out.) EOP's directors had not shopped the company around because they were worried that word would leak out, but they had fiduciary duties to their shareholders to try to get the best price. If they were going to sign a deal with Blackstone without inviting other bids up front, the cost of getting out of that agreement had to be cheap.

Breakup fees are meant to reward the first bidder for putting in the work to formulate a bid—a sort of token of appreciation for the loser. Typically they run 2–3 percent of the total value of the target's stock. Gray grudgingly agreed to a $200 million fee, or just 1 percent of EOP's market capitalization—not high enough to deter a serious bidder. The takeover agreement was wrapped up on Sunday, November 19.

Financing the EOP deal proved to be a cinch. It took Blackstone just five days to round up $29.5 billion in debt financing from Bear Stearns, Bank of America, and Goldman Sachs. As with Freescale, the terms on the loans were extraordinarily easy. In addition to the debt, the banks agreed to invest several billion dollars in equity, which Blackstone would repay at a small premium when it sold EOP assets. The banks would earn a return on that temporary equity, but they also bore part of the risk if the sales fell through and EOP ended up stuck with too much debt. Also, as it had with Freescale, Blackstone made sure none of EOP's new debt would fall due before 2012, giving EOP latitude if there were a downturn.

In size the deal would handily outstrip the $31.3 billion KKR paid for RJR Nabisco in 1989, and the $33 billion KKR had just agreed to pay for the hospital operator HCA. The unassuming, publicity-shy Gray was not only on top of the real estate world but was breaking records in private equity set by none other than Henry Kravis.

But he didn't have EOP locked up yet.

Blackstone was offering just a small 8.5 percent premium to EOP's stock price before the deal was signed, but Zell and Kincaid were happy because they were convinced that real estate values were peaking. Zell, always the trader, was content just to lock in the price for shareholders, including himself. "We thought the valuations were, frankly, excessive," Kincaid says.

Moreover, Zell and Kincaid knew something Blackstone did not: Zell's old friend Steven Roth, who had built Vornado Realty Trust into a major rival of EOP's, had approached Zell that summer about buying EOP. That was why Zell had insisted on a low breakup fee. He hoped that the Blackstone agreement would simply serve as the opening salvo in a bidding war.

A deal between Vornado and EOP would have been a personal as well as business proposition for Zell and Roth, who enjoyed a close, if quirky, friendship. They and their wives regularly dined together, and the two got a kick out of skewering each other publicly. At one real estate conference where they shared the stage, Roth called Zell a "bald-headed chicken fucker." Roth, whose own bare pate has been compared to Mr. Clean's, was poking fun at himself as much as at Zell. "I like Steve very much, and he likes me very much," Zell says.

Like Zell, Roth had started off down-market, raising money to develop strip malls in New Jersey, and had cut his teeth early on distressed property. He won control of Vornado through a proxy contest in 1980, when the company was an air-conditioner maker and retailer, shut its stores, and then rented out the space. In 1992, he and other creditors of the ailing Alexander's department store in New York forced the company into bankruptcy. Vornado kept Alexander's prime property next to Bloomingdale's department store on New York's Upper East Side, which Roth later developed into the headquarters for Bloomberg LP, the news and financial information firm owned by New York City mayor Michael Bloomberg.

As EOP had hoped, on November 24 Vornado's president, Michael Fascitelli, contacted EOP's banker, Doug Sesler at Merrill Lynch, to say Vornado was considering an offer. Yet, bizarrely, EOP would hear nothing more from Vornado for weeks. Zell grew alarmed. He had read newspaper reports about a Department of Justice investigation of possible collusion among buyout firms in bidding wars and began to wonder if Blackstone was freezing out competitors. When Gray arranged a get-to-know-you meeting with Zell over coffee one day when Zell was passing through New York, he found himself on the receiving end of a tirade from Zell, whom he hardly knew. For the sake of his career, Zell told Gray, he better not be doing anything to stifle rival bids. "No fucking around," Zell told him, employing "a lot of colorful language," as Zell recalls it. "The clear, unequivocal point" was to scare Gray, Zell freely admits. (Nothing ever came of the government investigation.)

The rant rattled Gray, who cultivated a reputation of rectitude, but it did nothing to elicit an offer from Vornado. Finally, in mid-December, Zell called Roth and asked, "Where the hell are you?" Roth confided that he had been tied up in unsuccessful talks with a potential bidding partner. Several more weeks passed without word from Vornado until on January 8, 2007, seven weeks after the Blackstone–EOP agreement was announced, Fascitelli rang Sesler to say that Vornado wouldn't bid for EOP after all. Instead, Vornado wanted to speak to Blackstone about buying specific properties. It looked like Blackstone had EOP to itself.

A week later, on January 15, Vornado did an about-face. Fascitelli called to say that Vornado was again weighing a takeover bid. By the morning of the seventeenth, the markets were rife with rumors that Vornado would soon unveil an offer and Zell banged out an e-mail to his friend: "Dear Stevie: / Roses are red / violets are blue / I heard a rumor / Is it true? / Love and kisses, / Sam."

The Vornado side was amused but flummoxed. None of Vornado's executives or bankers or lawyers could come up with a clever rhyme. Finally, Roth made a lame stab at e-mail poetry: "Sam how are you? / The rumor is true / I do love you / And the price is $52."

Zell had his auction. "We were obviously thrilled," says Kincaid.

The joy soon was tempered when Zell, Kincaid, and the EOP team saw the details of the proposal, which was backed by two other investors, Starwood Capital Group Global and Walton Street Capital. Zell and Kincaid had made it abundantly clear that they wanted a cash bid because they were convinced that real estate stocks, like property itself, were topping out. If they sold EOP for Vornado shares and the stock fell, EOP's shareholders wouldn't have locked in the peak-of-the-market price.

Vornado's $38 billion offer, though, was 40 percent in stock. Moreover it was nonbinding, and Vornado had not yet lined up debt financing, as Blackstone had when it signed its deal. To make matters worse, Vornado demanded that EOP sell off assets Vornado didn't want before the deal closed. Finally, for legal reasons, Vornado's own shareholders would have to approve the deal, and it was far from certain that they would agree to Vornado's borrowing more money and issuing so many new shares. Even if it had been a binding offer, there were so many conditions that it was far from a sure thing. It was really just a sketch of a possible deal, and not a very appealing sketch at that.

EOP's management made the best of it they could. "Of course, we immediately went back to Blackstone and said it was terrific," Zell says.

Vornado's posture was understandable. Vornado's market capitalization was only slightly bigger than EOP's, and it would have had to borrow a lot of money to make an all-cash bid, which likely would have knocked down its stock price. Its stock was trading at an all-time high, and at a much higher earnings multiple than EOP's, so it had every reason to prefer to pay with stock. But Zell had been clear with Roth the previous summer and was clear in his own mind. He wanted cash and only cash.

"You know how when you're in a discussion with your spouse?" says one person who was involved in the talks about Roth's bid. "Sometimes you hear what you want to hear."

Zell hadn't managed to ignite the bidding war he expected, but another one was heating up at Blackstone, where the phones were ringing off the hooks. Everyone in the commercial property business was clamoring to pry loose a piece of EOP. Gray and Frank Cohen were caught off guard shortly after the deal was announced when they had lunch with a property mogul who unexpectedly began to quiz them about what they would sell. None of the men had notepaper. They had to summon a waiter and borrow his order pad to jot down a list of the cities.

The inquiries and offers vindicated Blackstone's bet that it could off-load assets to finance the buyout. The flood of calls also made it clear to Gray's team that they could sell much more than the one-third or so of EOP's square footage they had projected. The godfather bids it was receiving for the buildings would make it possible to raise Blackstone's offer for EOP if it needed to.

It turned out that it soon would. Just as Blackstone had been forced to boost its bid for Freescale a few months earlier to preempt a firm offer from KKR and Silver Lake, Blackstone found itself under pressure to lift its offer for EOP even though there was no other binding bid from Vornado on the table. EOP's share price had risen past Blackstone's $48.50 offer, which meant some investors had paid more than that for their stock and wouldn't want to sell at a loss into Blackstone's offer. Blackstone was now bidding against market expectations as much as against Vornado.

The solution was to firm up the offers Blackstone was receiving for EOP's buildings so it could elevate its offer for EOP. To do so, Gray needed permission to share EOP's internal financial information with the real estate firms that wanted pieces of EOP. EOP quickly gave it.

Just as in Freescale, Blackstone had the jump on the competition because it had the support of the target's board and had had access to the target's internal financial information for months. Vornado had neither, and Blackstone would have to exploit its advantage. Gray's group launched a hectic round of talks, negotiating with real estate firms by day and then convening at night to deal with the EOP side of the deal. It quickly became clear that Blackstone would have to sell far more than the one-third of EOP it had planned, but the lofty offers Blackstone was fielding were nearly impossible to refuse.

The decisive factor was a jaw-dropping bid from Harry Macklowe, a New York office baron, who offered to buy most of EOP's New York buildings for $6.6 billion, a cap rate of between 3 and 3.5. That was equivalent to a cash-flow multiple of 29 to 33—well into nosebleed territory. Macklowe would have to pay more than 3.5 percent interest on the loans to buy the buildings, so he was guaranteed to lose money at least in the short run. It made sense only if he could sharply boost the rents he collected or if the buildings were destined to rise in value.

The New York portfolio was one of EOP's jewels, and one of the chief lures to Blackstone in the first place, but Macklowe's offer was irresistible. The $6.6 billion would go a long way toward Gray's goal of owning the rump of EOP for far less than its current value. He was now ready to offer EOP a bit more.

On January 22, Blackstone's bankers told EOP that Blackstone would pay $53.50 a share—a $5 boost over the price they had agreed on in November—provided EOP would increase the breakup fee to $700 million, or 3 percent of EOP's market capitalization. EOP's board held out for more, and eventually Blackstone agreed to $54 a share and settled for just a $500 million breakup fee. At that level, the fee amounted to $1.40 per share, effectively raising the cost to Vornado by that much.

Now it was crucial to keep pressing hard toward the EOP shareholder vote on February 5, just eleven days away, because Vornado was still posing questions to Kincaid and EOP's advisers. "We had a big timing advantage," says Brian Stadler, one of the two lead lawyers at Simpson Thacher & Barlett on the deal for Blackstone. "We wanted to keep the momentum."

When the *Chicago Tribune* reported January 31 that Vornado was going to bid $58.50—$4.50 more than Blackstone—the Blackstone team feared that, notwithstanding their push, the game was over. "That was the low point for us," Gray says. But Vornado's next proposal, once again, fell short of its advance billing. Bidding solo now, Vornado offered just $56 a share, and it lowered the cash portion to 55 percent from 60 percent.

To Zell and Kincaid, this was not really an improvement, and in some ways was worse than the disappointing January 17 proposal. Roth and Fascitelli seemed to be haggling as they might with another real estate firm over a building sale. They didn't seem to realize they were dealing with the board of a public company that had to have a compelling offer to present to shareholders.

For the moment, Blackstone stood pat and didn't up the ante. But

EOP's shares continued to rise in anticipation of another round of bidding, and neither Gray nor the EOP executives were confident that shareholders would go for its $54 offer.

On Super Bowl Sunday, February 1, on the eve of the EOP shareholder vote, Gray was at home in Manhattan glued to the TV as his hometown team, the Chicago Bears, faced off against the Indianapolis Colts. He had just watched the Bears' Devin Hester run back the opening kickoff for a ninety-two-yard touchdown when word came that Vornado had made another offer. Within minutes Gray and his fellow Chicagoan, Kincaid at EOP, were commiserating about the interruption to the game. "Can you believe this?" Gray said to Kincaid. They would miss the rest of the big game trying to figure out what Vornado was up to.

As it turned out, the offer was less dramatic than the runback. Vornado had stayed at $56 but offered to buy up to 55 percent of EOP's outstanding shares in advance of Vornado's shareholder vote. That would guarantee EOP's shareholders some cash immediately, but there was a downside: If Vornado's own shareholders voted down the full merger, Vornado would win control of EOP without paying for the whole company, and EOP's investors would be left as minority shareholders. What's more, even this offer was not legally binding; Vornado was free to back out.

Vornado's nickel-and-diming played into Blackstone's hands. "We hoped that Vornado's final bid for EOP would be flawed—riddled with conditions, not legally binding, not all cash—and it was," says James. "When Vornado's proposal was announced, we said, 'Aha! We could really put a stake through the heart of it.' They gave us that opening by their weak half measure and we took it."

Gray huddled with Schwarzman and James. Blackstone had already been forced to come up 11 percent from its original $48.50 offer in the fall, to $54. Did it make sense to increase its offer again, particularly when the Vornado bid seemed so unattractive? Time and again in Blackstone's internal meetings, Schwarzman invoked the memory of KKR's overpaying for RJR Nabisco. "We don't want another RJR," he would tell Gray.

"We talked about putting the firm's reputation at risk in so big a deal," Gray said. "If we had overpaid and the deal had gone spectacularly badly, we could have really hurt a franchise that took twenty years to build." But the offers for EOP properties were so high that the leftovers would end up costing Blackstone less than they would have at the original, November price, Gray demonstrated to Schwarzman and James.

Blackstone went back to EOP and offered another $1.25, or $55.25 a share. EOP's board pushed for an extra 25 cents, and the deal was struck at $55.50, with the breakup fee lifted to $720 million. The buyout would now be worth $38.7 billion, topping RJR Nabisco by an even wider margin than the original deal would have.

Vornado folded. Two days after the shareholder vote, which had been postponed to February 7, Blackstone owned EOP.

Gray's team had no time for a victory dinner. Gray's wife, Mindy, came to his office with a double magnum of Veuve Clicquot and a box of chocolate-covered raisins. The weary deal makers spent ten minutes toasting their accomplishment before turning to the daunting task of finalizing $19 billion of property sales they had in the pipeline. The biggest piece was already done: Macklowe's $6.6 billion deal for most of EOP's New York portfolio closed with the main buyout. A $6.4 billion sale of the Washington and Seattle holdings to Beacon Capital—the company headed by Alan Leventhal, whose theories of replacement value had inspired Gray—was nearly in the bag. But EOP emerged from the buyout with $32 billion in debt and the $3.5 billion of equity bridge financing, and knowing how torrid the market was, Gray sensed he had only a small window to sell off what he didn't want to get those numbers down.

From February to June, Blackstone unloaded sixty-one million of EOP's roughly one hundred million in square footage for about $28 billion and was left holding only properties in prime markets. The prices it received were so extraordinary that its effective cost for the remainder was far below their market value. With the benefit of leverage, Blackstone's $3.5 billion equity investment was worth about $7 billion when the sales were complete. It had doubled its money on paper simply by breaking up EOP.

Having pulled off by far the biggest deal Blackstone had ever attempted, Gray, Cohen, and Caplan could now turn their attention back to Hilton, the company they had been wooing on and off before EOP consumed all their energies.

CHAPTER 22

Going Public—Very Public

I'm not going to get beat twice," Schwarzman promised Michael Puglisi, Blackstone's longtime chief financial officer, after KKR raised a $5 billion investment pool on the Amsterdam stock exchange in May 2006.

That offering demonstrated that public investors were hungry to buy into private equity, but KKR's success in soaking up all the demand for such funds in Europe and preempting the field stung. Behind the scenes, amid the frenzied bidding for NXP, Freescale, Clear Channel, and Equity Office Properties, Schwarzman and James began crafting their response. This would be an even more groundbreaking deal: an IPO of Blackstone itself.

By 2006 the rivalry between Schwarzman and Henry Kravis had passed into legend—perhaps even myth. Was it a deeply personal mano a mano thing? Or just a run-of-the-mill testosterone-charged competition between Wall Street chieftains—Coke versus Pepsi with a financial twist? It was clear there was no love lost between them, and no professional camaraderie, but there were partisans of each who claimed their man didn't give the other much thought and that any melodrama was a creation of the press. After all, their firms collaborated on some of the largest buyouts of the decade, including the data company SunGard, the TV ratings firm VNU/Nielsen, and TDC, Denmark's telephone company, and they had teamed up for the unsuccessful bid for Clear Channel.

The two men were certainly different in background, temperament, and tastes. Kravis, who had grown up wealthy, was only three years older than Schwarzman but had a decade's head start in the buyout business and was already fabulously wealthy in his own right by the early eighties, when Schwarzman was a little-known banker at Lehman. KKR's deals had made Kravis an A-list celebrity in the eighties, and with his second wife, the fashion designer Caroline Roehm, on his arm, he had gained entrée to New York's elite social circles. He had worked the charity circuit for decades and his third wife, Marie-Josée Drouin, a Canadian economist and TV personality, made a name for herself hosting dinner parties sprinkled with intellectuals. Kravis seemed comfortable with his position and had retreated from the public eye after the 1980s. Schwarzman still had something to prove.

One didn't have to scratch hard to see the antipathy. Schwarzman never missed a chance to put down KKR, as he did when he called it "a one-trick pony" to *BusinessWeek*, and he conspicuously neglected to invite Kravis to his birthday party in 2007. While it was hard at times to distinguish between what was a genuine blood feud and what was simply good newspaper copy, there was nonetheless more than a bit of truth to the quip of someone who knows them both that "the psychodynamics of Steve and Henry drove an entire industry."

The notion that a major private equity firm would soon go public was in the air by early 2006. The previous December, Art Peponis, a banker at Goldman Sachs, had floated the idea with Schwarzman, but Peponis had tossed out a possible valuation of just $7.5 billion, far less than what Schwarzman had in mind, so that discussion went nowhere.

By the spring of 2006, a chorus of bankers was serenading Blackstone with the same tune, and with the momentum of buyouts building and in the wake of the KKR Amsterdam fund-raising, the value the market would put on a business like Blackstone was rising. Michael Klein, a senior Citigroup banker whose job it was to liaise with buyout firms, brought it up with Schwarzman over lunch at Schwarzman's weekend home in the Hamptons. Klein didn't know how profitable Blackstone was, but he knew that it had roughly $70 billion in assets under management and was in the best niches of the alternative asset management business. It collected both its steady 1.5 percent management fee plus 20 percent of the profits on its biggest funds, buyouts and real estate, and the investors in those committed their money for up to ten years; they couldn't cut and run like mutual fund or hedge fund investors if the firm had a rough year or two. "It made them decisively more valuable than hedge funds," Klein says. As a rough number, he suggested to Schwarzman that Blackstone might be worth upward of $20 billion—a figure that was much more to Schwarzman's liking.

James meanwhile was batting around the same ideas in more detail, with three senior bankers from Morgan Stanley: Ruth Porat, Edward Pick, and Michael Wise. In five brainstorming sessions in May 2006, they debated the merits both of raising a fund like KKR's and of Blackstone itself going public. The benefits of an IPO were clear enough. It would raise money for the firm and allow partners to "monetize" their stakes—turn them into cash. James pressed the bankers instead to focus on the downsides to going public. Jotting prodigiously on yellow notepads, with a can of Diet Dr Pepper invariably at his side, James conducted a Socratic interrogation of the trio.

"Please tell us how bad this could be?" was the thrust, says Porat, Morgan Stanley's head banker for financial services clients at the time and later the bank's chief financial officer.

An IPO would make sense only if the price were right, but there was no way James and Schwarzman were going to open up Blackstone's books to Morgan Stanley—not even to Porat, whom James had known for twenty years and had once tried to recruit to DLJ. No one outside the firm—not even rank-and-file Blackstone partners—knew what the firm as a whole made. And Morgan Stanley was a competitor in private equity, real estate investing, and merger advice. James's solution was to give Morgan Stanley some theoretical numbers. "We told them they would be disguised" but representative of the business, James explains. "Then we created a fictional set of numbers that reflected trends, mix, and margins but did not give absolute levels." Based on the valuations the bankers came back with, Blackstone would get a sense of what it might be worth without tipping its financial hand. From Morgan Stanley's response, James could see that they would end up not far off Klein's $20 billion figure.

Porat heard nothing back after the last meeting and thought perhaps James had cooled on the whole idea. In fact, she and her team had been so enthusiastic about the prospects that in early June, Schwarzman and James summoned Blackstone's CFO, Puglisi, and Robert Friedman, its general counsel, and asked them to figure out what needed to be done to prep the firm to go public.

Schwarzman laid out a couple of conditions. Control of Blackstone would have to remain with him and management. He didn't want to upset the system of benign dictatorship that had gotten the firm to this point and had suppressed internal rivalries. ("You have to understand where they came from—Lehman," says Puglisi.) Second, the IPO would have to be engineered to retain employees and not to provide a means for them to cash out and walk away. However the IPO was structured, it also had to be done in a way that didn't subject Blackstone to corporate taxes. (Blackstone was organized as a partnership and partnerships generally don't pay corporate taxes. Instead, their partners pay income tax on their respective shares of the partnership's profits.)

The top-secret project was dubbed Project Puma, an echo of Project Panther, the aborted bid to list a fund in Amsterdam. Only this small band and a handful of outside advisers would be let in on it. "I was fixated on confidentiality, in large part because I wasn't completely sure I wanted to do this. I wanted to make sure that virtually no one at the firm knew," Schwarzman says. "I didn't want to raise expectations. It could be a diversion." Joshua Ford Bonnie, a young IPO specialist at Simpson Thacher, Blackstone's law firm, was brought in to work on the legal issues, and Deloitte & Touche, Blackstone's audit firm, was consulted. But Blackstone required each individual outside lawyer, accountant, and banker to sign a personal confidentiality agreement—a virtually unprecedented demand. Other partners, even Peterson, would not learn about the plan for months.

There was no small irony in the move to take Blackstone public at a time when the firm was playing a starring role in a sweeping privatization of American and European business. But there were powerful reasons for Blackstone itself to move in the opposite direction. While its partners spent their days trying to devise ways to sell the assets Blackstone owned at a profit, they had no way of capturing the value in the business they had built. The issue was particularly acute for Peterson, who turned eighty in 2006. Under his original 1985 agreement with Schwarzman, if one of them died, his estate was entitled to receive income from the firm only for five to seven years; he could not pass on his stake in the firm to heirs, let alone sell it. Allowing the public to buy in would provide a route for Peterson to cash out and would help the firm ease out a founder who was de facto retired even though he shared fifty-fifty voting power with Schwarzman in its core businesses and continued to collect a sizable chunk of their profits.

Getting Blackstone into some form that could be taken public entailed a herculean effort by the lawyers and accountants. To begin with, there was no one Blackstone. The "firm" was a cluster of a hundred or so partnerships and corporations and funds with contractual ties and overlapping management and ownership but no single parent company whose shares could be sold to the public. Control was complicated, too. Peterson and Schwarzman alone had voting rights in the buyout and M&A businesses. They divvied up the profits to the partners in those groups and consulted them, but the other partners had no legal right to a say in management. By contrast, the managers of the real estate arm—including its founder, John Schreiber, who was not even a Blackstone partner or employee—controlled half of the voting rights for that business, with Blackstone holding the other half. To go public, Blackstone would have to create a single entity—and ultimately two entities—at the top of the corporate pyramid.

The restructuring posed a thicket of tax, regulatory, accounting, and governance barriers through which Blackstone had to navigate. The firm wanted to list on the New York Stock Exchange, but it did not want to submit to the exchange's rules giving shareholders the right to nominate, elect, and depose directors. On the regulatory front, Blackstone had to be an operating business that took a hands-on role in managing its holdings so that it would not fall under the onerous regulations governing passive stock market investors such as mutual fund managers. But for tax purposes, Blackstone wanted to be treated as a passive fund collecting income so it could avoid paying federal corporate taxes.

Going public also raised profound intangible issues: Would it alter the firm's culture and change the incentives for management? Would Blackstone over time concentrate more on producing predictable short-term profits for shareholders instead of bigger, but less predictable, long-term gains for the investors in its funds?

Schwarzman and James had many qualms about going public, but they knew that if Goldman, Citi, and Morgan Stanley had talked to them about it, bankers would assuredly be knocking on the doors at KKR, TPG, Apollo, and Carlyle as well.

"If we don't do it, someone else will" was the consensus around the table at the first Project Puma meetings, Puglisi recalls. "If someone else does it, everyone will have to follow. That's the law of Wall Street."

"There was an expectation that all the dominoes would fall," says Morgan Stanley's Porat.

Moreover, there were huge benefits to going public. Not only would it allow Peterson, Schwarzman, and other partners to sell down their stakes and diversify their wealth. It would give the firm "acquisition currency"—stock with which it could buy other businesses and lure talent. With stock it could afford to add much larger new businesses than it could if it had to pay in cash or with an illiquid ownership stake in Blackstone. That advantage would soon be demonstrated with GSO Capital, a debt fund manager formed by former colleagues of James's from DLJ. In January 2008, after the IPO, Blackstone agreed to buy GSO, which managed $10 billion in assets, paying for it largely with stock.

James also saw other, less obvious payoffs. Unlike most of their counterparts at other private equity houses, Blackstone's partners became fully vested in their profit stakes the day an investment was made. If they left the firm the next day, they would still collect their share of any gains when a company was sold years later. An IPO would allow the firm to create incentives for people to stay for the long haul. Under the plan that emerged, partners would receive their new stock in the company over eight years, forfeiting what they hadn't yet received if they left sooner.

James also saw going public as a chance to break down the silos in the organization—the tendency of its units to operate in isolation. Instead of just being paid a share of the profits from their own units, partners would now be awarded stakes in the entire enterprise, binding them together economically.

Still, the prospect of being public was daunting. "Everyone was a bit ambivalent," says James. "Do we want to live in a fishbowl? Do we want to disclose net worth and private compensation? This was a fundamentally different kind of decision" than raising a new fund on the stock market as KKR had.

To pull off an IPO, management would have to satisfy a multitude of constituencies: the investors in its existing funds (who might worry that the firm's priorities would be altered), the partners (whose financial interests would be completely restructured), as well as potential public investors. "A couple of times a week, Steve and I would sit down and say, 'Do we really want to do this?'" says James.

For all his concerns, James was convinced that it made sense for the firm, and acted, in Puglisi's words, as "the coach and quarterback" of the effort. Schwarzman, who would make the final call, reserved judgment through the fall and winter. "I didn't invest myself personally," Schwarzman says. Although he was involved in the discussions throughout, he "wanted to stay objective to make a balanced decision once all the facts were in."

Like prosecutor and judge, James would make the case and Schwarzman would take it under submission.

By the end of the summer of 2006, the lawyers at Simpson Thacher had drafted a plan to reform Blackstone as a master limited partnership, a structure commonly used for oil and investment partnerships. The public investors would be limited partners, or unit holders, and the partnership would be managed by a second partnership owned by Blackstone's existing partners. In this form, Blackstone would pay no corporate taxes and the public unit holders would have few rights. They would have no vote on directors, for instance, and it would be very difficult for them to dislodge management.

There was just one problem. Partners would have to swap their share of future profits for equity in the unified Blackstone. To do that would involve estimating the future gains on each investment, because partners had joined at different times and thus were entitled to different slices of the pie. Projecting future investment profits would be a dicey and a monumental exercise, and one potentially fraught with politics since individual partners might argue that the investments in which they had a stake were more promising than others.

James devised an end run around the difficulty. Partners would keep their stakes in most existing investments, and the public company would own only the profits on the most recent investments and those made after the IPO. This bypassed the need to predict the success of older investments, but there was a catch: The firm would have few if any investment profits in the first few years after the IPO, as it would take time for current investments to ripen and be harvested.

The solution was a new accounting rule, Financial Accounting Standard 159, which allowed firms in some circumstances to book income based on projections of future profits. Each quarter, Blackstone would appraise each investment in its portfolio, based on cash flows and values for similar businesses, and using complex financial models, it would calculate the present value of the carried interest—its 20 percent of the profit—that it was likely to collect down the road. It would be a stupendous feat of theorizing and speculation, but the new accounting rules seemed to authorize it. James did much of the number crunching himself to put the plan together.

By October 11, he had mustered enough information that he called Porat and told her he wanted Morgan Stanley to begin work in earnest on an IPO. One of the bank's primary tasks was to estimate more precisely what price Blackstone could command in the market. This was no small challenge. Investors and stock analysts typically look to comparable companies, but there weren't any public private equity firms that truly compared. In Britain there was 3i Group plc, but it was smaller and focused on midsized, not large, companies. Then there was Onex Corporation in Canada, but like 3i, it invested heavily in its own funds, so that buying its shares amounted to taking a stake in an investment fund whose profits and value could oscillate, rather than a piece of a fund manager, whose income and value tended to be more steady. Moreover, Blackstone wasn't just a private equity firm. It had its M&A and restructuring businesses, and its hedge fund-of-funds business.

None of the normal measures for assessing stocks worked well either. Assets under management—the benchmark for mutual fund companies and many other money management firms that derive their income from fixed management fees—wasn't an apt measure for Blackstone, because two-thirds of its profits in 2006 were investment gains. Likewise, price-earnings multiples, a standard benchmark for stocks, were pretty much meaningless because Blackstone's earnings took unconventional forms and fluctuated so widely quarter to quarter. It would take some ingenuity, then, to make the case for any valuation of the business.

Project Puma got an unexpected boost in November 2006 when Fortress Investment Group, a smaller private equity and hedge fund manager, filed papers to go public. Fortress had adopted a parallel legal structure and its business was similar enough to Blackstone's that it would be a useful trial balloon to gauge which way the market winds were blowing.

Through the late fall and winter, the lawyers and accountants ground away on the particulars. By January 2007 the planning was far enough along that Schwarzman finally met with Peterson to inform him of the IPO and to discuss the delicate issue of reducing his stake. It was a measure of how marginalized Peterson had become that six months of groundwork had been laid before he was made aware.

Though Peterson stood to gain the most from the IPO because he would be able to sell part of his stake, he wasn't keen on the project.

"I had run a public company, so I knew a lot about what public companies were about," Peterson says. "Steve and I must have had a two-hour discussion one day and I said, 'Look, I'm about to retire and, while I have the power [under the founders' agreement] to block it, I'm not going to do that. But I am going to insist that you have really thought this thing through. And I'm going to tell you how being public is very different from being private. You're used to the privacy of your compensation and all your arrangements and so forth. You're used to privacy in your private life. You as a CEO will become a center point or lightning rod and you'll have to become beholden to a board of directors. You're going to have to be meeting endlessly with equity analysts, [making] investor telephone calls, spending an enormous amount of time. If there happen to be any public problems, you're going to be the focal point.'"

By then the process was gaining momentum, and Blackstone was ready to bring in a second bank because the offering would be too big for Morgan Stanley to market single-handedly.

Adding bankers was more than an exercise in spreading the risk. It was also a division of spoils. The IPO would yield $246 million in fees and commissions for its underwriters, and every major investment bank would want a piece of the action. The first bone was thrown to Michael Klein, the Citi banker who had first floated the $20 billion valuation figure the spring before over lunch with Schwarzman. In January, Schwarzman chose Citi to colead the IPO with Morgan Stanley.

James summoned a team of Citi's capital markets bankers to Blackstone's headquarters on the evening of January 15, the Monday of the Martin Luther King Jr. holiday weekend, to let them in on the plans and to sign up Citi as an underwriter. Schwarzman and James were still so obsessed with secrecy that they didn't tell Morgan Stanley that Citi had been hired, or vice versa, for several weeks. As leads, each bank would be responsible for selling 20 percent of the shares, but Morgan Stanley would receive a bigger part of the fees because its bankers had labored for months laying the foundation.

As the IPO date drew close, Blackstone repaid favors to other banks that had backed its investments, adding Credit Suisse, Lehman Brothers, and Merrill Lynch & Co., each of which got a 14 percent slice. Deutsche Bank, which had financed many of Blackstone's LBOs but did not have the retail brokerage network needed to market large blocks of shares like those in Blackstone's offering, was tacked on at the end, after complaining about being left out. It was allocated just 5 percent of the stock and appeared one symbolic line further down in the list of banks on the cover page.

While the IPO preparations were moving ahead in secret, Blackstone was everywhere in the public eye in the first months of 2007. Jon Gray's real estate team was waging an all-out war for Equity Office Properties in January and February, and in Britain, Blackstone, KKR, TPG, and CVC Capital Partners were pursuing a closely watched $22 billion bid for J Sainsbury plc, one of the country's leading supermarket chains— a deal that, had it come to pass, would have set a new buyout record for Europe.

Meanwhile, Schwarzman had gone on the conference circuit and had become something of a quote-meister. That January at the World Economic Forum in Davos, Switzerland, the annual conclave of business, financial, and political leaders from around the globe, he expounded on how executives dreaded the headaches of managing a public company. The CEO of an unnamed $125 billion corporation, he told the audience, was tired of the hassles of answering to the public markets and said to him, "Geez, I wish you could buy us, but we're too big."

It was Schwarzman's sixtieth birthday party on February 13 that elevated him from being one more Wall Street bigwig to a symbol. It transformed him into a cliché for the age and a punching bag. The scale of the bash stunned even jaded Wall Streeters, and to the man in the street the extravagance reinforced every negative stereotype of financiers. It was the reality version of *Bonfire of the Vanities,* and the press had a field day, for the event encapsulated the power and wealth of private equity and of the small band of men who controlled its biggest firms.

The potential political fallout from the party worried Henry Silverman, the ex-Blackstone partner who had left to run Cendant. He says he bluntly asked Schwarzman, "Why would you do this?" Silverman was involved in a business group that lobbied in Washington and he knew that there were people in Congress who were looking at ways to raise taxes on hedge fund and private equity partners. "I said to Steve, 'This is a very bad idea because these guys read the newspapers, also.'"

It wasn't just the party. In the month that followed, Schwarzman continued on what seemed from the outside like an orgy of self-promotion. Just a week after the party, a cover story in *Fortune* dubbed him "the New King of Wall Street." Arms crossed, poker-faced, in his trademark blue-striped shirt with white collar and a navy pinstripe suit, Schwarzman looked every inch the Master of the Universe. "Steve Schwarzman of Blackstone wants to buy your company and has a $125 billion war chest to do it," the subhead read. A few weeks later, on March 16, Schwarzman showed up on CNBC in a lengthy interview with the network's glamorous anchor Maria Bartiromo.

Some of the press coverage was a fluke. *Fortune* had compiled a package of stories about private equity and whipped out the profile of Schwarzman at the last minute, without his knowledge, relying on a stock photo for the cover. But in the wake of the party, the exposure had made Schwarzman the very public face of the high-rolling world of leveraged buyouts.

Going into February, Schwarzman still hadn't given the final go-ahead for the IPO. "The very last thing we wanted to do was file the papers to go public and then change our minds," James says. "You get all the negatives of being public and none of the positives." They didn't want to launch an IPO "until we were absolutely sure we could complete it."

When Fortress went public on February 9, it became clear that Blackstone's plan was viable. Fortress priced its shares at $18.50, at the top of the estimated range, and they more than doubled on their first day of trading, hitting $38 at one point.

"Not only did they get public, but they got public with great success—with great fanfare and a great valuation," says James.

Now there was a sense of urgency, for Schwarzman and James had learned that KKR had designs to go public and there were rumblings that TPG had sought out bankers for advice. They also were concerned that the window of opportunity might slam shut. "Steve and I both instinctively felt that the public markets are inherently flighty," says James.

The publicity from the steadily escalating wave of buyouts unveiled that spring was bound to help, conveying that private equity was on a tear. On February 26, KKR and TPG announced they would buy TXU Corporation, a Texas electricity and gas utility, for $48 billion, eclipsing the record Blackstone had set just weeks earlier when it closed the buyout of Equity Office Properties. Three days later, KKR clinched the largest LBO ever in Europe, an $18.5 billion takeover of the publicly traded drug store chain Alliance Boots plc.

By then, a number of other partners had been consulted about Blackstone's IPO or had caught wind of it, but Schwarzman and James still hadn't officially informed rank-and-file partners when CNBC broke the news on TV on March 16 that Blackstone would soon file offering papers—the first leak since the planning had begun more than nine months earlier. Three days later Schwarzman and James convened partners in the thirty-first-floor conference room at Blackstone's headquarters, with partners in other offices beamed in on video monitors, to explain the IPO and the restructuring that would precede it.

On March 22, Blackstone made it official, lodging a draft prospectus with the Securities and Exchange Commission for an offering that could raise up to $4 billion. The 363-page document was long on words but short on the kinds of juicy details others really wanted to know, such as how much Peterson, Schwarzman, and James made and what their stakes in the firm were. (Under SEC rules, details like that do not have to be disclosed until later in the months-long process of going public.)

The thirty-three pages of financial statements were exceedingly opaque, if not perverse. A summary showed $2.3 billion of net income—profit in lay terms—but just $1.12 billion in revenue. How could that be? It made more than it took in? One had to burrow twenty-nine pages into the financials to find a line showing $1.55 billion in investment gains that fell outside the definition of "revenue."

Once the prospectus was on file, the SEC's "quiet period" rules kicked in and Schwarzman and others at the firm were barred from giving interviews. It should have been smoother sailing, but the project instead lurched forward and back as a succession of out-of-the-blue events caught Schwarzman, James, and the rest of Blackstone off guard.

The first was utterly fortuitous. Through friends, Antony Leung, the newly hired head of the firm's Asian operations and Hong Kong's former finance minister, contacted the managers of a new Chinese government sovereign wealth fund that was being formed to invest the billions of surplus dollars China was accumulating because of its yawning trade deficit with the West. Leung had in mind that the fund might buy a few Blackstone shares, but the managers of the new fund, later named China Investment Corporation, or CIC, instead expressed interest in buying a major stake.

Schwarzman wasn't sure at first if the offer was worth the potential complication and delay of negotiating a side deal, but the Chinese offered to invest $3 billion and their terms turned out to be simple. All they wanted was the chance to buy in without paying the investment banks' fees and commissions. They didn't seek any special access to information beforehand or a seat on Blackstone's board, and they agreed to keep the stake under 10 percent so that the investment didn't have to go through a national security review in the United States. In addition, their shares would be nonvoting.

On May 20, barely three weeks after Leung first spoke to CIC's head, Lou Jiwei, on April 30, a deal was signed for CIC to invest through a subsidiary optimistically named Beijing Wonderful Investments, Ltd. One person familiar with CIC calculated that in those three weeks of talks China accumulated $15 billion in new reserves and so he figured that its managers were just too busy putting out their money to haggle.

For Blackstone, the investment was a huge coup. The firm was several years behind competitors like Carlyle, KKR, and TPG developing its business in Asia. Now it had won the imprimatur of the Chinese government without any real strings attached, a link that promised to give it the inside track on many investment opportunities in China. The investment solved another problem as well: how to cash out Peterson. Up to then, the banks had figured that $4 billion was toward the upper limit of what Blackstone could raise in the IPO based on investor demand, and much of that money would go into the firm's coffers rather than partners' pockets. With the additional $3 billion from the Chinese, Blackstone would be able to sell 75 percent more shares than it had first planned, enough to allow Peterson and other partners to sell much bigger portions of their holdings. Now Blackstone would sell nearly $7.6 billion of stock and almost $4.6 billion of that would go to partners.

In exchange for Peterson's selling a higher proportion of his stake than other partners, James asked him to cut his equity stake ahead of the IPO. Peterson's son, a banker, negotiated the terms, and after some back and forth, they agreed he would give up 15 percent of his holding.

"I said I wanted to be able to look my partners in the eye," Peterson says. "What I get in liquidity they don't get." After he unloaded shares in the IPO, Peterson's stake in the firm would drop to 4.2 percent, and he confirmed that he would formally retire from Blackstone at the end of 2008. Schwarzman would be left with 23.3 percent, James with 4.9 percent.

The other surprises were not as auspicious as the Chinese overture.

While Blackstone was negotiating with the Chinese, the staff at the SEC, which vets prospectuses and the financial statements in them, was raising objections to Blackstone's quirky method of booking income based on projections of future profits. Blackstone's bankers had never been enthusiastic about the idea, because they thought it would be hard to explain to investors. Now the regulators thought it was too clever by half and threatened to nix the idea. Just when the hard work of getting the initial IPO prospectus on file, with all the financials, was complete, James was forced to go back to the drawing board and rethink both the accounting and the restructuring of the firm. Once again doing much of the math himself, he came up with a new scheme in which partners would exchange their shares of the profits on past investments for more equity in the new entity—the tricky swap he had tried to avoid originally. Ultimately the firm used a formula based on the average multiple of its money it had earned on its investments historically. The arrangement was clear and fair enough that partners went along, and on May 21, when the prospectus was next amended, it contained revamped financial statements. On page 83, the document mentioned in passing that Blackstone would not rely on the new accounting rules after all.

That was a headache, but another problem brewing in Washington threatened to derail the IPO altogether.

Private equity had long enjoyed two big tax advantages. First, its companies can deduct the interest on their debt, which gives them an advantage over companies that finance themselves with a higher portion of equity. Second, because most of the money that the partners in private equity firms make takes the form of carried interest—their 20 percent share of any investment gains—most of their income is taxed as capital gains. Instead of paying the top rate in the United States of 35 percent for high earners, buyout executives paid the 15 percent capital gains rate on most of their income. Similar rules apply in Britain, so that in both countries private equity kingpins, as one British investment fund manager pointedly put it, pay lower tax rates than their cleaning ladies.

On top of those long-standing tax traditions, Fortress and Blackstone were taking advantage of tax laws used originally for oil and gas and investment partnerships to avoid corporate taxes when they went public.

Off and on over the previous year, various senators and congressmen had brought up the idea of altering the treatment of carried interest for private equity and hedge fund managers. The press was filled with stories of hedge fund gurus who made more than $1 billion in 2006, and Fortress had revealed during its IPO that its three founders, Wesley Edens, Peter Briger Jr., and Michael Novogratz, and two other senior managers had received $1.7 billion from their firm shortly before Fortress's IPO.

The capital gains advantage was not unique to private equity or hedge funds. It stemmed from general principles of tax and partnership law and the gaping differential between the tax rates on ordinary income and capital gains. Carried interest by definition consists of investment profits, which are capital gains for tax purposes, and partnership law allows profits to be allocated to different classes of partners as the partnership chooses. In many family and other businesses organized as partnerships, for instance, managers receive a bigger share of the profits—whether ordinary income or capital gains—than the passive owner-partners, regardless of whether the managers invested their own capital. The same thing is true of many real estate investment partnerships. Changing the law for private equity and hedge fund managers thus would have required creating an ad hoc law targeting them or a much larger revamping of the tax code.

Still, it seemed unfair. How could the richest of the rich pay tax at the lowest possible rate? Even former U.S. treasury secretary and former Goldman Sachs cochairman Robert Rubin argued that carried interest was essentially compensation and should be taxed as ordinary income. From a political standpoint, too, raising taxes on a bunch of wealthy private equity and hedge fund managers was tempting because it would raise revenue and placate voters resentful of the huge profits being earned by financiers.

The political situation for private equity was only exacerbated by a string of deals in the hospital and nursing home industries by KKR, Carlyle, and others. The Service Employees International Union, a feisty group that had been working to unionize that sector, saw a chance to win concessions from the new owners by holding a political hammer over their heads, and it threw its support behind the tax reform effort. In May, SEIU officials charged before Congress that private equity treated employees badly and would put nursing home residents at risk. A few days later, the larger American Federation of Labor–Congress of Industrial Organizations joined the antibuyout chorus, dropping a thirteen-page letter on the SEC arguing that Blackstone came under the Investment Company Act of 1940, which governs pure investment funds.

Though the pressure tactics from unions were a powerful goad, the catalysts that spurred Congress to action were Schwarzman's birthday gala and the looming Blackstone IPO, say people who followed the congressional discussions.

"It was Steve's party," says Henry Silverman, "because they were getting pressure from their constituents—'Look at these fat cats and look at the way they're living their lives!'" Senator Max Baucus, who was behind one of the proposals, had a particular antipathy toward Schwarzman, people on the industry side say.

The political forces all converged the week of June 11, just as Blackstone's senior management was dispersing around the globe for the IPO road show, to woo investors in person.

As it happened, June 11 was the day that Blackstone finally revealed Schwarzman's pay: $398.3 million in 2006 alone. The figure was mind-boggling. It was nine times what Lloyd Blankfein, Schwarzman's counterpart at Goldman Sachs, made that year in cash and stock, though Goldman had thirty times as many employees and was universally acknowledged to be the most successful firm on Wall Street. Schwarzman's pay was twice what the top five executives at Goldman together took home. It attested to the profits private equity was churning out and revealed how rich Schwarzman had become owing to his nearly 30 percent stake in Blackstone.

That by itself might not have fanned the political fires much more, but a front-page profile of Schwarzman in the *Wall Street Journal* two days later made him the poster child for the campaign to sock the new barons of finance.

A cascade of headlines made the story an irresistible read: "Buyout Mogul—How Blackstone's Chief Became $7 Billion Man; Schwarzman Says He's Worth Every Penny; $400 for Stone Crabs," and Schwarzman obliged the *Journal* with quotes conforming to every stereotype of the financial shark.

"I want war—not a series of skirmishes," he was quoted as saying. "I always think about what will kill off the other bidder. . . . I didn't get to be successful by letting people hurt Blackstone or me." Nor was it just his competitors he treated mercilessly. The article implied that he was nasty to the help as well.

Once, while sunning by the pool at his 11,000-square-foot home in Palm Beach, Fla., he complained to Jean-Pierre Zeugin, his executive chef and estate manager, that an employee wasn't

wearing the proper black shoes with his uniform, according to
Mr. Zeugin, who says he has great admiration for his boss. Mr.
Schwarzman explains that he found the squeak of the rubber
soles distracting.

The *Journal* portrayed him as a Marie Antoinette, nonchalantly
spending hundreds of dollars on a casual lunch at his mansion:

He expects lunches consisting of cold soup, a cold entrée such as
lobster salad or fresh grilled tuna on salad, followed by dessert,
Mr. Zeugin says. He eats the three-course meal within 15 minutes, the chef says. Mr. Zeugin says he often spends $3,000 for a
weekend of food for Mr. Schwarzman and his wife, including
stone crabs that cost $400, or $40 per claw. (Mr. Schwarzman
says he had no idea how much the crabs cost.)

Like the *Fortune* cover, the *Journal* piece came out of the blue. The
interviews had been conducted months earlier, before the IPO plans
were disclosed, and Blackstone assumed the story was dead. Now it surfaced at the worst possible moment.

The next day, Thursday, June 14, two senators, Baucus, a Democrat
from Montana, and Charles Grassley, a Republican from Iowa, targeted
the legal structures that Fortress and Blackstone were using to escape
corporate taxes. Under their measure, any partnership that went public
after January 1, 2007, would be taxed as a corporation. In practice,
that meant Fortress and Blackstone, because the measure grandfathered
in firms that had gone public earlier, and it quickly became known as
the Blackstone Tax. It would have taken a big bite out of Fortress's and
Blackstone's profits, and Fortress's shares dropped more than 6 percent
the following day. It was now open season on Blackstone and the rest
of the buyout industry.

The evening Baucus and Grassley announced their proposal, as
James waited at Kennedy airport in New York for an overnight flight to
London for the next leg of the road show, Schwarzman caught up with

him by phone. Should they call the whole thing off? To them, it seemed the entire world was lining up against the IPO. Drained from a week of numbing back-to-back, dawn-to-dusk presentations, the two pondered what to do. The firm's lobbyists were assuring them that no bill was likely to pass soon, so they decided to press on.

They were in the home stretch now, just a week away from going public, but they would encounter ever more bizarre problems.

Early Saturday morning, when James arrived in Kuwait for meetings, he was in pain, those around him could see. He was whisked off to a hospital where tests confirmed he had a kidney stone. He was urged to stay in the hospital but returned to lead the presentations in Kuwait and more later that day in Saudi Arabia.

When the news got back to New York, the IPO team was alarmed. "I'm now going to speak to you like a mom," Ruth Porat told James when she tracked him down by phone at the hospital. "What are you doing going to road shows!"

Schwarzman got into the act, calling David Blitzer in London. "Blitz, Tony won't admit this, but he's really sick," Schwarzman told him. "He'd shoot me for saying this, but you need to get on a plane right now." Blitzer caught the first flight out, arriving in Dubai in time to kick off the meetings scheduled there Sunday morning. No sooner were they under way than James walked in. "I did start a meeting or two without him, but he showed up straight from the hospital and just plugged his way straight through, as only Tony can do," says Blitzer.

After one last day of meetings Monday, the exhausted troupe boarded a chartered corporate jet for the return to London only to confront one last, alarming hiccup. An hour or so into the flight, the plane suddenly dropped sharply—enough to wake up the dozing passengers. A few minutes later, the pilot came back into the cabin. "I don't want to panic you," he began, and then went on to explain that the plane had lost an engine. In ordinary circumstances, the pilot said, he would land at the nearest airport, but they were in Iranian airspace and it was the middle of the night. He thought they could reach Athens on one engine, but he left it to James and Blitzer to decide what to do. They called

Schwarzman and, after debating their choices, decided that it would be tempting fate for top executives of a pillar of American capitalism to make an unscheduled landing in Iran in the middle of the night. They told the pilot to try for Athens.

They made it there in the wee hours, and after boarding a replacement plane that had been sent for them, they headed for London, touching down as the sun was coming up. There was just enough time for James to dash to an 8:00 A.M. meeting with investors at Claridge's, the posh Mayfair hotel that Blackstone had once owned.

Back Stateside, the political bombardment continued. On Wednesday, June 20, Peter Welch, a Democratic congressman from Vermont, offered a bill to tax fund managers' carried interest as ordinary income rather than as capital gains. The next day, as Blackstone and its banks were finalizing the price for its shares, two new congressional hand grenades were lobbed at them. Democratic representatives Henry Waxman of California and Dennis Kucinich of Ohio wrote the SEC asking it to halt the IPO, arguing that Blackstone's investments were too risky for ordinary investors. Meanwhile, in a letter to the treasury secretary, the secretary of homeland security, and the chairman of the SEC, Democratic senator James Webb of Virginia demanded that the offering be postponed so that the government could investigate the national security implications of a foreign government taking a "reported" 40 percent stake in Blackstone. Never mind that it was a matter of public record that the Chinese were taking just a 9.9 percent, nonvoting stake.

"Every gun was pointed at us that week, trying to stop this thing," says Jon Gray, who was in Los Angeles that week for the road show and had to be briefed every morning on the latest bombshell from the capital.

The SEC had already signed off on the prospectus, so the last-minute objections came to nothing. By Thursday, June 21, the only thing that remained was to set the price. The banks had earlier estimated they could sell out the offering at $29 to $31 per unit. Around a table in Blackstone's boardroom that afternoon, James asked each of the Morgan Stanley and Citi bankers to write down on a piece of paper the price they would recommend, then reveal their numbers and explain their thinking. The Citi bankers each said $30; the Morgan Stanley bankers had written $31. Schwarzman asked if it might be better to price it at $30. He said he didn't want to be accused of taking every last dime if the stock later fell below the IPO price. But there was so much demand for the issue that the group finally agreed that they could easily sell out several times over at $31, and there was no reason to charge less.

That evening the banks bought the shares from Blackstone and sold them to their customers. The next day, when the new shareholders were free to trade their units on the New York Stock Exchange, the price soared to $38 as investors who hadn't been able to buy shares directly from the underwriters bid up the price. (The price settled back to $35.06 by the end of the day.)

When the accounts were tallied up, Peterson walked away with $1.92 billion and Schwarzman collected $684 million. James, who had been at Blackstone less than five years, pocketed $191 million. Tom Hill, Blackstone's vice-chairman and manager of the hedge fund arm, got $22.9 million and Mike Puglisi, the CFO, $13.8 million. The other fifty-five partners received $1.74 billion, or an average of almost $32 million each.

The offering was not simply a breakthrough for private equity, but was the biggest IPO in the United States in five years, and it put Blackstone squarely in the top tier of Wall Street firms. Blackstone was now worth as much as Lehman Brothers, where Peterson and Schwarzman had launched their banking careers, and a third as much as Goldman Sachs. Blackstone had arrived.

Eleven days later, on July 3, KKR filed to go public, but Kravis's firm was too late. The very day that Blackstone units began trading, Bear Stearns announced that it would lend $3.2 billion to a hedge fund it managed that was facing margin calls as the value of its mortgage-backed securities tumbled, and the bank said it might have to bail out a second, larger hedge fund. It was an omen. By mid-July, the credit markets were in full retreat and it was hard to muster financing for big

LBOs. The growing losses on mortgage securities were unnerving hedge funds and other investors, and buyout debt looked a little too similar, so banks could no longer raise money through CLOs to make buyout loans.

Peterson and Schwarzman had closed Blackstone's first fund on the eve of the market crash of 1987. With the IPO, too, they had sneaked in just under the wire.

CHAPTER 23

What Goes Up Must Come Down

For ten days after Blackstone's IPO, the buyout juggernaut rolled on, seemingly gaining speed. On June 30, a new record was set when BCE, Inc., Canada's biggest phone company, agreed to a $48.5 billion buyout led by the private equity arm of Ontario's teacher pension plan, edging out the $48 billion record KKR and TPG had set four months earlier with TXU, the Texas power company. Days later, on the eve of the July Fourth holiday, after ten months of off-and-on talks, Jon Gray finally cinched his deal to buy Hilton Hotels for $29 billion, Blackstone's second-largest LBO ever after EOP. At the end of that day, as people were filing out of their offices for the holiday, KKR at last filed its papers to go public.

It was a spectacular finale—like the climax of a Fourth of July fireworks—followed by silence. As the fallout from subprime mortgages spread that spring, the larger edifice of debt that had built up over years began to teeter. The floors were creaking and cracks were emerging in the walls, and the markets were spooked. In early June, the spread on junk bonds—the difference between their interest rates and ultrasafe U.S. treasury bonds—fell to its lowest level ever, below 2.5 percentage points, indicating that investors saw little risk in the debt. But then it abruptly switched directions. By mid-August, the spread was nearly 4.6 points, as demand for CLOs evaporated and investors balked at buying debt of highly leveraged companies, particularly when there were few covenants on the loans and bonds and the borrowers could opt to pay interest on bonds by issuing more paper. It was eerily familiar to veterans of the buyout world who had lived through 1989. Risk, which had been virtually banished from the financial lexicon, had returned to the discussion, and now the term "credit crunch" was being bandied about.

There was no single event that triggered the shift, as there had been in 1989, when the collapse of the financing for the employee buyout of United Airlines sent the debt markets tumbling, but the pivot in 2007 was nearly as swift, and just as disastrous for private equity's investment banks as it had been in 1989. As underwriters and loan arrangers, the banks had issued legally binding promises to provide loans to finance dozens of still-to-be-completed LBOs and had assumed the risk of peddling that debt to others.

Until then the buyout boom had been an absolute bonanza for the banks, generating hundreds of millions of dollars each year in investment banking fees. So long as investors were soaking up whatever CLOs the banks could offer, the banks could keep creating and selling those securities, funneling the money into buyout loans and bonds and passing on the risk to outside investors. But suddenly they couldn't sell them at the low interest rates everyone had expected. If a bank had agreed to float 7.5 percent bonds and the market rate was now 10 percent, it would have to sell the bonds at a discount that would yield that higher amount: A $1,000 bond on which the company paid 7.5 percent would have to be discounted to $750 so the buyer would earn a 10 percent yield on its investment. With hundreds of billions of dollars in loan and bond commitments outstanding, selling them at a loss could wipe out years of bank profits. By late June, banks were begging private equity firms to make concessions that would make the debt easier to sell so they wouldn't be saddled with billions of debt they hadn't bargained on holding.

As unsold debt piled up, interest rates spiked and new buyouts halted. The difference between 7.5 percent and 10 percent interest amounted to $25 million a year on every billion dollars of debt, which simply didn't compute in the finely tuned spreadsheets that underlay the deals. Pending deals, too, looked vulnerable. After two years of speculating about which big company would go private next, the financial world was now on death watch, as shareholders and traders bet on which buyouts would come unstuck.

The first LBO to fall victim to the crunch was SLM Corporation, the student loan company better known as Sallie Mae, which alerted share-holders on July 11 that its $25 billion take-private by two private equity firms, J.C. Flowers and Company and Friedman Fleischer & Lowe, and two big banks, JPMorgan Chase and Bank of America, was in jeopardy. The buyers said they were worried about a reduction in federal loan subsidies, but it was widely suspected they had gotten cold feet because of the fact that Sallie Mae borrowed money constantly to buy loans from banks and other lenders and might not be able to do so at afford-able interest rates. After SLM sued, JPMorgan Chase and BofA agreed to help refinance the company in lieu of the buyout and the private eq-uity firms dropped out.

A few weeks after the SLM deal began to unravel, Home Depot, Inc., revealed that it was in talks with Bain Capital, Carlyle, and Clayton Dubilier and would likely have to reduce the $10.3 billion price tag on its wholesale division, HD Supply, which the three sponsors had agreed to buy two months earlier, because of slumping sales. At the end of Au-gust, the price was slashed to $8.8 billion.

Bain Capital and Thomas H. Lee Partners' mammoth $25.5 billion Clear Channel deal was nearly scuppered, too, the next winter. Citi and Deutsche Bank, which had come up with an extra billion of financing in the spring of 2007 so the buyers could increase their offer, later dragged their feet about supplying the money. After the company, Bain and Thomas H. Lee, sued, everyone came back to the table, Clear Channel agreed to lower the buyout price, which reduced the debt needed, and the deal finally closed. In the renegotiations, the private equity firms man-aged to reduce their equity investment to $3 billion, so that in the end the buyout was financed with a meager 13 percent of equity.

Like many financial crises, this one began with a product that was at first benign: the subprime mortgage. There had long been niche players that offered mortgages to buyers with low incomes or poor credit histories, but over the course of the decade, mainstream banks and mortgage companies had moved onto this turf, envisaging millions of new customers. The mortgages paid high interest rates, and banks bundled them into newfangled securities that were then sliced and diced into multiple layers of equity and debt with different interest rates and risks. The most secure, senior tier of debt had first dibs on income from the underlying mortgages and came with insurance in case there was a default, which ensured that they carried strong credit ratings. The whole was supposed to be safer than the sum of the parts—less likely to default than the underlying mortgages were. In fact, the entities that were created to hold the mortgages shouldered so much debt that many layers could be wiped out if things didn't play out precisely according to plan.

The resulting mortgage securities, like the CLOs backed by corporate debt, were so seemingly safe and proved so popular with investors that money flooded into the mortgage companies. To drum up even more business and keep fees rolling in, lenders lowered credit standards so that even more borrowers qualified. Many banks and mortgage companies stopped bothering to verify the borrowers' jobs or income, and they offered adjustable-rate mortgages with such low initial rates that even those with marginal incomes could afford to pay, at least for a while. Other home mortgages had negative amortizations: the buyers' monthly payments were less than the interest owed so that the loan balance rose each month. The optimistic premise behind it all was that housing prices would continue rising and the mortgages could be refinanced a few years later, or the home could be sold at a profit to pay off the loan.

In four short years, the mortgage market was transformed. From 2001 to 2005, subprime lending leaped from 8 percent of all new home mortgages in the United States to 20 percent, and more than 80 percent of mortgages were securitized. It was a house of cards that kept rising until mid-2006, when housing prices crested and began gradually to fall. This coincided with step-ups in the interest rates on adjustable mortgages taken out a year or two earlier, which squeezed many home owners. Meanwhile, thousands of buyers who had lied about their incomes or had never been asked simply stopped paying. By the end of 2006,

10 percent of all subprime loans were in default, throwing all the calculations behind the mortgage-backed securities askew. The defaults first cut into the lower layers, which had to absorb the first losses if defaults exceeded projections. But soon the default rates were so high that they threatened even senior tranches that had top credit ratings and were supposed to be insulated from mortgage defaults. In the cascade of unforeseen consequences, the jump in defaults in turn threatened to bring down the bond insurers that had sold protection on the senior layers, figuring there was a one-in-a-million chance that the damage would ever penetrate that far.

As each month went by, more mortgage companies failed, and several steps down the financial chain, more margin calls were issued to investors who had borrowed to buy mortgage-backed securities that were no longer worth enough to suffice as collateral for the loans. Eventually the elaborately engineered mortgage securities that Wall Street had invented came home to roost, inflicting losses at the source—the banks. There was the collapse of the two Bear Stearns hedge funds the week of Blackstone's IPO in June. The same month Germany's IKB Deutsche Industriebank, which had invested heavily in American subprime securities, had to be bailed out. In Britain, which had seen its own subprime boom, there was a run on the giant British savings bank Northern Rock in September 2007 when it could not sell new debt to fund itself. As newspapers filled with photos of depositors lined up around the block at Northern Rock branches waiting to retrieve their money, the British government finally stepped in.

Until the spring of 2007, there had been a collective sense of denial about the mortgage problems and a persistent hope that they would not spread to other types of debt. But it was hard not to see the parallels to buyout lending—the escalating prices for companies, the extreme leverage, the loose lending terms, and the narrow margins for error. The securitization apparatus that had pumped up the mortgage markets since 2004 had gassed up the LBO market as well, so it was no surprise when the banks, hedge funds, and other investors that were already choking on subprime losses recoiled at taking on more LBO debt.

By the end of the summer, private equity firms, too, were getting skittish, and there was an epidemic of buyer's regret. Buyout firms and their banks—which by then were on the hook for more than $300 billion of LBO financing they couldn't sell—were squirming, looking for excuses to escape the deals they had struck. In some cases, like Home Depot's wholesale subsidiary, where the target's business dropped severely, there were legitimate legal grounds for calling things off or cutting the price. But many times the reasons looked like mere pretexts, and the targets cried foul and sued to try to force the buyers to go through with the deals so that their shareholders would get the benefit of the generous offers. The companies generally lost in court, because the takeover agreements had been drafted to make the buyers liable only for a fixed termination fee if they walked away—typically 2 percent or 3 percent of the deal value. Forking over hundreds of millions of dollars for nothing was a stiff penalty (that was the point), but it was better than being forced to pay a price that, as the economy and the markets headed south, now looked extravagant.

In one notorious case, Apollo was pilloried when it tried to back out of a $10.8 billion agreement to buy Huntsman Corporation, a chemical company in Texas. Huntsman had already agreed to merge with another company when Hexion Specialty Chemicals, a company owned by Apollo, topped that offer in July 2007. Hexion's bid, orchestrated by Apollo, was almost 50 percent higher than Huntsman's share price just a few weeks earlier, before the first merger was announced. In the months that followed, as the price of oil, a key raw material, soared and the economy began to slow, the offer looked like a dreadful miscalculation on Apollo's part, and Hexion sued to get out of the deal, arguing that the merged Hexion–Huntsman would be insolvent because it would carry so much new debt at a time when profits were falling. Huntsman countersued.

Unfortunately for Apollo, Huntsman had negotiated a nearly airtight agreement, which specifically provided that the merger couldn't be called off because of industry-wide problems, and the judge who heard the dispute came down hard on the buyout firm. He ruled that Apollo and Hexion had deliberately breached the agreement and that, consequently, the legal damages would not be limited to the $325 million breakup fee. Facing billions in potential liability, Apollo and Hexion paid $1 billion to Huntsman to settle the case. Credit Suisse and Deutsche Bank, which had sided with Apollo and Hexion, later chipped in another $1.7 billion to settle Huntsman's claims against them for trying to call off the deal.

Blackstone aborted two of its deals. One, to buy the mortgage arm of PHH Corporation, fell apart when the banks financing it said they would not lend as much as they had originally indicated. Blackstone coughed up the $50 million termination fee and walked away.

It had a much harder time extricating itself from its $7.8 billion deal to buy Alliance Data Systems Corporation, a credit card transaction processor. The May 2007 deal—one of the few big LBOs Blackstone's buyout group signed up that year—was delayed by federal bank regulators, who were concerned that a highly leveraged Alliance would not be able to back up its bank subsidiary if the bank got in trouble. They demanded that Blackstone provide more than $600 million in financial guarantees to Alliance's bank operation in case that occurred. But because buyouts are structured legally so that neither the fund nor the private equity firm that manages it is liable for the portfolio company's debt, providing a guarantee was problematic. Blackstone eventually made an unusual offer to have its buyout fund issue a $100 million guarantee, but that didn't satisfy the regulators.

When Blackstone pulled the plug on the buyout in April 2008, Alliance sued, charging that Blackstone hadn't lived up to its obligation to make its best effort to complete the deal. The case was thrown out in 2009 on the grounds that the buyout agreement didn't require Blackstone to provide any guarantees, and the firm got off without having to pay the breakup fee. Still, it was a costly episode. Blackstone had laid out $191 million to buy Alliance shares at $78 a share while the offer was pending, and the stock then slumped. Three years later, its investment was still underwater.

In a coda for the age, the mother of all buyouts, that of the Canadian phone company BCE, was canceled in December 2008, after a year and a half of regulatory and financing delays. The company's auditors took the deal off life support when they said they might not be able to certify the company's solvency, as required. That saved the buyers—the Ontario Teachers' Pension Plan, Providence Equity Partners, Madison Dearborn Partners, and Merrill Lynch's private equity fund—from what might have turned into the biggest private equity blunder ever. KKR and TPG were left holding the dubious record for history's biggest LBO, with TXU.

Whatever the merits of the legal positions, the cancellations and the wrangling took a toll on private equity's reputation. For a decade, private equity had sold itself as the fast and sure solution for sellers. Buyout firms had been pitching themselves as solid corporate citizens, telling companies that it was easier to do business with them than a corporation, where decisions had to filter through committees and boards of directors and sometimes were subject to shareholder approval. They may have won in court when challenged, but the fact was that many of the industry's stars—Apollo, Bain, Blackstone, Carlyle, Cerberus, Clayton Dubilier, Fortress, Goldman Sachs Capital Partners, and KKR—had all bailed out of deals or cut their prices when the going got tough.

CHAPTER 24

Paying the Piper

Market conditions worsened steadily as 2007 dragged on, and buyout firms breathed a sigh of relief every time they wiggled out of a deal. Most of the time, though, they couldn't undo the mistakes they had committed or weren't yet persuaded that they had overpaid. But soon the leverage that magnified returns when the markets were moving up began to work in reverse. The value of private equity–owned companies fell, but the debt on their books remained the same, a combination that threatened to pulverize billions of equity that buyout firms had plowed into their megadeals. It was payback time for an industry that had gorged on the debt it was offered and flagrantly bid up companies, trying to grab as much as it could while the going was good.

The dividend recaps that had yielded such quick, rich profits just a few years earlier caught up with some firms. Apollo had been particularly aggressive about ratcheting up the debt on its companies in order to pay itself dividends, milking a whopping $2 billion from twelve of its companies in late 2006 and 2007. Two of them, Noranda Aluminum Holding Corporation and Metals USA Holdings Corporation, saw their revenues collapse in 2008 and 2009 and ended up short of cash. Blackstone, too, had engineered two large dividend recapitalizations at the top of the market: a $1.1 billion payment from its travel reservations company Travelport after Travelport sold a big piece of Orbitz.com, its online travel website, in an IPO, and a $173 million payout from Health

Markets, a health insurer catering to small businesses and the self-employed. Neither company sank under the added debt, and Travelport in fact held up well in a very difficult market.

Private equity was in nowhere near as much trouble as the banking industry. Many banks, finance companies, and corporations relied on short-term borrowing that had to be refinanced constantly. When the capital markets froze up, institutions such as Bear Stearns, Lehman Brothers, and Merrill Lynch—even the giant Citigroup and the prestigious Morgan Stanley—faced insolvency when their debts came due unless they could find new capital in some other form. By contrast, buyout firms themselves bear essentially no debt, and the financing for their portfolio companies—both the equity and the debt—was safely locked in for years. Furthermore, even the most extreme LBOs were modestly leveraged compared with investment banks, many of which by 2007 were geared thirty to one. At that level, if the value of a bank's assets fell by even one-thirtieth, just 3.3 percent, its capital was wiped out. Compounding matters, the banks were investing their own equity in leveraged investments—baroquely structured mortgage securities, real estate, and LBOs. It was leverage on leverage, which put their thin slivers of equity capital at extreme risk.

Still, as shudders passed through the financial system in 2008 and the economy began to slow, problems accumulated for private equity. By the time Bain Capital and Thomas H. Lee Partners finally closed the Clear Channel buyout in July 2008, two years after trumping Blackstone's bid, advertising at the radio chain was evaporating. A year later, Clear Channel's revenue had fallen by almost a quarter. The company the buyers had labored so hard to acquire, like RJR Nabisco twenty years earlier, began to look like a clunker.

Apollo, which had loaded up on cyclical businesses in 2006 and 2007, was hit particularly hard. In addition to the costly Hexion Chemical debacle, where it lost its court battle to get out of buying Huntsman Corporation, the struggling housewares retailer Linens 'n Things went south on Apollo. The chain was such a shambles when it filed for bankruptcy that it was quickly liquidated. Across Apollo's portfolio, the results were dismal. At least five of its companies saw revenues plunge by 30 percent or more. They included Realogy, Incorporated, which licensed real estate brokerage brands such as Century 21, Coldwell Banker, and Sotheby's and Realogy's counterpart in Britain, Countrywide plc. When housing prices fell and fewer homes were sold, both companies saw franchise fees tumble. Creditors took over Countrywide in 2009.

Another Apollo casualty was Harrah's Entertainment, the casino operator it bought with TPG. Harrahs saw a similar fall-off in revenue—the first time in memory that gambling had declined during a recession. (Blackstone's buyout and real estate funds also took small, 2.5 percent stakes in Harrah's because the firm thought the casino industry was attractive and it had no other investments in the sector.)

In an earlier era, under covenants in the companies' loans, creditors could have stepped in and taken control if the companies' cash flows fell below specified levels. Not this time. The "covenant lite" loans for many of the big LBOs had so few restrictions that there was little bondholders or lenders could do until a company actually ran out of cash and stopped paying. Companies like Freescale and Clear Channel that had pay-in-kind debt had even more flexibility. They could choose to pay their creditors with more paper, as both eventually opted to do—escalating rather than paying down their debt. So long as a company didn't stop paying interest in some form, its day of reckoning would not arrive until 2011 to 2014, when its loans matured, giving its owners several years to turn things around. Blackstone's due dates were fairly typical. Its companies had virtually no debt maturing before 2013, but that year $34 billion was scheduled to come due and would have to be refinanced if the companies hadn't been sold by then.

Even with that latitude, the crunch took its toll. Scores of companies went bust, wiping out their owners' investments.

Cerberus, the vulture debt firm that morphed into a major private equity investor, suffered the most catastrophic and public losses. Cerberus led a consortium that bought 51 percent of General Motors' finance arm, GMAC, in 2006, at a time when GMAC's mortgage lending operation was throwing off $1 billion in profits annually, much of it from subprime lending. Soon that business began to hemorrhage hundreds of millions and nearly brought down the whole company. Then auto sales collapsed. In 2009 GMAC took a government bailout that reduced Cerberus to a 15 percent voting position.

Cerberus's buyout of the automaker Chrysler from its German parent in 2007 was even more disastrous. The investment had mystified most people in the financial and auto worlds, where the company's problems were seen as incurable. No one could understand how Cerberus thought it could turn around the smallest of U.S. automakers or how it could make a profit on it. Even Cerberus's investors were kept in the dark: It refused to share financial information when it raised the $7 billion in equity for the deal and told potential backers they would not receive regular financial reports even after they invested. "It was a blind-faith request—trust us," says one investor who was approached but turned down the chance to join in. The same institutions that invested in buyout funds were demanding the opportunity to invest directly in companies alongside firms like Cerberus and Blackstone, because they then would not have to hand over 20 percent of the profits to the buyout firm as they would if they invested through a fund. With that enticemment, Cerberus had no trouble rounding up the money. When Chrysler went into bankruptcy in 2009, Cerberus and its coinvestors lost almost all their money.

More established buyout firms had investments go down the drain, too. KKR lost Masonite, a building products maker, and Capmark Financial Group, Inc., an $8.8 billion commercial real estate finance firm that it bought from General Motors with Goldman Sach's private equity group, and Aveos Fleet Maintenance, an aircraft maintenance company it owned, went under. KKR also had to invest more equity in a German auto repair chain, the mattress maker Sealy, and in KION, a forklift maker, to prop them up.

Carlyle had five complete LBO wipeouts: Hawaiian Telcom Communications, that state's main phone company, which had had severe operational problems after Carlyle separated it from its former parent in

2005; Edscha AG, a German auto-parts maker; SemGroup LP, an oil transport and storage company that had made bad bets trying to hedge the risk of oil prices; Willcom, Inc., a Japanese wireless phone operator that used a nonstandard technology; and IMO Car Wash Group, Ltd., a British chain of car washes.

TPG lost Aleris International, Inc., an aluminum company it bought in late 2006, to bankruptcy, and suffered a $1.3 billion rubout in Washington Mutual, a wobbly savings bank it tried to shore up.

Thomas H. Lee Partners had a particularly poor track record. On top of its near-death experience with Clear Channel, five of its companies slipped into bankruptcy: an ethanol producer, an air-conditioning equipment maker, a printing and advertising firm, an auto-parts maker, and Simmons Bedding, the mattress maker that had gone through five successive LBOs.

Forstmann Little, KKR's main rival in the eighties, which nearly vanished after it made two massive, disastrous investments in telecoms at the peak of the market a decade earlier, lost one of its last holdings, the radio chain Citadel Broadcasting Corporation, to bankruptcy in December 2009.

In Britain, Terra Firma Capital Partners, one of that country's most high-profile buyout firms, was forced to tap its investors for more money to save its struggling recording company EMI Group, Ltd., and sued Citigroup, which had financed the deal.

In most cases the companies lived on, taken over by their creditors or by new investors. Very few were shut down altogether like Linens 'n Things, but in most cases the buyout owners lost all their money, and the lenders and bondholders often took a haircut as well in the restructuring.

It wasn't just the portfolio companies that were in trouble. In Britain there had long been a handful of publicly traded private equity vehicles like KKR's Amsterdam fund that fed money into conventional LBO partnerships. That structure tripped up two of that country's oldest and largest private equity houses, Candover Investments and Permira, when the credit crisis hit. Rather than keep billions of cash on hand waiting for capital calls from Candover and Permira, the public funds had lines of credit they could use when they had to write a check for a new deal. The system broke down when the market tanked because the value of the feeder funds' assets—their stakes in the buyout funds—dropped and they were receiving no cash back from the funds, so their credit was cut off. They thus could not meet capital calls when Candover and Permira issued them. The collapse throttled Candover, which was forced to sell some holdings and for a while considered winding down. Permira survived but agreed to release all its investors from a portion of their capital calls to relieve pressure on the public fund. Its capital base shrank, and a key source of its funds was drained.

The deals done in the heady days of 2006 and early 2007 inflicted enough harm to last for years, but a string of misgauged bailouts of financial services firms in late 2007 and 2008, made before the financial system bottomed out in early 2009, cost investors billions more. At the time, the turmoil looked to many firms like a terrific opportunity to buy on the cheap, and they leaped at the chance to shore up banks and other destabilized financial businesses. Warburg Pincus sank $800 million into a troubled bond insurer, MBIA, Inc.; Thomas H. Lee Partners and Goldman Sachs Capital Partners agreed to provide MoneyGram International with $1.2 billion after it took big losses on mortgage securities; J.C. Flowers and Company pumped $1.5 billion into Hypo Real Estate AG, a Munich bank that invested in American subprime mortgages; and TPG fronted $1.3 billion of a $7 billion bailout of the savings bank Washington Mutual.

They were too early. When the crisis deepened, much of their bailout capital was lost. MBIA's stock slid from $31 to barely $2, and the Money-Gram deal had to be rejiggered when the company's assets deteriorated. The German government seized Hypo Real Estate, obliterating almost all of Flowers's investment.

The rescue of Washington Mutual that TPG orchestrated was the most costly misjudgment of all. The $1.3 billion TPG invested in April 2008 was completely vaporized five months later when there was a run on the bank and regulators stepped in. It was an uncharacteristic misstep for the veteran turnaround investor David Bonderman, who had made his name originally spearheading a bailout of one of Washington Mutual's predecessor banks in 1988 and who sat on Washington Mutual's board after it absorbed the other bank. Executives at two other private equity firms that sized up Washington Mutual thought it needed $25 billion or $30 billion of new capital to ride out the storm. They were right. With hindsight, TPG underestimated the risk that customers would pull their money out and overestimated the bank's ability to regain its footing.

Even the investments that survived were in many cases now worth far less than what their owners had paid. The paper losses were alarming. One of Blackstone's coinvestors in Freescale wrote its investment down by 85 percent in 2008. KKR wrote off 90 percent of its chip maker, NXP, and its German satellite TV company ProSiebenSat.1 Media. The deal makers who had fought fierce bidding wars two or three years earlier to snare companies now faced the prospect of spending years laboring to keep them afloat and trying to devise a way to eke out even a small profit. It often was hard to see how they could, given the inflated prices they had paid and how steeply market values had fallen. If you paid ten times cash flow for a company, and valuations in its industry then recede to an historical norm of 7.5 times (a common scenario in 2009 and 2010), you would have to lift the company's cash flow by a third just to get back to break-even on your investment. In a protracted and weak economic recovery like the one many people were anticipating, that feat would tax the skills of the ablest corporate executives.

Many buyouts done at the market peak may turn out to be dead money—investments that may not lose money but tie up capital for years because they can't be sold, dragging down returns. TXU, the record-breaking buyout of a utility by KKR and TPG, looked to be such a case. Regulators set TXU's electricity rates based chiefly on the price of natural gas, but the company relied heavily on coal to generate power. It had minted money when gas prices were high relative to coal, but gas prices unexpectedly dropped after the buyout because of new gas discoveries and falling demand, squeezing the utility's profit margins severely. At the same time, electricity usage tumbled as the economy slowed.

By 2009 the company was barely making enough money to cover its expenses, including interest payments, and its outstanding loans and bonds likely exceeded the company's value, extinguishing the value of the equity, at least on paper. Little of the debt would come due before 2014, but the company started to renegotiate and extend its loans and bonds. It appears that it will take years of hard work for the owners just to preserve their investment, let alone make a profit. It could easily go down in the books like RJR Nabisco: the largest deal of its era and the biggest dud. KKR ultimately booked more than 20 percent loss on RJR when it unloaded the last piece of the investment eighteen years after the buyout closed.

In the rosiest scenario for the buyout business, values and cash flows generally will recover over several years. But the longer that takes, the lower the investment returns will be: Selling at a 50 percent profit after two years yields a robust 25 percent return. After five years, it's a mere 10 percent. Returns on most of the megabuyouts that epitomized the boom times are therefore likely to be dismal. Many industry insiders predicted that, collectively, private equity funds raised in the mid-2000s would not break even, performing even worse than funds raised at the end of the 1990s that were invested during the last market high.

The push by some firms like Apollo, KKR, and Carlyle to diversify away from LBOs into other asset classes by launching business development companies and publicly traded debt funds also proved calamitous. A $900 million mortgage debt fund that Carlyle raised on the Amsterdam exchange, shortly after KKR launched its $5 billion equity fund, was leveraged with more than $22 billion of debt and capsized in 2008 when its lenders issued margin calls and seized all its assets. It was a complete wipeout. KKR Financial, a leveraged mortgage and corporate debt vehicle in the United States, had to be propped up by KKR and barely survived. Its shares sank from more than $29 in late 2007 to less than 50 cents in early 2009. Apollo Investment Corporation, the business development company that Apollo created in 2004, beating Blackstone and others to the punch, took huge write-downs. Meanwhile, the shares of KKR Private Equity Investors, the landmark Amsterdam fund, lost more than 90 percent of their value by late 2008.

In addition to the choke hold the faltering economy put on highly lever-aged companies, the buyout industry faced two other crises: Its investors were tapped out, and there was a looming mountain of debt to be refi-nanced beginning in 2011 and 2012.

For a decade, pension funds, endowments, and other institutions had stoked the LBO business by reinvesting their profits back into new funds. When the markets turned, there were no buyers for private equity–backed companies and no demand for IPOs, so there was no way to cash out of investments. The steady profits that had streamed back to inves-tors for years dried up, depriving them of money to recycle back into private equity. Worse still for the investors, the distributions petered out while some of the biggest buyouts, including Hilton, Harrahs, Clear Channel, and TXU, were still pending in late 2007, and they faced the wrenching prospect of having to ante up amounts they couldn't really afford. "By December [2007] distributions basically came to a screech-ing halt, but the capital calls kept coming, which burned a hole in [lim-ited partners'] pockets," says one investor.

Pension funds had to scramble to muster cash to pay retirees, and university endowments told their institutions they had nothing to give. Investors were forced to liquidate stocks and bonds into a falling market, widening the sell-off. California's giant teachers' pension plan, CalSTRS, was so cash-strapped that it pleaded with private equity firms not to call on existing commitments.

The colossal sell-off of stocks and bonds that ensued only com-pounded private equity's fund-raising problems. As investors dumped stocks, bonds, and other liquid assets at fire-sale prices, the value of their overall portfolios sank relative to their private equity holdings, which were valued based on their long-term potential and thus didn't slump as much. As a result, private equity rose as a percentage of the investors' total assets, which threw the investors' asset allocations out of whack. Private equity's investors had to curtail new commitments to buyout funds in order to rebalance their accounts.

Private equity also faced another enormous problem. More than $800 billion of leveraged bank loans and junk bonds were due for refinancing from 2012 to 2014. Even if the economy turned up by then, many companies might still be worth less than the bloated sums paid for them, meaning that there might not be enough collateral to refinance their debt. If not, the equity might be wiped out, and the companies' creditors might seize control. There was a danger, too, even if the companies were worth more than their debts by then, that the debt markets would not have recovered enough to absorb all the scheduled refinancings, in which case there might not be enough credit to go around.

Any way you looked at it, private equity faced a forbidding landscape.

Blackstone was not spared when the financial roof caved in. With no investment profits on the horizon, and fewer new investments in the pipeline, the firm laid off 150 employees at the end of 2008, and its business remained in limbo the next year. As a public company, Blackstone's stock price served as a daily referendum on the firm and its prospects. In February 2009, with the future in doubt, the stock dipped to $3.55, down more than 90 percent from its peak on the triumphant opening day. Peterson felt so badly about the money his assistant and his driver lost on their Blackstone stock that he reimbursed them for their losses.

That month the firm announced that its earnings had dropped so much that it would not pay a dividend for the final quarter of 2008—the dividend that had been a key selling point for the IPO. Schwarzman, who had designed his own compensation to consist almost entirely of investment profits so that his interests would be aligned with those of Blackstone's investors, collected only his base pay of $350,000 in 2008 and 2009—less than one-thousandth of the $398 million he made in 2006.

Its stock price notwithstanding, Blackstone fared better than many competitors. Three years after the credit crisis began, only one of its holdings had gone bankrupt: Freedom Communications, the parent of the *Orange County Register* newspaper, in which it had invested $280 million for a minority stake in 2004. But Blackstone also wrote off its $343 million investment in Financial Guaranty Insurance Company, the bond insurer that had expanded from covering state and local government bonds to riskier mortgage-backed products. FGIC was still in business, but like other bond insurers it faced potentially ruinous claims on securitized investment products it insured. A slew of other investments looked in 2009 like they might end with losses, too: the crafts retailer Michaels Stores, a socks maker, Gold Toe Moretz, and the German plastic films producer Klöckner Pentaplast—all bought in late 2006 or 2007. The $749 million Blackstone invested in 2006 to buy a 4.5 percent stake in Deutsche Telekom, Germany's main phone company, was also deep underwater.

The biggest worry in Blackstone's private equity portfolio was Freescale Semiconductor. Blackstone had rounded up more than $4 billion of the $7.1 billion of equity needed for the deal, including $1.2 billion from its own fund plus a large chunk from its fund's investors. This was the deal Blackstone partner Chip Schorr had nearly sewn up when KKR dropped in a last-minute bid, forcing Blackstone to jack up its offer by $800 million. Blackstone and the three other private equity firms that invested alongside it—Carlyle, Permira, and TPG—knew the semiconductor industry was cyclical and anticipated that business from Motorola, Freescale's biggest customer, would taper off, and they put up 38 percent of the price in equity to keep the company relatively lightly leveraged.

Things quickly veered off course. Motorola's cell phones were eclipsed by competitors' models, and its market share, which peaked at 22 percent in 2006, the year Blackstone signed up the deal, fell to 14 percent in 2007 and just 8 percent in 2008. Simultaneously, Freescale's second-biggest business, selling chips to carmakers, went into free fall.

"In every fund you get one or two deals where literally everything goes wrong. Freescale was that deal in our fund five," says Schwarzman. "The last time something like that happened was HFS [the Ramada and

Howard Johnson franchisor], where we listed all the things that could go wrong and every one of them happened in the first six months: an invasion in the Middle East, oil prices spiking to then-unprecedented levels, the world being thrown into a global recession and, as a result of that, the [franchise] agreement was thrown into default."

Motorola's drastic loss of business "alone would have been problematic," he says, and no one foresaw the downside on the auto-parts side. "The idea that the number of cars manufactured in the United States was going to plunge from 17 million at the top to 8.5 million units annually was unprecedented in my experience. In our lifetimes, I can't remember when volumes went into single digits. A depressed year was twelve million."

In early 2008, barely a year after the Freescale buyout closed, Michel Mayer, the CEO Schorr had cultivated for years, was pushed out by the private equity owners. In 2009 the phone-chip business was reeling so badly that Freescale unwound its supply contracts with Motorola and said it would sell or close the unit. Freescale shuttered plants in Scotland, France, and Japan. Chip sales, which had run $6.4 billion in 2006, the year Blackstone pursued and won the company, nose-dived 45 percent to just $3.5 billion in 2009. In 2009 some of Freescale's bonds traded around 10 cents on the dollar because investors feared a default. The company went into the crisis with large cash reserves and no debt due for several years, and it restructured and bought in debt to ensure it remained solvent. By 2010 chip sales were rising again, and it looked like the company might be out of the woods. But unlike the HFS investment, which after its brush with disaster ultimately proved to be a roaring success, Blackstone will struggle just to recoup what it invested in Freescale.

"The game on a deal of this sort is basically to keep it alive," Schwarzman says. "With all the things that went wrong, this is like a military operation where your platoon is cut off behind enemy lines. You've got to stay alive, you've got to fight your way out, you've got to get reinforcements. If you do that right and you're a wise commander, a lot of your people will live to fight again some other day."

*   *   *

Real estate was also a big concern. Jon Gray had called the market perfectly when he sold off two-thirds of Equity Office Properties' towers in early 2007, but the prospects for commercial real estate had turned so bleak by 2009 that a pall hung over Blackstone's investment.

EOP had proved to be a disaster for the moguls who had bought buildings from Blackstone. Gray's deal had left a trail of carnage across the real estate industry. Harry Macklowe, who paid an unfathomable $6.6 billion for EOP's Manhattan office towers, lost them all a year later when his interim loans came due. By then, the mortgage market was frozen and the properties were worth far less than he had paid, so he was forced to turn them all over to his lenders, along with another trophy property, the General Motors Building on Fifth Avenue in Manhattan, which he had pledged as additional collateral.

The fallout from EOP was felt all across the nation. Brian Maguire, the founder of Maguire Properties, which bought many of EOP's southern California properties, was booted out as CEO after the purchase left the company overextended. Thomas Properties, which acquired EOP's Austin, Texas, portfolio with Lehman Brothers, found itself in a bind when Lehman went bankrupt and couldn't supply some of the financing it had promised. Morgan Stanley's real estate fund handed its lenders the keys to five ex-EOP buildings in San Francisco two years after the bank bought them, and Tishman Speyer Properties defaulted on loans for three towers in Chicago it acquired from Blackstone.

Even the crafty Sam Zell, who had personally pocketed $1 billion selling his EOP shares, came away a loser. He redeployed some of that money in a wildly overleveraged $8.2 billion buyout of Tribune Corporation, the publisher of the *Chicago Tribune* and the *Los Angeles Times,* which went bust in 2008. It was a particularly devastating collapse, for Zell financed the LBO in part with an employee stock ownership plan, and some employees lost both their jobs and their savings.

Because Blackstone received such extravagant offers for the EOP buildings it sold, it ended up paying only half what the properties were worth in 2007, in effect earning a $3.5 billion gain on paper. But with office rents falling and few new leases being written, the rump of EOP was worth far less two years later. There was $3.5 billion of equity on the line—the most Blackstone had ever risked on a single deal. In mid-2010 Blackstone took the first steps to negotiate extensions on EOP's debt so it wouldn't all come due in 2012–14, when so many other companies will be trying to refinance.

An even bigger question mark was Hilton Hotels, in which Blackstone's buyout and real estate funds and co-investors had sunk $5.5 billion of equity. Gray and Michael Chae, who led the deal for the buyout group, saw a chance to capitalize on an underdeveloped brand and turn around a poorly managed company. A year before the Blackstone takeover, Hilton had purchased its sister company, Hilton International, which owned the rights to the Hilton brand overseas. The namesake brand hadn't been fully exploited abroad, and the American company's lower-cost, limited-service brands such as Doubletree, Hilton Garden Inn, and Embassy Suites hadn't been licensed at all overseas. As a result, there was room to expand the business at the same time costs were being trimmed. Under Blackstone, the company franchised fifty thousand new rooms a year in 2008 and 2009, in places like Turkey, southern Italy, and Asia, which lifted cash flow sharply in 2008 and promised to elevate it permanently. Blackstone also moved Hilton's headquarters from pricey Beverly Hills to unglamorous but cheaper suburban Virginia.

But with travel falling off sharply in the recession, Hilton's business suffered badly. The company was in no danger of failing, because Gray had insisted on a financing package that wouldn't trip up the company if there were a downturn. The firm knew from bitter experience how cyclical the hotel business could be. Not only had it narrowly staved off disaster in 1990 at HFS, when travel fell off during the Persian Gulf War and Schwarzman and Henry Silverman had had to fly to Hong Kong to beg for a break from the owner of the Ramada brand. It also had another scare in 2001 with the Savoy hotel chain, when the chain's creditors threatened to foreclose after bookings dried up in the wake of the September 11 attacks.

This time there were no loan covenants, and Hilton had no debt due until late 2013, giving Blackstone six years to make something out of the business. Even so, the recession pounded Hilton and in April 2010, after long negotiations with Hilton's lenders, Hilton underwent a debt restructuring. Blackstone agreed to invest an additional $800 million to prop up the chain, and the banks, which had never been able to syndicate most of the debt from the deal and were stuck holding it, agreed to take a haircut. The accord reduced the $20 billion of debt on Hilton's books to $16 billion.

On top of the slump in travel, Hilton became embroiled in a dispute with one of its biggest competitors, Starwood Hotels & Resorts Worldwide, Inc., which charged that two executives Hilton had hired from Starwood had stolen one hundred thousand Starwood documents and, with the knowledge of Hilton's CEO, used the information to plan a new chain to compete against Starwood. Soon federal prosecutors launched an investigation as well. (Hilton and the executives denied wrongdoing.)

An economic recovery would give Hilton a lift. But the deal certainly was not going as Blackstone had expected.

CHAPTER 25

Value Builders or Quick-Buck Artists?

T he financial crisis called into question everything about private equity—its future, its role in the economy, and its capacity to create value. The business had expanded over three decades in benign economic conditions, with generally rising markets and low interest rates, and that growth plainly owed a lot to the rising economic tide. The debt crisis of the late 1980s and bursting of the equity bubble in the early 2000s were small corrections compared with the global meltdown in 2008 and 2009, which put to the test the industry's claims that it is a catalyst for value creation.

Despite rebranding itself as "private equity," and notwithstanding its attempt to cast itself as a business of corporate craftsmen who create value by reshaping businesses, the buyout industry has never outrun the reputation that stuck to it in the eighties. The image of buyout artists was enshrined then in books like *Barbarians at the Gate* and Oliver Stone's movie *Wall Street*. In the public's mind, they were ruthless job cutters who loot their companies of cash and assets for the sake of short-term profits. Fifteen years after the *Wall Street Journal* won a Pulitzer Prize for its story about the fallout for employees from KKR's restructuring of Safeway, *Business Week* reprised the theme that private equity hurts the businesses it buys. In "Buy It, Strip It, Then Flip It," a 2006 feature about the buyout of Hertz Corporation the year before, the magazine told readers to be wary of buying stock in Hertz's upcoming IPO because the "fast-buck artists" hadn't "been shy about backing up the Brinks truck" to the rental car company, milking it for a $1 billion dividend.

But is it a game of stripping, slashing, and flipping that hurts companies and the economy?

Even if buyouts don't inherently harm companies, do private equity firms actually add value to businesses while they control them? Or are they instead just like other successful equity investors, such as mutual funds or hedge funds, which buy and sell at a profit without altering the businesses in which they invest?

The answer to the first question is clearly no. Private equity as an industry does not harm the economy.

The answer to the second and third is that they do sometimes add fundamental economic value, but a good portion of their profits derive from buying and selling at the right moments and leveraging up to accentuate their gains. But that's no sin.

Despite the persistence of the bogeyman, strip-it-and-flip-it image, it isn't borne out by the facts. Take *Business Week*'s portrayal of the Hertz case.

Hertz was a classic case of an orphan subsidiary crying out for new management when Clayton Dubilier, Carlyle, and Merrill Lynch bought it from Ford Motor Company in December 2005. Ford viewed Hertz as a captive customer for its slow-selling cars and had paid it little attention.

The new owners rethought the way Hertz financed its fleets, saving money by buying more cars outright rather than leasing them, and lowered its borrowing costs by issuing bonds backed by the vehicles instead of unsecured corporate bonds. Under Ford, in the quest for market share, Hertz had opened non-airport rental offices in the United States that lost money. Many were shut. Overhead costs in Europe, which were several times higher than in the United States, were slashed. Employees' suggestions for more efficient cleaning and car return procedures were adopted, and consumers were encouraged to book online or use self-service kiosks, which cut costs. Executive compensation, which had been tied to market share—a factor in opening the money-losing offices— was changed to focus on cash flow and other metrics.

The changes quickly paid off. Hertz's revenue rose 16 percent in the two years after the buyout and cash flow was up 24 percent or 35 percent, depending on which measure you use. The $1 billion dividend that the magazine lambasted the owners for taking was actually no strain on the company, which threw off $3.1 billion in cash that year, and its cash flows were rising. Despite the payment of two dividends, in the two years after the buyout the company paid down more than a half-billion dollars of its debt. The bulk of the improvement took place with only minimal job cuts—barely 2 percent in the first year, despite the office closures. (When home construction slowed in 2007, severely hurting Hertz's large equipment rental businesses, there were bigger cuts. The company ended that year with 9 percent fewer employees than it had at the time of the buyout, but by then the economy was in recession.)

Investors who heeded *Business Week*'s warnings to shun Hertz's IPO lost out, for Hertz's shares nearly doubled in the year and a half after they were offered. When the economy and travel slowed further in 2008, Hertz's stock fared at least as well as its main competitors'. Plainly investors did not see Hertz as hobbled by its LBO.

It pays to be skeptical, then, about the potshots that are routinely aimed at the industry. Many are simply false.

Hertz could be dismissed as an anomaly, but a growing mound of academic research refutes the charge that private equity damages companies for the sake of profiteering.

In a study of 4,701 IPOs in the United States over a twenty-three-year span to 2004, a French business professor commissioned by the European Parliament found that the stocks of private equity–backed companies did better than comparable companies, belying the notion that LBOs leave companies in tatters. It stands to reason. How could a form of investment that relies on selling companies for a profit survive if it systematically damaged the companies it owned? Why would sophisticated buyers like corporations acquire companies from private equity firms if they were known to strip them bare? The oft-repeated suggestion that buyout firms foist their companies on unsuspecting investors in

IPOs likewise makes no sense. Most IPO investors are institutions such as mutual and hedge funds, banks, and insurers, which would have caught on long ago if private equity–owned companies were weak and overpriced. Moreover, buyout firms almost always retain substantial stakes in their companies for years after they have gone public, as Blackstone did with Celanese and TRW, KKR did with Safeway, and Clayton Dubilier did with Hertz, so their profits hinge on sustaining the companies' success over the long haul, not on dumping the stock at an inflated price and hightailing it.

Academic studies also debunk most of the other standard knocks on private equity: that it kills jobs, strips vital assets, and takes a short-sighted view of research and development.

To be sure, buyouts often are followed by job cuts. But companies cut jobs all the time, with or without a takeover, so the test of private equity's impact is how it stacks up against the corporate world at large. The most exhaustive survey of the impact of private equity ownership on employees, which looked at more than forty-five hundred investments from 1980 to 2005, found that private equity–backed companies tended to slash jobs at a slightly higher than average rate in the first two years after a buyout but over time created more jobs than they eliminated. Contrary to what critics say, in the first four years following a buyout, companies owned by private equity firms add new positions at a faster clip than their public-company peers, though the gap then narrows, according to the 2008 study led by Harvard Business School professor Josh Lerner and funded by the nonprofit World Economic Forum of Switzerland. The exception is in manufacturing, where the job growth is on a par with other companies.

As for quick flips, there are relatively few of those. Investments of less than two years accounted for just 12 percent of private equity–backed companies, while 58 percent of the companies were held five years or more. The survey also found that contrary to common wisdom, private equity–owned companies generally don't stint on crucial research and development spending, though they do focus research dollars on core product lines, where the stakes are highest, while deemphasizing more speculative, peripheral research.

There are risks, of course, to leverage, which elevates a company's fixed costs, potentially endangering the business in a slowdown. In every recession since 1990, scores of companies have given way under their LBO debt loads. Still, the overall casualty rate for private equity–owned companies has been remarkably light. The World Economic Forum study found that on average 1.2 percent of private equity–owned companies defaulted each year from 1970 to 2007—a thirty-seven-year span that included three recessions. That was higher than the overall rate for all U.S. companies, which was 0.6 percent, but still low, and it was well below the 1.6 percent for all companies that had bonds outstanding, which is arguably a more comparable pool than the set of all companies. Another study by the credit-rating agency Moody's Investors Service in 2008 found that private equity–owned companies had defaulted at much lower rates than other similarly leveraged companies while the economy was expanding in the mid-2000s. Any way you figure it, only a small fraction of companies that have gone through LBOs have failed. Those that have were often forced to cut jobs, but few of the businesses ceased to exist. Most were simply taken over by other companies, by new investors, or by their creditors. (The latest recession, which has seen defaults spike, could put those comparisons to the test, of course.)

There is little support, then, for the contention that private equity ownership generally harms businesses. But how do buyout firms make their money if not by slashing costs to lift profits? And do they contribute anything to the economy at large in the process, besides generating profits for their investors?

Private equity executives, hoping to share some of the plaudits that venture capitalists garner for funding new technologies, often claim that their firms make their money by making businesses better, creating fundamental economic change that benefits society. David Rubenstein, the cofounder of Carlyle, has gone so far as to pitch yet another rebranding. Private equity should be called "change equity," he has argued. (So far, there don't seem to be many takers.) The boast is that private equity firms do not just make well-chosen, well-timed investments and plump up the gains with some leverage; they have learned how to manage and transform businesses to create lasting improvements.

There are doubters. Even many limited partners and private equity executives are cynical about the source of the profits. "The bulk of the money that's been made in the private equity industry is from declining interest rates, which started in 1982," says the head of one established midsized buyout firm. "The use of leverage and the declining interest rates, I believe, are responsible for 75 percent of the value created in the last twenty-five years."

Academics who have analyzed the nature of the profits, however, have found that leverage contributes a surprisingly small part of investment profits overall. The European Parliament's study of IPOs concluded that while roughly a third of the gains on successful buyouts trace directly to leverage, the rest derive from long-term increases in companies' values. A more detailed study of thirty-two highly successful European buyouts (they had an average internal rate of return of 48 percent) found that just 22 percent of the profits were due to leverage. Another 21 percent resulted from increases in valuation multiples; that is, the multiples of earnings that investors think companies are worth. The remainder, more than half, came from sales growth and profit-margin increases. (The study didn't attempt to break out what portion of the gains in sales, cash flows, and profit margins stemmed from the business cycle—i.e., from buying at the bottom of the market and selling after a rebound.)

The truth is that private equity's profits arise from a mixture of all these factors—leverage and other types of financial engineering, good timing, new corporate strategies, mergers and divestitures, and operational fine-tuning—some of which create more fundamental economic wealth than others. Big private equity has grown not only because debt was plentiful for most of the last twenty-five years, but also because these firms have been adaptable, squeezing profits out by pushing up leverage in good times to pay for dividends, wading in to perform nuts-and-bolts overhauls of underperforming businesses at other points, and when the economy was down, trading the debt of troubled companies and gaining control of others through the bankruptcy process. Private equity firms are nothing if not opportunistic, and their techniques vary with business and market cycles.

Playing market swings doesn't create new wealth in the same way that wringing out inefficiencies, funding research, or repositioning a company to make higher-value products does, but it has produced high returns for pension funds, endowments, and other investors. If LBOs don't tend to hurt businesses, there's no more social harm to this form of ownership and capital structure than there is to a mutual fund that trades public stocks. Moreover, even bottom-fishing in a recession provides capital to companies when it's hard to come by and provides liquidity to sellers when there are few buyers—a different form of economic and social contribution.

It's an overstatement, though, to claim that private equity's profits today come primarily from building better companies. Tony James frequently boasts that two-thirds of Blackstone's gains come from increases in cash flow, implying that the businesses have improved fundamentally under Blackstone. But Blackstone can't take credit for all of that. Perhaps even more than its competitors, Blackstone has made its money investing at troughs in the market, so that a larger share of the financial improvement at its companies can be traced to the business cycle than to operating refinements.

In an internal analysis of its investments through 2005, Blackstone calculated that more than 63 percent of its profits had come from cyclical plays like UCAR, American Axle, Celanese, and Nalco, though less than 23 percent of its capital had been invested in that kind of deal. By contrast, where Blackstone attempted profound transformations of the companies it bought, as it did with Collins & Aikman, Imperial Home Decor, Allied Waste, and the Callahan cable systems in Germany, its record was dismal. Fourteen percent of its capital had gone to such investments, and together they had lost 2 percent of all the capital the firm had deployed over seventeen years.

Even so, Blackstone and other big buyout shops have concluded that the only way they can outperform the stock market over the long haul is to systematically improve the companies they own. Bain Capital, which grew out of the Bain and Company consulting group, was one of the first to take that notion seriously and has the largest staff of experts and seasoned managers assigned to its investments. TPG long ago built a deep team of operational experts because it had a tradition of tackling messy turnaround situations that required a lot of know-how and attention. KKR, too, formed an internal team of managers in 2000 that now numbers forty, and Carlyle built up an inventory of executives on its payroll.

Blackstone was a laggard in that regard and has been playing catch-up since 2004, when it hired James Quella, a former management consultant who had worked at DLJ Merchant Banking, Credit Suisse's private equity business, to set up what resembles a captive consulting firm. Quella's twelve-member team of corporate managers vets companies before Blackstone invests, and its members are often assigned to work with portfolio companies when Blackstone takes over.

That shift toward a more hands-on approach to reshaping portfolio companies can be seen in Celanese and three case studies of other successful Blackstone investments in the mid-2000s. These examples show how much the emphasis has evolved over time from a crude paring of expenses at portfolio companies to laboriously improving their operations and expanding and reorienting them.

Gerresheimer AG

Call it a makeover. That was the gist of Blackstone's strategy for the German packaging company Gerresheimer, which over the course of a decade shed its skin as a glass bottle maker and emerged as a producer of sophisticated, high-margin pharmaceutical containers. The result was one of Blackstone's most profitable deals. In less than four years, it made more than seven times its money.

Some of the credit goes to two prior private equity owners, Investcorp and Chase Manhattan Bank, which rescued the company in 2000 from an ungainly ownership structure. When they bought Gerresheimer it was 51 percent owned by the German industrial and utility company Viag AG, which was preoccupied with its pending merger with another utility company. The balance of Gerresheimer's stock was publicly traded, so management had to answer to public shareholders as well as its parent.

Gerresheimer's CEO, Axel Herberg, a onetime management consultant, had lobbied his bosses at Viag to take Gerresheimer out of the beverage bottle business, where competition was intense and profit margins
were low. To no avail. Viag had scant interest in Gerresheimer and even
less appetite for the painful layoffs the entrepreneurial Herberg felt were
necessary to convert Gerresheimer from a humdrum packaging business
into a much sexier health-care-oriented packager. "We were part of a
German conglomerate," Herberg says. Closing German factories, which
he envisioned, "would have been too much bad news for Viag."

Under Investcorp and Chase, Gerresheimer sold its beverages-
packaging factories and focused instead on specialized products where
there was less competition and the customers were loyal. Plants in Germany and the United States were closed, and a new one with cheaper
labor was opened in Mexico. But the process slowed when the economy
turned down in 2002 and 2003, at a time when the company's owners
had their own distractions. The Investcorp partner who had steered the
deal had left, and Chase had recently merged with J.P. Morgan. "From
their point of view, it was not the time to put more capital into the business," Herberg says, and they began looking for a buyer.

Herberg met with Tony James and Doug Rogers, a Blackstone adviser on health-care investments, in 2003 but it was another year, after a
drawn-out auction, before Lionel Assant of Blackstone's London office
finally inked the $705 million deal. The price was a modest 6.8 times
Gerresheimer's cash flow.

Because quality is crucial to drug makers and packaging is a small
component of the total cost of a drug, Gerresheimer's customers were
unlikely to squeeze it on price. Herberg's goal was to carve out a niche
by offering big drug makers a wide variety of containers and to keep those
customers so happy that they would not shop their business around.
With Blackstone's backing, over the next two years, Herberg aggressively
expanded Gerresheimer's range of pharmaceutical packaging by buying
other businesses. Most of the acquisitions were small—a factory in New
Jersey, three joint ventures in China, a Danish plant—but they added
products such as pre-fillable syringes and specialized plastic containers.

Negotiating privately, without going through auctions, Gerresheimer was able to snap up the assets at low multiples—just four to seven times cash flow. It was the same tactic that conglomerates had used in the 1960s and underlies many "roll-up" investments by private equity firms: Namely, buy assets at low multiples and merge them into a bigger company that will be valued at a higher multiple. Unlike the conglomerates, Gerresheimer was realizing synergies because its purchases were all in the same industry.

In one final, dramatic stroke in early 2007, Herberg arranged to buy the family-owned Wilden AG, which generated sales of more than $300 million a year making inhalers and other products. Wilden's market was increasingly global, but the brothers who ran the business recognized that their company didn't have the wherewithal to compete effectively on a global scale, Herberg says. The deal boosted Gerresheimer's revenues by some 40 percent and broadened its product lines.

That set the stage for Gerresheimer to go public, which it did in May 2007. In the less than two years since Blackstone had bought the company, revenue and cash flow were each up roughly 80 percent and there were 71 percent more employees. Most of the increase stemmed from the acquisitions, but Gerresheimer had also boasted strong organic growth, with sales rising 13 percent and cash flow up 18 percent excluding the new plants and businesses.

The IPO, which raised more than $1.4 billion, was the biggest new issue in Germany so far that year. With the trend lines at Gerresheimer moving so firmly upward, and stock prices rising globally, the company was valued at more than 10 times its 2007 cash flow, almost half again the 6.8-times ratio Blackstone had paid. Blackstone made back almost 5 times its money selling shares in the IPO. When it sold the last of its shares in 2008, it came away with 7.5 times the $116 million it had invested.

Having run the business as a subsidiary of a public conglomerate, under two sets of private equity owners, and as a stand-alone public company, Herberg believes the private equity stage was essential to the transition that created a bigger, more specialized, more profitable company. Gerresheimer couldn't have reached that point as a public company, he says. "If you miss a quarter, you get beaten down immediately. You have more time under private equity so you can take more risk." Contrary to the image of private equity backers as looking for a quick buck (or euro), they actually create wiggle room for managers to execute difficult strategies, he says. "You have long-term financing—six or eight years. You have a lot of stability under private ownership, which is underestimated because all you see is the leverage."

Once the business was more predictable, it made sense for the company to be public. "We're on a different plateau. The value creation by transformation is done," he says, and the company will now grow organically. Its stock performed in line with other German industrial stocks in the year after the IPO.

Merlin Entertainments Group, Ltd.

With Merlin Entertainments, Blackstone did not so much buy a business and reshape it as concoct one from scratch. With a quick succession of acquisitions, it took a small, domestic English aquarium operator and in two years made it into the second-largest amusement park and visitor-attraction operator in the world after the Walt Disney Company. Blackstone's handiwork was the very antithesis of a cost-slashing, asset-stripping scheme.

When Blackstone first eyed Merlin in 2005, it was a British company operating twenty-two Sea Life marine theme parks and the London Dungeon tourist attractions, all but a couple of which were in Britain. Like Gerresheimer, Merlin had an entrepreneurial CEO who had once been shackled by the management of its parent. Nick Varney had been running the business since the late 1990s, when it was owned by Vardon plc, whose core business was health and fitness clubs. He pressed to sell or close some of the smaller Sea Life parks and use the proceeds for capital expenditures on more promising attractions, but his bosses didn't want to forego the parks' cash flow during the time it would take to develop new properties.

"In a [public company] we were the Cinderella's sister in the nest, not getting the [capital expenditures], not getting the attention," Varney recalls. The stock market "was in love with health and fitness and out of love with visitor attractions."

With financial backing from the big British buyout firm Apax Partners, Varney bought the business from Vardon in 1999 and began building new Sea Life sites. The expansion continued when Apax sold the business to Hermes Private Equity, a smaller firm, in 2003. Merlin was still a minnow, with just $27 million of cash flow in 2004, and Varney had his sights set on something grander: the Legoland theme parks, which had been put up for sale by its parent, the Danish toy maker Lego. Hermes couldn't afford to finance the takeover of the much larger Legoland, but it was willing to sell Merlin if a buyer made an attractive offer.

Enter Blackstone, in the person of Joseph Baratta, a young partner in the London office. Blackstone knew the amusement parks industry, having invested in the Six Flags and Universal Orlando theme parks. Across Europe, there were midsized attractions, many owned by private equity firms, but no big operators. The properties were likely to come onto the market, since their owners would one day want to sell, and Baratta saw the chance to create an operator with heft.

Schwarzman and James weren't sure Merlin was big enough to bother with. It was "a tiny, bitty little $50 million equity investment," Baratta explains. ("The equity check was probably less than they usually spend on [deal] fees," jokes Varney.) But with the Legoland assets, there was the chance to create a more diversified and substantial business, and Baratta persuaded Blackstone's investment committee to give him the go-ahead. He began to negotiate simultaneously with both Merlin and the Kristiansen family that controlled Lego, and in back-to-back deals in mid-2005, Blackstone agreed to buy Merlin for about $200 million and then got Legoland for about $450 million. Blackstone stumped up another $100 million in equity to fund the Legoland purchase, and the Kristiansens took a 25 percent stake in the combined business in lieu of cash for part of the price, reducing Merlin and Blackstone's outlay.

In management argot, Legoland was a transformative merger. It made Merlin a substantial player in Continental Europe, and added a mix of indoor Legoland Discovery Centres and outdoor Legoland parks with miniature Lego buildings, roads, and trains, giving Merlin a hedge against northern Europe's fickle weather. "When the sun shone, we didn't do so well [at the indoor sites]," Varney explains. "When it poured with rain, [the outdoor attractions] didn't do so well."

He and Baratta thought Legoland could quickly be made more profitable. It was a strong brand, but its previous owners had seen it in part as a marketing tool for Lego toys and had not managed it aggressively. The parks "attract a very well-heeled crowd, [and] they had underpriced the property," Baratta says. In other words, prices could be raised. Moreover, the management hadn't timed advertising to coincide with improvements at the parks, so the company wasn't reaping the full benefits when it made upgrades.

Two more major acquisitions rounded out Merlin in 2006 and 2007. First, Blackstone invested another $140 million to fund the purchase of Gardaland, a water and theme park on Lake Garda at the base of the Italian Alps near Milan, which brought a sunny outdoor venue. The next year Merlin merged with the Madame Tussauds wax museum chain, which gave it a new chain of internationally known indoor attractions. The former had been owned by an Italian private equity group and the latter by an investment fund run by the government of Dubai.

The Tussauds business, like Legoland, dwarfed Merlin in value, but Baratta hatched a financing scheme to make the deal affordable. Borrowing a page from two other buyouts he'd worked on in the United Kingdom—of the Spirit pubs chain and the NHP/Southern Cross nursing homes—he sold some of the enlarged group's valuable real estate to investors who then leased it back to Merlin. The investors were willing to pay a rich price because they thought the properties would rise in value, and they were glad to lease them at advantageous rates in exchange for the potential appreciation. Selling the real estate at the top of the market, Merlin raised enough to pay the Dubai fund $2 billion in cash. Like the Kristiansen family, the Dubai fund took a 20 percent stake in the merged business rather than cashing out entirely. Merlin's biggest purchase by far was thus self-financed. Blackstone did not have to inject any new equity, retaining a 54 percent stake.

With the Tussauds attractions, by 2008 Merlin had become a major international business, drawing thirty-five million visitors annually and churning off some $300 million a year in cash, fourteen times what it did the year before Blackstone bought it. It had grown from seven hundred employees to more than thirteen thousand, including one thousand hired to fill new jobs stemming from organic growth unrelated to the mergers. Merlin was flourishing, with profits at existing properties ticking up at double-digit rates for ten years, not counting the add-ons.

Varney and Baratta say the company is now poised to generate more growth internally. With "chainable, brandable" attractions like Legoland and Sea Life, new sites can be rolled out at a fraction of the cost of a Disneyland-scale park. And with its big acquisitions under its belt, Merlin set out to expand in the United States, where it was building new Legoland and Sea Life sites. In 2010, it also bought the Cypress Gardens park in Florida, where it planned to create another Legoland. Like Disney's parks, Merlin's are aimed at families, but Merlin's are in or near major urban centers and cater to day visitors, so they are cheaper.

Private equity ownership itself was an essential element in turning Vardon's small-time Sea Life business into a major international company, Varney says. "In terms of the speed and focus of what we've done, you just couldn't do that in the public arena. . . . We could not be where we could be without private equity."

Merlin planned an IPO in early 2010, but called that off when European markets were shaken by worries about Greece's solvency. Instead, Blackstone sold a 20 percent stake to CVC Capital Partners, a big London buyout firm, in a deal that valued Merlin at $3.6 billion. Including the 34 percent stake it retained, Blackstone's original investment was worth three and a half times what it invested.

Travelport, Ltd.

In an era when lean operations are a mantra in the corporate world, there are fewer and fewer companies crying out to have their operations streamlined. The travel reservations company Travelport, Ltd., however, was riddled with the sort of inefficiencies that whet the appetites of private equity investors. Moreover, it threw off a bounty of cash—$554 million in 2006—that could support several billion dollars of LBO debt. In short, it was an ideal LBO candidate.

When Travelport's parent, Cendant Corporation, put Travelport on the block in 2006, Blackstone's Chip Schorr was eager to bid. At Citicorp Venture Capital, where Schorr had worked before Blackstone, he led a 2003 investment in Worldspan Technologies, one of Travelport's chief competitors, and had wrung costs out there. His plan for Travelport called for a similar dose of old-fashioned cost-cutting plus a merger and a spinoff that would produce a bigger but more svelte Travelport.

The deal brought Blackstone full circle with one of its formative investments, for Cendant was the reincarnation of the HFS hotel franchise business Blackstone had owned in the early nineties and was still headed by Henry Silverman, the Blackstone partner whom Prudential had forced to resign in 1991. Through scores of acquisitions, Cendant had morphed into a sprawling franchising and travel business, with brands ranging from Wyndham hotels to the Avis and Budget car rental chains, real estate brokerages such as Coldwell-Banker and Century 21, and Travelport and its online reservations subsidiary, Orbitz.com.

For years, Cendant had quenched the stock market's thirst for relentless and predictable gains in revenues and profits by acquiring scores of companies. Unfortunately, that strategy was sometimes at odds with maximizing the potential of the businesses, because restructuring can stunt revenue, increase expenses, and lead to write-offs that depress earnings in the near term. By 2005, Cendant's buy-buy-buy strategy was no longer paying off in the stock market and Silverman, who had devoted fifteen years to building the empire, concluded that Cendant would be worth more in pieces than as a whole, and the company announced it would split itself into four businesses. When Cendant auctioned Travelport the next year, Blackstone beat out Apollo with a $4.3 billion offer. Blackstone supplied $775 million of the $900 million of equity and Technology Crossover Ventures, a venture capital firm, put up the balance. (Five months after the deal closed, One Equity Partners, the private equity arm of JPMorgan Chase, put in $125 million. Blackstone later lifted its investment to just over $800 million.)

Shortly before the sale, Silverman installed Jeffrey Clarke, a veteran cost slasher, as Travelport's CEO. Clarke had led the integration of Compaq Computer into Hewlett-Packard after the rival PC makers merged in 2002. The twenty-five thousand jobs eliminated yielded more than $3 billion in annual savings and paved the way for HP to later overtake Dell as the world's largest PC maker.

Travelport, which was the product of twenty-two acquisitions in four years, was ripe for Clarke's scalpel, and when the buyout closed in August 2006, Clarke set to work, aided by Patrick Bourke, a veteran technology executive Schorr recruited because of his success chopping expenses at Worldspan under Schorr's old firm. A first wave of cuts zeroed in on obvious excess. The twenty-five data centers Travelport had piled up during the buying jag were whittled to three, resulting in hundreds of employees and contract workers being let go. Other information technology jobs were cut when Clarke dumped hundreds of costly new-product research projects and channeled resources instead to twenty or so projects deemed most critical. Two further moves saved another $60 million a year: Travelport ditched the thousands of dedicated, leased phone lines that it had used to communicate with travel agents and switched to far cheaper Internet links, and it ended an expensive outsourcing contract with IBM to run mainframe computers, replacing them with a network of cheaper server computers it could operate in-house. By the spring of 2007, cash flows were so robust that Travelport borrowed $1.1 billion and paid most of it out as a dividend. With that, Blackstone and Technology Crossover recouped virtually their entire investment seven months after they invested.

As Clarke worked on the internal streamlining, Schorr was out making deals, negotiating to buy Worldspan from its private equity owners and preparing to spin off its Orbitz retail travel website in an IPO. Adding Worldspan would beef up Travelport's core business, catering to travel agents and airlines. Splitting off the consumer-focused Orbitz, which accounted for about 30 percent of revenues, would leave Travelport as a

pure back-end business-to-business enterprise and resolve lurking con-
flicts between the consumer and wholesale sides of its operations. (Orbitz
competes both with Travelport's travel agent customers and with other
travel websites that rely on Travelport's reservations system.)

Worldspan would substantially boost Travelport's market share
among travel agents, particularly in Europe, and Worldspan had better
technology that could be incorporated into Galileo, Travelport's reservation system. The companies also had dovetailing airline customer
bases. Travelport hosted United Airline's data and Worldspan serviced
Delta and Northwest. Together they would vie as an equal against the
two biggest back-office reservations systems at the time, Sabre, which
was number one in the United States, and Amadeus, Europe's market
leader.

A $1.4 billion agreement for Worldspan was sewn up in December
2006, to be paid for almost entirely with new borrowings, and in July
2007, Travelport sold 41 percent of Orbitz to the public, netting $477
million, which it used to pay down debt. Less than a year after the buyout, Travelport was a very different business.

When the Worldspan merger closed in August 2007, a second round
of cuts began as overlaps were eliminated, producing another $195 mil-
lion of savings. By Clarke's tally, Travelport whacked $390 million a
year in operating expenses in the three years after the buyout—a staggering amount. That was 54 percent of its cash flow in 2008, the first
full year after Worldspan was absorbed. Put another way, the cuts together with the addition of Worldspan doubled Travelport's cash flow.

Along the way, there were sixteen hundred layoffs and six hundred
more jobs shed through attrition, but the company also added sixteen
hundred jobs after the buyout, including programmers familiar with the
Linux operating system used by the new servers, who replaced programmers specializing in IBM mainframe computers. The net loss of six hundred jobs amounted to about 10 percent of the Travelport and Worldspan
workforce, excluding Orbitz. The new hires, some of whom were in
Eastern Europe, India, and the Middle East, were generally younger and
lower paid than the ones they replaced.

"Buying and integrating Worldspan has been the biggest single value driver since I've been here," says Clarke. After the synergies from combining the two companies, he figures that Blackstone "in effect bought it for under four times cash flow, so it was a fantastic buy."

Silverman had seen the potential years earlier in Worldspan and had contemplated buying it, but to realize the cost savings, Cendant would have had to take big write-offs, hurting its earnings. "There are a lot of things we might have done [with Travelport] that we, as a public company, could not do," says Silverman. Blackstone, which was focused only on building the long-term value of the company, didn't have to worry about Travelport's booking expenses tied to the makeover that would cripple its share price. Blackstone was thus able to capture the benefits of the restructuring.

Even when it was pummeled by the drop-off in travel in the recession, Travelport spewed off cash—roughly $650 million in 2009. It was therefore able to take advantage of the meltdown in the credit markets and bought in some of its own bonds, with a face value of more than $1 billion, at a bargain-basement price of 46 cents on the dollar, shrinking its total debt to $4 billion. At that level, its cash flow was nearly 2.5 times its cash interest expense, giving it a healthy margin of safety.

Since Blackstone recovered virtually all its investment via the dividend in 2007, anything it collected after would be almost all profit. If Blackstone had sold in the recession in 2009, it might well have doubled its money. As the travel market rebounded and valuations headed up in 2010, the deal was primed to deliver a still greater payoff when Blackstone chooses to sell.

None of these investments was a pure cost-cutting play. In each case, Blackstone spearheaded acquisitions that enlarged and radically reframed the business. Only with Travelport was cost reduction a major element of the strategy, and even there the biggest cuts came when overlaps were eliminated as Worldspan was absorbed.

In fact, none of these three deals fits the simple LBO model. Many other Blackstone investments likewise deviate from the paradigm. When the firm seeded two reinsurance companies after 9/11, those were pure equity plays, without leverage. Other major investments like Kosmos Energy, an oil and gas exploration company Blackstone formed with Warburg Pincus in 2004, and Sithe Global Power, which builds and operates electric power plants, were start-ups. Blackstone's ill-fated investment in the cable TV systems in Germany in 2000 and 2001, too, had more in common with a start-up investment than a standard LBO built upon existing cash flow. The companies were leveraged, but the equity Blackstone and the other backers put in was used to finance the upgrading of their networks so that they could become full-fledged telecom companies offering phone and Internet service as well as cable TV.

The common strand that runs through all these cases is that Blackstone saw the companies through tricky transitions that public-market forces and their prior owners would have made difficult, if not impossible. The CEOs Herberg, Vernay, Silverman, and Clarke, like Celanese's David Weidman, testify to the impediments they faced trying to undertake big changes when their businesses were part of public companies that felt pressure to maintain steady earnings, even if the changes would improve financial performance in the long term. Under private equity owners, the managements were free to look out several years. The investors assumed the risks of making the changes because they controlled the company. As stand-alone businesses, with private equity owners, the companies were able to achieve much more of their potential.

Apart from the pressure public-company executives face from shareholders to deliver fast results, the compensation systems at public companies often fail to create incentives for managers to maximize long-term value. Too often, they make short-term success paramount—the most glaring example being the bonus programs at major banks, which in the years leading up to the financial crisis rewarded bankers and traders for taking huge short-term risks that sank (or nearly sank) the institutions.

The contrast between public-company pay packages and the ones private equity firms install is striking. Under buyout firms, bonuses may be rewarded for increases in cash flow or other benchmarks over the midterm. But the real payoff for managers comes from their equity stakes, and they collect those gains only when companies are sold—a strong inducement for them to focus on improving the companies to make them more attractive to buyers. Moreover, CEOs and other senior managers are usually required to invest money in their companies and not just collect stock or options for free. Hence, they have their own money at risk.

Furthermore, if a manager doesn't measure up, he or she is much more likely to be turfed out quickly because the company's directors are chosen by the owners, not by the CEO, as they often are in practice at big companies, and the executive won't walk away rich. At public companies, too often stock options vest when an executive is fired, so he or she receives a windfall for failing. Private equity firms typically structure the pay packages so that executives forfeit unvested equity, and severance is usually miserly compared with that of public companies—a year or two of base salary at most.

It's hard to measure how much the alignment of interests between managers and shareholders contributes to private equity–owned companies, but it is a crucial component of this alternative form of ownership, particularly when a company needs to chart a new course.

CHAPTER 26

Follow the Money

It was easy to understand why obituaries were written for big private equity. Heading into the second decade of the new century, the business looked to be in a dire, even terminal, state. Some thought it was destined to suffer the same fate that venture capital had in the 2000s, shriveling to a fraction of its former size. Market conditions had eviscerated the buyout business once before, at the end of the eighties. More than eighteen years passed before the records KKR set with the buyouts of Beatrice Foods and RJR Nabisco in 1986 and 1988 were eclipsed, and it wasn't until 2002 that KKR topped its $6.1 billion 1987 fund.

The competitive landscape within private equity is bound to change as limited partners tally up whose portfolios held up and whose suffered unforgivable or catastrophic losses. Apollo, Cerberus, Fortress, Thomas H. Lee Partners, and other firms that miscalculated more often than the rest will face skeptical investors the next time they go to raise money unless they somehow recoup their losses by making smart investments at the bottom of the market.

For all its wounds, though, private equity was weathering the crisis better than other essential suppliers of capital. It emerged with most of its capital intact while commercial and investment banks were hobbled by astronomical losses on mortgage products and derivatives. The buyout funds raised in 2005 to 2007 may end up delivering disappointing returns, just as many funds raised at the peaks of the market at the end of the eighties and nineties did. But the real test for private equity will be how it performs as an asset class against other investments. Notwithstanding the risks of leverage and the private equity–backed companies that went under, private equity funds have beaten the overall average returns at major pension funds over the last three, five, and ten years. For pension managers who need to make up for losses in stocks and real estate in 2007 to 2009, private equity will seem very tempting.

Even without new contributions, though, private equity firms have roughly $500 billion in their coffers at a time when other institutions are struggling to raise capital. The vast reserve ensures that private equity will play a major role as the economy recovers. By late 2009 private equity had started to reemerge, just as it had in 2002 when the economy and markets were still in the dumps after the end of the tech boom and 9/11.

The first signs were a string of distressed debt plays—typically the opening round of a new cycle of investments. Veteran vulture investment firms such as Oaktree Capital Management, Ares Management, and Cerberus were snatching up debt of distressed companies in hopes of gaining control of them. Many of the targets had been owned by buyout firms. Apollo, which made its name as a vulture in the early 1990s picking up the pieces of Drexel-backed companies that got in trouble, quickly joined in the scavenging, snatching control a failing German roofing materials maker, Monier Group, from one of France's biggest private equity shops, PAI Partners. It also teamed up with Ares to buy Aleris, an aluminum company formerly owned by TPG, out of bankruptcy, and partnered with Cerberus and Goldman Sachs to take over the British casino operator Gala Coral Group, which had been owned by three of the biggest British buyout shops, Permira, Candover, and Cinven. But the vulture game works both ways, as Apollo discovered when Ares took control of the former's ailing British real estate brokerage franchiser, Countrywide, by buying up its debt.

In most cases where the vultures descended, the companies continued in business. The owners and vulture creditors were simply fighting over who would lose how much and who would emerge with control—Wall Street at its opportunistic, merciless best.

In addition to the debt plays, beginning at the end of 2008 there was also a trickle of private equity–sponsored bank bailouts. J.C. Flowers and Company, a buyout firm that invests exclusively in financial institutions, and other investors bought a collapsed California mortgage lender, IndyMac, from federal bank regulators. After looking at more than forty institutions, in May 2009 Blackstone joined with Carlyle, Centerbridge Partners (the buyout shop founded by ex-Blackstone partner Mark Gallogly), and turnaround artist Wilbur Ross to buy Florida's BankUnited, another deal orchestrated by the regulators.

Late in 2009, Blackstone began making more conventional investments. It bought the Busch Gardens theme parks for $2.7 billion from the brewer Anheuser-Busch InBev NV, adding more visitor attractions to its portfolio alongside Merlin Entertainment and Universal Orlando. Another of its companies, Pinnacle Foods, which owns well-known brands such as Swanson and Armour meats, bought the Birds Eye frozen-foods business for $1.3 billion. Blackstone's real estate group, meanwhile, came to the rescue of two overstretched commercial property companies, buying a half-interest in the Broadgate office complex in London from British Land and a 60 percent stake in two shopping malls owned by a property firm in Ohio.

Perhaps more important than the new investments for the future of the business were the exits from older investments. The IPO and credit markets reopened just enough beginning in the fall of 2009 that there was a chance again to take some profits after a two-year drought. The first big company out of the gate was Dollar General Corporation, a discount retailer KKR bought in July 2007. KKR made a 150 percent gain on paper, showing that some investments made at the peak of the market could turn a hefty profit. Blackstone quickly followed with an IPO of Team Health, which provides health-care staff to hospitals and other institutions, more than doubling its money on paper after four years. Soon after Graham Packaging, which Blackstone had held since 1998, went public, yielding a modest profit on paper. Carlyle, Cerberus, TPG, and others also managed IPOs of portfolio companies in late 2009.

Around the same time, corporations came out of hibernation and began making acquisitions again, creating another avenue for exits. The pharmaceutical giant GlaxoSmithKline paid $3.6 billion for Stiefel Laboratories, Inc., a dermatological drug maker that was one-quarter owned by Blackstone. Blackstone booked a 40 percent gain barely two years after investing. A few months later, Blackstone doubled its money on a 2006 investment in Orangina Schweppes Group, the soft drink company, when the Japanese drinks company Suntory Holdings, Ltd., bought it for $2.7 billion. Kosmos Energy, the company exploring for oil off the west coast of Africa that Blackstone and Warburg Pincus had seeded in 2004, meanwhile, received an offer for one of its fields where it had confirmed big oil deposits. That promised to yield a huge profit for Kosmos's backers.

Even dividend recapitalizations staged a comeback. While credit in general was tight, healthy companies could borrow again, and private equity firms jumped at the chance to take some money out of their companies. Vanguard Health Systems, a hospital operator owned by Blackstone, borrowed to pay a $300 million dividend. Astonishingly, HCA, Inc., the hospital chain KKR had bought for $33 billion in 2006, was doing so well that it borrowed to pay its backers two dividends in early 2010 totaling $2.3 billion. HCA followed that by filing to go public.

The profit taking was crucial for the industry, because it would prime the fund-raising pump again. Every dollar returned to an investor was one less dollar in their private equity allocation and had to be replaced. It was the first step toward restoring the virtuous circle of profits and fresh fund-raising that sustained the business in the 2000s.

In the short term, private equity will have less capital at its disposal because its investors' assets have fallen in value and, with them, the absolute amounts they can invest. After two years of knocking on investors' doors, by July 2010 Blackstone had raised just $13.5 billion for its next buyout fund, a huge come-down from the $21.7 billion fund it closed in 2007. KKR postponed its fund-raising plans altogether in 2009 because its investors were tapped out. Until buyout firms realize profits and send money back to the pension plans and other investors, their asset pools will slowly shrink.

Even so, the longer-term trends work in the favor of private equity, for as populations in the developed world age, pension plans will have more money to deploy, and private equity is likely to gain a bigger share of a bigger pot. In 2009, when private equity was taken for dead, three of the largest public pension funds, the trendsetting CalPERS and Cal-STRS in California and New York State's pension plan, each decided to raise the portion of their assets going to private equity.

In the postcrisis era, private equity won't look like it did in 2006 and 2007, to be sure. Even the protagonists recognized at the time that it was a freakish period—too good to be true. With hindsight, the $20 billion–plus deals may look as anomalous as RJR Nabisco was in its day, when it was nearly four times the size of the next biggest LBO to that point. It may take a generation before there are buyouts on the scale of TXU, EOP, or Hilton again, many people in the business believe. The big question for private equity and its importance in the capital markets is not when the next $40 billion buyout occurs, but how long it takes before there are $5 billion or $10 billion deals—deals big enough to sustain private equity organizations on the scale they had operated at before the crash.

The securitization of buyout loans and junk bonds, and other debt like mortgages, created a credit bubble, so when leverage returns, it will not be on the same monumental scale seen in the mid-2000s. Still, the debt markets are vastly more sophisticated and deeper than they were in the 1980s, when the collapse of one firm, Drexel Burnham, put the buyout business on ice for years. Two decades on, LBO financing is provided by scores of institutions around the globe.

Notwithstanding the contraction of credit, the private equity business will rebound for no other reason than its $500 billion capital stockpile. Blackstone alone went into 2010 with $29 billion to invest in corporate buyouts, real estate, and debt—the largest pool of any of the big private equity houses. If history is a guide, that money will earn rich returns because investments made when the economy was weak have performed best. Buyouts in 1991 and 1992 and 2001 and 2002 earned returns near 30 percent on average, about double what investments in other years made, and the most successful funds ever were those raised and deployed at earlier troughs in the business cycle.

It isn't just the enormous war chest that ensures the industry's long-term survival, though. Private equity has carved out a unique role for itself. Today private equity is best understood as a parallel capital market and an alternative, transitional form of corporate ownership. Unlike the money a company raises in the stock or bond markets, or with a bank loan, this capital comes with an agenda attached, and the supplier of the capital has the power to see that plan carried out. Put another way, private equity takes risks that other investors don't want to shoulder, in exchange for control and high returns.

The LBO continues to be the paradigm and will come to the fore again when the debt markets recover, but it no longer defines the business. At lows in the business cycle, buyout capital is used to *de*leverage struggling or bankrupt businesses or to buy debt at big discounts, because undercapitalized and distressed companies have the most upside for investors in a bad economy. In better times, investment flows to companies that need operational improvements. Some money will also go to stake start-up businesses, as it did with the two reinsurers Blackstone helped form after September 11 and with Kosmos Energy, the oil exploration company.

The common thread in all these, except for pure debt trading, is that private equity serves as a bridge between two stages of the company's life. Just as venture capitalists fund young companies and lend management and market know-how, private equity has developed into a form of ownership where other forms of capital and ownership have fallen short. Sometimes the target is a public company like Celanese or Safeway that has not rationalized its businesses to maximize long-term value, or a major subsidiary of a public company, such as Travelport or Hertz, that hadn't received the management it deserved. In other cases, private equity firms step in when a subsidiary such as Merlin or Gerresheimer has had its ambitions thwarted by its parent. In distressed and turnaround investments, private equity buyers provide capital and bear the risks while a troubled business regains its footing.

Not only has the nature of private equity investing evolved beyond the LBO. The firms themselves have branched out. "All of these large buyout firms are now in the process of transforming themselves from being just private equity firms into alternative investment management firms," says David Rubenstein, the cofounder of Carlyle. Since the last downturn, Blackstone and most of its peers have become global businesses, managing a variety of asset categories and investing in emerging economies such as China and India. Three firms, Fortress, Blackstone, and (after a long delay) KKR, have gone public and Apollo hopes to soon, a process that forced them to complete the transition from secretive personal fiefdoms to mainstream institutions.

Private equity still must contend with the refinancing crunch that looms in 2012 to 2014, when the companies bought in the peak years will need to repay their loans and bonds and find new financing. Some companies, worth less than their debts, will surely be forfeited to creditors, their backers writing off their investments. But predictions of catastrophic waves of failure are probably overstated. Lenders and private equity firms alike have several years to renegotiate and postpone maturities. Billions in loans were modified, reduced, or extended in 2009 and 2010, and billions more were certain to be replaced or extended by the time the original due dates come around. By the spring of 2010, for instance, the $34 billion in debt that was originally scheduled to come due at Blackstone companies in 2013 had been reduced to just $15 billion through a combination of restructurings, extensions, and debt purchases. Its competitors had similarly worked down their totals in order to avoid a refinancing crisis. There will be a day of reckoning, but it won't sink the private equity business or the economy.

Meanwhile, new regulatory constraints on banks may work to private equity's benefit, forcing big banks to retrench in the areas where they encroached on private equity's turf. Some of the biggest competitors of Blackstone's real estate group, for instance, were the property investment arms of Goldman Sachs, Morgan Stanley, Merrill Lynch, and Lehman Brothers. Each has severely shrunk or disappeared from real estate private equity altogether after suffering big losses. The financial reforms of

2010 will limit how much of their own capital banks can invest in buy-outs, which could curb rivals such as Goldman Sachs Capital Partners and the private equity operations of other banks such as Citigroup, Morgan Stanley, and Credit Suisse.

At the same time that banks pull back, private equity firms are pushing further onto what had been the banks' exclusive territory, as Blackstone had from the beginning with its M&A and restructuring groups. KKR served notice in 2007 that it was setting up its own securities arm to sell shares and bonds. In part, this was a bid to service its own companies, cutting banks out of the loop and generating underwriting fees for itself, but KKR aims to be more than an in-house service unit. By 2010, it had participated in more than fifteen offerings, including floating bonds for Britain's leading sports franchise, the Manchester United soccer team, in which KKR had no stake.

"If we don't reinvent ourselves continually, we're dead," Schwarzman likes to tell his troops. At the end of the day, there are thousands of sources of pure capital. The trick is to supply something extra.

Amid the financial upheaval, Blackstone was observing that maxim, elaborating on the concept of private equity through new investments and investment vehicles in China. On the heels of the investment by China's sovereign wealth fund, Chinese Investment Corporation, in Blackstone in 2007, Blackstone took a minority stake in China Bluestar, a state-owned specialty chemicals company, for $500 million and agreed to work with it to acquire chemical makers elsewhere in the world. Two years later, Blackstone's real estate group invested with a local Chinese developer to build a shopping mall, and the firm followed that by launching a $730 million private equity fund denominated in the Chinese renmimbi currency that will invest in the Shanghai region. (Carlyle was forming a similar fund in Beijing.)

It wasn't Blackstone's capital that won it these roles; the Chinese have a surplus of capital. Instead, Blackstone was parlaying its financial, management, and real estate know-how into stakes in high-growth businesses. At the same time, CIC said it would invest a half-billion dollars in Blackstone's hedge fund-of-funds, suggesting a rich new vein of capital for Blackstone to tap.

Coming out of the crisis, Blackstone's buyout portfolio had withstood the crunch better than many of its competitors, and because it had fallen behind in the race to launch public investment funds, it dodged the meltdowns suffered by Apollo, Carlyle, and KKR's publicly traded debt funds. Blackstone remains the biggest firm, too—only Carlyle is close in the amount of capital it manages of all types—with by far the most diversified mix of businesses.

Twenty-five years on, Blackstone still conforms to the blueprint Peterson and Schwarzman drew up in 1985 for a new form of financial institution built around private equity with other niches added as opportunities arose. And, as the Chinese initiatives show, Schwarzman hasn't lost his knack for finding and supplying capital—and for spotting a way for Blackstone to get its cut.

ACKNOWLEDGMENTS

Even before we got under way in earnest with this book we had accumulated debts to many others. Leah Spiro at McGraw-Hill first set us thinking about a primer on private equity and then helped persuade us that David's barely conceived notion of a more time-consuming book on Blackstone alone would be much more interesting. From the start, Zoë Pagnamenta encouraged us and then won us entrée to three first-rate agents, including Larry Kirshbaum, who ultimately represented us.

We are enormously indebted to Larry for his savvy, for his understanding of the financial and book worlds, and for, well, just being Larry. His levelheadedness and e-mail wisecracks helped smooth out the inevitable bumps in the road in a three-year project.

In John Mahaney we were blessed with an editor who grasped the nuances of the subject yet had the perspective to keep us from losing our way among the trees. The manuscript benefited enormously from his comments and suggestions.

Bob Teitelman, our boss at *The Deal* and an author himself, from the start lent his moral and intellectual support. His thoughts on an early draft also helped steer us back toward the big picture. We owe thanks to Vyvyan Tenorio, Christine Idzelis, and Vipal Monga at *The Deal*, who were forced to take up the slack at many points when we were absent. John is also grateful to Arindam Nag, Susanna Potter, and the rest of his subsequent colleagues at Dow Jones, who indulged his preoccupation and erratic schedule as the book entered its later phases. All will be relieved that we are emerging at last from our Blackstone-centric world.

Kinsey Haffner, Sean Daly, and Adam Sachs each contributed

detailed, thoughtful comments on the manuscript that were incorporated in one form or another.

This book would not have been possible without the cooperation of Blackstone. From Steve Schwarzman, Tony James, and general counsel Bob Friedman on down through the ranks, people made themselves accessible and gave generously of their time, both in interviews and later in the lengthy process of fact-checking. Some were reticent at the outset, but without exception they respected our independence and never tried to turn the book into an authorized history. Steve Schwarzman gave more of his time than anyone else—more than a dozen extended interviews over nearly two years during which the financial world was upended. His candor and his exceptional memory allowed us to incorporate the firm's, and his, perspective on events over a twenty-five-year period to an extent we had not anticipated at the outset.

We are enormously indebted to John Ford, Blackstone's longtime press officer, whose integrity and courtesy had earned him the respect and affection of the financial press long before this book was conceived. His knowledge of the firm was a huge asset, particularly in the early stages of our reporting, and he shepherded the hundreds of fact-checking queries we submitted for a year after he retired officially. Two other people deserve special mentions: Stephanie Kokinos, John Ford's assistant, who miraculously buttonholed one partner after another for interviews during the early stages when we were reporting most heavily, and Christine Veschi, to whom fell the laborious task of checking dates, prices, and profits on scores of investments.

Many others in the financial world, named and unnamed, provided valuable background, recollections, and insights that informed the story and filled in details from other perspectives.

To all, our sincere thanks.

NOTES

Many basic facts about Blackstone's private equity investments—deal values, closing dates, the equity invested, profits and rates of return, the strategic plans behind individual investments, and accounts of how they played out over time—came originally from the confidential prospectuses known as private placement memorandums for Blackstone's fifth and sixth buyout funds, which were obtained by the authors. These documents are given to prospective investors in Blackstone's funds and are not publicly available. Details from these sources were later verified with Blackstone.

Hundreds of other facts pertaining directly to Blackstone were also checked with the firm in writing as the book neared completion. These ranged from simple dates and dollar amounts to the substance of discussions and sequences of events—information first obtained from interviews inside and outside the firm and from documents.

Blackstone did not at any stage review the manuscript, nor were the characterizations, observations, conclusions, or opinions here shared with or vetted by Blackstone.

As a condition of its cooperation, Blackstone required the authors to check all quotes and facts explicitly attributed to the firm or people there, a condition imposed by many sources and companies when dealing with journalists. In no case did the firm or the source substantially modify a quote except where it was factually mistaken, unclear, or ungrammatical. Of the hundreds of quotes from sources at Blackstone included in the book, only a handful were changed in any way. Because most Blackstone sources were interviewed on more than one occasion and the quotes were later verified in writing, dates are not listed for those interviews.

Some sources agreed to speak only if they were not identified. Because in many cases other portions of the same interviews were on the record and the source and the date of the interview are identified here, we have not included dates for interview material obtained on background.

Abbreviations

IPO Prospectus: Prospectus, Form 424B4, Blackstone Group LP, June 21, 2007, available at www.sec.gov/edgar.shtml.

PPM for BCP V: Confidential Private Placement Memorandum for Blackstone Capital Partners V fund (undated) and supplements in April and October 2005.

PPM for BCP VI: Confidential Private Placement Memorandum for Blackstone Capital Partners VI fund (undated) and updated investment results through December 31, 2008.

NYT: New York Times

WSJ: Wall Street Journal

Anders, *Merchants*: George Anders, *The Merchants of Debt: KKR and the Mortgaging of American Business* (Washington, DC: Beard Books, 2002; originally published by Basic Books, 1992).

Auletta, *Greed*: Ken Auletta, *Greed and Glory on Wall Street: The Fall of the House of Lehman* (New York: Warner Books, 1986).

Baker and Smith, *Capitalists*: George P. Baker and George David Smith, *The New Financial Capitalists: Kohlberg Kravis Roberts and the Creation of Corporate Value* (Cambridge, England: Cambridge University Press, 1998).

Bruck, *Predators*: Connie Bruck, *The Predators' Ball: The Junk Bond Raiders and the Man Who Staked Them* (New York: The American Lawyer/ Simon & Schuster, 1988).

Burrough and Helyar, *Barbarians*: Bryan Burrough and John Helyar, *Barbarians at the Gate: The Fall of RJR Nabisco* (New York: Harper & Row, 1990).

Finkel and Geising, *Masters*: Robert A. Finkel and David Geising, *The Masters of Private Equity and Venture Capital* (New York: McGraw-Hill, 2010).

Peterson, *Education*: Peter G. Peterson, *The Education of an American Dreamer: How a Son of Greek Immigrants Learned His Way from a Nebraska Diner to Washington, Wall Street, and Beyond* (New York: Twelve, 2009).

Stewart, "Party": James B. Stewart, "The Birthday Party," *New Yorker,* February 11, 2008.

Wasserstein, *Big Deal*: Bruce Wasserstein, *Big Deal: The Battle for Control of America's Leading Corporations* (New York: Warner Books, 1998).

Citations to company financials refer to quarterly and/or annual financial reports (Forms 10-Q and 10-K) filed with the U.S. Securities and Exchange Commission, which are available at www.sec.gov/edgar.shtml. Where reference is made to something more obscure than the figures in the main financial statements, we have included the SEC's form or schedule number as well as the date of the filing so the reader can find the document online.

Chapter 1: The Debutants

1–2 **"More Rumors" . . . $1 million for such appearances:** Landon Thomas Jr., "More Rumors About His Party Than About His Deals," *NYT,* Jan. 27, 2007; Michael J. de la Merced, "Dealbook—Inside Stephen Schwarzman's Birthday Bash," *NYT,* Feb. 14, 2007; Richard Johnson with Paula Froelich, Bill Hoffmann, and Corynne Steindler, "Page Six—$3M Birthday Party Fit for Buyout King," *New York Post,* Feb. 14, 2007; Michael Flaherty, "Blackstone CEO Gala Sign of Buyout Boom," Reuters, Feb. 14, 2007; Richard Johnson with Paula Froelich, Bill Hoffmann, and Corynne Steindler, "Page Six—No Room for Henry At Bash," *New York Post,* Feb. 15, 2007; also background interview with an attendee.

2 **At the closing price:** The $38 billion includes the equity units held by Blackstone partners that were not publicly traded.

3 **Going public had laid bare:** IPO Prospectus.

3   **By 2007 private equity:** Thomson Reuters data compiled for the authors on May 26, 2009.

3   **There was even talk:** "Behind Home Depot Rumors," CNBC Faber Report, http://www.cnbc.com/id/16037251, Dec. 4, 2006.

4   **Blackstone alone owned all:** Blackstone.

4   **Goldman Sachs had 30,500 employees:** Goldman Sachs Group, annual report Form 10-K for fiscal year ending Nov. 30, 2007, Jan. 29, 2008, 15; Blackstone, annual report Form 10-K for 2007, Mar. 12, 2008, 11.

4   **In a telling episode:** David Carey and Vipal Monga, "Wielding the Club: The Warner Chilcott Affair," *The Deal,* May 19, 2005.

5   **It was bigger than KKR:** IPO Prospectus, 1; AIM Program Fund Performance Review, California Public Employees' Retirement System, as of June 30, 2007; Alternative Investments Portfolio Performance, California State Teachers' Retirement System, as of Mar. 31, 2007.

6   **The backlash against the buyout:** "German SPD Head Says to Fight Capitalist 'Locusts,'" Reuters, Apr. 17, 2005; Kerry Capell, with Gail Edmondson, "A Backlash Against Private Equity," *BusinessWeek,* Mar. 12, 2007.

7   **Even the conservative *Wall Street Journal*:** Alan Murray, "A Question for Chairman Bernanke: Is It Time to Yank the Punch Bowl?" *WSJ,* Feb. 14, 2007; "The Blackstone Tax" (unsigned editorial), *WSJ,* June 20, 2007.

8   **A growing body of academic research:** See chapter 25.

8   **Notwithstanding the controversy:** Julie Creswell and Vikas Bajaj, "$3.2 Billion Move by Bear Stearns to Rescue Fund," *NYT,* June 23, 2007.

9   **Like shopalcoholics:** Blackstone annual report Form 10-K for 2008, Mar. 3, 2009, 158.

10 **On the contrary:** Two background interviews.

11 **For starters, the industry was sitting:** Hugh MacArthur, Graham Elton, Bill Halloran, et al., *Global Private Equity Report 2010,* Bain & Co., Mar. 10, 2010 ($508 billion estimate); Heino Meerkatt and Heinrich Liechenstein, *Driving the Shakeout in Private Equity,* Boston Consulting Group and the IESE Business School of the University of Navarra, Navarra, Spain, July 2009 ($550 billion); Conor Kehoe and Robert N.

Palter, "The Future of Private Equity," *McKinsey Quarterly* 31 (Spring 2009): 11 ($470 billion).

11 **Though new fund-raising slowed:** California Public Employees' Retirement System (CalPERS) press release, June 15, 2009 (increased from 10 percent to 14 percent); Keenan Skelly, "Calstrs Raises Target Allocation to 12%," *LBO Wire*, Aug. 17, 2009; Mar. 8, 2010, e-mail from Robert Whalen, press officer for New York State Comptroller Thomas P. DiNapoli (confirming that the New York State Common Retirement Fund raised its allocation from 8 percent to 10 percent in November 2009).

Chapter 2: Houdaille Magic, Lehman Angst

13 **"I read that prospectus":** Stephen Schwarzman interview.

13–14 **"When Houdaille came along":** Richard Beattie interview, Aug. 5, 2008.

15 **Weeks after:** Michael M. Thomas, "Windfall—A Game of 1980s High Finance," *New York*, Aug. 8, 1983, 22ff; Ann Crittenden, "Reaping the Big Profits from a Fat Cat," *NYT*, Aug. 7, 1983.

15 **Simon himself called his windfall:** Crittenden, "Reaping the Big Profits."

16 **He couldn't help but pay attention:** Schwarzman interview.

16 **Virtually from the day:** Peter Peterson interview.

16 **But by the time Peterson arrived:** Warren Hellman, in Finkel and Geising, *Masters*, 55.

17 **When Peterson joined:** Ibid., 54.

17 **They even went so far:** Peterson and Schwarzman interviews.

17 **Schwarzman would invite:** Beattie interview.

18 **His rise up the corporate ladder:** Auletta, *Greed*, 35ff.

18 **Though Peterson had allies:** Peterson, *Education*, 147ff.

18 **At one point:** Ibid., 147–48.

19 **John Connally:** Ibid., 148–51.

19 **Nixon dumped Peterson:** Ibid., 193ff.

19 **But two months after being recruited:** Ibid, 218–19; Auletta, *Greed*, 48.

20 **The man responsible:** Peterson, *Education*, 218–19; Auletta, *Greed*, 48.

20 **"I argued that the guy":** Warren Hellman interview, June 4, 2008.

20 **In 1975 *BusinessWeek*:** "Back from the Brink Comes Lehman Bros.," *BusinessWeek*, Nov. 1975.

20   "He kept calling": Background interview with a former Lehman partner.

20   But with colleagues: Auletta, *Greed,* 16ff; background interview with a former Lehman partner.

21   At times, he seemed to inhabit: Background interviews with several former colleagues of Peterson's and with the head of a New York private equity firm.

21   Howard Lipson: Howard Lipson interview, May 29, 2008.

21   In his conference room: Personal observation.

21   "Pete was probably thinking great thoughts": David Batten interview, Oct. 1, 2008.

21   Since the death: Auletta, *Greed,* 32ff; Peterson, *Education,* 215ff.

22   One Lehman partner was rumored: Peterson, *Education,* 216.

22   In a case of double-dealing: Ibid., 236–37.

22   Robert Rubin: Hellman, in Finkel and Geising, *Masters,* 54.

22   "I don't understand why": Stewart, "Party."

22   The bitterest schism: Auletta, *Greed,* 3ff; Peterson, *Education,* 216.

22   Peterson tried to bridge: Peterson, *Education,* 225–32.

23   He was closest to Hellman: Ibid., 216–17.

23   Of the younger partners: Peterson interview.

23   Those qualities were prized: Peterson and Schwarzman interviews.

23   "I guess I was thought of": Peterson interview.

24   Harvester's CEO: Peterson, *Education,* 231; Schwarzman interview.

24   Similarly, Peterson landed Bendix: Schwarzman interview.

24   Schwarzman's family: Schwarzman interview.

25   That shone through: Karen W. Arenson, "Stephen Schwarzman, Lehman's Merger Maker," *NYT,* Jan. 13, 1980.

25   At a company outing: Stewart, "Party."

25   As one Lehman alumnus: Background interview.

25   "He had a pretty good ego": Hellman inverview.

25   Ralph Schlosstein: Ralph Schlosstein interview, July 25, 2008.

26   "We made it up": Schwarzman interview.

26   He sensed that Glucksman: Auletta, *Greed,* 70ff; Peterson, *Education,* 255ff.

27   "He had a corner on the trading area": Peterson interview.

27   Schwarzman and other Lehman partners: Peterson, *Education*, 260.

27   Some of Peterson's friends: Auletta, *Greed*, 69ff; background interviews.

27   Peterson owns up to being "naïve": Peterson, *Education*, 256, 266.

27   It was Schwarzman: Schwarzman interview; Auletta, *Greed*, 190ff.

28   Shearson insisted that most Lehman partners: Auletta, *Greed*, 208.

28   He yearned to join: Schwarzman interview.

28   Cohen agreed: Schwarzman and Peterson interviews.

28   "The other [Lehman] partners": Background interview with a former Lehman partner.

28   Asked why Schwarzman thought: Background interview with someone who knows Schwarzman.

29   In the months after: Background interviews with two former Lehman partners.

29   "Steve and I were highly complementary": Peterson interview.

29   Eventually, Peterson: Peterson interview.

29   "It was a brutal process": Peterson interview.

29   Shearson had drawn up: Peterson and Schwarzman interviews.

29   In Schwarzman's mind: Background interviews with three people who know Schwarzman.

29   "Steve doesn't forget": Background interview.

29–30   "The idea of giving": Peterson interview.

Chapter 3: The Drexel Decade

31   Corporate conglomerates: Wasserstein, *Big Deal*, 55ff; Baker and Smith, *Capitalists*, 16ff.

32   KKR, which opened its doors: Baker and Smith, *Capitalists*, 52ff; Burrough and Helyar, *Barbarians*, 133ff.

32   On his thirtieth birthday: Burrough and Helyar, *Barbarians*, 133.

32   In 1976, Kohlberg: Ibid., 136–38.

32   The trio's inaugural fund: Background interview with a KKR partner.

32   That success made KKR a magnet: IPO Registration Statement, Form S-1, KKR & Co. LP, Oct. 31, 2008, 233.

33   Goldman's partners agonized: Steven Klinsky interview, June 6, 2008.

33   It was only half KKR's size: Background interview.

33   **Ted Forstmann:** Burrough and Helyar, *Barbarians*, 235ff.

33   **He swiftly proved himself a master:** Forstmann Little & Co. undated confidential private placement memorandum, late 1990s.

34   **In the 1960s, conglomerates' stocks:** Wasserstein, *Big Deal*, 64ff.

35   **But reality caught up:** Ibid., 71ff; Baker and Smith, *Capitalists*, 48–49.

35   **A banner year:** Kohlberg Kravis Roberts & Co. undated confidential private placement memorandum, late 1990s; Forstmann Little & Co. confidential private placement memorandum, late 1990s; news reports.

36   **As KKR, Forstmann Little:** Kohlberg Kravis Roberts & Co. and Forstmann Little & Co. private placement memoranda, late 1990s.

37   **When Henry Kravis demurred:** Anders, *Merchants*, 85.

37   **"It was like falling off a log":** Daniel O'Connell interview, 1994.

38   **Renowned for his work ethic:** Wasserstein, *Big Deal*, 81–85; Anders, *Merchants*, 83–108; Bruck, *Predators*, 10ff.   ·

38   **After a breakout year:** Bruck, *Predators*, 78.

38   **KKR was one of the first:** Baker and Smith, *Capitalists*, 25; Anders, *Merchants*, 88.

38   **Kravis called Drexel's ability:** Anders, *Merchants*, 89.

39   **At their peak in the mid-1980s:** Ibid., 83; Wasserstein, *Big Deal*, 83.

39   **Investors in KKR's first five funds:** Amendment 6 to Form S-1, KKR & Co. LP, Oct. 31, 2008, 233.

39   **Jerry Kohlberg resigned:** Baker and Smith, *Capitalists*, 179–80; multiple news accounts.

40   **The hunted and the hunters:** An excellent summary of the verbal warfare between raiders and the corporate establishment in the 1980s, of how the press portrayed buyout artists, and of the political backlash against them can be found in Baker and Smith, *Capitalists*, 14–40.

41   **After buying up shares:** Wasserstein, *Big Deal*, 108–9; news accounts.

41   **Other times, the company:** Wasserstein, *Big Deal*, 109, 135; news accounts.

41   **Peltz ran National Can:** Wasserstein, *Big Deal*, 108–10; David Carey, "Can Raiders Run What They Raid?" *Fortune*, June 4, 1990.

42   **The device wasn't new:** Wasserstein, *Big Deal*, 57–58, 72ff, 618ff; Baker and Smith, *Capitalists*, 18ff.

42 **A giant of the M&A bar:** Bruck, *Predators,* 204ff; Wasserstein, *Big Deal,* 146.

42 **KKR touted itself:** Wasserstein, *Big Deal,* 95; Baker and Smith, *Capitalists,* 99.

42 **"We came into a contested situation":** Richard Beattie interview, Aug. 5, 2008.

43 **KKR used this tactic:** Baker and Smith, *Capitalists,* 84; Wasserstein, *Big Deal,* 97; news accounts.

43 **"We don't have assistants":** Carol J. Loomis, "Buyout Kings," *Fortune,* July 4, 1988.

43 **In a series of hearings:** Wasserstein, *Big Deal,* 79–80; Baker and Smith, *Capitalists,* 33ff.

43 **At a meeting:** Baker and Smith, *Capitalists,* 91–92.

44 **Though he had made his name:** Burrough and Helyar, *Barbarians,* 233–34 and 240–41; Theodore J. Forstmann, "Corporate Finance, 'Leveraged to the Hilt'—Violating Our Rules of Prudence," *WSJ,* Oct. 25, 1988.

44 **Forstmann would privately rant:** Burrough and Helyar, *Barbarians,* 234; see also Anders, *Merchants,* 125 ("Tall and athletic, Forstmann routinely called Kravis and Roberts 'the midgets' ").

44 **Kravis, for his part:** Burrough and Helyar, *Barbarians,* 129.

Chapter 4: Who Are You Guys?

45 **The name, Schwarzman's invention:** Peter Peterson and Stephen Schwarzman interviews.

45 **Their quarters:** Steven Mufson, "Creating Connections at Blackstone Group," *Washington Post,* July 30, 1989.

45 **The funding was similarly frugal:** Peterson and Schwarzman interviews.

45 **That was nothing to Peterson:** Auletta, *Greed,* 221.

45 **Schwarzman, too, had made:** Interviews with Schwarzman and his tax accountant.

45–48 **They worried that if they ran . . . Disheartened that his client:** Schwarzman interviews.

48 **KKR, the buyout front-runner:** Kohlberg Kravis Roberts & Co. confidential private placement memorandum, late 1990s.

49 **KKR, the biggest operator:** Form S-1, KKR & Co. LP, Oct. 31, 2008, 233.

50 **While the individual partners:** Dyan Machan, Stephen Taub, Paul Swee-
ney, et al., "The Financial World 100: The Highest Paid People on Wall
Street," *Financial World,* July 22, 1986, 21.

50 **"The problem was":** Peterson interview.

50–52 **"Pete and I expected" . . . By the winter of 1986:** Schwarzman interview.

52 **But Peterson had done business:** Peterson interview; Garnett Keith
interview, July 30, 2008.

53 **Prudential insisted:** Michael Puglisi and Schwarzman interviews.

53 **It paid off particularly in Japan:** Schwarzman interview.

54 **"We'd congratulate ourselves":** Schwarzman interview.

54 **In June, Peterson bumped:** Peterson interview.

55–56 **Even more momentous . . . "It was probably the luckiest":** Schwarzman interview. The $635 million figure for the fund is from a reprint of a
late 1987 Blackstone newspaper ad.

Chapter 5: Right on Track

57 **It took a ten-year lease:** Blackstone; Stephen Schwarzman interview.

57–58 **Peterson and Schwarzman:** Peter Peterson and Schwarzman interviews.

58 **Altman's coyness:** Background interview with a former Altman colleague.

58 **The 1981 article:** William Greider, "The Education of David Stockman,"
Atlantic, Dec. 1981, 27ff; David Stockman, *The Triumph of Politics:
Why the Reagan Revolution Failed* (New York: Harper & Row, 1986).

59 **He was recruited:** Schwarzman and Peterson interviews.

59 **At the time, Fink:** Steve Swartz, "First Boston's Mortgage Securities Chief
Leaves to Join Smaller Blackstone Group," *WSJ,* March 4, 1988.

59 **They accepted Fink's explanation:** Schwarzman interview.

59 **Peterson and Schwarzman offered:** Interviews with Schwarzman and background sources.

60 **Altman, who might have:** Background interviews with three people familiar with the matter.

60   **By the spring of 1988:** Schwarzman interview. Two investors in the fund later defaulted, reducing the fund's size to $810 million.

60   **There were more than sixteen hundred:** Scot J. Paltrow, "Nomura Buys Stake in Fledgling Investment Firm," *Washington Post,* July 28, 1988.

60   **A Wall Street bank:** Carol J. Loomis, "The New J.P. Morgans," *Fortune,* Feb. 29, 1988; news accounts.

60   **More than anyone else, Wasserstein:** Wasserstein, *Big Deal,* 179ff; Dennis K. Berman, Jeffrey McCracken, and Randall Smith, "Wasserstein Dies, Leaves Deal-Making Legacy," *WSJ,* Oct. 16, 2009; Andrew Ross Sorkin and Michael J. de la Merced, "Obituary—Bruce Wasserstein, 61, Corporate Raider," *NYT,* Oct. 16, 2009.

61   **Wasserstein Perella soon won:** Paltrow, "Nomura Buys Stake"; Michael Quint, "Yamaichi-Lodestar Deal Another Sign of the Trend," *NYT,* July 28, 1988; background interview with a former Wasserstein Perella partner.

61   **Most or all of that money:** Background interview with a former Wasserstein Perella partner.

61   **The other headline-grabbing:** Quint, "Yamaichi-Lodestar Deal"; other news accounts.

62   **It had recently amassed:** Loomis, "The New J.P. Morgans"; Form S-1, KKR & Co. LP, Oct. 31, 2008, 233. KKR's 1987 fund had a $5.6 billion first closing. KKR later added another $500 million in commitments to close the fund at $6.1 billion.

62   **In May 1988, Henry Kravis:** Kohlberg Kravis Roberts & Co. confidential private placement memorandum, late 1990s. The document puts KKR's gross profit on its $221 million investment in Storer at $658.2 milion. The firm's partners would have collected 20 percent of that profit, or $131.6 million, as their "carried interest."

62   **Early that year:** Michael Puglisi, written response to query; Peterson, *Education,* 274ff; news accounts.

63   **It began when Altman:** Donald Hoffman interview, June 30, 2009.

63–64 **Altman, Peterson, and Schwarzman . . . "We saw probably":** Peterson and Schwarzman interviews; Hoffman interview; David Roderick interview, June 16, 2009.

64 **Back in New York:** Schwarzman, written response to query.

64–65 **The big concern . . . "James did a perfect analysis":** Schwarzman interview; Howard Lipson interview, May 29, 2008.

65 **"Their mind-set was":** Lipson interview.

65–66 **Schwarzman put out calls . . . "But he said our offer":** Schwarzman interview; James Lee interview, July 24, 2008.

67 **"We really wanted":** Peterson interview.

67 **Blackstone got everything:** Schwarzman and Lipson (May 29, 2008) interviews.

68 **In 1989, in line:** Form S-1, Transtar Holdings LP, Apr. 27, 1994.

69 **"You could argue":** Background interview with a leveraged-finance banker.

69 **It helped establish:** Peterson interview.

69 **"In every way":** Howard Lipson interview, June 9, 2008.

70 **With the prices:** Schwarzman interview.

70 **"We always thought":** Background interview with a buyout specialist who was active in the 1980s.

70 **Schwarzman's preoccupation:** Background interviews with four former Blackstone partners.

71 **Schwarzman acknowledges as much:** Schwarzman interview.

Chapter 6: Running Off the Rails

72 **Stockman was a relentless advocate:** Background interviews with a banker and with a deal maker who worked with Stockman, and with two of his former Blackstone colleagues.

73 **An early sign of trouble:** Background interview with a former Blackstone employee.

73 **"What we found":** Stephen Schwarzman interview.

74 **"He had a habit":** Background interview with a former Blackstone partner. Two other former colleagues said the same thing.

74 **"Right or wrong":** David Batten interview, Oct. 1, 2008.

74 **Its profit margins . . . "It turned out":** Schwarzman interview.

75 **"That's where I saw":** Background interview with a former Blackstone partner.

75 In a phone conversation: Schwarzman interview.

75 He castigated him: Background interviews with three former Blackstone partners.

75 Anything from misspelling: Background interview with a former Blackstone employee.

76 In the early years: Howard Lipson interview, May 29, 2008.

76 "After Bruce did that deal": Schwarzman interview.

76 Instead of taking a straight: Schwarzman and Michael Puglisi interviews.

76 Mergers had rebounded: Puglisi interview.

77 McVeigh's résumé: Randall Smith, "Blackstone Group Leaving Arbitrage as Deals Dwindle," *WSJ*, Jan. 29, 1990.

78 Ten months after McVeigh: Puglisi and Batten interviews.

78 But it's safe to say: Background interviews with two former Blackstone partners; Stewart, "Party."

78 Winograd and McVeigh: Background interviews with three former Blackstone partners.

79 "He was a terrific manager": Background interview with a former Blackstone partner.

79 Junior staff members: Background interview with a former Blackstone employee.

79 "Steve was a very tough boss": Henry Silverman interview, May 13, 2008.

79–80 Realizing that a second . . . "Had we not had Edgcomb": Schwarzman interview.

Chapter 7: Presenting the Steve Schwarzman Show

81 "I was extremely active": Peter Peterson interview.

81 Starting with essays: Peter G. Peterson, "The Morning After," *Atlantic,* Oct. 1987.

82 *Newsday* columnist: Allan Sloan, "LBO Ends Up on Scrap Heap," *Newsday,* Sept. 9, 1990.

82 An article in *Barron's*: Joe Queenan, "The Cadillac Cassandra—Peter Peterson's Quixotic Quest for Fame and Fortune," *Barron's,* Jan. 16, 1989.

82 During investment: Jonathan Colby interview, Dec. 14, 2008; background interviews with two former colleagues of Peterson's.

83 **Peterson rarely deigned:** Background interviews with three former Blackstone employees.

83 **"He was absolutely a presence":** Lawrence Guffey interview.

83 **In a revealing anecdote:** Stewart, "Party."

83 **"I saw the business":** Stephen Schwarzman interview.

83 **"He could fly, man!"** Bobby Bryant interview, Feb. 19, 2009.

84 **He was a solid A and B student . . . Schwarzman also won:** Jeffrey Rosen interview, May 28, 2008; Schwarzman interview; Stewart, "Party."

84–85 **Fresh out of Yale . . . Donaldson, Schwarzman says:** Schwarzman interviews.

85 **Donaldson says:** William Donaldson interview, Feb. 12, 2010.

85 **When the bank's president:** Schwarzman interview.

86 **"He would often call":** James Lee interview, July 24, 2008.

86 **Former partner Bret Pearlman:** Bret Pearlman interview, Oct. 22, 2008.

86 **"When I worked":** Background interview with a former Blackstone partner.

86 **A banker recalls:** Background interview with a leveraged-finance banker.

86 **The head of another:** Background interview with the head of a private equity firm.

87 **He took pains:** Howard Lipson interview, May 29, 2008.

87 **When Steven Fenster:** Rosen interview; background interview with a Blackstone partner.

87 **On the eve:** Pearlman interview.

87 **"I just remember":** Mario Giannini interview, Feb. 13, 2009.

88 **Schwarzman had an "unfiltered" quality:** Background interview with the head of a private equity firm; personal observation.

88 **"Steve is not the sort":** Simon Lonergan interview, Jan. 22, 2009.

88 **In 1990 he told:** Randall Smith, "Fast Talk, Connections Help Make Blackstone a Wall Street Success," *WSJ*, Oct. 24, 1990.

88 **At Blackstone's annual meeting:** Peter Lattman, "Steve Schwarzman's Take on the Subprime Mess," *WSJ* Blog, May 8, 2008; background interview with a Blackstone limited partner.

89 **Schwarzman "always has":** Background interview with a Blackstone limited partner.

Chapter 8: End of an Era, Beginning of an Image Problem

90 **Another fountain of fees:** Form S-1, BFM Holdings, Inc., May 19, 1992.

91 **Immediately after catching wind:** Background interview with a former DLJ executive.

91 **UP's chairman:** Peter Peterson interview.

94 **DLJ found itself:** Background interviews with two former DLJ executives.

94–96 **So it was . . . "He was gracious":** Schwarzman and Hamilton James interviews; background interview with a former DLJ executive; IPO Prospectus, Chicago and North Western Holdings Corp., March 31, 1992, 9ff.

97 **It had everything:** Burrough and Helyar, *Barbarians;* Wasserstein, *Big Deal,* 113–16; background interview with a KKR partner.

98 **"The firm's partners":** James Sterngold, "Buyout Specialist Bids $20.3 Billion for RJR Nabisco," *NYT,* Oct. 25, 1988.

99 **But KKR ended:** Anders, *Merchants,* 255; RJR financial filings, 1990.

99 **By the spring:** Ibid., 263.

99 **The rip-roaring bestseller:** Burrough and Helyar, *Barbarians.*

99 **Years later:** Background interview with a person familiar with the investment.

99 **Investors in KKR's:** Form S-1, KKR & Co. LP, Oct. 31, 2008, 233.

100 **A devastating front-page story:** Susan Faludi, "The Reckoning: Safeway LBO Yields Vast Profits but Exacts a Heavy Human Toll," *WSJ,* May 16, 1990.

101–104 **The true consequences . . . By 1989, three years:** Anders, *Merchants,* 115–18, 166–68, 184–85, 206–12, 228–29; Baker and Smith, *Capitalists,* 92–95, 107–113; Government Accounting Office, *Case Studies of Selected Leveraged Buyouts—No. 91–107,* 1991; "LBOs: The Good, the Bad and the Ugly," *BusinessWeek* online, Dec. 3, 2007, http://images .businessweek.com/ss/07/12/1203_lbo/index_01.htm (slide 7) (based on Standard & Poor's RatingsDirect report); company reports.

104 **KKR made more:** KKR confidential private placement memorandum, late 1990s.

104 **Spurred by new business:** interview with Rand Garbacz, former managing director at Deloitte Consulting and corporate strategy and restructuring officer, Nov. 14, 2009.

104 **"These people were":** Robert Bruner interview, Dec. 2, 2009.

Chapter 9: Fresh Faces

107 **In 1990, just $1.4 billion:** Securities Data Corporation, cited by Michael Siconolfi, "Year-End Review of Bond Markets: Merrill Retains Underwriting Crown in Shaky Market," *WSJ*, Jan. 2, 1991.

107 **Federal regulators seized:** Timothy Curry and Lynn Shibut, "The Cost of the Savings and Loan Crisis: Truth and Consequences," *FDIC Banking Review*, Dec. 2000, 2.

107 **Schwarzman embellishes:** Stephen Schwarzman interview.

109 **Carlyle notched:** Confidential report to Carlyle's limited partners, June 2000.

109 **From its quick flip:** Thomas Hicks interview, Nov. 1992.

110 **When the economy revived:** Davan Maharaj, John-Thor Dahlberg, staff writers, "Tycoon Has Law Hot on His Heels: California Accuses Francois Pinault and Others of Illegally Acquiring an Insurer's Assets," *Los Angeles Times*, July 6, 2000. Black and his financial backers later sold part of the Executive Life bond portfolio to Francois Pinault, the "tycoon" in the headline. Apollo and Pinault together made a $2.5 billion profit on the deal, the paper reported. Black and Apollo were never charged in the scandal involving Pinault.

110 **Apollo Advisors:** Form S-1, Apollo Global Management LLC, Aug. 12, 2008, 187.

110 **Bass would turn:** Background interview with a person familiar with the American Savings Bank and Continental Airlines deals.

111 **Four years before:** Norm Clarke, "Money Man Really Means Business When He Celebrates His Birthday," *Las Vegas Review-Journal*, Nov. 13, 2002; "$7 Million Birthday Bash," *New York Post*, Nov. 13, 2002.

111 **The following year:** Leslie Wayne, "The R.T.C.'s Point Man in Distressed Real Estate," *NYT,* Mar. 10, 1991.

111–12 **Batten, who had been charged . . . Robertson wasn't fired:** David Batten interview, Oct. 1, 2008.

113 **The apartment's buyer:** Michael Gross, "Where the Boldface Bunk," *NYT,* March 11, 2004.

113 **Moreover, Blackstone:** Henry Silverman interview, Jan. 20, 2010.

113–15 **"Our reservation volume" . . . Schwarzman was so relieved:** Schwarzman interview; Henry Silverman interview, May 13, 2008.

116 **The IPO price:** IPO Prospectus, Chicago and North Western Holdings Corp., Mar. 31, 1992; CNW's cash flow (its earnings before interest, taxes, depreciation, and amortization, known as EBITDA) in a given year can be computed by adding the company's depreciation and amortization expense, on p. F-4 of the prospectus, to its operating income, on p. F-2.

116 **"CNW didn't hit one":** Howard Lipson interview, June 9, 2008.

116 **"When Henry joined us":** Schwarzman interview.

117 **"Because of the people":** Silverman interview, May 13, 2008.

117 **Rounding up pledges wasn't easy:** Kenneth Whitney interview.

Chapter 10: The Divorces and a Battle of the Minds

118 **On the op-ed page:** Peter G. Peterson, "The Budget: From Comedy to Tragedy," *NYT,* Sept. 16, 1990.

118 **In a glossy "Men's Fashions":** "Store Styling," in "Men's Fashions of the Times," *NYT,* Sept. 16, 1990.

118 **To some people's eyes:** Background interview with a former Blackstone partner.

119 **"Steve and Pete were very close":** Jonathan Colby interview, Dec. 14, 2008.

119 **Over time, however:** Background interviews with three people who know Peterson and Schwarzman.

119 **"I felt it was fair":** Peter Peterson in an e-mail.

119 **"With Pete, it wasn't the money":** Background interview with a friend of Peterson's.

120 **"Pete doesn't believe the point":** Background interview with a person who knows Peterson and Schwarzman.

120 **Schwarzman very much liked:** Stephen Schwarzman interview.

121 **"Pru felt it would be":** Gary Trabka interview, Oct. 2, 2008.

121 **Prudential's Blair Communications:** Henry Silverman interview, Jan. 20, 2010.

121–22 **Altman had paid dearly ... For years Altman:** Background interviews with three former Blackstone partners.

122 **Peterson, Altman's mentor:** Austin Beutner interview, Oct. 9, 2008.

122–23 **Schwarzman was less forgiving ... For a high-level Treasury:** Background interviews with three former Blackstone partners.

123 **When Altman returned:** Background interview with a friend of Altman's.

123 **"That he wasn't asked back":** Background interview with a former Blackstone partner.

123 **By early 1992, BFM's assets:** Form S-1, BFM Holdings Inc., May 19, 1992.

124 **But Fink and Schwarzman soon ... finally relented:** Background interviews with former Blackstone partners.

124 **In June 1994, the business:** PNC press release, June 16, 1994.

124 **Blackstone's partners made out well:** Background interviews with three former Blackstone partners.

124 **Though the size:** Leah N. Spiro and Kathleen Morris, "Blackstone: Nice Is for Suckers—Its Good Cop–Bad Cop Team Grabs the No. 2 spot in LBOs," *BusinessWeek*, Apr. 13, 1998.

125 **Schwarzman would later freely admit:** For instance, during a Jan. 10, 2008, conference call with analysts and reporters to discuss Blackstone's acquisition of GSO Capital Partners, Schwarzman said: "One regret we have is that we sold BlackRock too early."

125 **Blackstone partner Chinh Chu:** Chinh Chu interview.

126–27 **At an investment committee ... "Exactly!" said Lipson:** Background interview with a person who sat in on the meeting.

127–29 **"James's IQ" ... As a result, Mossman:** Recollections and quotes concerning Mossman, his face-offs with Stockman, his work habits, and his influence within Blackstone came from interviews with J. Tomilson Hill III, Kenneth Whitney, Chu, and Simon Lonergan (Jan. 22, 2009), and background interviews with several former Blackstone partners and others Mossman worked with.

Chapter 11: Hanging Out New Shingles

131 **"I told him I had no interest" . . . In his place, Schreiber:** John Schreiber and Stephen Schwarzman interviews.

132 **The firm tried in 1991:** Kenneth Whitney and Schwarzman interviews.

132 **Through his long-standing ties:** Case study of the DeBartolo deal in the PPM for BCP V.

134 **From the moment Altman left:** Blackstone press release, Nov. 18, 1993.

134 **Merger activity:** U.S. M&A activity rose from $153 billion in 1992 to $451 billion in 1995 according to Securities Data Corporation.

135 **"The animosity between Michael and Steve":** Background interview with a former Blackstone partner.

135 **"I thought we did well":** Michael Hoffman interview, May 20, 2009.

Chapter 12: Back in Business

137 **CD&R claims:** November 2006 speech by CD&R president and CEO Donald J. Gogel at the Astoria Private Equity Investment Forum; a transcript is posted on CD&R's website: http://www.cdr-inc.com/news/per spectives/private_equity_a_force.php.

139 **"David Stockman came up":** Howard Lipson interview, June 9, 2008.

139 **"I told him it made sense":** Peter Peterson interview.

139–40 **"The only way we're going to talk" . . . With Chemical in its corner:** James Lee interview, July 24, 2008.

140 **By the late 1990s:** Ellen Moody, "King of corporate debt moves into equities," Bloomberg News, Oct. 4, 1999.

141 **Says Lipson:** Lipson interview.

142 **In an April 1998 interview:** Leah N. Spiro and Kathleen Morris, "Blackstone: Nice Is for Suckers," *BusinessWeek*, Apr. 13, 1998.

143 **"We preserved capital":** Lipson interview.

144 **"These were all medium-sized":** Stephen Schwarzman interview.

145 **When oil prices rose:** Background interview with a former Blackstone partner.

145 **"I'm thinking":** Background interview with a banker.

146 **When Bar Technologies:** Steel industry analyst Charles Bradford, quoted by Len Boselovic, "Heavy Metal Buyout Owners of Former Johnstown Steel Plant Make a Bid for Company that Owns Beaver Falls Plant," *Pittsburgh Post-Gazette,* July 25, 1998.

146 **"The pension payouts":** Background interview with a source involved in the Republic deal.

146 **In addition to the stream:** Information on the events leading up to Stockman's departure from Blackstone came chiefly from background interviews with two former Blackstone colleagues and another person who worked closely with Stockman.

Chapter 13: Tuning in Profits

148 **The world's largest insurance:** AIG press release, "AIG to Invest $1.35 Billion in The Blackstone Group and Its Funds," Aug. 30, 1998.

148 ***Forbes* and *BusinessWeek*:** Matthew Schifrin, "LBO Madness," *Forbes,* Mar. 9, 1998; Stanley Reed, "Buyout Fever! LBOs Are Changing the Face of Dealmaking in Europe," *BusinessWeek,* June 14, 1999.

148 **The IPO of Netscape:** David Henry, "Netscape Investors Bet on a Dream," *USA Today,* Aug. 9, 1995.

149 **The next year Yahoo!:** Rose Aquilar, "Yahoo IPO Closes at $33 after $43 Peak," *CNET News,* Apr. 12, 1996.

152 **Gallogly was the odd one out:** Personal observation; background interviews with a Blackstone investor and with three former colleagues.

152 **Gallogly became intrigued:** Mark Gallogly interviews, July 17, 2008 and Feb. 24, 2009; Bret Pearlman interviews, Oct. 22, 2008 and Feb. 11, 2009; Simon Lonergan interview, Jan. 22, 2009; Lawrence Guffey interview.

153 **The first deal:** Gallogly interview, Feb. 24, 2009; Pearlman interview, Oct. 22, 2008; Lonergan interview.

154 **Beginning in 1998:** David Carey, "Short Circuited or Hard-Wired?" *Deal,* Feb. 28, 2003.

154 **Convinced that new technology:** Guffey interview, confirmed by Blackstone.

155 **"Paul Allen seemed to believe":** Lonergan interview; Pearlman interview, Feb. 11, 2009.

155 **In fact, the prices:** Carey, "Short Circuited."

155 **But Allen's folly:** Confirmed by Blackstone.

155 **On top of the cable deals:** Gallogly interview, Feb. 24, 2009; Lonergan interview.

155 **Gallogly's very success:** Stephen Schwarzman interview; Gallogly interview, Feb. 24, 2009.

156 **"There was a growing concern":** Peter Peterson written response to fact-checking query.

156 **"We hit a fork" . . . "There was more risk":** Peterson, Schwarzman, and Robert Friedman interviews.

157 **It also wasn't clear:** Lonergan interview.

Chapter 14: An Expensive Trip to Germany

158 **Microsoft had displaced:** "The FT 500—Global 500, Section One," *Financial Times,* May 4, 2000.

158 **With some venture funds:** See, e.g., Regents of the University of California, *Alternative Investments as of March 31, 2003.*

158 **Venture firms, which had attracted:** Venture Economics/Thomson Financial and National Venture Capital Association press release, "Strong Fund Reserves Diminish Need for Venture Capitalists to Raise Additional Capital," May 6, 2002.

159 **This rearranged the map:** John Gorham, "Go West, Rich Men," *Forbes,* Oct. 12, 1998. "Forbes 400 Richest in America," *Forbes,* Oct. 1999. Peterson and Schwarzman may well have deserved to be included toward the bottom of the list, based on the valuation of Blackstone implied by AIG's investment in 1998 and the profits they had earned from the firm over the years.

159 **Blackstone couldn't help but feel:** Stephen Schwarzman interviews; Bret Pearlman interviews, Oct. 22, 2008, and Feb. 11, 2009.

160 **Schwarzman threw a bone:** Schwarzman interviews; Pearlman interview, Oct. 22, 2008; $7 million figure from Blackstone.

160 **It plowed $227 million:** Pearlman interview, Oct. 22, 2008.

161–62 **The grandest plan . . . The physical networks:** Interview with William Obenshain, former Bank of America executive, Feb. 29, 2009; Simon Lonergan interview, Jan. 22, 2009; background interviews with two other sources involved with the investment.

162–63 **But the management team . . . "These [meetings] were very unpleasant":** Obenshain interview; background interviews with three sources involved with the investment.

164 **"Where's my fucking money?":** Background interview with a source with ties to Callahan.

164 **"I was really furious":** Schwarzman interview.

164 **Two-thirds of the investments:** Materials for offsite meeting of Blackstone private equity group, volume 1, part II, 18, Apr. 21, 2006.

164 **"The pain we took":** David Blitzer interview.

165 **From there it was all downhill:** Dealogic data compiled for the authors on Apr. 7, 2009 (IPO and junk-bond issues).

165 **As stinging as Blackstone's losses:** David Carey, "Why the Telcos Burned the Buyout Shops," *Deal,* Nov. 17, 2000.

166 **Exacerbating its woes:** Vyvyan Tenorio and John E. Morris, "Ted Forstmann Testifies in Trial," *Deal,* June 1, 2004; "Jury Finds Forstmann Little Liable on All Counts," Reuters, July 1, 2004.

166 **When Tom Hicks:** Jonathan Braude and David Carey, "Hicks Europe Wing on Its Own," *Deal,* Jan. 21, 2005; David Carey, "Class of '98," *Deal,* Aug. 1, 2003.

166 **The carnage extended:** David Carey, "AMF Rolls a Gutter Ball," *Deal,* July 3, 2001.

166 **Meanwhile, KKR:** David Carey, "Regal Cinemas Near Prepackaged Bankruptcy," *Deal,* Jan. 12, 2001.

167 **Sixty-two major private equity–backed companies:** David Carey, "Older, but How Much Wiser?" *Deal,* Dec. 6, 2001; David Carey, "Bust-Up Update," *Deal,* Aug. 8, 2002.

167 **Blackstone narrowly escaped:** Chad Pike interview.

167 **By 2002, the default rate:** Edward Altman, New York University Stern School of Business, "Review of the High Yield and Distress Debt Mar-

kets," presentation at Boston College Center for Asset Management Conference, June 5, 2009.

168 From the summer of 2000: PPM for BCP V.

Chapter 15: Ahead of the Curve

171 At the time, it looked: Stephen Schwarzman interview.

172 "When you look at distressed deals": Chinh Chu interview.

172 "We're value investors and we're pretty agnostic": Schwarzman interview.

173 Blackstone tested its new strategy: Lawrence Guffey and Arthur Newman interviews.

173 "At that point, cable": Schwarzman and Guffey interviews.

174–75 Together with its coinvestors . . . Adelphia and Charter yielded: Summary in PPM for BCP V; William Obenshain interview, Feb. 29, 2009; Guffey interview.

175 The communication fund: PPM for BCP VI.

176 When Blackstone took a minority stake: John E. Morris and David Carey, "DLJ, Blackstone Cash In on Nycomed," *Deal*, Mar. 10, 2005.

176 Likewise, the financing . . . TRW Automotive: Neil Simpkins interview; Kelly Holman and Lou Whiteman, "Blackstone Inks TRW Auto Deal," *Deal*, Nov. 19, 2002.

176 In another instance, Blackstone: Lou Whiteman, "PMI Leads Buyout of GE Unit," *Deal*, Aug. 4, 2003.

Chapter 16: Help Wanted

179 Between 1996 and 2000: Blackstone (employee count).

179 For all intents and purposes: Stephen Schwarzman interview; Howard Lipson interview, May 29, 2008.

180 Lee was at the very top: Robert Lenzner, "Meet the New Michael Milken," *Forbes,* Apr. 17, 2000.

180 Yet within weeks of Lee's: Robert Clow, "Jimmy Lee Banks Again—To Hunt M&A in His Own, Separate Shop at Chase," *New York Post,* Nov. 7, 2000; Erica Copulsky, "At Chase Manhattan, a Study in Contrasts," *Deal,* May 31, 2000; Laura M. Holson, "Chase's Investment Banking Hopes Ride on a Goldman Exile," *NYT,* June 29, 2000.

180 **"At the defining moments"**: Bret Pearlman interview, Feb. 11, 2009.

180–82 **Lee, who had spent . . . "Jimmy's an exceptionally loyal person"**: Schwarzman interview; James Lee interview, Oct. 17, 2008.

182 **An executive recruiter**: Schwarzman interview.

182 **On paper, James**: IPO Prospectus, 193–94.

182 **When Schwarzman reached out**: Massachusetts Pension Reserves Investment Board, list of private equity partnerships and internal rates of return as of Dec. 31, 2003, provided by fax on Aug. 25, 2004, in response to query (DLJ Merchant Banking); California State Teachers' Retirement System, Statement of Investments as of June 30, 2002, provided by fax on Dec. 13, 2002, in response to query (Blackstone Capital Partners II).

183 **"He wasn't running"**: Sabin Streeter interview, Feb. 25, 2009; background interviews with three former DLJ bankers.

183 **When a new CEO**: Andrew Ross Sorkin and Patrick McGeehan, "First Boston Plans a Shakeup in Its Banking Unit," *NYT,* Feb. 19, 2002; Landon Thomas Jr., "The New Color of Money," *New York,* May 27, 2002; Erica Copulsky, "CSFB Big Gun James Jumps to Blackstone," *New York Post,* Oct. 18, 2002; background interviews with two ex-CSFB sources.

184–88 **To Schwarzman, James possessed . . . ahead of schedule in early November**: The account of the discussions and their thoughts is based on Schwarzman and Tony James interviews; personal details verified by James; summary of personality from authors' observations and interviews.

187 **Friends say that James**: Background interviews.

188 **James wasted no time**: Pearlman interview.

188 **His mandate from Schwarzman**: James interview; David Carey, "Stirring the Pot at Blackstone," *Deal,* Aug. 8, 2003.

189 **He also pressed partners**: James interview.

189 **James hammered home**: Lawrence Guffey interview.

190 **"Eight train tracks ran"**: Chinh Chu interview.

190 **It came as no surprise**: Materials for an offsite meeting of Blackstone's private equity group, vol. 1, pt. II, 56, Apr. 21, 2006.

191 **James also reexamined**: James interview.

191 **"Tony said, 'We're not' "**: Background interview with a leveraged-finance banker.

191 **"we were run"**: Chad Pike interview.

191 **"This was not Tony [coming]"**: Schwarzman interview.

192 **Some partners were anxious:** Two background interviews.

192 **Mossman was the person:** Three background interviews.

192 **"Before, everyone had their own relationship"**: Lipson interview.

193 **For Bret Pearlman and Mark Gallogly:** Matthew Craft, "Elevation Part-
ners Raises $1.8B Fund," *Corporate Financing Week,* July 1, 2005;
Henny Sender, "Centerbridge over Troubled Waters: New Fund Mixes
Buyouts, Bad Debt", *WSJ,* Dec. 15, 2006.

195 **"He's pretty self-aware"**: Background interview with a leveraged-finance
banker.

Chapter 17: Good Chemistry, Perfect Timing

196 **As they sized up each other:** Stephen Schwarzman and Tony James interviews.

196 **Theirs was a contrarian view:** Mario Giannini interview, Feb. 13, 2009.

197 **"We got very active"**: James interview; Dealogic data compiled for the
authors on May 7, 2009.

197 **The first big cyclical play:** Neil Simpkins interview.

198 **Chu had followed:** Chinh Chu interviews and written response to query.

199–200 **When Chu first began . . . back on track:** Chu interviews; Celanese
financials. Quotes and thoughts attributed to Chu in this chapter are
based on interviews with him.

200 **"It did take some time"**: David Weidman, written response to query,
mid-2009.

201 **Scaring up the equity:** Chu interview.

201 **In December 2003:** Chu interview; Blackstone press release, Dec. 16, 2003.
The 2.8 billion ($3.4 billion) deal value excludes pension liabilities.

202 **The next morning:** Blackstone press release, Mar. 30, 2004; Celanese
press releases of Aug. 3, 2004, Aug. 19, 2005, and Dec. 22, 2006.

203 **The problem was exacerbated:** Chu interview.

204 **The move to Dallas saved:** Chu interview.

205 **Two months after the dividend:** Form S-1, Celanese Corp., Nov. 3, 2004,
and Form 424B4, Celanese, Jan. 24, 2005; PPM for BCP V.

205 **By the time they sold:** Blackstone recorded a $2.9 billion gain on BCP IV's $405.6 million investment in Celanese.

205–206 **By Chu's reckoning . . . on Blackstone's watch:** Chu interview and written response to fact-checking queries (source of profits and employee count); BASF, Dow Chemical, and Eastman Chemical financial reports (comparative cash flows); Celanese financials (productivity).

206 **The economic slowdown:** David Weidman, written response to query, mid-2009.

206 **The Nalco investment:** PPM for BCP V.

206 **"You've got to have":** Chu interview.

206 **It was a lesson:** Schedule 14A, TRW Automotive Holdings Corp., Apr. 3, 2009 (Blackstone's remaining stake); TRW press release, Mar. 1, 2010 (stock sale).

Chapter 18: Cash Out, Ante Up Again

208 **The mood shift:** Dealogic data compiled for the authors on Apr. 7, 2009.

210 **The high-yield bond market:** Dealogic data compiled for the authors on Apr. 7, 2009.

210 **That's what happened with Nalco:** Nalco financials; background interview with a source involved in the buyout.

211 **Still, there had never before been:** Vyvyan Tenorio, "The Dividend Debate," *Deal,* Apr. 16, 2009; press reports on bond spreads.

211 **The secondary buyouts:** John E. Morris, "Sealy Hops from Bain to KKR," *Deal,* Mar. 4, 2005.

212 **Nevertheless, Simmons's three other:** David Carey, "How Many Times Can You Flip This Mattress?" *Deal,* Jan. 23, 2004. A lengthy *NYT* story about Simmons's bankruptcy in 2009 stressed how debt had increased through the successive buyouts but nowhere mentioned the simultaneous rise in cash flow or the growth of the business: Julie Creswell, "Profits for Buyout Firms as Company Debt Soared," *NYT,* Oct. 5, 2009.

212 **Even though Sealy's growth:** Sealy financials; Morris, "Sealy Hops from Bain to KKR."

212 **Blackstone's buyout funds:** Blackstone; Carlyle press release, Feb. 14, 2005 (2004 payouts); Amendment No. 6, S-1A, KKR & Co., LP, Oct.

31, 2008, 232; Nathalie Boschat, "Carlyle and Blackstone in Record Payouts," *Financial News,* Jan. 27, 2006 (Carlyle 2005 payouts). KKR had more buyout capital under management in the late 1990s and early 2000s than Blackstone and hence had more investments to exit in this period. Carlyle's figures include venture capital, real estate, and mezzanine debt funds. Blackstone's figures do not include its real estate funds.

213 **By the end of 2005:** California Public Employees Retirement System, AIM Program Fund Performance Review (hereafter CalPERS Fund Report) as of Dec. 31, 2005 (Apollo 2001 fund: 39.8 percent; Blackstone 2002 fund: 70.8 percent; TPG 2003 fund: 41.8 percent); Washington State Investment Board, Portfolio Overview by Strategy, Dec. 31, 2005 (KKR 2002 fund: 50.5 percent). Beginning in the early 2000s many state pension funds were required to disclose returns on individual private equity and venture capital funds in which they had invested, making the returns a matter of public record for the first time.

213 **Blackstone's 2002 fund:** CalPERS Fund Report as of Dec. 31, 2008; Oregon Public Employees' Retirement Fund, Alternative Equity Portfolio as of Mar. 31, 2009.

214 **By the late 1990s, banks:** Center for Private Equity and Entrepreneurship, Tuck School of Business at Dartmouth, *Note on Private Equity Asset Allocation*, Case #5-0015, updated Aug. 18, 2003 (hereafter *Note on Allocation*), 14.

214 **The typical pension fund:** 2009 Wilshire Report on State Retirement Systems: Funding Levels and Asset Allocations, Wilshire Associates, Inc., 11–12; *Note on Allocation*, 2–3.

214 **Giant pensions:** Ibid., 1; CalPERS Fund Report as of Dec. 31, 2005.

214 **Between 2003 and 2008:** 2009 Wilshire Report on State Retirement Systems, 11.

215 **But those whose profits:** Heino Meerkatt, John Rose, Michael Brig, Heinrich Liechenstein, M. Julia Prats, and Alejandro Herrerra, *The Advantage of Persistence—How the Best Private Equity Firms "Beat the Fade,"* Boston Consulting Group and the IESE Business School of the University of Navarra, Navarra, Spain, Feb. 2008; *Note on Allocation*, 12.

215 **As a consequence:** Conor Kehoe and Robert N. Palter, "The Future of Private Equity," *McKinsey Quarterly* 31 (Spring 2009): 15.

215 **From the low ebb:** National Venture Capital Association/Thomson Financial press release, Jan. 16, 2007.

215 **The industry wasn't as concentrated:** Kehoe and Palter, "The Future of Private Equity," 15. In 2006 the U.S. Department of Justice launched an investigation of possible collusion among big private equity firms. Later, some shareholders of buyout targets brought an antitrust suit against most of the largest private equity firms, charging that they agreed not to bid against each other in several major corporate auctions. As of early 2010, nothing had come of the government investigation, and the evidence in the civil suit was under seal, so no public evidence of collusion had been revealed. Peter Lattman, " 'Club' Suit Dogs Buyout Firms," *WSJ,* Mar. 9, 2010.

216 **In the previous decade . . . Private equity's share:** Dealogic data compiled for the authors on May 28, 2009.

Chapter 19: Wanted: Public Investors

219 **Leon Black's Apollo Management:** N-2, Apollo Capital Corp., Feb. 6, 2004. The company was renamed Apollo Investment Corporation before it went public.

220 **When Apollo said in early April:** Vipal Monga, "Blackstone Locks Up BDC Market," *Deal,* May 19, 2004.

220 **It was "the pack moving":** Background interview.

220 **As things played out:** Vipal Monga, "This Goose Is Cooked," *Deal,* Oct. 1, 2004.

221 **"The golden goose":** Ibid.

221 **In March 2005:** Jonathan Braude, "Ripplewood Stock Rises," *Deal,* Mar. 24, 2006.

221 **In early 2006:** "KKR Starts Roadshow for $1.5bln Listing—source," Reuters, Apr. 19, 2006.

222 **"There were twenty other":** Michael Klein interview, Nov. 14, 2008; background interview with an adviser on several offerings.

222 **At the original $1.5 billion:** Stephen Schwarzman interview.

222 **Competitors soon found:** Schwarzman and Klein interviews.

223 **There were mixed emotions:** Edward Pick interview, Oct. 22, 2008.

223 **The lesson:** Schwarzman interview.

Chapter 20: Too Good to Be True

224 **For Chinh Chu:** Chinh Chu interview.

224 **The $2.6 billion in gains:** Calculations based on figures in PPM for BCP V.

224 **"The debt [offered] on that deal":** Chu interview.

225 **After peaking that year:** Tronox annual report for 2007.

225 **At $11.3 billion:** David Carey, "Silver Lake Leads SunGard Buyout," *Deal,* Mar. 28, 2005.

226 **The Sarbanes-Oxley law:** Daniel Rosenberg, "Sarbanes-Oxley Slows IPO Rush in Boom to Private-Equity Funds," *WSJ,* Mar. 31, 2005.

228 **CLOs quickly came:** Statistics in PowerPoint presentation provided by Meredith Coffey, senior vice president, Research and Analysis, Loan Syndications & Trading Association, June 17, 2009, in response to a query.

229 **In 2004 the average large company:** Standard & Poor's / Leveraged Commentary & Data figures, June 9, 2009, provided in response to query.

230 **"Inevitably when people look back":** Carmel Crimmins, "Carlyle's Rubenstein Sees No Buyout Crash," Reuters, Jan. 25, 2006.

230 **That year private equity firms initiated:** Dealogic data compiled for the authors on May 28, 2009.

230 **"It's not that you see":** Tony James interview.

231 **It began in May 2006:** Paul Schorr IV interview. The account of the negotiations for the buyout, through "no one emerged to trump Blackstone's offer," is based on that interview and the Freescale proxy statement cited below.

232 **Freescale agreed to let Schorr's team:** Schedule DEFM14A proxy statement, Freescale Semiconductor, Oct. 19, 2006, 19–31 ("Background of the Merger"). The filing includes a day-by-day account of the offers, demands, negotiations, and board of directors meetings from the company's perspective.

233 **"We were prepared to sign":** Schwarzman interview.

234 **It was a steep price:** Freescale annual reports for 2006 and 2008.

234 **To give the company:** Freescale annual report for 2007, Mar. 13, 2008, 59–60.

235 **"Semiconductors, you knew, was cyclical":** James interview.

235 **Even with the hefty equity investment:** Balance sheets in Freescale's report for the quarter ended Sept. 29, 2006, and in its annual report for 2007.

235 **"It was frustrating sometimes":** Chu interview.

235 **In late August:** The identities of the bidders and their bids, as well as the chronology of the bidding war, come from the original proxy statement for the merger: Schedule DEFM14A, Clear Channel, Jan. 29, 2007, 24–36.

236 **"The banks were offering":** James interview.

236 **Bain and Lee's agreement:** Schedule DEFM14A, Clear Channel, 6–7.

236 **After a group of hedge funds:** Chris Nolter, "Clear Channel Warms to Bid," *Deal*, May 18, 2007.

237 **Similar scenarios played out:** E-mail from Blackstone partner Prakash Melwani, Aug. 28, 2008. Blackstone confirmed the companies' identities and provided its offer price for each. In some cases, its bid was disclosed in the proxy statements of the targets.

237 **"We lost seven out of eight":** Prakash Melwani interview.

237 **Blackstone outspent rivals:** Blackstone annual report for 2008, Mar. 3, 2009, 70, 72; Amendment No. 6, Form S-1A, KKR & Co., LP, Oct. 31, 2008, 25 ($6.7 billion of limited-partner capital invested in 2006); Amendment No. 2, Form S-1A, Apollo Global Management, LLC, Nov. 23, 2009, 32 ($2.9 billion of limited-partner capital invested in 2006).

237 **"It's very hard":** James interview.

Chapter 21: Office Party

239 **Chapter 21:** Portions of this chapter were adapted from a Nov. 30, 2007, story in the *Deal* by the authors titled "New Kids on the Block."

239 **"You should buy EOP":** The conversation with Kaplan and other exchanges involving Jonathan Gray in this chapter, and the details concerning EOP not otherwise footnoted, are based on interviews with Gray.

241 **In 1998, for instance:** Chad Pike interview.